THE OFFICIAL RED BOOK®

A Guide Book of GOLD DOLLARS

Complete Source for History, Grading, and Values

Q. David Bowers

Foreword by
David W. Akers

Valuations Editors
Lawrence R. Stack

A Guide Book of

GOLD DOLLARS

Complete Source for History, Grading, and Values

www.whitmanbooks.com

3101 Clairmont Road, Suite C, Atlanta, GA 30329

Correspondence concerning this book may be directed to the publisher, Attn: U.S. Gold Dollars, at the address above.

ISBN: 0794826644
Printed in the United States

Disclaimer: Expert opinion should be sought in any significant numismatic purchase. This book is presented as a guide only. No warranty or representation of any kind is made concerning the completeness of the information presented. The author and valuations editors sometimes buy, sell, or hold certain of the items discussed in this book.

Caveat: The value estimates given are subject to variation and differences of opinion. Before making decisions to buy or sell, consult the latest information. Past performance of the numismatic market or any coin within that market is not necessarily an indication of future performance, as the future is unknown. Such factors as changing demand, popularity, grading interpretations, strength of the overall market, and economic conditions will continue to be influences.

About the cover: United States gold dollar designs were variations on two basic Liberty motifs: one with a tiara and one with a feathered Native American headdress. The result was three major types by which collectors identify the gold dollar. On the cover, at center, is the reverse of 1849, the first year the series was minted; at top left and right, Type I, the "Liberty Head," produced in both Small Head and Large Head varieties, respectively; at bottom left, Type II, the "Indian Princess Head, Small Head"; at bottom right, Type III, the "Indian Princess Head, Large Head."

WCG™ Pricing Grid
OCG™ Collecting Guide

Contents

About the Author

Q. David Bowers became a professional numismatist as a teenager in 1953, later (1960) earning a B.A. in Finance from the Pennsylvania State University, which in 1976 bestowed its Distinguished Alumni Award on him. The author served as president of the American Numismatic Association (1983–1985) and president of the Professional Numismatists Guild (1977–1979); is a recipient of the highest honor bestowed by the ANA (the Farran Zerbe Award); was the first ANA member to be named Numismatist of the Year (1995); in 2005 was given the Lifetime Achievement Award; and has been inducted into the ANA Numismatic Hall of Fame, today being one of just 12 living recipients with that distinction. Bowers has received the highest honor of the Professional Numismatists Guild (The Founders' Award) and more "Book of the Year Award" and "Best Columnist" honors of the Numismatic Literary Guild than any other writer. In 2000 he was the first annual recipient of the Burnett Anderson Memorial Award for writing. In July 1999, in a poll published in *COINage*, "Numismatists of the Century," by Ed Reiter, Bowers was recognized in this list of just 18 names. He is the author of more than 50 books, hundreds of auction and other catalogues, and several thousand articles including columns in *Coin World* (now the longest-running by any author in numismatic history), *Paper Money*, and, in past years, *The Numismatist*. His prime enjoyments in numismatics are knowing "coin people," from newcomers to old-timers, and studying the endless lore, technical aspects, and history of coins, tokens, medals, and paper money. As co-chairman of Stack's (New York City and Wolfeboro, New Hampshire) and numismatic director for Whitman Publishing, LLC, he is at the forefront of current events in the hobby.

Foreword author **David W. Akers,** of Stuart, Florida, has been prominent in numismatics since the 1970s. For many years he was an executive of Paramount International Coin Corporation, serving as its president from 1981 onward. In addition to his regular duties at Paramount, he supervised the production of the firm's auction sales, including its participation in the cooperative "Apostrophe Sales" of 1979 and onward. In 1975 he began his *United States Gold Coins: An Analysis of Auction Records* series, commencing with gold dollars, and completing the sequence in 1982 with volume 6. In 1996, then trading as David Akers Numismatics, Inc., he was awarded the auction of the John H. Pittman Collection, one of America's largest and finest old-time cabinets. A series of three sales realized about $30 million. Today, the catalogs are valuable reference sources. He is the recipient of awards and honors, including the Founders' Award and the Lifetime Achievement Award from the Professional Numismatists Guild, of which he is member 279.

Credits and Acknowledgments

As the author has studied gold dollars for many years, certain credits are for people who helped long ago and may not be living today (these being so noted):

John W. Adams loaned auction catalogs of Thomas L. Elder. The **American Numismatic Association,** Colorado Springs, Colorado. The **American Numismatic Society,** New York City, New York, provided accommodations for research and coins for study. The late **Harry W. Bass Jr.** shared his wealth of knowledge on gold-dollar characteristics and varieties. **Wynn Bowers** reviewed the manuscript and made suggestions. The late **Walter Breen** discussed die varieties, Proofs, and other aspects. **Roger W. Burdette** provided information from the National Archives. **John Dannreuther,** eminent student of the gold-dollar series, reviewed the manuscript and made suggestions. The late **John J. Ford Jr.** shared information and recollections. **R.W. Julian** furnished information on Proof mintages and helped in other ways. **Richard Doty** and **Jim Hughes** of the **Smithsonian Institution** helped in many ways, including providing numerous coins for study. **Stack's,** incorporating the former American Numismatic Rarities, was the source of many photographs. **Douglas Winter** reviewed the manuscript and made suggestions.

FOREWORD

I have to admit that gold dollars are by far my favorite series of United States coin. I have studied, handled as a professional numismatist, and personally collected them for most of my life. In the foreword I wrote for Q. David Bowers's book on double eagles a few years ago, I noted that, for many collectors, size matters, and I commented on the fact that double eagles are considerably more popular than gold dollars at least partly because of their much larger size. However, personally, I love the small size of gold dollars and find them to have a particularly appealing jewel-like cameo quality. The designs of all three types of gold dollars are also outstanding, with the Type I looking like a miniature Liberty Head double eagle and the Type II and Type III designs being the first in a long line of popular "Indian head" motifs that have appeared on U.S. coinage.

I saw a gold dollar for the first time in 1950 at Hisken's coin store in Seattle. It was a lightly circulated 1856, but the price of $7 was simply out of my price range, so I had to settle that day with buying an Uncirculated 1832 Capped Bust half dollar instead, using up my entire $3 coin-buying budget to do so. To be sure, the half dollar was an exciting purchase because it was by far the most expensive coin I had ever bought at that point. But it still didn't compare to the gold dollar, which made a deep and lasting impression on me and turned out to be the genesis of my lifelong interest and involvement in the field of U.S. gold coins in general and gold dollars in particular.

Two years after that first encounter with a gold dollar, my mother and I visited Seattle Stamp & Coin, where I met Don Zearing who, over the next few years, took me under his wing and became my earliest and most influential numismatic mentor. I explained to him that I wanted to buy a U.S. gold coin but didn't have very much money to spend, although my coin-buying budget by then was up to $10! I told him that I had thought a lot about this and had come up with a few basic criteria (with my mother's help), and that I wanted his recommendation based on those criteria if possible. First, I wanted something very old, preferably from the 19th century, since I associated rarity with a coin's age at that time. Second, it had to be in "really good" condition; I didn't know anything about grading or even what terms to use, but Mr. Zearing knew what I meant. Third, I wanted a coin of which not many had been made, that is, one with a low mintage (although I didn't know enough to use the correct term "mintage" either). And finally, the coin had to be cheap, since, after all, my budget was only $10.

So there were my four criteria for buying my first U.S. gold coin: old, "really good" condition, low mintage, and cheap. I am sure that Don Zearing got a good chuckle out of the whole matter, but he listened carefully to what I had to say and immediately came up with the suggestion that all four of my criteria could be met by only one U.S. gold coin: an Uncirculated, late-date gold dollar from the 1880s. Of course, he also just happened to have a few in stock, and so my gold dollar collecting and passion began that day in 1952 with the purchase of a very nice, Uncirculated 1889 gold dollar for $9. As I carefully counted out my nine one-dollar bills, my mother asked me if I was sure that I really wanted to spend so much money on just one single coin, and an awfully little one at that. I assured her that I did. My love and interest in gold dollars continues unabated to this day. In fact, I still have many of the gold dollars I purchased 30, 40, and even 50 years ago, and I always first turn to the gold dollar section of every new auction catalog I receive—perhaps mostly out of habit, but always with the true collector's hope of seeing something offered that I have never seen before.

In 1975, after years of research and keeping detailed notes on everything I had seen, read about, or just heard of, I wrote a book on gold dollars. It was the first in a series of six volumes I wrote over a seven-year period covering all of the U.S. gold coin series and individual issues, *United States Gold Coins, an Illustrated History* (1982). Before then, the only work that had ever been published focusing solely on the gold dollar series was a 24-page monograph, *Major Varieties of U.S. Gold Dollars*, written by Walter Breen in 1964. Although it was a ground-breaking work with a lot of worthwhile information in it, its primary focus was die varieties, and it did not fully, or even correctly in many cases, address the subject of rarity, usually quoting only mintage figures (which are not particularly reliable indicators of actual rarity).

Something much more was needed. The intent of my book was to answer questions that a true gold dollar specialist might have about the series, especially the questions about rarity. I am pleased and proud that my book was so well received in 1975 and that it has stood the test of time, having been a commonly used reference work for more than three decades. Once again, however, a new book offering much more was needed. A definite step in that direction was taken a few years ago with the publication of Jeff Garrett and Ron Guth's *Encyclopedia of U.S. Gold Coins* (Whitman, 2006), which included a tremendous amount of valuable information about the gold dollar series. I recommend this volume very highly.

But the gold dollar enthusiast in me would not have been fully satisfied without a new, in-depth volume concentrating only on gold dollars, and this new addition to the *Official Red Book®* series is just what I have been waiting for. It is written by Q. David Bowers, who is, in my opinion (and the opinion of just about everyone else in the hobby), the most important numismatist of the past 50 years and unquestionably the greatest and most prolific numismatic author in history. In fact, if one had a library consisting only of the books and auction catalogs that Dave Bowers has written, the field of U.S. numismatics would be quite thoroughly and satisfactorily covered. Such a claim could not be made about any other person, past or present.

Having been a full-time professional numismatist since the 1950s, Dave has seen and handled many of the greatest collections ever assembled, including Garrett, Eliasberg, Brand, Norweb, Bass, and countless others. As a result, he has bought and sold more than his fair share of gold dollars and, even more important, he has studied them as only a scholar and enthusiast would do. With this new book, he communicates his knowledge about the gold dollar series in a way that is every bit as entertaining as it is informative.

The book contains all the information one could ask for about each individual issue, such as rarity (including estimates of the numbers of examples known in various grades), die characteristics, striking and minting quality, current certified population report numbers, present market values, and important auction records. In addition to this essential data, Dave has also included a great deal of historical information about gold dollars and each year of the 40-year era in which they were minted, as well as chapters on mints, the minting process, and grading. One of my favorite sections of the book covers "How to Be a Smart Buyer of Gold Dollars." The valuable advice Dave gives in this chapter is equally applicable to being a smart buyer of coins in any series.

Before writing this foreword, I read this book from cover to cover several times, and I can honestly say that I enjoyed it and learned more from it with each successive reading. In my opinion it is a wonderful book—in fact, the finest volume that Dave Bowers has yet written in the *Official Red Book®* series. Based on the very high standard he has already set with his previous volumes, that is high praise indeed.

—David Akers

Introduction

In all of American numismatics the gold dollar possesses a special charm. First minted in 1849, and very popular at the time, its production continued through 1889, by which time it had become an anachronism.

Today, this is perhaps the most collectible of the gold denominations, in terms of the opportunity to acquire a very extensive collection of dates and mintmarks or one that is absolutely complete. While there are a number of scarce and rare varieties, none are "impossible."

A nicely preserved gold dollar is beautiful to behold. The liberty-head design of 1849 to 1854 is a miniature, cameo version of the motif used on the double eagle. The Indian-head design, made in two variations from 1854 to 1856 and from 1856 to 1889, has long been a favorite. It may be worth noting that in 1905, President Theodore Roosevelt, in discussing designs being created by sculptor Augustus Saint-Gaudens, commented: "Far and away the best coin we ever had is the little gold dollar with the feather crowned Indian on it."[1]

Along the way, as you will see in the following pages, the series is anything but simple. Coins produced at different mints are apt to have widely different characteristics. There is little resemblance in striking quality or general appearance between a coin struck in 1857 at the Charlotte Mint and one made in Philadelphia. A few years after that came the 1861-D, a curiousity in that it was the only gold coin whose entire mintage was struck by the Confederate States of America, when it had control of the Dahlonega Mint. Again, these pieces, while rare, are collectible and available.

There are many puzzlements and paradoxes in the series. Sometimes an issue with a relatively high mintage, such as the 1857, can be scarce in Mint State today, with perhaps 500 or so known. In curious contrast, the 1880, of which just 1,600 circulation strikes were minted, is actually *common* in that grade, with more than 1,000 in existence.

Along the way, America went through many transitions—the Gold Rush, political controversy, the Civil War, monetary crises, and more, all of which had a profound effect on gold dollars, how and where they were minted, and in what quantities. A single issue—take your pick—is apt to have a rich story in addition to its assigned grade and visual appearance.

As a professional I have enjoyed buying and selling gold dollars for a long time, and had the privilege of cataloging (with assistance from a fine staff) the Eliasberg, Norweb, Bass, and other notable collections that will forever echo in the halls of numismatic history. I have also had the opportunity to study and correspond about the series in detail, with such scholars as R.W. Julian and John Dannreuther, to mention just two. A special nod also goes to David Akers, author of a memorable book on gold dollars published in 1975 and contributor of the foreword to the present book.

A Guide Book of United States Gold Dollars is now in your hands. I enjoyed creating it. I hope you will share the same enjoyment as a reader.

1
Chronicle of Gold Dollars

Introduction

Interestingly, the first American gold dollars were not struck by any federal coining facility but, instead, were produced circa 1832 by a German metallurgist and private coiner, Christopher Bechtler, who had a small mint at Rutherfordton, North Carolina. There he processed gold that had been mined from hills and stream beds of the nearby region. Bechtler produced just three denominations, whose simple designs consisted only of lettering and numerals. However, they served well and were popular in the Carolinas and Georgia and were occasionally seen farther afield.

Gold dollar struck by Christopher Bechtler in Rutherfordton, North Carolina, in the 1830s (actual size about 16 mm; shown enlarged).

In the same decade, Secretary of the Treasury Levi Woodbury was very interested in the coinage of a gold dollar by the United States, a passion not shared by Mint Director Robert Maskell Patterson.[2] In fact the director did everything he could think of to dissuade the Treasury from even considering such an idea. One of his principal arguments was that only second-rate countries issued gold coins of such small size. Woodbury remained convinced that he was correct and persuaded President Andrew Jackson to let him have patterns struck to illustrate the idea. In January 1836, Patterson reluctantly ordered Mint staff engraver Christian Gobrecht to drop his work on a revised silver dollar obverse die (with which he had been making great progress), to concentrate on the gold dollar.

Pattern gold dollars were struck in the first two weeks of March 1836. Their attractive design—liberty cap and rays—was different from any motif theretofore used in the U.S. series. The arrangement was reminiscent of Mexican coinage, and was also used on Hard Times tokens and, later, on a distinctive medalet die by James A. Bolen—a Springfield, Massachusetts, engraver active in the private sector. The reverse of the 1836-dated U.S. pattern dollars displayed a palm branch arranged in a circle or loop. Examples were struck in gold as well as other metals. Despite the seeming success of the patterns, gold dollars were not adopted at the time. Specimens from this and subsequent restrike mintages became highly prized as collectors' items. On June 5, 1855, an auction described in the catalog *Valuable Collection of American and Foreign Coins and Medals* took place in New York City at Bangs, Brother & Co., 13 Park Row, and included:

Pattern gold dollar of 1836 by Christian Gobrecht, of the variety cataloged today as Judd-67 (actual size 14 mm; shown enlarged).

> Lot 172. The beautiful gold dollar of 1836; a magnificent *Proof, and of the same degree of rarity* [as the preceding lot], *viz., the first, in morocco case.* [Realized $5.75]

At the same time the gold dollar dies were being executed, Gobrecht and Franklin Peale (melter and refiner at the Mint) collaborated on the production of a pair of medal dies to celebrate the introduction, scheduled for Washington's birthday anniversary, February 22, 1836, of steam coinage at the Philadelphia Mint. The dies were ready in time, but the ceremony was delayed for mechanical reasons and was not actually held until March 23. Gobrecht altered the date-side die from FEB. 22 to MAR. 23. Copper cent planchets served as blanks. Quite a few of the medals were struck for visitors and official purposes. A few were struck before the die was changed, and may have been given out earlier. Most in existence today have the altered date. Later copies sold by the Mint were from new dies and have the date MAR. 23, with no trace of an earlier inscription.

In 1844 there was more discussion concerning a federal gold dollar. On January 22, Mint Director Robert Maskell Patterson wrote to Secretary of the Treasury John C. Spencer:

> Sir,
>
> I have been called upon to present my views to the Committee of Ways and Means as to the propriety of introducing the coinage of gold dollar pieces, and I have done so, in a letter sent to the Chairman [James McKay, a representative from North Carolina] by yesterday's mail.
>
> As one of the elements on which they are to form their judgment, I have caused some pieces to be struck, from dies prepared for a similar occasion in 1836. It is right that the head of the Treasury Department should also be furnished with one of these specimens, and I therefore send you the enclosed piece. Its weight is 25.8 grains; its volume but little more than two thirds of that of the half dime, the smallest of our coins.[3]
>
> The opinion to which my reflections and inquiries have led me is adverse to the proposed innovation in our coinage. If it should be ordered, however, the piece sent to you is not offered as a model to be followed. The obverse should bear the head of Liberty, like our other gold coins. In the reverse, however, I think that the figure of the eagle should be omitted as in the dime and half dime.

Patterson's desire for a gold dollar was minimal at best. In a subsequent letter the director criticized the denomination as too tiny and too easily counterfeited.

However, during the next several years nothing further was done on the subject. In the meantime, in North Carolina the Bechtler "mint" continued making its own gold coins. The three gold denominations struck at the federal mints continued to be $2.50, $5, and $10.

THE GOLD RUSH

Gold was discovered at Sutter's Mill on the American River in California on the morning of January 24, 1848, when James Marshall glimpsed a glittering flake in the tailrace that was to power the mill. Soon, the news spread, and by the summer there were thousands of fortune seekers panning and washing gold from the American River and its tributaries.

In December 1848, gold bullion from the West reached the Mint by special courier, and it was confirmed that all the rumors were indeed true. There was gold in California, and a lot of it. The Gold Rush was on! The next year, the "Forty-Niners" followed the western sunset in search of fortune. Many families and those with large numbers of possessions elected to go overland by one or another of the trails. By summer and autumn, thousands of wagons drawn by oxen or horses crossed the plains, then the desert, eventually reaching California.

Other gold seekers departed by steamer from Boston, New York, New Orleans, and other ports, traveled south through the Caribbean Sea to the eastern side of Panama, journeyed over the land strip by river boats and wagons, arrived on the Pacific shore, and took another steamer north to San Francisco. Heavy cargoes as well as passengers who were not in a hurry went entirely by ship, around Cape Horn at the southern extremity of South America, then through the Pacific to San Francisco—a trip typically taking somewhat more than 100 days.

Travel by any route was less than serene, and many were the tales of adventure and hardship endured by the pioneers.

GOLD DOLLARS AUTHORIZED

By early 1849 it became apparent that gold metal, once quite scarce in America, might become plentiful. Steps were taken to facilitate expanded coinage of gold, including the initiation of two new gold denominations.

A hand-engraved pattern gold dollar of 1849, the variety known as Judd-115 (actual size 16 mm; shown enlarged).

In January 1849, Chief Engraver James B. Longacre created, on gold discs, several patterns for a dollar. To increase the diameter of the coin but retain the same metallic content, a square hole was put in the center, in the manner of Chinese coins. While these handmade patterns were interesting and still are, it would have been very difficult to have prepared planchets with center holes and strike them properly. Moreover, it would have taken some ingenuity to have created a design that, per the still-effective Mint Act of April 2, 1792, would have included a "device emblematic of liberty."

On March 3, 1849, the gold dollar denomination was authorized by Congress, and at the same time the $20 denomination became a reality. The weight of the gold dollar was established at 25.8 grains, to consist of 90% gold and 10% copper (with traces of other metals).

In the meantime, it is probable that the Mint dusted off some old dies for Gobrecht's pattern 1836 gold dollar with the liberty cap design and made new strikings, possibly to illustrate what the size and general concept of a gold dollar would be. In April 1849, the *Ohio State Journal* carried this item:

> We were shown, on Saturday, a gold dollar, just from the Mint. If Congress passes the bill now before the House, we will soon have a plentiful supply of this description of small change. The dollar piece is a little larger in circuit than the half dime, but not quite as thick. On one side there is a wreath of leaves, and around it the words, "UNITED STATES OF AMERICA, 1836."[4]

Longacre, working with assistant engraver Peter F. Cross, worked on a new gold dollar design in the spring of 1849, creating wax models. The motif featured the head of Miss Liberty wearing a beaded tiara or coronet, with a circle of 13 six-pointed stars around the border. The reverse illustrated a wreath enclosing the denomination 1 / DOLLAR in two lines. The inscription UNITED STATES OF AMERICA was lettered around the border.

Longacre's Diary

These entries in Longacre's personal diary pertain to gold dollars:[5]

> *Monday, April 30, 1849:* Got my Liberty punch from Dougherty for the gold dollar.
>
> *Thursday, May 3, 1849:* Finished my first working die of the face for the gold dollar.
>
> *Friday, May 4, 1849:* At work on the hub for the reverse.
>
> *Saturday, May 5, 1849:* William Dougherty left his bill for punches for the engraver $69.25. At work on hub of the reverse g.d. [gold dollar]
>
> *Monday, May 7, 1849:* Finished hub for reverse of G.D.
>
> *Tuesday, May 8, 1849:* The Gold Dollar first coined today. (I made the design and finished the dies since the beginning of March.)

THE GOLD DOLLAR BECOMES A REALITY

Records kept in the Medal Department noted: "Struck the first gold dollars May 7th 1849."[6] This is a day earlier than mentioned by Longacre. In any event, the new denomination was born.

The new federal gold dollar of 1849 (actual size 12.7 mm; shown enlarged).

The new coins appeared in circulation the same month and were an immediate success, although there were some complaints that they were too small to handle easily. In 1849 and for the next several years, gold dollars were struck at the Philadelphia Mint and the three branches at Charlotte (each coin with a "C" mintmark), Dahlonega ("D"), and New Orleans ("O"). Beginning in 1854, gold dollars were also struck in San Francisco ("S").

The first gold dollars had the wreath tips on the reverse distant from the numeral 1, the style known today as the "Open Wreath" variety. Soon thereafter, the wreath was modified so that the tips were near the 1 ("Close Wreath").

During the first few weeks of coinage at Philadelphia, before the branch mints began making gold dollars, some modifications were made to the portrait of Miss Liberty. The earlier issues, including those of May 8, have the stars in different relation to the head, as well as being more lightly punched into the master dies.

PRESS REVIEWS OF THE GOLD DOLLAR

The *New York Weekly Tribune*, Saturday, May 19, 1849, included this:

> THE GOLD DOLLAR. It has come at last! Adams & Co.'s Express brought on the 9th from Philadelphia several of the glittering diminutive gold drops, and through this source we are indebted for a sight of it.
>
> In size it is somewhat larger than a Tuscan *quattrino* (one-sixth of a cent) which you never find again after you drop it into your pocket, but it is considerably smaller than a half-dime, heretofore the smallest of all American coinage. The dies are exquisitely cut, which accounts for the length of time in preparing them.
>
> The gold dollar is undoubtedly the neatest, tiniest, lightest coin in this country, if not—value considered—in any other. There is no "hard money" feeling about it. It is too delicate and beautiful to pay out for potatoes, and sauerkraut, and salt pork.

> Oberon might have paid Puck with it for bringing the blossom which bewitched Titania. Ladies might wear one pendant in each ear, or a number of them as a bandeau, like the women of the Greek Archipelago. The only objection they could have would be that rival belles could tell the exact value of their *parure.*
>
> The principal convenience of the gold dollar consists in its adaptation for making small remittances by letter. In this respect it will no doubt have a wide circulation. Its appearance strengthens our original notion that the little dollar will prove a great favorite. In spite of the poets, we all have a weakness for the "shining dross," while very few are able to indulge it otherwise than homeopathically.
>
> The gold dollar therefore meets a universal want, and will be generally welcome. Wherefore, gentlemen of the Mint! Be pleased to "shell out!"

What an auspicious welcome!

The preceding account was reprinted in Raleigh on May 23, by the *North Carolina Standard,* with this appended commentary:

> We hope the members of Congress from this state will use their exertions to have the gold dollar coined at the Mint in Charlotte. North Carolina produces more of the "raw material" than any region this side of California, and we think therefore that she has a right to make this request of the general government.
>
> Our own banks are not permitted to issue any bills of a less denomination than three dollars; and the consequence is that we are now flooded, and have been for years, with ragged one and two dollar emissions from South Carolina and Virginia. The gold dollar, if issued, as it might be, in sufficient quantities from the Charlotte Mint, would soon do away with this evil; and in the place of these bills, many of which wear out in the pockets of the people and are thus a dead loss to them, we should have a neat and beautiful medium of exchange, always good, and never liable to depreciation.

In September 1849, *Banker's Magazine* included this item, reprinted from *Willis' Bank Note List:*

> *The New Gold Coins.* The gold dollars have made their appearance in very limited quantities. One hundred thousand dollars only have been coined. The directors of the Mint issue them only in exchange for bullion; therefore but few have been circulated among the people. The government have recently ordered the balance on hand to be sent to Washington.
>
> By the single piece they command 2 to 5 percent premium, as a matter of curiosity. There is no probability of their ever getting into general circulation; they are altogether too small. The quarter eagles are a much handsomer coin, but even those are not much used in the common currency. The great number of banks creates a very extensive interest in favor of bank note currency. The liability of bank failures is not much considered, and the greater convenience of the paper inclines the mass in its favor. The liability of loss by counterfeits is greater in the gold coinage than in paper. The gold double eagles have not made their appearance; they will be more popular than the dollar pieces.

Gold Dollars Very Popular (1850–1853)

As gold bullion from California poured into the mints, the precious yellow metal became "common" in relation to silver. Soon thereafter, large gold discoveries were made in Australia, bringing additional amounts of gold into international markets. By 1850, silver coins were worth a premium over face value in terms of gold coins. In other words, a silver dollar traded at a value higher than a gold dollar. The rise is evident from these melt-down values of single silver dollars:

1849: 1.013

1850: 1.018

1851: 1.034

1852: 1.025

1853: 1.042

At the 1853 price, the melting of $1,000 in silver coins would yield a $42 profit.

By spring 1853, silver half dimes, dimes, quarter dollars, half dollars, and dollars had virtually disappeared from circulation, because speculators and exchange brokers snapped them up to be melted. Mintages of new silver coins diminished sharply. In the years 1851 and 1852, only 1,300 and 1,100 silver dollars, respectively, were struck.

The gold dollar quickly became a substitute for silver dollars and other coins, and large quantities were made, amounting to 3,317,671 gold dollars in 1851 and 2,045,351 in 1852. The years 1850 through 1853 were the high-water mark of the gold dollar, the glory years of the denomination when the little gold coins took the place of half dollars and silver dollars in everyday transactions.

The Act of February 21, 1853, reduced the authorized weights of the silver coins from the half dime to the half dollar.[7] No longer was the silver content of these denominations worth more than face value in terms of exchange with gold. By summer 1853, millions of these new lightweight silver coins, no longer worth a premium, were common in the channels of business and banking, and the need for gold dollars faded—but not before a record 4,076,051 gold dollars were struck.

A new lightweight silver coin, the three-cent piece (or *trime*), was introduced in 1851, but the face value was so low that it did not materially affect the demand for gold dollars. However, the trime, when used in multiples, took the place of smaller silver coins such as the half dime and dime.

In the years after 1853 and 1854, gold dollars continued to be minted in fairly large numbers, although the totals were much lower than in the peak period. Gold dollars remained readily available at banks and were frequently seen in circulation through and including the year 1861.

Gold Dollar Design Changes

In the early years, from 1849 through the Civil War, the gold dollar was a workhorse denomination. Those of the first major design, with Miss Liberty wearing a beaded coronet, are called Type I or Coronet issues by collectors today. Measuring 1/2 inch (12.7 mm) in diameter, these little coins were used intensively in everyday commerce. As a result, most examples seen today show evidence of wear.

The Type II design introduced in 1854 was slightly larger than the earlier design, but caused problems during the striking process (actual size 14.3 mm; shown enlarged).

In 1854 the diameter was enlarged slightly to 9/16 inch (14.3 mm), to make the coin more convenient to handle. The Indian Princess or Type II design, introduced in that year, replaced the Type I or Coronet style. Miss Liberty was decked out in a headdress of feather plumes.

Unfortunately, the new Type II motif created problems, since it was not possible for the metal in the dies to flow into the deep recesses of Miss Liberty's portrait on the obverse and at the same time into the central date digits on the reverse—with the result that the majority of pieces seen today are weakly struck on the central two digits (on the 85 in the date 1854, for example).

To correct this, the Type III portrait, with Miss Liberty, still as an Indian Princess, but now slightly larger and in shallower relief, was created in 1856. The lettering of the obverse also was moved closer to the edge, which allowed the reverse to strike up completely because it enabled better metal flow into the wreath. The reverse was unchanged and the diameter remained the same. The problem of sharpness was neatly solved, and nearly all Type III gold dollars showed excellent design details when first minted. (The resulting better strike led previous researchers to the conclusion that the reverse design was modified, but it is clearly the same as used on the Type II.)

The Type III gold dollar of 1856 was the final design in the series (actual size 14.3 mm; shown enlarged).

THE CIVIL WAR AND LATER

Following the bombardment and evacuation of Fort Sumter in the harbor of Charleston, South Carolina, in April 1861, the Union declared war against the Confederate States of America. The Civil War erupted in full force, and throughout the rest of the year there were many bloody encounters. At first, the "Yankees" in the North thought the situation was an easy win, but by the time that autumn and early winter set in, it was realized by both adversaries that a long struggle was ahead, and the victor would by no means be certain. The public became frightened, and widespread hoarding of gold and silver coins began.

On December 28, 1861, faced with a bottomless demand for gold coins, the leading eastern banks stopped paying them out, and the suspension of gold payments was complete by December 31. Silver coins began to be hoarded in quantity, and eventually disappeared. The Treasury Department withheld newly struck coins, and before long, commerce in the East and Midwest was conducted primarily with paper money, then entirely by paper. By mid-July 1862, no coins of any kind were in general circulation, and even the copper-nickel Flying Eagle and Indian cents were nowhere to be seen. From this time until December 17, 1878, gold coins did not circulate. The situation with silver coins was somewhat parallel, except that silver denominations began being released back into circulation slightly earlier—in a large way on April 20, 1876. By mid-1878, a glut of quarter dollars, half dollars, and other silver coins existed—there were so many, in fact, that beginning in 1879, production figures dropped sharply.[8]

In the meantime, Legal Tender notes, Fractional Currency notes, National Bank notes, and other government bills flooded circulation. For smaller transactions, the private sector furnished many currency substitutes, including encased postage stamps, cent-sized Civil War tokens, and private paper-money scrip notes in small denominations.

Gold coins could be purchased during the 1862 through 1878 period at a sharp premium in terms of paper money, and sellers included banks, bullion and specie dealers, and the Treasury Department itself. In the months after the Civil War ended, in the summer of 1865, it took more than $2 in Legal Tender "greenback" notes to buy a gold dollar.

Interestingly, gold and silver coins still circulated in the West, but paper money was traded at a proportional discount. It took $2 in Legal Tender bills to buy a single gold dollar in the East. In the West, gold dollars circulated at par. Accordingly, there was no advantage in sending either coins or currency from one coast to the other.

Demand for gold coins was primarily from merchants who wanted larger denominations for use in the export trade. At the time, gold coins were not struck on speculation by the Treasury (except for a small number to keep on hand for payment against bullion deposits). Rather, those bringing gold bullion to the Mint specified the denomination(s) they desired, and this usually was the $20 double eagle. Call for gold dollars was minimal, and mintages fell to very low levels. After 1861, it cost more than face value in bullion to make gold coins. Because of this, they were ordered only for export, where they were valued on their gold content, and the imprinted denomination was not important. (Today we have the same situation with gold bullion "Eagle" coins bearing denominations, such as $50, that are not relevant to their gold content or market value.)

For a time in 1873 and 1874 it seemed that gold coins would again be paid out at par by the Treasury, and quantities of gold dollars were minted of these two dates—the source of bullion being primarily the melting of old worn coins (under a section of the Coinage Act of 1873). However, suspension remained in effect, and mintages fell back to low levels, touching an unbelievably low figure of just 400 circulation strikes in 1875.

After December 17, 1878, gold dollars again traded at par with paper money. However, there were so many currency notes in circulation, plus a flood of recently released silver coins and newly minted Morgan-type silver dollars, that there was little call for the gold dollar. Really, there was no demand all for them, except from jewelers and numismatists.

Sunset Years of the Gold Dollar

Beginning in autumn 1879, a speculative interest arose in certain coins, most particularly Proof trade dollars and regular-issue (circulation-strike) gold dollars. Quantities were hoarded by those who ordered them through banks or coin dealers. The fever continued, but somewhat diminished, through the next decade. Although the Philadelphia Mint was still striking gold dollars, it seems that a small premium or "thank-you tip" was charged by bank tellers and others who had them.

Rather than strike very few or none at all, the Mint, fearful that coin collectors, dealers, and investors would realize a profit, struck at least a few thousand gold dollars in most of the years from 1879 through 1889. These low mintages were recognized by the numismatic community, and dealer Ebenezer Locke Mason Jr., for one, used them as a sales tool to market gold dollars to collectors—this being the opposite of what the Treasury had intended.

Production rose in 1888 and 1889 because such coins were still trading at a premium, and numismatists, jewelers, bankers, and others were aware of the situation and endeavored to lay in stocks of them. It seems likely that jewelers, unable to easily procure current circulation strike coins, simply ordered Proofs in quantity from the Mint, beginning in 1884. This explains why Proof mintages were exceptionally high—but not why few of those extra Proof coins survive unimpaired today.

Gold dollars were discontinued in 1889, and their official authorization was terminated by a legislative act in 1890. Soon thereafter the specimens still held by the Treasury Department, apparently including many of the final date (1889), were melted.

Official Commentaries

In 1889, James P. Kimball, director of the Mint, sent the following communication to the House Committee on Coinage, Weights, and Measures. Among other things, the commentary reiterates that later mintages were made to prevent numismatists from acquiring rarities:

> Observing by the *Congressional Record* (p. 1696) that the bill (HR 7214) prohibiting the coinage of the three-dollar piece was reported back with a favorable recommendation. . . . Referring to the proposal to discontinue coinage of the gold dollar piece, I may say that such a measure commends itself to my judgment. Since 1862 (except for two years) the coinage, at a single mint, of this piece has been limited to such a number as would satisfy the demand for it as a "Proof coin" and to such a supplementary coinage as was deemed sufficient to prevent an undue enhancement of value of the Proof coin.
>
> The practice of the [Treasury] Department, therefore, for twenty five years, except 1873 and 1874, has been in harmony with the measure now proposed, and for the reason that little practical use has been found for this coin except for special purposes, such as souvenirs and for manufacture into articles of personal adornment. No encouragement by the Department has been given to the demands of manufacturers, on account of the mutilation incidental to the use of coin for the purpose indicated.[9]
>
> A notable demand for this coin for shipment to China and Japan for manufacture into necklaces, bracelets, etc., has for many years existed, and still exists. Indeed, a premium is often put by dealers on this coin, so that in spite of the efforts of this Department the larger part of the supplementary [circulation-strike] coinage is believed still to be absorbed by manufacturers of articles of the kind indicated and for shipment.
>
> A measure in the terms of the bill in question would relieve this Department from the necessity of issuing Proofs, which have a tendency to become enhanced in value from the absorption of the illegitimate purposes of the supplementary coinage designed to prevent such enhancement.

The preceding commentary also reveals that Director Kimball viewed the making of Proof coins as a nuisance.

In his *Annual Report* for fiscal year 1889, Kimball's successor (confirmed on December 19), Mint Director Edward O. Leech, commented:

> I have the honor to recommend that legislation looking towards the discontinuance of the coinage of the 3-dollar and 1-dollar gold pieces and the 3-cent nickel piece be requested of Congress. . . .
>
> The same objections apply to the 1-dollar gold piece, with the additional ones that it is too small for circulation, and that the few pieces issued annually from the Mint are used almost exclusively for the purposes of ornament. So long as statutory authority exists to coin this latter denomination, the suspension of its coinage by the Secretary of the Treasury is of doubtful legality. The most he has ever felt warranted in doing was to limit its coinage to pressing demands about the holiday season, and to maintain, unbroken, the series of coin sets sold by the Mint. The very limitation of its coinage leads to favorites in the distribution of the few pieces struck annually, and to speculation in them.

MINTAGE TOTALS OF $1 GOLD COINS

The following figures—grand totals for all U.S. gold denominations—are cumulative and are from the *Annual Report of the Director of the Mint*, 1934, by which time U.S. gold coinage had ceased. Totals for various denominations span 1795 to 1933.[10]

> *$1 gold*—$19,499,337 face value (19,499,337 coins). If commemoratives are added, $19,874,754 (19,874,754 coins).
>
> *$2.50 gold*—$50,541,475 face value (20,216,590 coins). If commemoratives are added, $51,067,082.50 (20,426,833 coins).
>
> *$3 gold*—$1,619,376 face value (539,792 coins).
>
> *$5 gold*—$397,684,345 face value (79,536,869 coins).
>
> *$10 gold*—$582,619,850 face value (58,261,985 coins).
>
> *$20 gold*—$3,473,202,120 face value (173,660,106 coins).

Gold dollar coinage, broken down by Mint:

> *Philadelphia Mint*—18,223,438 regular issues plus 350,383 commemoratives, for a grand total of 18,573,821 pieces coined.
>
> *Charlotte Mint*—109,138 pieces coined.
>
> *Dahlonega Mint*—72,529 pieces coined.
>
> *New Orleans Mint*—1,004,000 pieces coined.
>
> *San Francisco Mint*—90,232 regular issues plus 25,034 commemoratives, for a grand total of 115,266 pieces coined.

2
Mints and the Minting Process

Introduction

From 1849 to 1889, gold dollars were struck each year at the Philadelphia Mint. In addition, for certain years they were made at the branch mints at Charlotte, Dahlonega, New Orleans, and San Francisco. While the history of these mints is well known, brief sketches of each are appropriate here.[11]

The Philadelphia Mint, 1849-1889

The Philadelphia Mint was the focus of activity for gold dollars, which were made each year from 1849 to 1889. This was the home of the Engraving Department, where Chief Engraver James B. Longacre created the design in 1849, modified it in 1854, and modified it again in 1856. All dies were made in Philadelphia, including those for use at the branch mints.

This was the second Philadelphia Mint, the successor to the Mint of 1792. Opened for production in early 1833, the new building incorporated many refinements and improvements and remained in use until autumn 1901.

Many procedures dated back to the 1830s. Appointed to the Mint staff in 1833, Franklin Peale, one of several sons of well-known Philadelphia museum owner and artist Charles Willson Peale, was commissioned to visit the mints of Europe and make notes and observations. This he did, returning with sketches, models of coining presses, and details concerning the availability of equipment. He submitted a detailed report to Mint Director Robert Maskell Patterson on June 17, 1835, that led to many improvements. Up to that time, equipment and many processes in use in America were archaic in comparison to the state of the art in England, France, and other European mints.

From France, a Contamin portrait lathe (tour à Portrait de Contamin) of sophisticated construction was ordered in November 1836, under the direction of

Obverse and reverse of an 1849 gold dollar struck at the Philadelphia Mint (actual size 12.7 mm; shown enlarged).

The second Philadelphia Mint as it appeared in 1873. This is where the gold dollar was designed, dies were made, and coins were struck continuously from 1849 to 1889. (*Leslie's Illustrated Newspaper*, November 15, 1873, supplement.)

Peale—to replace an earlier portrait-transfer machine. It arrived in March 1837, poorly packed and in damaged condition. Soon put in working order, it served well for several decades, including for the making of Longacre's $1 gold hubs. Peale, who had good political connections and was held in high esteem, was appointed as chief coiner in 1839, after which he greatly abused his positions and privileges, including using Mint personnel and equipment for his private profit. Peale and Longacre were not friends, and on occasion Peale would stymie the chief engraver's efforts (such as in the creation of the double eagle dies in 1849 and early 1850). Peale personally operated the Contamin lathe and protested that Longacre's models were unsatisfactory. Peale was fired from the Mint in 1854.

From time to time assistant engravers were employed, including Anthony C. Paquet, a supplier of letter and number punches who joined the staff in 1858. It is believed that he continued to make certain of these punches while employed at the Mint. After the death of Longacre on January 1, 1869, William Barber became the chief engraver, though he had no influence on the $1 series.

For the duration of the $1 gold coinage through 1889, the Philadelphia Mint turned out new issues each year, typically in small quantities after 1861, when such coins did not circulate in the East or Midwest (as noted earlier). Proof coins for collectors and for presentation purposes were also struck there. In 1875 the mintage was particularly small, and consisted only of 20 or so Proofs and 400 circulation strikes.

The Mint Cabinet, established in June 1838, was located at the Philadelphia Mint during the time that gold dollars were being struck (generations later, in 1923, it was transferred to the Smithsonian Institution). Each year samples of current coinage would be added to the display, including a set of Proof gold with the dollar denomination. The curators of the Cabinet were not interested in branch mint issues and did not acquire them.

The Charlotte Mint, 1849–1859

The Charlotte Mint in North Carolina was authorized by Congress on March 3, 1835, in the same legislation that created the branches at Dahlonega and New Orleans. Gold was abundant in the district, and it was anticipated that a mint would be useful to miners and merchants and would eliminate the costs of shipping and insurance and reduce the time needed to convert metal to useful form.

From 1835 until it closed in 1861, in the early era of the Confederate States of America, the Charlotte Mint produced gold coins in the denominations of $1, $2.50, and $5. There were no presses on hand with the capacity to strike larger-diameter pieces. Compared to Philadelphia, the planchet-making and coin-striking operations were primitive. Many of the coins were struck on poor planchets, using rough or imperfect dies, and otherwise carelessly made. There was no oversight for quality. Gold dollars were last struck at Charlotte in 1859.

Obverse and reverse of an 1849-C gold dollar struck at the Charlotte Mint (actual size 12.7 mm; shown enlarged).

The Charlotte Mint (drawn by George Osborn).

THE DAHLONEGA MINT, 1849–1861

The Dahlonega Mint (drawn by George Osborn).

The Dahlonega Mint, authorized under the Act of March 3, 1835, operated from 1838 until the early days of the Civil War in 1861, and struck coins in gold, but no other metals. Each piece bore a signifying D mintmark.

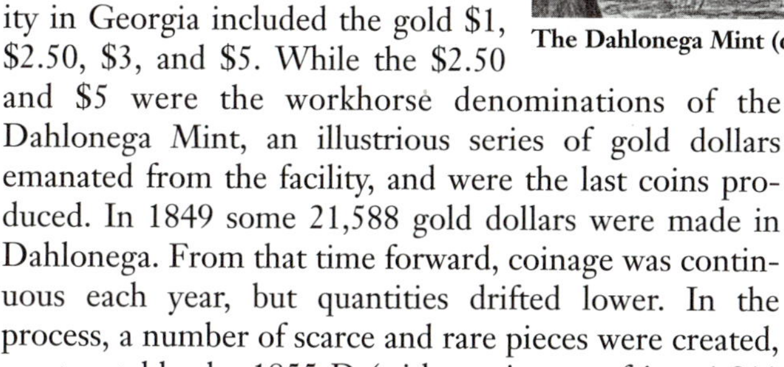

Denominations struck at this facility in Georgia included the gold $1, $2.50, $3, and $5. While the $2.50 and $5 were the workhorse denominations of the Dahlonega Mint, an illustrious series of gold dollars emanated from the facility, and were the last coins produced. In 1849 some 21,588 gold dollars were made in Dahlonega. From that time forward, coinage was continuous each year, but quantities drifted lower. In the process, a number of scarce and rare pieces were created, most notably the 1855-D (with a mintage of just 1,811 pieces—further distinguished as being the only Dahlonega Mint variety of the modified Type II design), the famous 1860-D, and the even more famous 1861-D.

Obverse and reverse of an 1849-D gold dollar struck at the Dahlonega Mint (actual size 12.7 mm; shown enlarged).

As at Charlotte, production at Dahlonega was often performed carelessly, resulting in many coins being struck on poor planchets and with incomplete detail. This rusticity, so to speak, has given a special numismatic charm to the coins of both of these mints.

After Abraham Lincoln was elected president in November 1860, many Southerners realized that the federal government would become increasingly hostile to the practice of slavery. On December 20, 1860, South Carolina seceded from the Union. Soon it was joined by others. Georgia seceded on January 19, 1861, after which time the Dahlonega Mint was in Confederate hands. Sometime after January 19, the Mint, occupied by troops under authority given by Governor Joseph E. Brown of Georgia, commenced striking coins from gold dollar dies that had been delivered on January 7, 1861, less than two weeks before the secession. Operations continued for a short time. The Mint could not be sustained, and on May 31, 1861, the facilities closed. In May, bullion on hand, struck coins, nitric acid (used in refining), and other assets were turned over to the Treasury of the Confederate States of America.

THE NEW ORLEANS MINT, 1849–1855

Of the three branches authorized on March 3, 1835, and opened for business in 1838, by far the most important in terms of building size and coinage output was the New Orleans Mint. This institution operated from 1838 until early 1861. Gold dollars were produced each year from 1849 to 1855 (except 1854). On January 31, 1861, the facilities were taken over by state troops of Louisiana and, later, on April 1, by Confederate troops. The mint soon closed, but would reopen in 1879 and produce coins through 1909.

Obverse and reverse of an 1849-O gold dollar struck at the New Orleans Mint (actual size 12.7 mm; shown enlarged).

From the early days, many difficulties attended the operation of the New Orleans Mint. Situated on "high ground" for New Orleans, the structure had many problems with its maintenance, possibly due to the high water table (New Orleans cemeteries are famous for their above-ground crypts). On April 17, 1854, Superintendent Charles Bienvenu wrote to Director Snowden to apprise him of the state of affairs, noting in part:

The New Orleans Mint as it appeared in the early 20th century.

> I believe it is my duty to call your special attention concerning the building of our Branch Mint, in order that you may take proper steps to present for the future an enormous expense for its preservation. I have taken great care to examine it with the other officers and some of our best architects of our city, and we all came to the conclusion that it was necessary in order to preserve the building to submit to your consideration the repairs absolutely required to be made to the same.

In response, a Senate resolution of May 31 of that year requested the secretary of the Treasury to determine whether it was better to remedy the defects in the original structure or whether it was "a wise economy [to] render it expedient to erect a new building."

Further: "The foundation is defective, causing the walls to spread, same being of insufficient strength to support the arches below the floors. To correct this and other problems the estimated sum of $25,000 is required." The repairs commenced in 1855 and continued until September 30, 1858, by which time the remarkable total of $588,812.70 had been spent.

Likely, the poor condition of the New Orleans Mint was responsible for the fact that no gold dollars were struck there after 1855.

The San Francisco Mint, 1854–1870

In March 1854 the San Francisco Mint opened for business in the premises earlier used by Curtis, Perry & Ward, the partnership that had operated the private coining firm of Moffat & Co. and, under Treasury contract, the United States Assay Office of Gold. The building had been refurbished and expanded, and new equipment had arrived by sea via the Cape Horn route. The first dies for coinage were delivered on March 15. By the time the mint opened in late March, a staff of nearly 70 people was on hand, including more than a dozen women to work in the adjusting room to verify the correctness of gold coin planchets.

The San Francisco Mint in the 1850s.

The facilities were small, cramped, and poorly ventilated. In time severe health problems were sustained by some of the workers. Production of gold dollars commenced in the first year, skipped 1855, continued from 1856 to 1860, then ceased. A decade later in 1870, gold dollars were made once again, after which time no more were produced. In 1870 the cornerstone was laid for a new San Francisco Mint at Fifth and Mission streets. Its cornerstone included a newly made gold dollar.

Obverse and reverse of an 1854-S gold dollar struck at the San Francisco Mint (actual size 12.7 mm; shown enlarged).

MINTS AND DIFFERENCES

Gold dollars struck during the same era, but at different mints, can have widely varying characteristics. Further, coins struck from the same dies at the same mint, but at different times, can have different characteristics. There is no consistency across the gold dollar era.

The following are general observations relevant to gold dollars and lend to their understanding. There are exceptions, but the following comments apply to most of the issues of a given design, mint, and time and explain the "personality" that various coins display, those from the Charlotte and Dahlonega mints being the most "rustic."

PLANCHET CREATION AND PREPARATION PROCESSES

Circular blanks to be made into planchets were prepared by taking gold ingots and running them between two steel rollers. Several pass-throughs were done, each time with the rollers spaced more closely together, creating an ever-thinner strip. Finally, by use of the drawing bench, the strip was pulled through an opening to create the desired final thickness.

As the strip grew ever longer during this process, small inclusions of carbon or foreign material, or imperfectly mixed copper added to the ingot as an alloy, or air bubbles, became distended or lengthened. Sometimes, flakes or distended pieces of the metal would separate, causing a recess or depression in the planchet surface.

Blank discs were cut from the strip by the use of a metal punch, in the manner of a cookie cutter. Next, the blanks were individually weighed. Those found to be too light were rejected and melted. Those found to be slightly overweight were "adjusted" by drawing a file across the surface. Such adjustment marks are rarely seen on gold dollars—a few Charlotte and Dahlonega coins being exceptions.

The next step was to run the blanks through a milling machine, which compressed the discs horizontally between a steel roller and the vertical inside edge of the machine, imparting a raised rim. At this stage the blank became a *planchet.* Planchets were then heated to a high temperature, and cooled very slowly, to make the metal soft, to permit better metal flow during the striking process. Planchet quality varied by mint, as follows:

> Philadelphia Mint—Generally, planchet preparation was excellent with regard to smooth surfaces. In the 1880s in particular, there was imperfect mixing of the copper alloy, causing "copper toning" or "copper spots" on the finished coins, including Proofs.

Charlotte Mint—Planchet preparation was generally poor, often with flaking and laminations. Quality deteriorated further after the mid-1850s. Annealing may have been improper in some instances, contributing to light striking of details.

Dahlonega Mint—Planchet preparation was generally poor, often with flaking and laminations, but generally better than at Charlotte. Quality deteriorated further after the mid-1850s. Annealing may have been improper in some instances, contributing to light striking of details.

New Orleans Mint—Planchet preparation was excellent with regard to smooth surfaces.

San Francisco Mint—Planchet preparation was excellent with regard to smooth surfaces.

Preparing Dies for Gold Dollars

Overview

Gold dollars were struck using two working dies, an obverse and a reverse. At the mints these were often called a *face die* and a *tail die*, although these terms are not popular in numismatic circles now.

Early in the procedure leading up to the manufacture of working dies for striking coins, a model was created by Chief Engraver James B. Longacre. The usual way to create a design was to make a model of a size much larger than the finished coin, to permit the artist to carefully finesse the details. Longacre preferred to work in wax. When completed, a model up to four or five inches in diameter was coated with graphite or another conducting substance and immersed in an electrolytic bath. By electrodeposition, a *galvano* was made in copper. This consisted of a mirror image of the model with the features recessed. By further transfer, a positive galvano would be made.

The large galvano model, now with a hard surface, was placed on a Contamin portrait lathe. This device consisted of a stylus with a pointed tip that traced over the contours of the model, up and down or level, as the model was very slowly rotated, much in the manner that a phonograph needle moves up and down in a slowly spiraling path—except that the slow spiral on the portrait lathe started at the center and continued outward to the rim. A mechanical arm connected to the stylus was directly connected to another arm that had a tiny rotating cutter at its end, which cut away at the face of a soft steel cylindrical blank. The position of the secondary arm could be adjusted to reduce the design of the model to any diameter required. For the gold, the reduction was to the same size as the finished coin.

From the reduction, the process continued, culminating in the making of working dies for coinage, as described below.

The Hub Die

The portrait lathe created an actual-size die, called a *hub*, which featured the raised image of Miss Liberty on its face. The hub was then given to Longacre or an assistant, who, using magnification, studied its features carefully. If some details of Miss Liberty's portrait did not transfer properly, or if a few lines or details required strengthening, this was done by hand, using engraving tools. A similar procedure was followed for the reverse.

This reduction then had LIBERTY punched into the empty space between the beading. Variously called a reduction, master hub, punch, puncheon, etc., this positive was used to create a master die by impressing it into soft die steel. For the 1849 gold dollar, a metal compass or scribe was placed at the center of the hub die, and tiny circles were scratched around the periphery, to serve as guide lines. Then, on the obverse die 13 stars were punched in by hand, and on the reverse die, lettering was placed around the periphery. Dentils (toothlike projections inside the rim, adjacent to the field) were then added by machine. The die was then finished by light grinding and polishing, to remove the raised burrs that rose around the letters and other features as metal was displaced. The date 1849 was also added (but in later years, 1850 onward, dates were punched in by hand). The result in 1849 was a *master die* with all of the features of a finished coin.

Master Dies

The master die was then hardened. The next step was to impress a soft steel cylinder into the master die, using a powerful slow-acting press. This soft cylinder became a *working hub*, with the design in raised relief—appearing as a finished coin, but without a date (excepting 1849, as noted). Often, several working hubs were created, although another could be created from the master die upon notice. Nomenclature has varied over the years. The working hub was then hardened.

Making the Working Dies for Coinage

The *working dies* for coinage were prepared by slowly and powerfully impressing a hardened steel working hub into the face of a soft cylinder of steel. The impressions from the working hub, which were in relief or raised (as on a finished coin) were transferred directly into the working die, becoming recessed or incused into the working die. This was done for both the obverse and reverse.

Then (excepting for 1849) the date was punched into a reverse die. Interestingly, in Mint records this side is sometimes called the obverse or face, in contravention to numismatic practice at the time and today, in which the "head" side is the obverse (as used in this book). If the die was intended to be shipped to a branch mint, a mintmark was added to the reverse.

If, during the transfer process of making working dies, there was a slight jiggling, a *doubled die* was produced. Such a working die showed doubling of some details. Most often, die making was done precisely, without any doubling.

Adding the Date to a Die. On gold dollars (except 1849) a four-digit logotype with the entire date, such as 1850, was separately punched into the working die. Positioning was done by eye, resulting in some variations of date placement.

It was standard practice to use just one punch for all dies of a given year. Exceptions occurred in 1856, 1859, and 1873 (see appropriate information under those entries). Sometimes the same date punch was used on dies of other coins of about the same diameter, such as the half dime.

If there was jiggling or a second tap during the entering of the date punch, a slight doubling of the numerals would occur, although this did not happen often.

Technical Notes. Various factors can affect the appearance of a logotype. If it is punched deeply into the die, the numerals on a struck coin will appear to be closer together, possibly even touching each other, whereas if it is punched lightly into the die, or if a die has been relapped (surfaces lightly ground down) or resurfaced, the numbers can appear to be thin and farther apart. If an engraver held the punch at a slight angle, the left or right side, or top or bottom of the logotype in the die can be deeper or shallower than its opposite. As an example, a date logotype may feature a numeral 8 having top and bottom loops of the same size. Depending on how it is punched into the working die, the loops can appear to be of different sizes on a finished coin. If the top of the logotype is punched deeply and the bottom less deeply, the top loop on a struck coin will seem smaller than the bottom one. If the logotype is punched more deeply at the bottom and less deeply at the top, the bottom loop will appear to be the smaller.

Various aspects of individual numbers can vary due to the same considerations—including the aforementioned appearance of the loops of the 8; the distance of the ball on a 5 from the vertical element above it; the size of the spaces within the numerals 3, 4, 5, 6, and 9; and others. However, within a given logotype punch, the relative positions of the numerals will not change. If, for example, the 1 in the date is tilted on a particular logotype, it will be tilted whether the date appears to be light or heavy on a particular coin. The description of the space between two digits is based on the closest point of each digit to the adjacent digit. For the first two digits, 18, this point is the distance from the tip of the lower right serif of the 1 to the curve of the nearby 8.

If a die is later relapped, the numerals which were once deeply cut into the die will become thinner and farther apart on the struck coin.

Adding the Mintmark to a Die. At the Philadelphia Mint the Engraving Department kept on hand a supply of letter punches for use in adding mintmarks. These were of different sizes to suit different diameters of coins. Generally, a large diameter coin such as a silver dollar or gold double eagle would use the largest size of mintmark punch, while a half dime, gold dollar (as here), or other small coin would use the smallest size.

It was usually the job of an assistant engraver to add the mintmarks. Probably, in Longacre's era this was done by one of several helpers he had from time to time. Positioning was done by eye, without a guide or a jig. For a typical branch mint reverse die, a letter punch was held over a spot above the dentils and below the wreath and tapped with a small hammer. Positions of the letters were apt to vary slightly: high or low, centered, or to the left or right. Sometimes a mintmark would be tilted slightly.

Preparation of Dies for Coinage Use

The dies sent to the branch mints were *not hardened for use*, but were sent "raw." This was said to have been done for security reasons: if they were lost en route, they would not be usable for any extended amount of coinage. Upon arrival at the branch mints, the dies often showed light rust. It was the job of the machine shop to prepare them for coinage. Dies were cleaned and lightly dressed. Then each was "basined," or given a gentle curve to the fields, curving upward toward the border. Afterward, the dies were heated to cherry red, then rapidly quenched in cold water or oil. Each die was then dressed or prepared for use by grinding the face to remove scale (from the hardening process) and, sometimes, to remove grinding and basining marks by light polishing. The final preparation varied from mint to mint, as follows:

> Philadelphia Mint—The final preparation of dies was of a high order of excellence. Die surfaces were made smooth and ready for coinage.
>
> Charlotte Mint—Dies were dressed or finished by rough grinding, with the result that there were many irregularities. Some dies were not basined, but remained with flat fields, this being most noticeable at the center on coins of the Type I design. It is likely that certain "planchet roughness" per conventional wisdom is really evidence of rough die surfaces; the comparison of two or more specimens of the same date and die state will verify this if the "planchet roughness" is identical on each.

Dahlonega Mint—As at Charlotte, at Dahlonega some of the dies were not basined. The finish given to dies ranged from careless or casual to quite good, with no single rule applicable to all. Generally, preparation at Dahlonega was better than at Charlotte, but it was still significantly below the quality of preparation at Philadelphia, New Orleans, or San Francisco.

New Orleans Mint—Final preparation was of a high order of excellence. Die surfaces were made smooth and ready for coinage. Some were lightly polished, imparting a prooflike surface to the finished coins.

San Francisco Mint—Final preparation was of a high order of excellence, sometimes with even more care taken than at Philadelphia (the 1854-S gold dollar is a paragon of die excellence). Die surfaces were made smooth and ready for coinage.

ASPECTS OF COINING AND STRIKING

The Coining Process

After the dies were readied for use and a supply of planchets was on hand, the dies were placed into a steam-powered coining press. A technician adjusted the obverse and reverse dies so that as the press went through its cycle, and the hammer (top) die came toward the anvil (bottom) die, it would travel far enough down to strike the gold dollar, but not too far.

If the dies were placed too close together, metal would be squeezed out of the collar (creating a "wire" rim, called a *fin* in Mint documents), and the dies would wear more rapidly. On the other hand, if the dies were spaced too far apart, they would last longer, but the planchet metal would not completely fill the deepest recesses of the dies. Adjustments were made each time a new die or pair of dies was put into the coining press, and sometimes during the process of a given press run.

The coining process varied among the different mints as follows:

Philadelphia Mint—Presses were usually well adjusted and the dies closely spaced, yielding excellent striking details (except for 1854 and 1855 Type II). Dies were usually replaced soon after significant cracks developed.

Charlotte Mint—Presses were casually adjusted, often with the dies set too far apart, resulting in lightness of design details on most issues. Poor annealing may have caused planchets to be too hard, resulting in weak striking and accelerated die wear. Dies were kept in service long after significant cracks had developed.

Dahlonega Mint—Presses were casually adjusted, often with the dies too far apart, resulting in lightness of design details on many issues. Poor annealing may have caused planchets to be too hard, resulting in weak striking and accelerated die wear. Dies were kept in service long after significant cracks had developed. This said, the procedures, as careless as they may have been, were somewhat better than those used at Charlotte.

New Orleans Mint—The presses usually were well adjusted and the dies closely spaced, producing coins with excellent striking details (except for 1855-O Type II, which was a result of the design). The dies usually were replaced soon after significant cracks had developed.

San Francisco Mint—The presses usually were well adjusted and dies closely spaced, yielding excellent striking details (even the solitary Type II issue at this mint, the 1856-S, was fairly well made). The 1856-S dies were kept in service long after significant cracks had developed. Other coinages were small enough that die cracks were not a problem.

GOLD DOLLAR DESIGN TYPES AND STRIKING SHARPNESS

The sharpness of details and the general appearance of a given gold dollar were the result of a combination of many factors, including the relief and arrangement of the design details as well as the differences among mints described above.

1849–1854, Type I—The relief of the Liberty Head is high at the center, sometimes causing incomplete striking of details. This is most evident at the highest hair points. On the reverse there can be weakness at the center of the word DOLLAR.

1854–1856, Type II—The new Liberty Head, called the Indian Princess by numismatists, is small and in very high relief. In the coining press the head is opposite the center of the reverse, which included the center of the word DOLLAR and the two central figures of the date, 85. Since the planchet metal could not effectively fill the deepest areas in the obverse and reverse dies simultaneously, the central features usually show weakness. Charlotte and Dahlonega coins in particular are *miserably* struck—this being of no concern to the specialist who expects this, but which can be quite disconcerting to a newcomer to the hobby or an uninformed investor. Because of this weakness, the Type II design was abandoned after just a short use.

1856–1889, Type III—The Indian Princess head is larger and in shallower relief and has the lettering moved closer to the edge. The reverse is unchanged. On most Type III coins from the Philadelphia and New Orleans mints the striking is usually excellent, although on some the dentils may be mushy, and on the reverse there may be slight weakness at the center digits, 85. Many Philadelphia Mint issues of the 1870s and 1880s are highly prooflike and have often been confused with Proofs. Charlotte issues of this type are usually weakly, even downright miserably, struck in some areas—due not to the design, but to the die preparation and coinage procedure. Dahlonega coins are also often sub-par, but somewhat better than those minted in Charlotte. The rusticity of Charlotte and Dahlonega gold dollars has endeared them to numismatists, just as "folk art" is popular with collectors of antiques. Accordingly, what might be perceived as a negative for C and D mint coins is not—except that within a given date and mint, a sharp coin is always preferable to a weak one.

3
Proofs for Collectors

Introduction

From 1849 onward, the vast majority of gold dollars were struck for use in commerce. In addition, for some early years and for all years after 1853, special Proof-finish coins were struck for collectors or for presentation purposes. These were struck from deeply polished dies, at slow speed on a special press, using specially prepared planchets. Most are Cameo Proofs with frosted designs and lettering set against the mirrored field. The finished details on a Proof coin are needle sharp, including the both the high areas of the design and the dentils.

Proof gold dollars were made for 1849 and for every year from 1854 (Type II) to 1889. Prior to 1860 it was general practice to sell Proofs for face value to interested collectors. The Mint was very accommodating, and the Mint Cabinet, curated by Jacob Reese Eckfeldt and W.E. Dubois, was an object of pride. Beginning in June 1838, when the Cabinet was started, examples of coins, mineral ores and samples, and other items related to coins and precious metals were added. The gallery served as a focal point for numismatists in an era prior to organized coin clubs and the issuance of periodicals related to the hobby. Records have not been found, but it stands to reason that an interested numismatist could obtain Proof gold dollars from 1849 onward by contacting the curators and paying a small premium over face value.

Ordering Proof Gold Dollars From the Mint

Proof coins, until 1859, were sold at face value, but at the start of 1860 a fee of 25¢ per coin was added.[12] One could buy gold pieces individually or, for $43, in a full Proof set consisting of the $1, $2.50, $3, $5, $10, and $20 denominations–with a total face value of $41.50. Generally, official Mint records of gold Proofs list the number of *sets* produced, such as 20 in 1875. However, auction catalogs and other records of the time demonstrate that most dealers and collectors who bought and sold Proof gold dollars were not interested in the higher denominations, particularly not the $5, $10, and $20. Likely, single Proof gold dollars were most often sold at $1.25 each to those who wanted them. This is certainly true from the mid-1880s to the end of the series in 1889, for gold dollar Proof mintages were reported at far greater numbers than for other Proof denominations. Again, few specific records survive.

In 1862 and the ensuing years, when gold coins traded at a sharp premium in terms of paper money, Proofs could be purchased only by paying for them with other gold and silver coins (which in turn could be purchased easily enough at a premium from an exchange broker). Presumably, certain types of paper money specifically payable in gold coins would have been accepted as well. It was not until December 17, 1878, that gold coins and paper money were again on a par, and not until 1880 that the Mint changed its ordering requirements for Proofs.

How Many Proofs Were Made?

Proof gold dollars were made in small numbers in the early years. Mintage figures are not known, but estimates can be made by extrapolating the number of confirmed Proofs that exist today. The Mint published figures from the 1860s onward but, as noted above, for some years these were for the number of full gold Proof sets made, not counting any individual gold dollars that may have been struck as well.

Prior to the 1880s, Proof gold dollars were produced in relatively small numbers in comparison to circulation strikes. Apparently in response to demand from the jewelry trade, plus investor interest, Proof production went through the roof in 1884, when 1,006 were made. In that year dealer Ebenezer Locke Mason Jr., for one, had publicized that no circulation strikes would be made (which proved to be incorrect). It was an exciting prospect to lay away a few "rare" Proofs for investment. Proof mintages continued above the 1,000 mark, rising to unprecedented heights in 1889 when the Mint declared that 1,779 had been struck. However, such numbers belie the actual availability, and today the 1889 Proof is considered to be the rarest date of the late 1880s! Most probably, most of these were bought by jewelers, and not many by numismatists, because the market was in a slump at the time (following frenetic activity earlier in the decade). Gold dollars were very popular for use in necklaces, bracelets, and other fancy goods.

The Making of Proofs

To strike Proof coins, in many instances a "stock" obverse Proof die was paired with a new Proof die carrying the date of a given year, such as 1858 or 1859. For some years in which the production of circulation strikes was very limited, it was a simple measure to take a reverse die that had been used in this regard, and to polish it for a further production of Proofs.

In addition, many circulation strike gold dollar dies were given a prooflike finish in the normal course of business. Such coins very closely resemble Proofs, and sometimes can be distinguished as circulation strikes only by very careful study of the die characteristics. Some, but hardly all, such pieces intended for circulation have areas with lightly struck or mushy details, unlike Proofs, which are needle-sharp. Adding to the puzzle are *inadvertent* Proofs—coins made from circulation strike dies that clashed (came together without an intervening planchet, creating incuse marks on both dies) and then were relapped or polished to remove the clash marks.

Pursuit of such information has been an interest of several researchers in the past, most notably David W. Akers, Harry W. Bass Jr., Walter Breen, and John Dannreuther. As an example of a finding, Akers posited (and Breen picked up) that Proofs of the year 1875, of which just 20 or so were struck, have deep mirror surfaces, as do most of the small mintage of 400 circulation strikes, but the latter have a tiny thorn-like projection extending into the field from the lower jaw of Miss Liberty. In the following date descriptions, Proof die characteristics are enumerated.

While not everyone agrees on what is a Proof vs. a prooflike circulation strike, guidelines formulated by the above scholars are generally used by the certification services. Absent such information, generations of early collectors and dealers have attributed thousands of prooflike circulation strikes as Proofs. Accordingly, historical catalog listings cannot be used as a guide, except in the few instances in which gold dollars have been a part of full gold Proof sets, from the dollar to the double eagle.

SURFACES OF PROOFS

The finish on Proofs is best described as deep mirrorlike in the fields or flat areas. The higher areas such as lettering, the date, Liberty Head, and wreath are satiny or frosty, sometimes made so by light acid etching. This gives them "cameo" contrast.

Many Proof gold coins have what has been widely described as "orange peel" surface on the fields. A catalog description of orange-peel texture on a Proof 1885 $5 gold coin included this: "The fields appear perfectly reflective to the unaided eye, but when a magnifier is used, the fields break up into tiny interlocking facets which have an appearance similar to sun dried mud which has cracked into millions of fragments."[13]

This piqued the interest of long-time researcher Chris Pilliod, who with assistance from James D. Bonn Sr., prepared an article, "Observed 'Orange Peel' Effect on 19th Century U.S. Proofs," which appeared in *Longacre's Ledger*, June 2007. The authors studied a similar coin, a Proof 1881 $5, under a scanning electron microscope, but found that the texture was too subtle to be discerned. Then:

> We switched to DIC microscopy (Differential Interference Contrast). This type of light illuminates the surface of the piece at high magnification and reveals the topography. . . . Our observations are summarized below:
>
> Metals form different phases when they solidify and cool. Gold is an austenitic phase metal. Austenitic alloys are characterized by superior ductility and deformability. However, if not closely controlled, they are also prone to large grain size growth on a microscopic level. The DIC was able to capture the original austenitic grain size, and it was observed to be very large on this 1881 piece. We measured an ASTM grains size of #1 on a scale of 0 to 14. As a comparison die steels are of a martensitic phase and typically exhibit a grain size of 13 or 14. A major cause of an extreme grain size such as this is an improper anneal. If a metal is heated too high during annealing the grains can grow at a rapid rate. . . .
>
> When austenitics are deformed, such as during striking, the grain boundaries deform at a different rate than the intragranular regions, and this can be observed on the surface as "orange peel" . . . Surfaces that are mirror-like and heavily deformed, such as the fields of a Proof coin, will exhibit the effect in a more pronounced fashion. . . .
>
> All four major coining metals—nickel, copper, gold and silver—are austenitic in structure and therefore subject to the same phenomenon. So why have I never observed "orange peel" on silver or nickel Proofs, I wondered. [M]y initial answer to this lies in annealing temperatures associated with each of the metals. Perhaps gold and copper have the lowest annealing temperatures, and somehow occasional blanks or strips were annealed too hot, perhaps at the temperature used for nickel annealing. Or even more intriguing, perhaps the copper and gold blanks used for business strikes or intentionally annealed at a higher temperature to make them softer and with low proof mintages perhaps the Mint in those days merely grabbed a few annealed business planchets and polished them for making Proofs. While this is an intriguing and credible explanation, it is obvious I still have more homework to do on this subject, so stay tuned!

While the preceding is an initial inquiry, it furnishes a logical explanation for a surface quality that has puzzled generations of numismatists. "Orange peel" surface, which has a "curdled" mirrorlike surface, has long been viewed as a plus by collectors—an added element of attractiveness. The article also pictured something not mentioned by the authors—microscopic criss-cross polish lines visible along with the reticulated surfaces. This seems to indicate that the dies also may have contributed to the "orange peel" effect.

4
Collecting Gold Dollars: Tradition and Overview

Gold Dollars Prized by Collectors

Numismatics became a popular hobby in the late 1850s, when the discontinuation of the "large" copper cents in January 1857 evoked a wave of nostalgia for the "pennies" of childhood. All across America, thousands of people looked through their change and picked out as many different dates as they could find. This interest quickly expanded as collectors wondered what other coins would be interesting to save. Newspapers and the newly launched *Historical Magazine* included many questions and answers about coins, their rarity and value.

In 1858 the American Numismatic Society was formed, becoming the first truly important collectors' organization in the country. In the same year the demand for Proof coins resulted in an estimated 210 silver sets being sold, plus a larger number of one-cent pieces. A few dozen, or perhaps even more, collectors who could afford to do so added gold dollars to their cabinets. At the time there was also interest in all early 1795 to 1834 gold, but scarcely any notice at all for the high denominations of $5, $10, and $20. Gold dollars became increasingly popular. Numismatic auction sales commenced in a significant way in 1859, when Augustus B. Sage cataloged three events—launching a venue that by the mid-1880s saw nearly one coin auction sale per week. Today as you read these words, dozens of sales are held each year via printed catalogs, and many more, large and small, on the Internet.

As noted earlier, gold dollars were not seen in circulation in the East and Midwest from 1862 through late 1878. Collecting enthusiasm for them continued, with all purchases being made at a premium. Then in 1879, they became a popular speculation, after which many coins were saved as investments. Today, dates from 1879 to 1889 are among the most common in choice and gem Mint State, although the overall mintages are low. Thousands of others were sold as jewelry and lost forever.

Almost immediately after gold dollars were discontinued in 1889, they became even more desired by numismatists. Ever-increasing premiums were paid for them. By the early 1890s many of the earlier dates were already regarded as being scarce. Jewelers continued to be big buyers and acquired countless thousands from the public.

Mintmark Issues

Of all gold denominations, dollars continued to be the most popular with numismatists during the 19th century. Remarkably from today's viewpoint, back then virtually all attention was paid to the coins *by date*, with few if any collectors caring whether a coin had a C, D, O, or S mintmark on the reverse. Typically, catalogers and dealers did not even bother to notice. An 1849 gold dollar was an 1849 gold dollar. Period. Further, it mattered not if it was "Open Wreath" or "Close Wreath." There were scattered exceptions, and some auction catalogs offered mintmark varieties.

In 1893, Augustus G. Heaton, an author, commercial artist, and important figure in the recently formed (1891) American Numismatic Association, published his *Treatise on Mint Marks*. Included was this:

> Since the suspension of the gold dollar coinage in 1889, the piece has been much used for ornament, and regardless of date or condition, now commands nearly 50 cents' premium. It has attracted great attention from many collectors who have sought no other gold series, and its mint marks have become generally very rare.

He continued by listing the varieties of which he was aware–such information not being readily available in any other single numismatic publication. He suggested that his little treatise might stir interest in collecting mintmarks, by finding pieces in circulation or at banks, stating that if they "should establish correspondence and exchange, one might soon hear of far advanced gold mint mark collections which would be an honor to the enterprising numismatists possessing them."

The notation by Heaton that gold dollars were "much used for ornament," reflected related comments in the popular press, dating back long before Heaton's booklet was printed. Officials of the Philadelphia Mint had been led to believe that most gold dollars of the 1880s were used as jewelry—on bracelets, necklaces, and the like. In addition to this demand, at any given time it was popular to give gold coins as presents, especially around the holiday season. After the gold dollar was discontinued in 1889, the $2.50 quarter eagle became the lowest current gold denomination and was widely used in gift-giving.

During the 1880s, the number of visitors to the Philadelphia Mint was typically in the range of 50,000 to 100,000 per year. From the cashier at the Mint, current coins could be purchased. While no records survive, it is likely that thousands of the low-mintage gold dollars circa 1879 through 1889 were sold in this manner. We also know that Philadelphia dealers such as the Chapman brothers, J. Colvin Randall, John Haseltine, and E.B. Mason Jr., bought quantities from the Mint. As already mentioned, the Mint would not sell to jewelers, likely prompting that industry to order *Proofs* in large quantities beginning in 1884. One of Virgil Brand's first coin purchases was 50 examples of the 1889 gold dollar (he also bought 50 three-dollar 1889 specimens at that time). Brand, who began his interest in numismatics as a teenager in the late 1880s, collected more than 350,000 coins, including duplicates of rarities, by the time of his death in 1926.

Continuing Numismatic Activity

Collecting gold dollars by date and mintmark soon achieved a degree of popularity, with perhaps one or two dozen numismatists aspiring to form such sets. It was found that certain Charlotte and Dahlonega dollars were especially hard to find. When located, they were nearly always well worn. At the same time, larger denominations continued to be nearly completely ignored. In 1893, Augustus G. Heaton was not aware of even a single collector who aspired to obtain mintmark varieties of $5, $10, and $20 gold coins![14]

A decade after their mintage was discontinued, U.S. gold dollars were bringing as much as $1.80 each, according to the February 1899 issue of *The Numismatist*, which noted that this obsolete coinage was in demand for "decorative purposes" and birthday gifts. While a premium of 80¢ may not seem significant to the modern reader, in 1899, a dinner at a fine restaurant could be bought for this price.

In the January 1904 issue of *The Numismatist*, Fort Worth, Texas, numismatist B. Max Mehl, whose initial advertisement had appeared the month before, was back again with a notice in which he proclaimed he specialized in American, colonial, and U.S. gold, silver, and copper coins, private and territorial issues of gold, and fractional currency:

> I deal in the above coins exclusively, and am always ready to purchase entire or part of collections at the highest prices. Send me your list of what you want to buy or sell. All letters promptly and cheerfully answered.

As if the reader didn't get the point, at the bottom of the notice appeared another comment: "Correspondence Solicited." On a facing page was another advertisement from the Fort Worth dealer, offering his *Premium List of United States Gold Dollars*, which showed "prices paid for all the U.S. gold dollars issued; including those issued at the branch mints. If you are a collector of gold dollars this last will certainly interest you." This catalog, available free of charge, was probably the first of hundreds of catalogs, leaflets, magazines, and other publications and periodicals that would eventually bear his name. Simultaneously, this little listing, very rare today, may have been the first specialized numismatic publication devoted entirely to the gold dollar.

The Numismatist for December 1905 carried news of a deposit of 100 American gold dollars, dated from 1849 to 1857, made at the Colonial Trust Company, Pittsburgh, Pennsylvania, which paid its client $1.60 each, crediting his account with $160, instead of the face value of $100. This reflected the awareness of bank tellers and officials of the scarcity of such coins.

In his sale of the Collection of a Southern Banker, September 4–5, 1908, Lyman H. Low noted: "In order to guide the collector in making his bids, I will state that the market price for common dates of gold dollars is $2. I will pay that sum for one or one hundred."

In January 1911 *The Numismatist* told of a hoard of gold coins unearthed in Ohio. Buried in glass fruit jars, the pieces had a face value of about $25,000, mostly double eagles, but including 651 gold dollars, all dated prior to 1862.

In 1907 this exchange or interview was printed, reflecting continued demand from the jewelry industry:

> "Got a gold dollar, have you?" said the jeweler. "Certainly, I'll give you something for it. It's worth a dollar to spend and a dollar and a half to sell. That's the fixed price for them, and practically any jeweler who makes use of them will give you $1.50 apiece for as many as you happen to have about you. What do we use them for? Oh, in a variety of ways; for bangles and pins and ornaments of one sort and another. There are more of them used in this way than are taken up by collectors.
>
> Of course, there are certain dates that are worth more than the regular market price for collectors. The war year issues, for instance, 1863, '64 and '65, bring from $2.50 to $5, according to condition. There are other dates that bring still higher prices. But for our purpose one date is as good as another, and a gold dollar is "as good as gold" for $1.50 at any time.
>
> Yes, they are growing scarcer all the time, of course. The government stopped coining them some six years ago [*sic;* actually in 1889], but I believe that something like 19,000,000 or 20,000,000 of them had been put into circulation up to that time, so there are still a good many tucked away in old pocketbooks and carried as pocket pieces.[15]

THE ELDER HOARD OF GOLD DOLLARS

A fascinating hoard was delineated by Thomas L. Elder in an article, "Four Thousand Gold Dollars Sold in Two Lots," printed in the January 1926 issue of *The Numismatist:*

A few details as to how over 4,000 U.S. gold dollars—those tiny coins of two sizes, coined between the years 1849 and 1889, covering a period of just 40 years—were disposed of to an American, and by him to Americans, may be of more than passing interest.

It took the World War, or, rather, its aftermath, to uncover these two hoards and remove them from their hiding places in old and dusty bags in foreign vaults and bring them again into the land of their origin. The vicissitudes of foreign paper tender must have had a great deal to do with it, possibly the shrinkage of the mark, or even the franc, but most likely the former.

At any rate, one day about two and a half years ago a tall young man with a slightly foreign accent, evidently British, drew a few samples of the coins from his pocket and extended his hand with them in its palm across the counter of a well-known New York dealer. Said he: "What will you offer for each? There are more of them—quite a few more." The price was quickly agreed on per coin and no limit was placed on the number.

The next day, in a spacious, well-furnished office resembling that used by directors in their meetings, three men sat around a table as two small bags were opened and 1,700 of the tiny coins were rolled out into view. They were counted into three piles, viz., the fine, the simply good and the damaged gold dollars. The deal being completed, the matter was thought to be ended, when, behold! some three months later the same tall Britisher telephoned the collector and asked if he would not come downtown, since another bag of gold dollars had arrived. Well, in that bag there were not only more than 2,000 gold dollars but perhaps 20 of our $3 gold pieces. Here a really remarkable find had been disposed of, and all to one individual in the city of New York.

Now, collectors, you will ask what did that immense lot of gold dollars contain and what did it prove as to the commonness or rarity of gold dollars? Surely this is a question of interest to at least those who try to keep close records on current prices of coins and priced catalogs of coin sales. One of the singular things about this big find was that the second portion of the collection contained only gold dollars of the small size. Another just as singular thing about this big find was that the second portion of gold dollars contained the rarest assemblage of dates and mintmarks, proving in a way, that in the long run the larger gold dollars—that is, the later dates—include more rarities than the smaller and older ones. The buyer paid no attention to what the lot might contain when he made the offer, because he had no way of finding that out in advance. The owner, or broker, or agent wanted a price per coin in a stated condition, and the buyer, in a business-like way, immediately made his offer and got the coins, taking a chance on what the lots might contain.

Well, in that lot of over 4,000 gold dollars there were almost all dates, not quite all, nor quite all the mintmarks. There were two 1863s, two 1864s, and all the other dates in the '60s, except 1865. The dollar of 1865 therefore, must be rated as one of exceptional rarity—not one in over 4,000! Neither was there an 1875, but all other dates in the '70s of the Philadelphia Mint were there, including an Uncirculated 1870 of the S mint. Just imagine coming across perhaps the finest 1870 of the San Francisco Mint in a pile of coins like this! But there was only one. In the first lot also were a few of the C and D mints, but not nearly all. There was no 1855, 1859, 1860 nor 1861 of the D mint. There were a considerable number of the San Francisco Mint, such dates as 1856, 1857, 1858, 1859 and 1860. There was only one 1850 of the New Orleans Mint. Strange to say the larger lot of the two, the one of over 2,000, contained very few rarities.

> Now, you may inquire, what became of all these gold dollars, and does the buyer still have them tucked in the little bags in his safe-deposit vault? Just here I will tell you how quickly those 4,000 gold dollars were absorbed—taken up so completely that not more than about 100 of them remain in the original buyer's hands. Were these gold dollars taken by dealers, to be scattered throughout the country, to keep down the value of gold dollars? Collecting Americans need not worry, for most of these coins rest today in collections which will not be sold, at least not for a good many years, for the dealers did not get them, and, except for a few scattering very small lots, they went into the hands of less than four collectors. In fact the biggest buyer of them has never been known to deal in coins or sell coins. If the knowledge that a large lot or two of gold dollars has been "around" during the past two or three years has tended to keep speculation in these coins slightly on the bear side, let not the numismatic gold dollar "bulls" despair, because the day of the gold dollar—its best day—has not yet come, but is surely coming.
>
> Knowing that this large lot is now off the market, and knowing that these little yellow pieces have always enjoyed favor among collectors, and still continue in favor, it is certain we are going to see less gold dollars in the future than we have been seeing and hearing about recently. Only the other day a big New York dealer said to me: "Gold dollars? Why, a gold dollar—we wouldn't sell one for less than $4!" I say the present craze for late-date quarter eagles is simply nothing compared with the craze that will one day seize the Americans in their search for gold dollars. The gold dollar is just as scarce as ever. It sold for $4 four years ago, and will sell for $4 for common issues in the very near future, I predict. See if I am not right.
>
> The popularity of the gold dollar has been very great, and is destined to become still greater as the supply diminishes. Mr. [Lyman H.] Low[16] told of having gone to the Philadelphia Mint in 1889, the last year of their coinage, and how the mint master urged him to take a thousand brilliant new gold dollars, which had just been struck, for their face value, but the numismatist either did not have the means or the inclination to accept this suggestion and passed up the wonderful opportunity.
>
> Since that day things have changed as regards the gold dollar, and as early as 1908 or 1910 the gold dollar of 1861 of the Dahlonega Mint made a record of $250 or more. The writer sold several for over $225 apiece. DeWitt Smith paid, I think, $280 for one specimen and valued its rarity extremely high. One of this mint and date came over the writer's counter back about 1910. Recent fluctuations in the prices of the common dates have shown very clearly how the law of supply and demand governs the price of coins.

Years later, in *Hobbies* magazine, May 1943, Elder printed a revised version stating that two groups of gold dollars, *7,000* in total, had come to New York during the World War, and he had bought them for $2 each, unsorted. Whether this was the group mentioned in 1927 *plus* another group was not stated.

Still later, in "The Cost of Gold Dollars," in the *Numismatic Scrapbook Magazine*, February 1946, Elder commented:

> During the First World War when the [value of the gold] dollar went up to $2.50, then when the depression of 1920–22 came it sagged a bit, but not much. Two large finds came on the market soon after, which were disposed of at from $2 to $2.10 per coin. After that came the Baltimore find of several thousand, which sold at the same

> figures. Since then the gold dollar has not been offered in any quantity, not even in lots of a hundred.
>
> An inquiry four years ago disclosed there were no large lots around, and the price commenced to rise. From $2.50 it rose rather slowly and has since gone to $5 for Fine and $7.50 to $8 for Uncirculated for common dates in recent coin sales. . . .
>
> The mintmarked gold dollars are at the present moment in great demand at rising prices. They have gone up faster than the regular mint [Philadelphia] series. Uncirculated gold dollars of 1863, 1864, and 1865 seem to be about as rare as the 1875, still they do not bring nearly as much as 1875.

Elder is personally responsible for rescuing many gold dollars from oblivion, because in the early 20th century he circulated buying lists of coins to bankers and jewelers stating that all coins of this denomination were worth a premium, and that some, such as Charlotte and Dahlonega coins, were particularly valuable. Vast quantities of gold dollars appeared in his auction catalogs from 1905 to 1940. Perhaps this book should have been dedicated to his memory!

Beginning in the 1930s, a passion arose for the collecting of gold coins of all denominations, up to and including the formerly neglected $5, $10, and $20 pieces. By that time, many opportunities were long gone.

The Baltimore Find

In 1934 two young lads found a remarkable cache of several thousand gold coins in the cellar of a house at 132 South Eden Street, East Baltimore. These pieces, the latest of which were dated 1856, must have been hidden in that year. Many of the dates just prior to 1856 were gems. No precise accounting of the "Baltimore Hoard" or "Baltimore Find" is known. The treasure has been the subject of great numismatic interest, meriting a section in my book, *American Coin Treasures and Hoards*, and several articles by researcher Len Augsburger.

The sale of the coins was conducted on May 2, 1935, at the Lord Baltimore Hotel downtown, with Perry W. Fuller serving as auctioneer. About 100 people attended including a few out-of-town dealers and many local curiosity seekers. Grouped into 438 lots and casually described (most pieces were simply called "very fine") in a printed catalog, the hoard realized $19,558.75.

On that day, per the auction catalog, the following gold dollars were sold, with the listing omitting mintmarks(!):

1849: 95 pieces

1850: 78

1851: 452

1853: 976

1854 Type I: 215 [curious that the next two are also 215]

1854 Type II: 215

1855: 215

1856: 296

Various damaged coins 1849–1856: 39

More than just a few coins from the Baltimore Hoard found their way to dealer Thomas Elder, either on the aftermarket or, possibly, from the many pieces that were sold privately by the finders, and of which no details are known today. M.H. Bolender also had quite a few in his mail bid sales.

Numismatic Considerations Today

Today, gold dollars stand high as collectors' favorites. They are collected in a number of ways, including in sets of three—one of each major design type—and in date and mintmark sequence. In recent decades, in which *high grade* has become the oriflamme for well-financed newcomers to the hobby, the concept of gem quality has propelled certain coins to record high price levels, never mind if they are *common* dates. To such buyers, a superb gem MS-67 1853 gold dollar—a date that is extremely common in lesser grade—is much more desirable than a rare 1853-D in "only" MS-60 grade. This has created a new market for buyers who acquire *selected gems* as "trophy coins," without any thought of completing a type set or series. The several types of buyers each contribute to a very strong market.

For the specialist or systematic collector there are numerous rare issues to contemplate. All from the Charlotte and Dahlonega mints are elusive, and several, including the 1853-D, 1854-D, 1855-C, 1855-D, 1856-D, 1857-D, 1858-D, 1859-D, and 1860-D, are rare. Most Charlotte and Dahlonega gold dollars are very weakly struck, this being especially true of issues struck after 1854. The same situation occurred with most quarter eagles and half eagles from the same two Southern mints.

One of the most famous of all gold dollar rarities is the 1861-D. This was struck after the Dahlonega Mint was captured by forces of the Confederate States of America. No coinage records were kept, but it is estimated that only about 1,250 or so were made. The 1861-D stands today as the sole gold coin known to have had its entire issue struck under Confederate auspices. Whenever one of these comes on the market, like as not it is accompanied by a sentence or two, or even a paragraph, of text mentioning its history—deservedly so.

To the specialist, weak and/or generally poor striking simply reflect the personality or charm of Charlotte and Dahlonega gold dollars. This statement may seem illogical—or to be a seller's apology or an excuse to the uninitiated numismatist such as the aforementioned gem-seeking buyer–but time and again in numismatics, coins that show evidence of rustic die surfaces or primitive striking often are the focus of attention. Remarkably in the view of an outsider, such coins often sell for sharp premiums, simply because they have an especially high degree of human interest.

Allow me to expand on this seeming paradox. Elsewhere in North American numismatics, there is an avid desire to acquire such naive pieces as the entire production of crudely-made copper coins from Machin's Mills (Newburgh, New York in the late 1780s); the "Indiana primitive" Civil War tokens created by Henry D. Higgins (Mishawaka, Indiana), and the even more enigmatic "Buffalo primitives" (Civil War tokens produced in Buffalo, New York, by a presently unchronicled maker, among which are the only known Civil War tokens to have *diagonally reeded* edges). To these can be added the extensive series of blacksmiths' tokens (usually associated with Canada), the rustic Hard Times tokens struck in Albany and Troy, New York, circa 1837, the 1652-dated Massachusetts silver Willow Tree coinage, and the 1795 *Jefferson Head* large copper cent—this being but a *short list* of pieces and areas that have captured the fancy of advanced collectors. The reason for dwelling on this is that someone just entering the hobby would probably be completely amazed to learn that Dahlonega and Charlotte coins can be eagerly competed for, eagerly sought, and cherished for a long period by discriminating numismatists, even though the pieces are poorly struck and on defective planchets. In the absence of the above information, a cover-up by the owners of C and D coins might be imagined!

Among all gold dollars produced at the various mints from 1849 to 1889, several varieties are relatively available in worn grades, but emerge as great rarities at the Mint State level. Examples include 1857-S, 1858-S, and 1859-S, among others. These gold dollars from the San Francisco Mint were strictly utilitarian when made: they were struck and passed out into circulation. So far as is known, not a single piece was saved as a numismatic souvenir!

All Philadelphia Mint gold dollars from 1863 to 1878 are scarce in any grade and rare in Mint State, the 1863 being especially so, although its elusivity is generally known only to numismatic scholars. In his 1926 article about the hoard of 4,000 gold dollars, Thomas Elder singled out the 1865 for special mention, and this remains a prized rarity today. Many gold dollars of the 1880s have the appeal of low mintage figures in combination with relative ease of acquisition today, simply because quantities were saved at the time by collectors, dealers, and investors.

More information will be found under "Ways to Collect Gold Dollars" in the next chapter.

HOW MANY GOLD DOLLARS EXIST TODAY?

Walter Breen, in *Major Varieties of U.S. Gold Dollars*, 1964, discussed the rarity of the denomination, noting (in part):

> There is no entirely safe basis for estimating the current total population of gold dollars. It is likely to be only a few hundred thousand, regardless of what Treasury redemption figures might say. Of these few hundred thousand, many thousands are mutilated by holing, plugging, looping or use (with soldered shanks) as buttons. This even includes the rare dates in the 1860s and 1870s.
>
> Characteristic Ratios (number extant / number minted) can be somewhat doubtfully estimated, such estimates based on censuses of the rare dates and mintmarks. Dahlonega Mint coins seem to have survived to the extent of 0.5% to 2%. Charlotte Mint perhaps a little more. . . . The census for 1849 Type I—swelled by the presence of a number of gem Uncirculated examples evidently saved as souvenirs—may be as high as 4% or a little over. That for some of the rarer Philadelphia dates in the 1860s and 1870s seems to be between 1% and 2%.

Breen's 1964 study was an early entry in research involving the survival of gold dollars and is viewed as being somewhat inaccurate today. For example, in 1964 Breen wrote of the 1860-D "Probably less than a dozen known." Later studies by David W. Akers (1975), Breen again (1988), and others have added a tremendous amount of information. Today, an estimate in the 100 range for 1860-D coins seems more reasonable.

AUCTION SURVEY

I have surveyed more than 5,000 auction catalogs and price lists issued since the late 1850s. These have ranged from the mainstream and well-known productions of W. Elliot Woodward, the Chapman brothers, B. Max Mehl, Numismatic Gallery (Abe Kosoff and

Abner Kreisberg), and others through the mid-20th century, and Stack's—which alone remains active from this era—continuing down to the individuals and companies of the present era. Included have been thousands of catalogs not surveyed by Walter Breen or other researchers, including, in particular, those published by Thomas L. Elder, the leading dealer and auctioneer in the gold dollar field from 1905 through the late 1930s—and just about everyone else.

Although many individual gold dollars are mentioned later under the different dates and mints, there is *one* memorable cabinet that included gold dollars in bulk. In February and March 1954, the coins of ousted and exiled King Farouk I were auctioned in Cairo, by Sotheby's, under the title of The Palace Collections of Egypt. The typical lot consisted of rare and common coins mixed together in bulk, with very little description. The Farouk gold dollars were described as follows:

> Lot 285—1849 (2) Open and Close Wreath, 1849-C, 1849-D, 1849-O, 1850, 1850-C, 1850-D, 1850-O, 1851, 1851-C, 1851-D, 1851-O, 1852, 1852-C, 1852-D, 1852-O, 1853, 1853-C, 1853-D, 1853-O, 1854, 1854-D, 1854-S. Mounted in a fitted case, cellophane each side of coins; an interesting set, all Very Fine or better. 24 pieces.
>
> Lot 286—1854, 1855, 1855-C, 1855-D, 1855-O, 1856 Upright 5, 1856 Sloping 5, 1856-D, 1856-S, 1857, 1857-C, 1857-D, 1857-S, 1858, 1858-D, 1858-S, 1859, 1859-C, 1859-D, 1859-S, 1860, 1860-D, 1860-S, 1861, 1861-D, 1862, 1863. Similarly mounted to last lot, mostly Very Fine or better, the 1863 a brilliant Proof. 27 pieces.
>
> Lot 287—1864, 1865, 1866, 1867, 1868, 1889, 1870, 1870-S, 1871, 1872, 1873, 1874, 1875, 1876, 1877, 1878, 1879, 1880, 1881, 1882, 1883, 1884, 1885, 1886, 1887, 1888, 1889. Similarly mounted to last two lots, a set all in beautiful condition and many brilliant Proofs. 27 pieces.

Today, auction listings of gold dollars are a dynamic part of the marketplace. The perusing of descriptions and examination of the illustrations can be an important guide to availability and rarity.

5
How to be a Smart Buyer

Overview of Grading

The ANA System

In today's numismatic world the assigned grade of a gold dollar (or other coin), particularly if that dollar is in a holder certified by a leading service, is the prime determinant of its value. While such aspects as sharpness of strike, planchet quality, and overall eye appeal are very important to connoisseurs and advanced specialists, to perhaps 90% of buyers, numbers are everything. This has an immense benefit in the marketplace, since coins that are unattractive from an eye appeal standpoint will find a ready market today, whereas several decades ago such pieces were apt to remain in dealers' stocks for a long time. I am not intending to be cynical, but simply to give a feeling for grade and the role it plays.

At present, nearly everyone uses the system outlined in the book, *The Official ANA Grading Standards for U.S. Coins.* Grade levels are assigned numbers along with descriptors. In the range of Uncirculated or Mint State coins, grades are continuous from MS-60 to MS-70 inclusive, covering 11 grades. At lower levels, grades are spaced more widely apart, such as Good-4 (G-4), jumping to Very Good-8 (VG-8), then to Fine-12 (F-12), and so on. See the ANA Grading Standards, discussed later in this chapter.

Generations Ago

When gold dollars first attracted the interest of numismatists at the inception of the popular coin market in the late 1850s, descriptions had little meaning with relation to the grades we know today. A coin might be described as "Good," which at the time meant "nice" or "worth having." Very Fine and Extremely Fine were used, but not About Uncirculated (AU). It was not unusual to see a description such as "Extremely Fine, lustrous." Today, a coin with much if not most luster would probably be called About Uncirculated or even Mint State. Although the *Mint State* nomenclature was in use in early times, until the 1970s, *Uncirculated* was the preferred form. Now it is *Mint State* nearly exclusively, following the ANA grading system.

Prices, Grades, and Descriptions in 1918

In the 1860s, or even in the 1910s, a large difference in grade did not necessarily mean a large difference in price. Examples are legion. Accordingly, while collectors and dealers yearned for a uniform grading system to be formulated, the financial effects of an overgraded or undergraded coin could sometimes be very slight.

In 1918, Elmer S. Sears, one of America's leading coin dealers (who until that time had been associated with Wayte Raymond in conducting the United States Coin Company), put out a fixed price list. Among professionals of his era, Sears enjoyed one of the finest reputations, and his grading could be relied upon.

At the time, nearly all numismatists sought "nice" examples of a given gold dollar. If an Extremely Fine specimen was acquired, that requirement was filled, and there was no need to search for an upgrade. At the time there were no reference books listing mintages, rarity, or prices of gold dollars. There was no competition to be the "best." While catalogers were often enthusiastic when a choice example was offered, the descriptions were usually brief. These examples from the Sears list reflect the small difference between the prices of Uncirculated gold dollars and those showing wear (modern comments added in brackets in some instances):

1849-D Uncirculated, mint lustre. $6.50; Very Fine, $3.50.

1849-O Uncirculated. $4; Fine, $2.65.

1850 Uncirculated, mint lustre. $3.50; Very Fine, $2.50.

1851 Uncirculated, mint lustre. $3.50; Very Fine, $2.50.

1851-C Uncirculated. $4; Very Fine, $3.50.

1851-D Die cracked at I of AMERICA and E of STATES, also at T of UNITED. Only specimen I have seen with these three die breaks. Uncirculated, mint lustre. $15. [Sears placed a premium on die cracks. Today in the early 21st century, the presence or absence of die cracks usually has no effect on prices, but many collectors find them to be interesting.]

1851-D Without die break at I of AMERICA. Uncirculated. Rare. $12.50.

1851-D Uncirculated. $6.50. [Sears offers no clue as to how this 1851-D at $6.50 differs from the two Uncirculated coins listed above.] Very Fine, $4.75.

1852 Uncirculated, mint lustre. $3.50; Very Fine, $2.50.

1853 Uncirculated, mint lustre. $3.50; Very Fine, $2.50.

1853-O Uncirculated. $4; Extremely Fine, $3.50.

1870-S Practically Uncirculated. Of great rarity. $110; Very Fine, extremely rare, $75.

The Contrast of Today's Prices

Fast forward to today, a century after Elmer Sears's listing, when the ANA grading standards are nearly universally used. Today, a coin is described as G-4, VF-20, EF-40, MS-66, or some other abbreviated grade followed by a number. The higher the number, the finer the coin. Absent the numbers, if the coins were described as Good, Very Fine, Extremely Fine, and Mint State, a newcomer to the hobby might not know how to rank them. "Good" is in fact a very low grade for a gold dollar. Few serious collectors would buy one at this level. However, an 1853 (common date) simply described as "Good" grade in an Internet listing might indicate that here, indeed, was a very worthwhile coin.

No longer do prices of gold dollars hover in about the same range for each variety, with an Uncirculated coin selling for just a small amount more than an Extremely Fine. Consider these values for gold dollars listed in the *Rare Coin Market Report—PCGS Price Guide*, December 2007:

1853–EF-40, $235. AU-55, $295. MS-60, $355. MS-63, $1,310. MS-64, $1,875. MS-65, $6,200. MS-66, $9,000. MS-67, $22,500. MS-68, $38,500.

1858–Proof-60, $3,525. Proof-62, $4,700. Proof-63, $9,000. Proof-64, $20,000. Proof-65, $35,000. Proof-66, $45,000.

1862–EF-40, $235. AU-55, $295. MS-60, $375. MS-63, $1,185. MS-64, $1,400. MS-65, $3,200. MS-66, $4,200. MS-67, $8,000.

1863–Proof-60, $3,400. Proof-62, $4,425. Proof-63, $5,750. Proof-64, $9,500. Proof-65, $18,500. Proof-66, $27,000.

1870-S–EF-40, $850. AU-55, $1,450. MS-60, $3,000. MS-63, $7,400. MS-64, $13,000. MS-65, $23,000. MS-66, $36,000.

1881–EF-40, $235. AU-55, $295. MS-60, $375. MS-63, $1,115. MS-64, $1,400. MS-65, $3,200. MS-66, $3,700. MS-67, $5,500. MS-68, $15,000.

1884–Proof-60, $2,800. Proof-61, $3,000. Proof-62, $3,300. Proof-63, $4,950. Proof-64, $6,100. Proof-65, $10,500. Proof-66, $15,000. Proof-67, $25,000.

It is seen that a small difference in grade can make a huge difference in price. Consider the first listing, an 1853 Philadelphia Mint coin, the same variety listed by Elmer S. Sears in 1918 for $2.50 in Very Fine (a notch below the EF-40 minimum given in the 2007 list) and $3.50 Uncirculated. An Uncirculated piece was less than 50% more than a Very Fine.

Today, assuming that Sears's coin was nice and equivalent to, say, MS-64, not unusual for an 1853, today's figures are $235 EF-40 and $1,875 MS-64. The last is about 800% of the price of the first.

"There is safety in the ANA numbers," you might think. And, you would be right, in a sense, because while today there may be differences of opinion, they are usually not as wide as they were a century ago. Still, a small, normal difference of opinion of one grading point in the Mint State or Proof categories can have a dramatic effect.

Focus on an 1855-D Gold Dollar

Consider this "case study," the detailed listing penned by Heritage Auction Galleries for a coin in its January 2004 Platinum Night Sale:

> 1855-D MS-62 (PCGS). Partial Date. Variety 7-I. The great majority of 1855-D gold dollars are quite poorly struck. However, the piece has much better detail than usual. The obverse has some weakness on the hair below LIBE with the rest of the strands showing clear separation The plumes in the headdress are fully detailed while most of the denticles are clear. The reverse is very sharp with the wreath displaying complete detail. The 8 in the date is weak, as usual, while the other three digits are fully brought up. Both sides show a number of clashmarks.
>
> Ex Hancock and Harwell; 1999 ANA (Heritage, 8/99), Lot 7627; Chestatee Collection (Duke's Creek Collection duplicates); Hancock and Harwell; Michigan Collection; Hancock and Harwell; Jeff Notrica; Doug winter; 1991 FUN Sale (Mid-American, 1/91), Lot 1727; Jascha Heifetz Collection (Superior, 10/89), Lot 3899; Connoisseur's Collection (Superior (1/89), Lot 256; Dr. Philip Weinstein; 1986 GNA Sale (Mid-American, 5/86), Lot 1817; Auction '82 (Paramount's session), Lot 1841; Donald Groves Collection (Stack's, 11/74), Lot 473; Ullmer Sale (Stack's, 5/74), Lot 340; and Miles Collection (Stack's, 9/68), Lot 27. Graded Mint State 62 by PCGS.
>
> This coin has been graded AU-50 to MS-63 in its numerous auction appearances. This is the plate coin in the second edition of Winter's book on Dahlonega gold and is listed as the third finest known in the updated Condition Census.

Notably, over a period of time in the late 20th century this coin had been graded by experts as AU-50 upward. Now that it is certified as MS-62, discussion comes to a halt! The coin is likely to remain in this holder forever, or if resubmitted, not taken out of the holder—as there is a chance as a "raw" coin it might be sent back to the About Uncirculated level. The Heritage cataloging, although it does not solve the grading problem, reflects a detailed description of the surface, allowing a buyer to learn more than simply a grading number.

The earlier-mentioned PCGS *Rare Coin Market Report* gives these values for the 1855-D gold dollar:

> 1855-D–EF-40, $15,000. AU-55: $27,500. MS-60, $47,500. MS-63, $90,000. MS-64, $145,000 [highest grade priced].

Going back to the Heritage comment, "The coin has been graded AU-50 to MS-62 in its numerous auction appearances," it seems evident that the holder determines the price. Interpolating the PCGS values given above, an 1855-D at AU-50 might be worth $22,500, while at MS-62 it might be valued at, say, $75,000.

The quality of this particular 1855-D is not in question. It is one of the finer known examples. As to whether you or I will agree it is MS-62 is not the point. Rather, the point is that if you as a buyer are looking at ANA grading numbers as being "scientific," you are sadly misled. Is this 1855-D a $22,500 coin or a $75,000 coin? Ponder the thought.

This is a great example of several concepts:

1. Over the years, experts have had divided opinions as to the grade of this coin, one suggesting as low as AU-50, another as high as MS-63. The most that can logically be said is that this is a high grade 1855-D, and that some experts consider it to be a low-level AU-50 (this being the lowest number in the About Uncirculated category), while others consider it to be Mint State, or a coin that has never been in circulation.
2. Now that the coin is in a PCGS holder certified as MS-62, it might be financially dangerous to remove it. What if the second time around, it is graded AU-50 once again? Accordingly, it is likely that the coin will be accepted in the marketplace as a Mint State coin at the 62 level. Its past grading history, nicely given by Heritage, is likely to be ignored in future offerings.
3. Since it may cost, say, $20 to have an 1855-D gold dollar certified, it is readily seen that the owner of a coin graded AU-50 could send it to a grading service dozens of times, paying $20 for each go-around, and if it eventually is certified as MS-62, that owner will hit the jackpot. On the surface this is a win-win situation. The owner of the coin makes thousands of dollars profit, and the grading service profits on the dozens of times it sees the coin.
4. A final note: While the Heritage description informs the buyer that this coin, while above average, has some weakness in the hair and a weak 8 in the 1855 date, anyone looking at the holder would not know this, for the striking and surface characteristics are not mentioned at all.

Often, there is far more to know than what is given on the label of coin holder. Now you know the story.

Details of the ANA Grading System

Background of the ANA Standards

The seemingly curious use of 1 to 70, rather than 1 to 10 or 1 to 100, originated in a market formula for large copper cents of 1793 to 1814, delineated in 1949 by William H. Sheldon in *Early American Cents*. At that time the market for cents was far different from what it is now, and an MS-60 coin was worth just twice as much as a VF-30 one. This was understandable and was not much different from the Elmer S. Sears pricing jumps used in 1918, and employed by everyone else in numismatics from the 1850s until toward the end of the 20th century.

By assigning a Basal Value (another Sheldon concept) to a cent in 1949, say a Basal Value of $2, then a numismatist could calculate that a VF-20 coin of a certain variety was worth $2 x 20 or $40, an EF-40 coin was worth $2 x 40 or $80, and an MS-60 coin was worth $2 x 60 or $120, and so on. Today, there is a huge difference between VF-30 and MS-60, and the Sheldon system is completely useless. In fact, only a few years after 1949, it was recognized as being pseudo-science and invalid. However, the concept of using numbers lived on, and today we have them.

At first, the *Official ANA Grading Standards* mirrored the Sheldon system of numbers, but extended to all other series beyond early copper cents. In successive editions intermediate numerical grades were added, such as AU-55, MS-63, MS-67, etc., then the full range of Mint State possibilities, including MS-61, MS-62, and so on, plus additions in lower categories as well. Tom DeLorey, first president of the ANA Certification Service (ANACS), pioneered many of these distinctions. Today in the About Uncirculated range we have AU-50, 53, 55, and 58. Perhaps someday we will also have AU-51, 52, 54, 56, 57, and 59. Who knows?

Upon close inspection, the ANA Grading system for VF-20 extends 10 points until VF-30 is reached, but there is not much market difference today between a 20 and a 30. The MS-60 grade extends 10 points to MS-70, with *extreme* pricing differences for many steps. Illogical, yes. Most people are not aware of how such numbers originated—but now you know. We still do not have explanatory adjectives added, as Howland Wood proposed way back in 1910.

A 100-point grading system might be more logical, in keeping with the grading of fine wine, antique automobiles, and a few other specialties. For the grading of *stamps* the Professional Stamp Experts (PSE) division of Collectors Universe (parent of the Professional Coin Grading Service) has developed a well-reasoned 100-point system that combines condition or evidence of wear and handling with appearance and centering. In my opinion a PSE-certified stamp is more solidly graded than is a coin by any commercial service.

For the present, it seems that the 70-point ANA scale for coins is here to stay. A light at the end of the tunnel was furnished by John Albanese in 2007 when he launched the Collectors Acceptance Corporation (CAC). This service reviews coins that have already been certified by various services. If the CAC observers believe that a coin is correctly graded and is of premium quality within that grade, it is given a CAC sticker. So far, this concept has been well received in the marketplace. However, whether a coin is weakly struck, sharply struck, or somewhere in between, is not stated. The determination of this very important (in my opinion) aspect is left up to the buyer. Perhaps CAC will refine its service to include that concept.

ANA Grading Standards for Gold Dollars

Type I 1849–1854

MINT STATE. *Absolutely no trace of wear.*

MS-70. A flawless coin exactly as it was minted, with no trace of wear or injury. Must have full mint luster and brilliance. Any unusual die or planchet traits must be described.

MS-67. Virtually flawless but with minor imperfections.

MS-65. No trace of wear; nearly as perfect as MS-67 except for some small blemish. Has full mint luster and brilliance but may show slight discoloration. A few barely noticeable nicks or marks may be present.

MS-63. A Mint State coin with attractive mint luster, but noticeable detracting contact marks or minor blemishes.

MS-60. A strictly Uncirculated coin with no trace of wear, but with blemishes more obvious than for MS-63. May lack full mint luster and brilliance.

ABOUT UNCIRCULATED. *Small trace of wear visible on highest points.*

AU-58, Very Choice. Has some signs of abrasion at hair near coronet and tips of leaves.

AU-55, Choice. *Obverse:* There is a trace of wear at upper hair line below coronet. *Reverse:* Trace of wear visible on tips of leaves. Three-quarters of the mint luster is still present.

AU-50, Typical. *Obverse:* There is a trace of wear on hair lines near coronet, and below the ear. *Reverse:* Trace of wear visible on tips of leaves. Half of the mint luster is still present.

EXTREMELY FINE. *Very light wear on only the highest points.*

EF-45, Choice. *Obverse:* Slight wear shows on highest wave of hair, hairline, and below ear. All major details are sharp. Beads at top of coronet are well defined. *Reverse:* Leaves show visible wear at tips, but central details are clearly defined. Part of the mint luster is still present.

EF-40, Typical. *Obverse:* Slight wear shows on highest wave of hair, hairline, and below ear. All major details are sharp. Beads at top of coronet are well defined. *Reverse:* Leaves show visible wear at tips, but central details are clearly defined. Traces of mint luster will show.

VERY FINE. *Light to moderate even wear. All major features are sharp.*

VF-30, Choice. *Obverse:* Beads on top of coronet are well defined. LIBERTY is complete. Hair around face and neck slightly worn, but strands fully separated. Star centers show some details. *Reverse:* There is light even wear on legend and date. Some details show in center of leaves.

VF-20, Typical. *Obverse:* Beads at top of coronet are partially separated. LIBERTY is complete. Hair around face and neck noticeably worn but well outlined. Some star centers show details. *Reverse:* Legend and date have light even wear. Only traces of leaf ribs are visible. Bow knot is flat on high point.

FINE. *Moderate to heavy even wear. Entire design is clear and bold.*

F-12. *Obverse:* LIBERTY is complete but weak. Ear lobe is visible. Hairlines and beads on coronet are worn smooth. Stars are clearly outlined, but centers are flat. *Reverse:* Legend within wreath is worn and weak in spots. Leaves and wreath are well outlined. Rim is full and edge is beveled.

VERY GOOD. *Well worn. Design is clear but flat and lacking details.*

VG-8. *Obverse:* Only the outline of hair is visible. Four letters in LIBERTY are clear. *Reverse:* Only the outline of leaves is visible. Legend and numeral are worn and very weak.

GOOD. *Heavily worn. Design and legend are visible but faint in spots.*

G-4. *Obverse:* Head is outlined with nearly all details worn away. Stars are weak. Full rim shows. *Reverse:* Date and legend well worn but readable. Leaves are outlined. Full rim shows.

Notes: The gold dollars struck at Charlotte and Dahlonega are crude compared to those of the Philadelphia Mint. Frequently they have rough edges, and the die work appears to be generally inferior. In grading coins from these branch mints, consideration must be made for these factors. The 1849-D is usually weakly struck.

Type II 1854–1856

MINT STATE. *Absolutely no trace of wear.*

MS-70. A flawless coin exactly as it was minted, with no trace of wear or injury. Must have full mint luster and brilliance. Any unusual die or planchet traits must be described.

MS-67. Virtually flawless but with minor imperfections.

MS-65. No trace of wear; nearly as perfect as MS-67 except for some small blemish. Has full mint luster and brilliance but may show slight discoloration. A few barely noticeable nicks or marks may be present.

MS-63. A Mint State coin with attractive mint luster, but noticeable detracting contact marks or minor blemishes.

MS-60. A strictly Uncirculated coin with no trace of wear, but with blemishes more obvious than for MS-63. May lack full mint luster and brilliance.

ABOUT UNCIRCULATED. *Small trace of wear visible on highest points.*

AU-58, Very Choice. Has some signs of abrasion at hair over Liberty's eye and bow knot.

AU-55, Choice. *Obverse:* There is a trace of wear on hair over eye. *Reverse:* Trace of wear visible on bow knot. Three-quarters of mint luster is still present.

AU-50, Typical. *Obverse:* There is a trace of wear on hair over eye, at curl below ear, and at top of feathers. *Reverse:* Trace of wear visible on tips of leaves and bow knot. Half of the mint luster is still present.

EXTREMELY FINE. *Very light wear on only the highest points.*

EF-45, Choice. *Obverse:* There is slight wear on hair at forehead, below ear, on tops of feathers, and on cheek. All major details are sharp. *Reverse:* Slight wear shows on tops of leaves, bow knot, wreath, and 1 DOLLAR. Part of mint luster is still present.

EF-40, Typical. *Obverse:* There is slight wear on highest wave of hair, on hairline, below ear, on top of feathers, and on cheek. All major details are sharp. *Reverse:* Slight wear shows on tops of leaves, bow knot, wreath, legend and date. Traces of mint luster will show.

VERY FINE. *Light to moderate even wear. All major features are sharp.*

VF-30, Choice. *Obverse:* Hair above forehead and around neck worn, but some details are visible. LIBERTY is complete. Legend is strong. *Reverse:* Wear shows on legend. Leaves and bow knot show some detail.

VF-20, Typical. *Obverse:* Hair, feathers, and curl tips are outlined with only slight detail. LIBERTY worn but visible. *Reverse:* Bow knot well worn. Slight detail visible in leaves. Some indentation remains on cotton bolls.

FINE. *Moderate to heavy even wear. Entire design is clear and bold.*

F-12. *Obverse:* Hair and some feathers smooth. Earlobe visible. TY in LIBERTY almost smooth. *Reverse:* Bow knot, leaves, and cotton bolls outlined only, with no details visible.

VERY GOOD. *Well worn. Design is clear but flat and lacking details.*

VG-8. *Obverse:* The headdress is outlined only. Earlobe is partially visible. Three or four letters in LIBERTY will be clear. *Reverse:* Wreath is outlined and lacks any detail. Legend and date are very weak, but visible.

GOOD. *Heavily worn. Design and legend visible but faint in spots.*

G-4. *Obverse:* Headdress is outlined only. Legend is worn but visible. LIBERTY is smooth. *Reverse:* Wreath outlined. Date and legend are well worn, but visible.

Notes: Clash marks are frequently seen and should be described. They do not alter the condition of the coin. Nearly all of these coins have weakly struck spots on the reverse, especially at LL in DOLLAR, and in the date.

Type III 1856–1889

MINT STATE. *Absolutely no trace of wear.*

MS-70. A flawless coin exactly as it was minted, with no trace of wear or injury. Must have full mint luster and brilliance. Any unusual die or planchet traits must be described.

MS-67. Virtually flawless, but with minor imperfections.

MS-65. No trace of wear; nearly as perfect as MS-67 except for some small blemish. Has full mint luster and brilliance but may show slight discoloration. A few barely noticeable nicks or marks may be present.

MS-63. A Mint State coin with attractive mint luster, but noticeable detracting contact marks or minor blemishes.

MS-60. A strictly Uncirculated coin with no trace of wear, but with blemishes more obvious than for MS-63. May lack full mint luster and brilliance.

ABOUT UNCIRCULATED. *Small trace of wear visible on highest points.*

AU-58, Very Choice. Has some signs of abrasion at hair over Liberty's eye and bow knot.

AU-55, Choice. *Obverse:* There is a trace of wear at hairline over Liberty's eye and bow knot. *Reverse:* Trace of wear visible on ribbon bow knot. Three-quarters of mint luster is still present.

AU-50, Typical. *Obverse:* There is a trace of wear at hairline and at top of feathers. *Reverse:* Trace of wear visible on tips of leaves and bow knot. Half of the mint luster is still present.

EXTREMELY FINE. *Very light wear on only the highest points.*

EF-45, Choice. *Obverse:* There is slight wear at hairline, hair near ear, tops of feathers, and on cheek. *Reverse:* Slight wear visible on tips of leaves, bow knot, wreath, and legend. Part of mint luster is still present.

EF-40, Typical. *Obverse:* Slight wear shows at hairline, on hair near ear, tops of feathers, and on cheek. All major details are sharp. *Reverse:* Slight wear shows on tops of leaves, bow knot, wreath, legend, and date. Traces of mint luster will show.

VERY FINE. *Light to moderate even wear. All major features are sharp.*

VF-30, Choice. *Obverse:* Hair above forehead and around neck worn. Feather curls are outlined but show some detail. LIBERTY complete. Legend strong. *Reverse:* Wear shows on legend. Leaves and bow knot show some detail.

VF-20, Typical. *Obverse:* Hair, feathers, and curl tips are outlined with only slight detail. LIBERTY worn but visible. *Reverse:* Bow knot well worn. Slight detail visible in leaves. Some indentation remains on cotton bolls.

FINE. *Moderate to heavy even wear. Entire design is clear and bold.*

F-12. *Obverse:* Hair and some feathers are smooth. Earlobe is visible. Part of LIBERTY is worn almost smooth. *Reverse:* Bow knot, leaves and cotton bolls outlined only, with no details visible.

Notes: This type is seldom found in grades below Fine. LIBERTY is sometimes weakly struck; occasionally it is missing, even on Uncirculated specimens.

$1 Gold, Type 1. Many dates come weakly struck in the hair below "LIBERTY" and behind the ear. Most Charlotte and Dahlonega pieces of all denominations come weakly struck to very weakly struck, 98% of the time. The 1849-D is a date that is usually weakly struck.

$1 Gold, Type II. The rule on both 1854 and 1855 (especially the 1855) is that the "LL" and "85" are weakly struck on the reverse. On some specimens, the middle digits are virtually nonexistent.

$1 Gold, Type III. The 1856 and 1857 are occasionally seen with very weak strikes on the upper half of the coin, and can come weakly struck in general. The same also applies to the 1874. After this date, Type III specimens are generally well struck and sometimes prooflike in appearance.

How to Be a Smart Buyer of Gold Dollars

If you've read and absorbed the grading and market information above, you are well on your way to becoming a smart buyer of gold dollars. To paraphrase a popular statement from some years ago, you will "question authority." You will see a grading number, but will know that the number in itself is not definitive. For a gold dollar, there is *much more* information you need in order to obtain good values in the marketplace.

In the following paragraphs I share my ideas on how you can build a truly superb collection of gold dollars, with due consideration that some varieties are easy to find in high grades with excellent eye appeal, and others are not. This is a reiteration of some items already mentioned, plus new ideas, followed by a summary. Gold dollars are very complex, and one rule does not fit all.

As will be seen later in this book in the discussion under the various gold dollar issues by date and mint, evaluating an 1857-C, which usually is poorly struck and on an unsatisfactory planchet, takes a different mindset than doing the same for an 1889, which usually is found Mint State, well struck, and very beautiful. You've already read of the complexities of a certain 1855-D that has been graded all the way from AU-50 to MS-63 by expert numismatists.

As no rule fits all gold dollars, in addition to the guidelines given below, you must consult the individual listings for characteristics of each variety. Although the ANA grading system does not have additional adjectives such as "weakly struck," "poor planchet," "prooflike surface," and so on, the adding of these terms, by the informed seller or by *you* when you consider purchase, is absolutely essential if you are to be a smart buyer.

Step 1: The Numerical Grade

When considering gold dollars, check market listings to determine what grade level you might like to buy for each of the varieties. This will be influenced by your budget plus the desire to obtain good value for your money. Consider, for example, these price levels (again from the *Rare Coin Market Report* published by PCGS):

> 1855-O–EF-40, $1,100. AU-55, $3,000. MS-60, $7,500. MS-63, $27,500. MS-64, $38,500.
>
> 1856-D–EF-40, $7,000. AU-55, $11,000. MS-60, $30,000.
>
> 1888–EF-40, $235. AU-55, $295. MS-60, $375. MS-63, $1,185. MS-64, $1,400. MS-65, $3,200. MS-66, $3,700. MS-67, $5,500. MS-68, $16,500.

How much do you want to spend? If your budget is unlimited—say you've won the sweepstakes or your bachelor Uncle Henry left you a fortune—by all means aspire to the high end of the scale: an MS-63 or 64 1855-O, an MS-68 1888, and so on. However, if you are like most of us, an element of practicality will enter your thinking. Even if you can afford an MS-68 1888 for $16,500, is it a good use of your money? Might an MS-66 at $3,700 be a better buy? Bear in mind that the MS-68 might be called that by a certain certification service, but that another might evaluate it as MS-66.

To reiterate, in forming a "want list" of what to look for, in grades beyond MS-65, for gold dollars having large quantities available in such grades, you may want to be careful, no matter how extensive your finances may be. A very small difference in grade, such as between MS-66 and MS-67 or between MS-67 and MS-68, can mean a very large difference in price. In actuality, two such certified coins viewed side by side may appear to be not much different.

The reason for determining the grade in Step 1 is that, for example, if you desire to purchase an MS-63 1888 gold dollar, there is no sense asking a dealer to send you, on approval, an MS-60 or an MS-67. Per the current price structure it seems that if your desire is to own an MS-63 1888, you might as well go for an MS-64 for just a slightly higher cost.

This reflects the situation that you should build your want list coin by coin, and not by a blanket rule, such as all EF-40, or MS-60, or MS-63. In addition, there is an element of availability. Even with your uncle's inheritance, you cannot buy an MS-65 1856-D if no such grade is available for that particular date and mintmark.

Once you set up a want list, it is time to explore the wide world of coins for sale—the numismatic marketplace—ranging from dealers' price lists, to auctions, to coin shops and conventions. I suggest that you spend some time in "field work," looking at coins at shows, studying sharp images (when you can find them) on the Internet, and exploring elsewhere. On the Internet, many images posted by professional numismatic firms are quite good. From the comfort of your favorite chair you can browse the Internet and learn a lot.

A good way to begin this is to start simply. Pick, say, the date 1853, and review all of the pictures and listings you can, including the Charlotte, Dahlonega, and New Orleans branch mint coins for that year. Use the appropriate pages in this book to gain basic information as you explore. Before you know it, you'll understand what is a "nice" coin and what is not! You will be well on your way to being a smart buyer.

With this in mind it is time to start your search.

Assume you have opted to buy an EF-40 1855-O ($1,100 in the above-quoted list), an EF-40 1856-D ($7,000), and an MS-64 1888 ($1,400)—these being reasonable grades for many specialists, and yielding good value within the grades. If you are at a coin show or are viewing auction lots, then ask to see coins in these categories.

I recommend that you stay with coins certified by one of the leading grading services. The two most popular are the Professional Coin Grading Service (PCGS), founded in 1986, and the Numismatic Guaranty Corporation of America (NGC), founded in 1987. Runners up are ANACS and Independent Coin Grading (ICG). There are at least a dozen or more other services, some of which are reliable, others of which are simply exploitative and give unreliable grades intended to deceive gullible buyers. As to which services are best, this is a hot potato subject. It would probably be best to "ask around" among collectors and dealers and get their ideas. The earlier-mentioned Collectors Acceptance Corporation (CAC) approval of a certified coin can be very valuable as well, as CAC is independent and has no connection with any service.

Take your time. Look at coins. Read this book. Reread the descriptions of interest. It is easier to buy a coin than to sell one. Before you buy a coin, you'll want to be sure it will be a "keeper," and not one that a year hence you will wish to upgrade.

Zero in on the coins you need, one at a time. Let's use the 1888 in MS-64 as an illustration. Look around and find one for sale. Then go through the following steps (which you can repeat for several 1888 dollars, or a dozen—until you find one that is just right). There are many dollars of this year and grade in the marketplace—perhaps not right now, today, but over the course of a year. As of press time for this book, ANACS, NGC, and PCGS have certified about 400 in MS-64. These are submission *events*, not necessarily all different coins. Still, it is likely that a couple hundred or so are in collectors hands.

Now, with a certified 1888 MS-64 gold dollar in hand, even better if it has a CAC sticker (but at present, only a few holders have these, as the service is new, having been launched in autumn 2007), you have a candidate for your further consideration.

STEP 2: EYE APPEAL AT FIRST GLANCE

At this point take a quick glance at the coin. Is it "pretty"? Is it yellow gold and pleasing to your eye, or is it dingy, or with some copper spots, or with red or black staining? Is it brilliant and lustrous, or is it dull? Is it prooflike, which is dandy, but is it also attractive in its other aspects?

If the 1888 is not pleasing to you, then reject it and go on. A general rule is that a coin that is very attractive to your eyes will be attractive to others when you sell your collection. A coin that is unattractive to you is likely to be rejected by some buyers in the future. There are a lot of unattractive or even downright ugly MS-64 coins in holders, and it is up to you to avoid them. Many 1888 gold dollars have copper stains or spots from improper mixing of the alloy. Avoid these.

Among gold dollars of the Philadelphia Mint, most in MS-63 or better grades have nice eye appeal, as do many at lower levels. Branch mint coins, particularly Charlotte and Dahlonega, can be a great challenge, with many as ugly as a toad (but not marked as such). Again, it is up to you to avoid these.

Now, with an attractive MS-64 1888 gold dollar in your hand, one with *great* eye appeal, it is a candidate for your further consideration.

STEP 3: EVALUATING SHARPNESS AND RELATED FEATURES

At this point you have a gold dollar that you believe to be more or less in the numerical grade assigned, a coin with excellent eye appeal. The next step is to take out a magnifying glass and evaluate its sharpness. When weakness is found on an 1888 gold dollar, it is usually on the higher parts of the design, such as the hair of Miss Liberty, or on the reverse at the two central figures of the date. Check the dentils, too. Most 1888 dollars are well struck, however.

While every gold dollar should be checked, by following the guidelines for each date and mintmark variety in this book you will know that most 1888 gold dollars are sharply struck (but still need to be checked), while most Charlotte and Dahlonega gold dollars of the mid- and late 1850s are poorly struck. For some varieties, fully struck coins do not exist. However, within those or other categories you will want to find the best that is generally available. A little secret is that since certified holders do not mention sharpness, when you find a sharply struck example, likely it will cost no more than a weakly struck one. This is the benefit of knowledge.

Examine the attractive MS-64 1888 gold dollar carefully, and reject it if there are any problems with the surface or planchet. No compromise of any kind need be made, as there are others in the marketplace to consider. If the coin you are considering buying has passed the preceding tests, it is a candidate for your further consideration.

STEP 4: ESTABLISHING A FAIR MARKET PRICE

Now, you have a very nice 1888 gold dollar candidate for your collection! Next comes the evaluation of its price.

For starters, use one or several handy market guides for a ballpark estimate. This book is a handy guide, but as prices change, sometimes rapidly, you should also consult one of the weekly or monthly listings, such as *Coin Values* (published by *Coin World*), the "Coin Market" feature of *Numismatic News*, or the *Certified Coin Dealer Newsletter*. The *Rare Coin Market Report*, published by PCGS, gives prices for coins of that service. Nearly all Philadelphia Mint gold dollars in grades up to MS-63 or 64 have standard values and trade within certain ranges, and some issues are bought and sold regularly in higher grades. In contrast, for certain rare Charlotte and Dahlonega gold dollars, AU-50, AU-58, MS-60, and MS-61 might be the range available, and there are no MS-64 or higher coins. For gold dollars in ultra high grades, and for which just a few have been certified, prices can differ widely. Be careful.

If a particular gold dollar is easy enough to find in a given grade—with sharp strike, fine planchet quality, and good eye appeal—then be sure the coin is being offered for about the going market price. This applies to the nice 1888 used as an example here. If the going price is, say, $1,300 to $1,500 (as an illustration only; check *current* prices when you buy), then if you are offered a beautiful 1888 for $1,500 it might be worth buying—for it is on hand, you've inspected it, and there is value of having a bird in the hand, so to speak. On the other hand, if the seller is asking $2,200, it would be best to pass it by, unless, by virtue of your own experience and perhaps consultation of an expert, it is found to be undergraded and really an MS-65 (these things do happen).

If the nice MS-64 1888 is offered at the bargain price of $1,000, then you'd better look at it again, and more carefully. Perhaps it has a defect you have not recognized. Or perhaps it is in a holder of a grading service with a questionable reputation. Usually, correctly graded certified coins with sharp strike and excellent eye appeal, certified by a leading service, are not priced as bargains. For sure (based upon my knowledge so far), those with CAC stickers will command strong market values.

As part of building your collection of gold dollars, it may be desirable to pick a dealer you like, of good reputation (check around with other collectors who have dealt with him or her), with reasonable prices, and buy as many as you can from this single source—then fill in any open spaces later. Take your time, and buy slowly.

Voila! Now, by careful consideration, you have a very beautiful MS-64 gold dollar, one without any problems, and acquired at a fair market value. Tuck it away in your collection and go on to the next coin!

Time Out for Enjoyment

Gold dollars are meant to be *enjoyed.* It would be no fun at all, even if you could afford it, to write a check and acquire in one fell swoop a complete collection of every date and mintmark from 1849 to 1889. Your interest would probably fade.

On the other hand, by viewing your collection as an adventure and gathering the coins one by one, and over a period of time, each will be a special "friend," with its own character and personality. Read as much as you can about gold dollars—here as well as in other books, auction offerings, and lists. As a collector of selected coins, tokens, medals, and paper money varieties, I keep these in a bank vault, but have sharp photographs or scans of each. I regularly enjoy viewing them on my laptop computer. Because the images are in high resolution I can see even the smallest details.

Take time to view the coins you have, then look at them again every so often. Each new purchase will be a treasure. Look, contemplate, read, study. You will find that as a smart buyer your numismatic life will be all the richer for the experience, and in time you will have a beautiful set of one of America's most interesting coins.

Take time to learn as much you can about the gold dollars you already own as well as those you hope to acquire. Books are an excellent source. David W. Akers' 1975 study, *United States Gold Coins: An Analysis of Auction Records, Gold Dollars*, provides a view of the availability of dates and mintmarks in various grades, in an era when there were no minute differences in grading, save for occasional adjectives such as *choice* and *gem.* This is also a good resource for contemplating the "gradeflation" that has occurred since then. Douglas

Winters' books on Charlotte, Dahlonega, and New Orleans gold coins give much information on gold dollars, including descriptions of die varieties, and are essential for the specialist. Information about gold dollars in the 1987 work, *Walter Breen's Encyclopedia of U.S. and Colonial Proof Coins, 1792–1977* has been superseded in many instances by modern research, but the text still remains valuable. Hereafter, this title will be referred to as Breen (*Proof* 1989) since 1989 was the most recent edition. *Walter Breen's Complete Encyclopedia of U.S. and Colonial Coins* also discusses gold dollars. Hereafter it will be referred to as Breen (*Encyclopedia* 1988). See the Selected Bibliography for other suggestions.

Reality check: If you've absorbed the information in this book so far, you have a good general knowledge of how gold dollars were minted and distributed, how they have been collected over the years, and how to be a smart buyer in today's marketplace. If you are like I am when I read a book on a new area of numismatics, you will want to go back and re-read some of the earlier information once you finish. I dare say that at this point you are better informed than 90% of the buyers who are looking for gold dollars!

Ways to Collect Gold Dollars

Introduction

Dozens of dates and mintmarks of gold dollars were minted from 1849 to 1889. Over a long period, dozens of numismatists have endeavored to acquire one of each date and mint. More often, they selected examples of the different types—one of each. Below are some of the possibilities.

A Type Set of Gold Dollars

Probably the most popular way to acquire gold dollars is to acquire one of each design, popularly known as Type I, Type II, and Type III. Of course, forming a type set is not seriously collecting gold dollars, what with just three coin types. Not much challenge here—not much to command your lasting attention. Gold dollars by the three types are usually sought as part of a larger type set that includes other denominations.

Focusing on the major designs, the following are some comments concerning their availability, and points to look for when buying.

Type I: Liberty Head (1849–1854)

A representative example of the first type is easily enough obtained in just about any grade desired. For a Mint State coin, the most obvious and least expensive possibility is a Philadelphia Mint issue. Circulated coins in grades from VF-20 to AU-58 are very common. Most collectors ignore the VF level and start at EF or AU. Within Mint State levels, MS-60 to MS-63 coins are very affordable. True gems at the MS-65 and higher levels, if sharply struck and with good eye appeal, are found with regularity, but cannot be called common in relation to the demand for them. The year 1853 is the easiest to find in all grades, although the first year, 1849, has a high survival rate and perhaps is the easiest to locate in gem Mint State, although 1851, 1852, and 1853 gold dollars appear frequently, as their large mintages suggest. The 1850 is very rare at the MS-65 or higher level.

Across the board, Type I gold dollars vary widely in sharpness of strike, quality of planchet, and eye appeal. There are enough in the market, however, that finding one that is just right will present no difficulty.

If you can afford to do so and want to add spice to your set, seek a branch mint gold dollar. These are generally available in circulated grades, but can be rare in Mint State—

especially if sharply struck, without flaws, and with good eye appeal. The Type I can be divided into two sub-types: 1849 Open Wreath, and 1849 to 1854 Close Wreath.

Type II: Indian Princess, High Relief (1854–1856)

This is the key type among the three designs. The most available are the Philadelphia Mint issues of 1854 and 1855. Choice Mint State coins are at once scarce and expensive. Nearly all are weakly struck, especially at the two central date numerals (85) on the reverse, but often on the highest details of the Indian Princess's head on the obverse. Some cherry-picking will yield a better-than-average strike for little in the way of an additional premium, for certification services do not take note of striking sharpness, and only connoisseurs seek such pieces. Branch mint coins are very elusive, especially in high grade—this being especially true of 1855-C and 1855-D—and are not usually sought for a type set.

When buying a Type II gold dollar, put your "smart buyer hat" on and be careful. It will take time to find a sharp strike, without flaws, and with superb eye appeal. Such coins are in the minority in all grades, and at the Mint State level, probably not one in 10 coins will pass muster. Challenge is part of the game! Enjoy the hunt.

Type III: Indian Princess, Low Relief (1856–1889)

Gold dollars of this type are readily available in Mint State, this being true of the Philadelphia issues to 1862 and, especially, of the later period, 1879 through 1889. Branch mint coins range from scarce to rare, with Mint State pieces being formidable rarities. The later years are especially popular, since the mintages are low, but the survival rates are high. Even though a date such as 1880 may be easily acquired at the gem level, there still is something special about contemplating the low mintage of just 1,600 coins. Never mind that 1,000 or more survive in Mint State! In contrast, for the 1863 gold dollar only about 30 to 50 Mint State coins survive from a mintage of 6,200. Such situations contribute to the fascination of collecting gold dollars.

While some Type III gold dollars have problems with striking, planchet quality, or other negatives, the vast majority are sharply struck and attractive. Still, it will pay to examine every detail carefully.

Specialized Collections of Gold Dollars

One of Each Date and Mint

A full set of gold dollars from 1849 to 1889 forms an interesting challenge to collect. For basic dates and mintmarks there are no "impossible" rarities, although certain of the Dahlonega and Charlotte issues from the mid-1850s onward are rare and expensive, as are the 1870-S and, among Philadelphia Mint coins, the 1875 in particular. If varieties are added beyond basic dates and mintmarks, a special challenge is the 1849-C with Open Wreath, of which just about a half dozen are known, far fewer than any of the scarce and rare standard date and mintmark issues.

Among circulation strike issues, as a general rule Philadelphia coins can be obtained in Mint State. Most are readily available in grades up through and including MS-64 and MS-65, although challenges are provided by certain dates in the mid-1860s, and the 1875 is both rare and expensive. The 1850 and several years in the 1860s and 1870s are hard to find in MS-64 or higher grades, with sharp strike and good eye appeal.

Charlotte and Dahlonega coins are another situation entirely. A complete Uncirculated collection has never been formed, and probably never will be, although it should be noted that some pieces certified today as MS-60, MS-61, and MS-62 might better be called AU, and are not Uncirculated by old time standards. By all logic, a Mint State coin should not show *wear*, but many lower level certified Mint State coins do—part of the grading game collectors and dealers seem to enjoy. Realistic expectations for Charlotte and Dahlonega coins are pieces grading EF-40 upward, carefully selected for striking sharpness, planchet quality, and eye appeal. Most advanced collectors would rather have a fairly sharp 1857-C on a fairly nice planchet and graded AU-58, than one graded MS-62, poorly struck, and on a miserable planchet. Such options are very realistic and examples appear frequently in the marketplace. Individual listings for the different varieties give further explanations.

Generally, New Orleans gold dollars, minted from 1849 through 1855, can be collected in high Circulated grades as well as various Mint State levels, although some are rare. The quality of New Orleans pieces tends to be quite good, with striking excellent and with nice eye appeal. San Francisco gold dollars, made from 1854 intermittently to 1860, and then again in 1870, can vary in striking sharpness, but are usually on nice planchets and have great eye appeal. Realistic expectations for advanced buyers range from AU through lower Mint State grades, although for some it is a possibility to acquire gems.

A full set of gold dollars of hand-picked quality (considering sharpness of strike, planchet surface, and eye appeal) will usually take several years to form, even in grades such as EF and AU. For higher grades, anything goes, and the endeavor can be a lifetime pursuit, as, indeed, it was for the late Harry W. Bass Jr., who enjoyed adding to his collection for more than 30 years, until his passing.

Gold Dollars From a Favorite Mint

For a long time, Charlotte and Dahlonega coins have attracted a strong following, not necessarily by those who collect only gold dollars from these two Southern mints, but as part of collections that include other denominations as well, up to the $5 half eagle. These are sought with passion, and constitute a separate and dynamic market, quite independent of the rarity-to-price ratio aspects of Philadelphia coins. Coin for coin, a Charlotte or Dahlonega dollar of approximately equal rarity to a New Orleans or San Francisco gold dollar will sell for much more.

As noted throughout the text, Charlotte and Dahlonega coins are often miserably struck, this being particularly true of issues from 1855 onward. This does not dampen the demand for them in the slightest, because the rustic nature of these pieces adds to their overall appeal—as curious as this may seem.

Gold Dollar Die Varieties

Among the various dates and mintmarks, gold dollars could be collected by die varieties with minor differences, but only a handful of people have ever done this. The Thomas G. Melish Collection auctioned by Abe Kosoff in April 1956 was laden with duplicates of certain dates, attributed with die cracks, repunchings, and other features. Similarly, the Harry W. Bass Jr. Collection included varieties. John Dannreuther, a particularly knowledgeable dealer, has spent much time studying gold dollar die varieties (especially the issues of 1849) and debunking Walter Breen's assertion that Proofs of 1865 were restruck.

Proofs

An expanded complete collection might include one of each Proof for Philadelphia issues, in addition to circulation strikes. Chapter 3 tells how such pieces were made and distributed. In the late 20th century, Harry W. Bass Jr. acquired Proofs in addition to circulation strikes, and was able to buy a number of rarities from the 1850s. Ed Trompeter assembled a full set of Proof gold dollars from 1858 onward, as part of his remarkable Proof gold collection of all denominations. John Jay Pittman was another Proof specialist.

Generally, Proof gold dollars can be collected from the 1854 Type II onward, with the first several years being very rare. Later issues are mostly elusive, through the early 1880s, but tend to turn up on the market rather frequently. This is because some people buy them as "trophy coins" and part with them relatively quickly—in contrast to dedicated collectors who may keep them for a lifetime. Proofs of the mid-1880s onward are much more easily found, except for the rare 1889.

"Trophy Coins"

In recent years, especially after the advent of certifying coins in sealed holders, many investors and collectors have sought trophy coins. These are gold dollars or any other coin that is rare, not necessarily because it is a scarce date or mint, but because it is in a particularly high grade, and thus is among the finest of its kind. As curious as it may seem to a long-time collector of the traditional turn of mind, a rare and historic 1861-D gold dollar (all of which were struck under the auspices of the Confederate States of America) in a grade such as AU-50 would not be considered a trophy coin, but a common-date 1853 gold dollar, of which thousands of Mint State pieces are known, would be considered a trophy in a grade such as MS-68 or MS-69, simply because at that particular level, not many have been certified.

David Hall, a founder of PCGS, initiated the brilliant marketing concept of the Registry Set, in which PCGS allows collectors and investors to register the numbers assigned to their PCGS coins (no consideration for striking, planchet quality or eye appeal), and then ranks them in order, with special appreciation being given to those who have examples at the highest level certified. This alone has prompted tremendous demand for trophy coins, and has had a resultant dramatic effect on the prices of such.

Owners of trophy coins tend to quickly tire of the novelty of ownership, a boon to coin auction companies. It is not unusual for a high-grade gold dollar to have appeared in auctions three, four, or even a half dozen or more times within a decade or two. This is in contrast to the "buy and hold" philosophy of most collectors forming type sets or specialized collections.

6
How to Use This Book

For each date and mintmark issue in the gold dollar series from 1849 to 1889, I have given extensive information, which includes the following narrative and data sections.

America and Numismatics. Each year-and-mintmark group is preceded by this feature, which includes items relating to politics, American life, economics, and other aspects, plus commentary on events in the numismatic field.

Circulation-Strike Mintage. This figure is taken from the *Annual Report of the Director of the Mint*, except for certain instances marked "estimate." In the latter situations, such as for the 1856 Philadelphia Mint varieties with Upright 5 and Slanting 5, the Mint report figures are not broken down into these groups, and thus estimates are given—based upon the author's experience, consultation with others, and an evaluation of the number known today. Statistics for the 1861-D are necessarily estimated since no records were kept.

Proof Mintage. Taken from the Mint report, modified by research in the National Archives by R.W. Julian. For some early Proofs, estimates are made by the author.

Key to Collecting. Gives a general overview of the issue with regard to circulation strikes and their availability in the numismatic market today, combined with suggestions of aspects to look for if you desire to build a high quality collection within whatever grade levels you choose.

Estimated Total Population (Mint State). The author's estimates, in consultation with others, of the number of gold dollars in existence today that could can be classified MS-60 or finer. Within the MS-60 to MS-62 range are many coins that, a generation ago, would have been called About Uncirculated. Figures for certified populations of MS-63 and higher give a better estimate as to the quantity certified without "gradeflation," and may better reflect the number of "nice" Mint State coins graded.

Estimated Total Population (Circulated Grades). The author's estimate of the number in existence in grades from very well worn up through and including AU-58.

Characteristics of Striking and Die Notes. Information is derived from the Mint reports, observations by the author, published texts, advisors, and other sources, plus examination of the coins themselves. For some issues, additional information is given under Numismatic Notes.

Population Report Totals for Circulation Strikes. The number certified, divided into categories, as reported by ANACS, NGC, and PCGS in early 2008. These figures will necessarily change as new coins are submitted and older coins are resubmitted. Moreover, since a cost is involved in submitting coins for certification, many lower grade issues of common gold dollars have not been certified. High-grade gold dollars of significant market value are often submitted multiple times in the hope of gaining an even higher grade, which in many instances can have an extreme financial impact. Accordingly, certified populations of very high-grade coins may overstate the number in existence, while for low-grade coins, the numbers may be understated. For example, the 1854 Type II and 1855 are both scarce, but since they are especially valuable, inordinate numbers have been certified, making them appear common in relation to certain other dates that in reality are much easier to find (but not in certified holders).

Current Market Values. Estimated values for a typical certified coin offered in the marketplace as of early 2008. Values are subject to change over time, as well as within a specific period. Prices depend upon demand, the appearance of the coin, and other factors. For current market transactions, auction and other records can also be consulted. Further, prices of coins in higher grades or of those that trade infrequently in certain grades are apt to vary widely as occasional pieces come on the market. Verification of this can be obtained by reviewing auction realizations.

Estimated Total Population and Key to Collecting for Proofs. Estimates of the number of different Proofs surviving today. Commentary as to their availability. For some issues, additional information is given under separate headings below.

Population Report Totals for Proofs. Certification events for Proofs reported by ANACS, NGC, and PCGS as of early 2008. Such numbers typically increase as more coins are certified or resubmitted. For the latest information check current population reports of the several services.

Current Market Values of Proofs. Estimated values for typical Proofs in the grades listed. Because Proofs are generally rare, actual transactions at auction or private sale can vary widely.

Numismatic Notes. These include die information, historical listings, and other information of interest to specialists and advanced collectors. Topics discussed in Numismatic Notes include, but are not limited to, the following:

Die Data. This includes a description of the four-digit date logotype punched into each working die. Over a period of time, the size and styles of the dates changed, in addition to the year itself. There are several instances in which, within a given year, multiple-date logotypes were used. These include 1856, 1859, and 1873. Apart from these, as a general rule the same logotype was used all year at all mints and also on circulation strike dies as well as Proof dies. Accordingly, details of the logotype are given under the first listing for the year, which is the Philadelphia Mint listing.

Auction Information. Includes commentary concerning selected auction appearances, often with citations of particularly interesting or significant items, or citations that reflect changing descriptions or opinions.

Examples of Characteristics of Coins

To aid in understanding the terms used throughout chapters 7, 8, and 9, the photos and descriptions below illustrate a variety of differences, features, and other aspects of gold dollar coins. Enlargements are made to varying scales.

Date-Logotype Differences. On all dies after 1849, the dates were punched into the working dies with a four-digit logotype. Accordingly, there are variations as to the orientation of the date up or down as well as left to right. The relation of the date in respect to certain letters of the word DOLLAR above and the wreath ribbon bow(s) below are aids in recognizing such differences. Dates, if punched deeply into the die, can appear heavy, while if punched lightly, or if the die was relapped, can appear light. These variations have no effect on the value of a coin.

Beginning in 1850, each different die for each mint or for the same mint had a slightly different positioning of the date logotype, since these were punched in by hand.

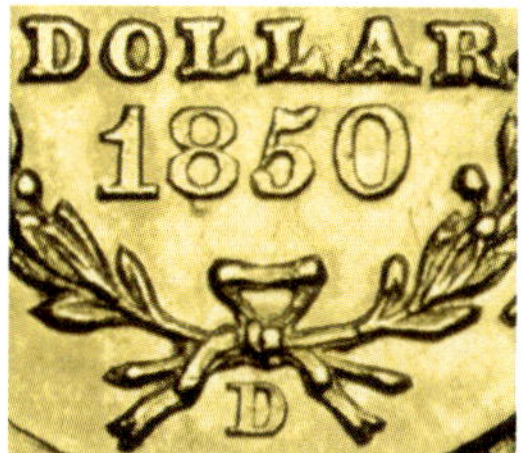

High date on an 1850-D gold dollar. Note that the date is closer to the word DOLLAR above than it is to the ribbon bow below. Note also the distance between the wreath leaf and the lower left serif of the numeral 1.

Centered date on an 1850 gold dollar.

Low date on an 1850-O gold dollar.

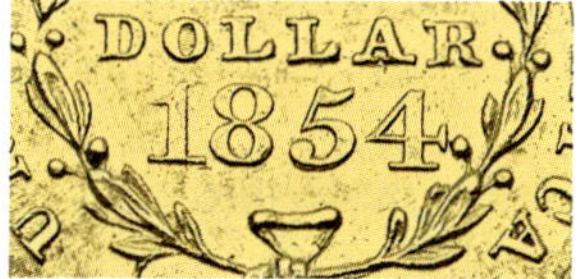

Date on an 1854 Type I gold dollar. On this and other illustrated dies, note the position of the 1 and its distance from the leaf, and the relation of the crossbar of the 4 to the berry; note also the distance from the date to the word DOLLAR.

1854 date on an 1854-D Type I gold dollar.

1854 date on an 1854-S Type I gold dollar.

1861 Proof with date logotype low, with 6 centered slightly to the left of the peak on the ribbon bow.

1861 circulation strike with date logotype higher in the field, with 6 centered slightly to the right of the peak on the ribbon bow.

The date logotype on the 1889 gold dollar was punched at a slant, with the 1 closer to DOLLAR than is the 9. Circulation strikes and Proofs both have this feature.

Clash Marks. When dies come together without an intervening planchet, features of the obverse die are transferred or clashed into the reverse die, and vice versa. These marks have no effect on the value of a coin.

The full outline in mirror image of the head of Liberty can be seen on the reverse of this 1854 Type II gold dollar—the result of clashing. Note the nose and lips near D (DOLLAR). (Inverted image.)

Unfinished and Relapped Dies. Many dies for circulation-strike gold dollars, especially in the 1860s, were lightly ground down, but not completely finished by polishing. As a result, early strikes from these dies show many tiny parallel *raised* lines, usually oriented upward at a slant from the vertical, in the obverse and/or reverse fields. As more coins were struck, the lines wore away and became less noticeable. The same striae are common on other gold denominations of the era and on many silver issues. Unlike hairlines and scratches, striae are raised on the surface of a coin and are only on the flat or field surfaces—not on the letters, numerals, or designs. These are not visible on certain photographs if the lines are oriented perpendicularly to the camera lens. Oriented crosswise, the striae are very prominent in an image. Little notice is usually taken of striae, and they have no impact on the value of a coin, because for certain years they are expected.

Occasionally a gold dollar is found struck from a die that has had very little grinding and is, in essence, "raw." Such coins show the letters, numerals, and other features much bolder and in higher relief than those struck from properly finished dies. Letters and numerals appear larger and closer together. There is no market premium or deduction for a coin struck from an unfinished die.

When dies became damaged (such as by clashing) or worn, they were often ground down to remove the old surface and create a smoother field. This process ground away some of the low-relief features such as berry stems (on Type I dollars), leaf stems, ribbon ends, and so on. Stars were made smaller. While it would seem that a coin struck from a perfect die would be more valuable than one made from a relapped die, in the marketplace, few buyers take notice either way.

Gold dollars of 1849 had the date in the master die and hub, with the result that there are no positional differences for this year only. However, the 1849 date can have different appearances depending on the depth of the impression into the working die and the finishing of the working die.

Illustrated is an 1849-C gold dollar for which the working die received very little finishing by grinding down and polishing, and therefore was essentially "raw" as received from the Philadelphia Mint—although it may have been hardened. The result is that the numerals appear to be heavier, closer together, and with certain interior areas filled or clogged.

Philadephia Mint 1849 gold dollar, this one struck from a die that was ground down properly and polished. The numerals appear lighter and more widely spaced, and their interiors are clear.

Extensive die striae on the obverse of a circulation strike 1862 gold dollar.

Extensive die striae on the reverse of a circulation strike 1867 gold dollar.

Heavy relapping on the reverse of this 1849-O dollar resulted in removing features in low relief in the die, including stems to the berries and parts of the ribbon, and weakening the date.=

Heavy relapping on the reverse die of this 1869 gold dollar has removed lower relief areas of the ribbon and some features of the wreath. The date is very bold, raising the possibility that the die was relapped before the date was punched in, an unusual procedure.

Sharpness of Strike. If dies are properly spaced in the coining press, and if the planchet is properly annealed (softened by heating, then cooling slowly), the result will be a coin with needle-sharp features. Dies spaced too far apart or planchets that are too hard from improper annealing will yield areas of light striking—typically on the features cut deepest into the dies. On the obverse these include the higher parts of the portrait of Liberty, and on Type II the tips of the ostrich plumes on the headdress. The reverse may be weak at the ribbon bow knot and on certain features of the wreath. On many coins the two center digits of the date are weak. In all instances a sharply struck coin is more valuable than a weakly struck one.

Sharply struck head of Miss Liberty on an 1851 Type I gold dollar.

Weakly struck head of Miss Liberty on an 1851-D Type I gold dollar. Note the lack of details in the hair below the coronet.

Weakly struck stars and border dentils on the obverse of an 1849-O Type I gold dollar.

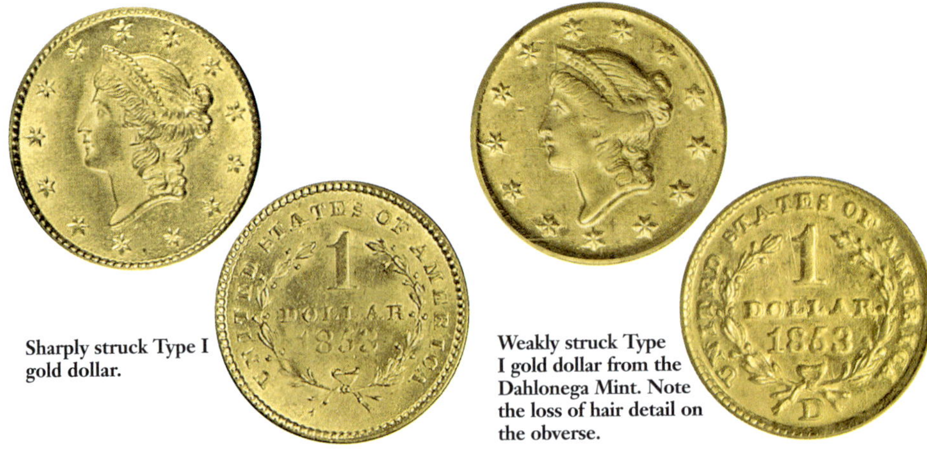

Sharply struck Type I gold dollar.

Weakly struck Type I gold dollar from the Dahlonega Mint. Note the loss of hair detail on the obverse.

Fairly well-struck head of Miss Liberty on a Proof 1855 Type II gold dollar. There is some slight lightness on a few hair strands. Only a few Type II dollars are this sharp, and hardly any are sharper. Problems with striking prompted the Mint to change the design in 1856.

Light striking on the hair details and feather tips of the portrait on an 1855-O Type II gold dollar.

Well struck head of Miss Liberty on a Proof 1857 Type III gold dollar.

Weakly struck head of Miss Liberty on an 1857-D Type III gold dollar.

Sharply struck reverse on an 1887 gold dollar. Note the delicate vertical details on the ribbon knot, a feature visible only on well-struck examples of Type II and III coins.

Weakly struck reverse on an 1876 gold dollar. The ribbon knot lacks details and the 8 is lighter than the other numerals.

Die Cracks. Occasionally, a gold dollar will be found showing evidence of cracks that occurred due to stress or wear of the die. Such a coin displays irregular raised cracks that are interesting to view. These have no effect on its value.

Die crack on the reverse of an 1849-D gold dollar.

Die crack on the reverse of an 1849 Open Wreath gold dollar.

Die cracks on the obverse of an 1849-O gold dollar.

Crack linking stars 2 to 4 (counting left from tip neck) on an 1851 gold dollar.

Planchet Quality. For many coins of the Charlotte and Dahlonega mints, rough or irregular planchets were used, often in combination with damaged dies or unsatisfactory striking. Some have laminations or pieces missing from the planchet. While such defects are to be expected, the occasional coin that is problem free will have a higher value if of a date that ordinarily is found with inadequacies.

1850-C gold with large lamination area at ITE (UNITED) at the left side of the reverse.

1853-C gold dollar with a large lamination or piece out of the planchet near the bottom border.

1853-C with small lamination, half-moon shape, at the left of the denomination numeral 1.

7
TYPE I GOLD DOLLARS
(1849–1854)
CORONET OR LIBERTY HEAD DESIGN

THE BEGINNING OF GOLD DOLLARS

The first gold dollar design, the Coronet or Liberty Head type, made its debut in May 1849 and its use continued through part of 1854. The design of Miss Liberty on the obverse was of the same style used on the pattern $20 gold coins of the year. She faces left with her hair tied at the back, and wears a coronet inscribed LIBERTY. Thirteen stars surround.

The reverse depicts a wreath open at the top and enclosing the numeral 1, the value DOLLAR, and the date. Varieties of 1849 gold dollars exist with "Open Wreath" and "Close Wreath," the latter style being continued through early 1854. The inscription UNITED STATES OF AMERICA surrounds.

Measuring just 1/2 inch (12.7 mm) in diameter, the gold dollar of the 1849–1854 type is the smallest U.S. coin, being even smaller than the 14.3 mm silver three-cent piece. Production was continuous from 1849 through 1854.

MINTS AND MINTAGES

Examples of Type I gold dollars were produced primarily at the Philadelphia Mint, but the facilities at New Orleans, Dahlonega, Charlotte, and San Francisco contributed as well. As a general rule, the coins of Dahlonega and Charlotte were made in small numbers.

Dahlonega Mint gold coins dated 1853 or earlier, of all denominations, are apt to have a yellowish "brassy" color, because the Dahlonega Mint used a very large proportion of silver to make up the 10% of metal beyond the 90% gold in the alloy. In addition, much California gold—also often brassy in color—was sent to Dahlonega in the early 1850s, before the San Francisco Mint opened for business (in 1854). The standard had been defined as 900 parts gold, 75 parts copper, and 25 parts silver. On September 29, 1853, Philadelphia Mint director James Ross Snowden advised Dahlonega Mint director Julius M. Patton that, at Philadelphia, the gold coins typically contained 900 parts gold, 92 parts copper, and 8 parts silver. In contrast, a modern evaluation of various Dahlonega Mint coins from 1838 to 1853, reported by Clair M. Birdsall, revealed 37 to 48 parts of silver per 1,000 parts of metal.[17] At Dahlonega in 1854, the situation was corrected somewhat, and coins of that year revealed 13 to 14 parts of silver. Exact percentages were difficult to achieve in the reality of the refining process, but after 1853, the coins no longer had their brassy color.

The San Francisco Mint opened in spring 1854, just in time to coin one variety of the Type I gold dollar, the 1854-S.

In August 1854, when the first shipments of the new Type II dollars were made, the Treasury Department began to call in the earlier small-diameter Type I coins minted since 1849. This does not seem to have applied to the 1854-S coins circulating in remote California.

By 1861, approximately 8,000,000 pieces had been redeemed, amounting to more than 60% of the Type I issues. These were reduced to bullion, and in 1861 and 1862 the metal was used at the Philadelphia Mint to strike gold dollars, quarter eagles, and double eagles.

During the Type I period, the total mintage of circulation strikes amounted to 12,496,215 coins. Proof quantities were not recorded, but were a few dozen at most, if even that many.

Type I circulation strikes were made as follows:

Philadelphia: 11,465,095	New Orleans: 949,000
Charlotte: 80,816	San Francisco: 14,574
Dahlonega: 55,730	**Total, all mints: 12,496,215**

The Elusive "1854-C" Gold Dollar

For a long time various 20th-century texts, including the *Guide Book of United States Coins*, listed the "1854-C" gold dollar and noted that only four were struck. Some excitement regarding this piece first developed in February 1909, when Edgar H. Adams, in the first appearance of his column, "Current American Numismatic Notes," commented that veteran numismatist Augustus G. Heaton, the well-known author of *Mint Marks* and a frequent contributor to the coin-collecting scene (and who had recently moved from Washington to New York City), had snared a unique prize: "One of Mr. Heaton's choice mintmarks is the Charlotte gold dollar of 1854. This in all likelihood is the rarest gold dollar, and it is the only specimen known, so far as can be learned."

In the August issue of the same magazine, Heaton informed the editor that, unfortunately, he owned no such coin. Further, "As a matter of fact, not a single specimen of this greatest rarity of the gold dollar series is known." Notwithstanding this, various mentions of the 1854-C crept into many later reference books.

Collecting Considerations

Examples of Type I Philadelphia Mint gold dollars are readily available in various grades from Very Fine to About Uncirculated. Uncirculated pieces are easy enough to find, but superb gems are elusive, especially if sharply struck and with good eye appeal. However, there are enough on the market that anyone caring to pay the market price will find a gem without difficulty. A major exception to the Philadelphia rule is the 1850, which is a rarity even at the MS-60 level and is an incredible prize if MS-64 or MS-65, although it is unheralded and unknown save to specialists. The 1854 Type I Philadelphia Mint gold dollar is also rare in Mint State, but is hardly in the same category as the 1850.

All of the Charlotte and Dahlonega coins are scarce today in grades from Very Good to Extremely Fine, and some are very rare. In About Uncirculated, any variety is important, and in Mint State nearly all are rarities. Charlotte and Dahlonega coins in particular are nearly always weakly defined in certain areas, this being true of examples in any and all grades. This "rustic" appearance has endeared them to specialists, but has probably turned away many investors—who might scratch their heads in amazement as to why anyone would want to own an 1853-C gold dollar in, say, Extremely Fine grade, for which the planchet quality is usually very poor and the striking weak! Of course, the knowing gold-dollar specialist will simply wink and eagerly buy this *rarity*.

The key variety among Type I gold dollars is the 1849-C with Open Wreath, of which only a handful are known to exist.

Large numbers of counterfeits of the Type I gold dollar, including Philadelphia issues of all years, were produced in Europe beginning by the 1950s. By the early 1960s, such fakes were commonly offered by banks, bullion exchanges, and even coin dealers. Most lacked the luster of authentic high-grade coins and were often poorly defined, especially at the dentils. However, there were exceptions, and many were highly deceptive. Today, certification by a grading service that guarantees authenticity (which not all services do; policies change; it is best to check) is your best protection.

A SPECIAL CASE: THE OBVERSE DIES OF 1849

Among 1849 gold dollars, Philadelphia Mint issues exist in several obverse varieties. At one time, Small Head and Large Head varieties were listed, but recent research by John Dannreuther revealed that the head sizes are the same, but star spacing varies. He provided the following synopsis of the 1849 master dies, in the order they were made, for the present text.

> *Dannreuther Obverse 1*—1849 No L. Designer's initial is not on the neck truncation. This style uses the *First Head* or portrait, differing very slightly from the *Second Head* in details, including placement of the word LIBERTY. This obverse was combined with two reverses, each of which cracked, probably leading to the subsequent modifications.
>
> *Dannreuther Obverse 2*—1849 With L, Narrow Border, Normal Stars, Concave Field. The *Second Head* was used on this and the next two styles. The relief appears to be ever so slightly lower than on the *First Head.* All *Second Head* dies have the same placement of LIBERTY. Longacre either modified the wax model or the reduction (punch/master hub). The *First Head* and the *Second Head* are the same in size. The relief change may be the depth the hub was punched into the master dies, not a reduction in the wax model or in the reduction/master punch/master hub, although there are slight "curl" changes. The fields are deeply basined, curving upward near the border. Tiny letter L on neck truncation. This is the style formerly called "Small Head" or "Small Stars."
>
> *Dannreuther Obverse 3*—1849 With L, Narrow Border, Distant Stars, Flat Field. Stars are distant from the head and close to dentils. Formerly called "Small Head" or "Small Stars."
>
> *Dannreuther Obverse 4*—1849 With L, Normal Border, Close Stars. Formerly called "Large Head" or "Large Stars."

The large versus small stars result from the depth of punching for each master die, because both marks appear to be made by the same punch. (The No. 4 has its stars more deeply punched.) However, the breakage of the two No L reverses led to the change to the less concave, lower relief head. The Distant Star, Flat Fields variety (No. 3) replaced the Normal Stars, Concave Fields variety (No. 2), because the latter reverse cracked. Only a single die of each of these variations has been found, each cracked, which led to the Close Star variety (No. 4), the former "Large Head." These were all tests that failed—except the last one, of course, which was used until 1854.

AMERICA AND NUMISMATICS IN 1849

America was focused on the California Gold Rush. In this year tens of thousands of "Forty-Niners" headed west by wagon and ship, soon redefining the boundaries of the United States. Gold began to pour into Eastern banks and the Philadelphia Mint. A proposal to establish a mint to coin gold in New York City captured news headlines for a while, then faded. The Coinage Act of March 3, 1849, created the new gold $1 and $20 denominations.

At the time coins in general circulation ranged from copper cents (and relatively few half cents) to gold eagles. Among silver and gold coins, issues of Spanish America dominated commerce, and remained legal tender until 1859. Still, Liberty Seated coins from half dimes to dollars were seen with frequency, and larger transactions were often carried out with gold coins. Paper currency issued by state-chartered banks was a mainstay of trade, but care had to be taken that the bills were genuine and from a bank with sound financial footing.

Numismatics was in its infancy. In Philadelphia the Mint Cabinet, a display opened in June 1838, continued to attract visitors. The curators, Jacob R. Eckfeldt and William E. Dubois, welcomed collectors. Proofs coins and sets were made available on request. There were probably fewer than 100 serious collectors in America at the time.

On March 5, Zachary Taylor was inaugurated as president, having won on the Whig ticket a contest with Democrat Lewis Cass the preceding November. His predecessor, James Knox Polk, went back to his home Tennessee, where, in poor health, he died a few months later on June 15. America was torn by the slavery question, this being the focal point of politics as well as many debates and discussions. In the recent election the Free Soil Party had promoted Martin Van Buren, who took votes away from Cass, handing victory to Taylor, who had not campaigned intensely. At a July 4 ceremony held at the Washington Monument, then under construction (as it had been intermittently since 1836), Taylor became ill, and died a few days later on July 9. Vice President Millard Fillmore succeeded him as chief executive.

The American economy, in a growth period since the end of the Hard Times era in 1843, was good and becoming stronger. Railroads were the hot ticket stock investment on Wall Street.

1849, Open Wreath, No L on Truncation

(Dannreuther Obverse 1)

Enlarged 2x
(actual size 13 mm)

Circulation-Strike Mintage
10,000 (estimate, of 688,567 total for year)

Proof Mintage
Fewer than 10 (estimate)

Whitman Coin Guide (WCG™)

VF-20	EF-40	AU-50	AU-55	MS-60	MS-63	MS-65
$200	$285	$350	$400	$1,000	$2,400	$7,500

CERTIFIED POPULATIONS

G-4–VF-35	EF-40–AU-58	MS-60–62	MS-63	MS-64	MS-65	MS-66	MS-67	MS-68–70
4	104	200	112	138	49	18	7	3
PF-50–58	**PF-60–62**	**PF-63**	**PF-64**	**PF-65**	**PF-66**	**PF-67**	**PF-68–70**	
0	0	0	1	0	0	0	0	

Note: An unknown but no doubt proportional quantity of other pieces were classified simply as "1849"; those quantities are not given here.

Key to Collecting. Among the Open Wreath gold dollars of the Philadelphia Mint there are four styles—this one without the initial L on the neck truncation, and three (separately listed) with the L, but having different borders. It is a matter of preference whether to collect just one 1849 Open Wreath gold dollar, as most numismatists have done over the years, or to seek all four.

Gold dollars of this variety without the L are basically scarce, but those that exist are most likely to be in Mint State and very attractive. Likely, these were struck only for a short time. The obverse outlasted two reverses that each cracked, probably causing Chief Engraver James B. Longacre to make modifications.

Although some writers have suggested that only 1,000 circulation strikes were minted, it is likely that 10,000 or more were struck. In terms of auction appearances in choice and gem Mint State, this is one of the *more plentiful* varieties of the year—a situation diametrically opposed to conventional wisdom.

Estimated Total Population (Mint State). 700 to 1,600. Relatively easily available, because undue numbers were saved for their novelty as the first year of the new denomination. Mint State pieces, being of greater value and interest than worn pieces, are more likely to have been certified and publicized. Many pieces are of choice or gem quality, often somewhat prooflike. The cameo-like appearance (due to the small size of the stars and their distance from the portrait) and the typical satiny surface of Mint State pieces are aspects that combine to create gold dollars of outstanding visual appeal. To see a choice or gem piece is to want to own it! This variety seems to be more plentiful than the With L, Open Wreath issue. *Certified population MS-63 and higher:* 320.

Estimated Total Population (Circulated Grades). 600 to 900, mostly in higher grades such as Extremely Fine and About Uncirculated. Elusive, but not extensively studied; thus, true rarity is not known. It is known, however, that such pieces are far rarer than 1849 gold dollars of the Open Wreath style.

Characteristics of Striking and Die Notes. This variety is usually fairly sharply struck, although many show some lightness at the obverse stars and at the dentils. Luster is more satiny than frosty, giving a very attractive appearance to the coins.

Proofs

Proofs of the 1849 Open Wreath, No L variety are not documented in Mint records. David Akers (1975) cited the appearance of two Proofs, but suggested that seven or eight are known. Walter Breen (*Encyclopedia*, 1988, p. 477) stated that "at least seven" are known, but did reconcile this with his earlier comment that about a half dozen were struck (*Major Varieties of U.S. Gold Dollars*, 1964). In his comprehensive work on Proof coins (1989), Breen stated: "About a dozen now known."

In 1870 when coins from the estate of Longacre were auctioned, two 1849 gold dollars were included. Breen surmised, without any evidence, that both were Proofs and were of this variety.

The Smithsonian Institution has an unquestioned Proof of this variety, although the American Numismatic Society's example has been reexamined (John Dannreuther, 1999) and is an early circulation strike with prooflike surfaces. Scattered others have appeared on the market over the years. The situation is not simple, for circulation strikes with prooflike surfaces may have been called "Proof" in some old catalogs.

Even today, there can be controversy. Reflective of the line of demarcation between Mint State and Proof coins, in the Stetson University Collection sale (B&M, May 1993) lot 571 was described: "Possible Proof. Deep prooflike surfaces exhibit all of diagnostics for the Proof of this date. Frosty design motifs form a pleasing contrast to the mirrorlike fields." At the viewing of the lot, qualified observers were divided in their opinions, but one suggested that all that was needed was to have it *certified* "Proof" and that would end the matter; today, it is not unusual for opinions to change into *facts* (sort of) by this method!

NUMISMATIC NOTES

Die Data. The tip of the coronet is between stars 5 and 6 (counting with star 1 slightly to the left of the bust tip), *closer to star 5.* Stars punched by hand into the obverse die, thus accounting for some variations. There is no L on the neck truncation (care must be taken when seeking this feature, because some later varieties have the L lightly struck or missing, leading to their misattribution as "No L"). The obverse die is in fairly high relief. Stars 1 and 13 are noticeably repunched, star 9 (opposite the lower part of the hair bun) lightly so.

Although other obverse dies have been described (Auction '80, lot 1411; Polis Collection, June 1991, lot 1433; and a coin in the Harry W. Bass Jr, Part III sale), it is John Dannreuther's opinion that just one obverse die is truly of the No-L style. The others are With-L varieties with the L not visible.

On all 1849 gold dollar reverses—Open Wreath as well as Close Wreath—the date 1849 was incorporated into the *master die* and thus has the same placement on all dies of all mints.[18] On all later gold dollar dies, a four-digit logotype was entered separately into the working die.

Auction Information. In the absence of pedigree links down to the present day, it is not known how many of the following would qualify as having the Dannreuther-1 obverse die or as Proofs:

> *1940: 54th Catalog Sale* (Barney Bluestone), lot 706: "1849 Open Wreath, Unc. Semi-Proof surface. Sharpest and most beautiful specimen I have ever handled. A rare gem, so choice. From the Brand collection."
>
> *1986: Spring 1986 Arizona State Invitational Auction* (Pacific Coast Auction Galleries), lot 420: "1849 Small Head, No L, Open Wreath, Proof or possibly prooflike first strike. Extremely sharp strike, full frosty devices and smokey prooflike fields. Very, very faint hairlines. Superb example of this first variety of the gold dollar."
>
> *1989: Auction '89* (Paramount [Akers]), lot 820: "1849 NGC MS-65. This intriguing gold dollar has deep prooflike fields (which NGC appears to have ignored in their grade designation) in addition to its eye-popping 'flash.' A 1983 letter from Walter Breen accompanies the coin. We will quote it in its entirety and let you decide: 'This certifies that I have examined the accompanying coin, and that I have compared it with others of its kind, and that I unhesitatingly declare it an authentic 1849 Type I Proof gold dollar (small head, No L). The coin in every particular matches other Proofs of this issue: surfaces, die state, die identity striking quality. It is superior to the specimen in ANS or to the scratched piece I formerly owned (later, owned by Lester Merkin, most recently in Kagin's Sale of the 70's, lot 1497). It is an exact match for the coin in Norman Stack's type set. To date 9 or 10 are traced, of which two are in museums and two in a Philadelphia estate.'" (Breen often sold "authentications" for a fee; certain of these have been discredited by later scholars, and in this present instance NGC has ignored it.)

1993: Stetson University Collection (Bowers and Merena Galleries), lot 571: "1849 Open Wreath. Small Head, Without L. MS-64. Possible Proof. Deep prooflike surfaces exhibit all of diagnostics for the Proof of this date. Frosty design motifs form a pleasing contrast to the mirrorlike fields."

1849, Open Wreath, With L on Truncation, Narrow Border

Flat or Concave Field
Former "Small Head"
(Dannreuther Obverses 2 and 3)

Circulation-Strike Mintage
20,000 (estimate, of 688,567 total for year)

Pricing and Population Data. Due to the recent nature of the identification of this variety, pricing and population information has been combined with the data for the Normal Border variety of this coin, which follows this entry. No image is available at this time.

Key to Collecting. No specific records exist of the mintage of this variety, because the Mint did not keep track of when dies and styles were changed on the presses. It seems that many fewer of these were minted than of the Open Wreath, Small Head, Without L.

Estimated Total Population (Mint State). 1,200 to 1,600. Many pieces are of choice or gem quality, often somewhat prooflike. In the course of research for this book, the author was surprised to learn that relatively few of this variety have ever been offered for sale. *Certified population MS-63 and higher:* 648. Present population reports are inconsistent, however, and probably include some apparent No-L coins on which the L is actually weakly struck.

Estimated Total Population (Circulated Grades). 2,000 to 3,000, mostly in higher grades such as About Uncirculated.

Characteristics of Striking and Die Notes. This variety is usually fairly well struck, although some show weak hair on Miss Liberty. Many are prooflike. Sometimes the L on the neck truncation is weak, leading to the misattribution of the variety as a No-L issue.

Certified Populations. See the populations chart for the next entry.

Numismatic Notes

Die Data. Borders are narrow. The 1849 Small Head dollar With L on truncation exists in two major styles: with flat obverse field and distant stars, and with concave obverse field and stars normally placed (in the same relation to the head as seen on the No-L variety). The concave field with normally placed stars style has the tip of the coronet between stars 5 and 6 closer to star 5 (the coronet point being level with the lower right star point). The flat field, distant stars style has the coronet tip approximately centered between the two (the coronet point being level with the lowest star point).

Dannreuther-2: Concave field, tip of neck same distance as No L variety—The fields are slightly basined or dished, although not as concave as in the No L variety. The portrait is in slightly lower relief than on the *without L* variety, but still rather high. Stars 3, 11, and 12 are noticeably repunched.

Dannreuther-3: Flat field, tip of neck distant from star—Miss Liberty's visage appears cameo-like in a large surrounding area of field with distant encircling stars, giving this variety a distinctive appearance. Fields are planar or flat. The cameo-like appearance is produced by the flat field "framing" the portrait more noticeably. No significant repunching of stars is seen.

Auction Information. In some instances definite correlation cannot be made between the following listings and today's Dannreuther obverse varieties.

1882: Property of J. Colvin Randall (George W. Cogan), lot 592: "1849 Star not directly under front of bust. Rev. Open wreath. 12 berries. Fine. (R.1.)" Realized $1.20. Lot 593: "1849 Star not directly under front of bust. Rev. Same as No. 1. Fine. (R.2.)" Realized $1.20. Lot 594: "1849 Star off from and not directly under the bust. Large planchet. Rev. Same as No. 1. Very Good. (R.3.)" Realized $1.25. (The "R" numbers were "Randall numbers" and were used for a short time. This is a very early effort to sort out the obverse varieties of the 1849 Open Wreath; doubtless the foregoing includes some that today are listed under later headings.[19])

1916: Clarence S. Bement Collection (Henry Chapman), lot 228: "1849 Diadem points directly between stars. Wide wreath, 6 berries on each branch. Brilliant semi-Proof surface. Perfection and a little gem of the first year of coinage." Realized $7.75. Lot 229: "1849 Diadem points slightly nearer one star than the other. R. As last. Unc." Realized $5.10.

2000–11: Harry W. Bass Jr. Collection Part IV (Bowers and Merena Galleries), lot 3: "1849 Open Wreath, Small Head, With L. MS-65 (PCGS) . . . Star 11 is sharply recut while star 12 is very slightly doubled. A few other stars show very slight recutting. Reverse has left ribbon and knot very slightly separated. Several very fine die cracks are present, most prominent from the border through D to the wreath. The dentil tips over S OF and from left stem end to U are connected by very light curved lines. Purchased from Julian Leidman, April 3, 1973." Lot 4 "1849 Open Wreath, Small Head, With L. MS-63. . . . Flat obverse field: . . . Same obverse die as previous lot with star 12 sharply recut. The reverse die also appears to be the same, although in an earlier die state without visible cracks. The lines inside border dentils are the same on both coins. Purchased from Julian Leidman, May 30, 1972." Lot 5: "1849 Open Wreath, Small Head, With L. Doubled 18 in date. MS-62 . . . Same obverse die as preceding [lot 4 in the sale] with star 11 sharply recut. Reverse has digit 1 sharply recut south and digit 8 very slightly recut south. A diagonal crack begins in the upper left reverse field and passes through left foot of large digit 1, second L in DOLLAR, and just touches top of 4 and lower left curve of 9, continuing to the inside right branch. Purchased from Stanley Kesselman, December 21, 1971."

1849, Open Wreath, With L on Truncation, Normal Border, Close Stars

Former "Large Head" (Dannreuther Obverse 4)

Enlarged 2x
(actual size 13 mm)

Circulation-Strike Mintage
540,000 (estimate, of 688,567 total for year)

Whitman Coin Guide (WCG™)

VF-20	EF-40	AU-50	AU-55	MS-60	MS-63	MS-65
$165	$210	$260	$285	$600	$1,750	$5,000

CERTIFIED POPULATIONS

G-4–VF-35	EF-40–AU-58	MS-60–62	MS-63	MS-64	MS-65	MS-66	MS-67	MS-68–70
19	488	667	327	226	63	16	1	1

Note: Totals here include both border types, as the Narrow Border style was only recently identified and does not yet appear separately in the population reports. In addition, an unknown but no doubt proportional quantity of other pieces were classified simply as "1849"; those quantities are not given here.

Key to Collecting. This is the last variety of the Open Wreath. On the obverse the stars were incorporated into the hub die, making their positions the same on all working dies. The border is wider, the stars are slightly larger due to their being more deeply punched into the master die, and the tip of the coronet is about centered between stars 5 and 6. The arrangement gives the optical illusion of the head being "large," because it is more crowded by the stars, which are very close to the portrait. Until John Dannreuther pointed out that the head size is the same on *all* 1849 obverses, but the stars and borders vary, this was called the Large Head style.

The circulation-strike mintage constitutes the majority of the total mintage of 688,567 for the year (specific number not recorded, but probably at least several hundred thousand or so). These were struck from May 9 through June 7, 1849, per Walter Breen (probably a guess, not a factual statement).

Estimated Total Population (Mint State). 3,000 to 5,000. Mint State coins are plentiful, but most are at lower levels such as MS-60 or close to it; this is unlike the earlier Open Wreath dollars that are often found in MS-64 or MS-65 grades. *Certified population MS-63 and higher:* 859.

Estimated Total Population (Circulated Grades). 12,000 to 18,000. Unlike the preceding, most specimens seen today are in worn grades. The typically encountered grade is Extremely Fine, although Very Fine and About Uncirculated coins are plentiful.

Characteristics of Striking and Die Notes. Gold dollars of this variety are generally well struck. Some show die cracks, especially on the reverse. Die striae are common on early strikings as well as on coins struck from relapped dies.

1849, CLOSE WREATH

Enlarged 2x
(actual size 13 mm)

Circulation-Strike Mintage
120,000 (estimate, of 688,567 total for year)

Proof Mintage
None

Whitman Coin Guide (WCG™)

VF-20	EF-40	AU-50	AU-55	MS-60	MS-63	MS-65
$165	$210	$260	$285	$600	$1,650	$4,500

CERTIFIED POPULATIONS

G-4–VF-35	EF-40–AU-58	MS-60–62	MS-63	MS-64	MS-65	MS-66	MS-67	MS-68–70
10	143	168	71	98	25	6	0	0

Note: An unknown but no doubt proportional quantity of other pieces were classified simply as "1849"; those quantities are not given here.

Key to Collecting. Examples of the 1849 Close Wreath are scarce in comparison to the Open Wreath variety. In choice and gem Mint State the Close Wreath coins are very rare, although this characteristic is not widely appreciated. The reason for this is that the Open Wreath pieces were widely saved as novelties upon release, whereas by the time the Close Wreath coins were issued, the excitement had passed.

These are called "Close Wreath" today, a term that dates back to the 19th century. However, "*Closed* Wreath" was a popular designation until a few years ago, when observers realized that the wreath tips were close to each other, but not "closed." "Long Wreath" was occasionally used years ago, but is seen no longer.

Estimated Total Population (Mint State). 1,400 to 1,900. Mint State coins are very scarce in comparison to Open Wreath coins. Most are in lower grades, MS-60 to MS-63. Higher grade coins are particularly scarce, and true gem MS-65 coins are rare, with MS-66 being even more so. *Certified population MS-63 and higher:* 203.

Estimated Total Population (Circulated Grades). 5,000 to 8,000. Very Fine, Extremely Fine, and About Uncirculated coins are abundant.

Characteristics of Striking and Die Notes. Some have die cracks, especially on the reverse. Some have one (usually the reverse) or both dies clashed.

NUMISMATIC NOTES

Die Data. The Close Wreath type, with 16 berries in the wreath, was created by adding two berries and three leaves at the top of the former highest leaf groups to a new master die (recessed images used to make the working hubs, which have relief images) and, in turn, the working dies (recessed images). All other features remained the same. On all 1849 gold dollar reverses—Open Wreath as well as Close Wreath—the date 1849 was incorporated into the *master die* and thus has the same placement on all dies of all mints.[20] On all later gold dollar dies, a four-digit logotype was entered separately into the working die.

Dies that have been relapped, or for which the master die was not impressed deeply into the working die, can have the head in slightly lower relief, with part of the bottom of the L (for Longacre) missing.

Breen's "Heavy Date" variety has the numerals impressed deeply into the dies. Since the date was in the master die, it is likely the 4-digit logotype was used to "strengthen" this particular working die. Breen's "Thin Numerals" variety was caused by light impression of the date logotype into the working die, or by relapping.

Notes About "Proofs." Walter Breen (*Proof*, 1989) suggested that three are known. David Akers (1975) found no Proof citations. Paul F. Taglione (1986) had this to say: "Three are reported, although one of these is quite possibly a carelessly cleaned and polished business strike."[21]

The Floyd T. Starr coin listed as Proof has recently been examined by John Dannreuther and is a circulation strike with relapped dies after clashing was noted. Walter Breen's attributions cannot be relied upon. No Proofs have been recognized by the leading certification services.

Auction Information. In February 1921, B. Max Mehl in his sale of the Dr. G.F.E. Wilharm Collection offered lot 4, "1849 So-called larger head, larger stars, closer to head; rev. heavier closed wreath. Brilliant Uncirculated, Mint luster. Rare." Realized $4.60. This was one of many listings referring to a "larger" or "large" head, nomenclature which was in effect for generations afterward and became standard (until John Dannreuther published his study in 2007, demonstrating that all heads are the same size). Star size was sometimes mentioned as well in early listings, as in the Wilharm catalog.

1849-C, Open Wreath

Circulation-Strike Mintage
Fewer than 125 (estimate)

Enlarged 2x
(actual size 13 mm)

Whitman Coin Guide (WCG™)

VF-20	EF-40	AU-50	AU-55	MS-60	MS-63	MS-65
$250,000	$350,000	$425,000	$500,000	$650,000	$900,000	

CERTIFIED POPULATIONS

G-4–VF-35	EF-40–AU-58	MS-60–62	MS-63	MS-64	MS-65	MS-66	MS-67	MS-68–70
1	4	0	1	0	0	0	0	0

Key to Collecting. Although the 1849-C Open Wreath gold dollar was not appreciated until the late 20th century, today it stands as a highly desired variety. Known examples show evidence of circulation. Only four have been confirmed. Beyond dates and mintmarks, this is the most important variety in the series. By reverse calculation, a conservation ratio of 3% to 4% would suggest a mintage of fewer than 125 coins. Perhaps the reverse die shattered, although no extant coin shows any evidence of this. The reason for such an abbreviated production is not known.

Estimated Total Population (Mint State). One. Graded MS-63, earlier graded Extremely Fine or About Uncirculated. Sold with the Richmond Collection by David Lawrence Rare Coins. *Certified population MS-63 and higher:* One.

Estimated Total Population (Circulated Grades). 3 or 4. These range from about Very Fine to About Uncirculated. At least one is scratched and was used as jewelry. Including the (now) Mint State coin listed above, four coins have been confirmed, with the possibility of a fifth or even a sixth.

Characteristics of Striking and Die Notes. Some subtle lightness of striking is seen at the centers of most coins, including at the hair of Miss Liberty and, on the reverse, the central two date digits.

NUMISMATIC NOTES

Die Data. Two pairs of dies were shipped from Philadelphia (where all dies including those for branch mints were made) to the Charlotte Mint on June 10 and 13, 1849, and are believed to have been of the early Open Wreath configuration. Only one pair of dies is known to have been used, although the dateless obverse could have been used later on other varieties.

The first coinage of gold dollars at Charlotte took place on July 3, 1849. From the first batch, two examples were sent to Mint Director Robert Maskell Patterson in Philadelphia, who replied that the coins were not well made, that the milling was too prominent, and that, in any event, new dies were being sent, and that two gold dollars recently minted at Philadelphia were being forwarded as samples of excellence.

Auction Information. For many years, numismatists thought all 1849-C gold dollars to be of the Close Wreath style, because these had appeared in many collections.[22] Apparently, few had thought to look for an Open Wreath variation.

The earliest publication of the 1849-C Open Wreath seems to have been in B. Max Mehl's February 1944 sale of the Belden Roach Collection, although auction descriptions indicate that Waldo C. Newcomer, a Baltimore collector who died in 1934, may have owned one.

In *The Numismatist*, March 1951, this letter from Robert F. Schermerhorn, Dallas collector and rare coin dealer, was published:

> About eight years ago I acquired an 1849-C mint gold dollar which I believe to be unique, for unlike all the others I have been able to locate, this one has an open wreath. It is the same weight and size as other gold dollars of 1849. I would very much appreciate hearing from other collectors who have seen or who own a similar specimen.

The matching of photographs identifies this as the Roach coin sold by Mehl (in Fort Worth, close to Dallas) in 1944, but it is quite curious that Schermerhorn did not mention Mehl in this regard. Here is Mehl's description for Lot 1083 of the Belden E. Roach Collection sale of 1944:

> 1849-C Mint letter C below wreath, as all are. This specimen seems to be of an entirely new variety. It is Open Wreath and the stars on obverse are smaller; the borders are raised making the coin appear somewhat thicker than the regular issue. Uncirculated with brilliant luster. Almost equal to a Proof. Struck in light yellow gold. I unhesitatingly say that this coin is of excessive rarity, if not unique. (Not listed in the new 1944 *Standard Catalogue*.)

This is the earliest mention I have located in print for this variety. Note that it is graded as "Uncirculated." Possibly it was sold to Charles M. Williams, a Cincinnati numismatist and insurance executive, one of the major buyers of the era. Williams may have obtained this coin in some manner and kept it until late in 1950, when he sold his collection *en bloc* to the Numismatic Gallery, operated by Abe Kosoff and Abner Kreisberg. Alternatively, it may have been sold to Schermerhorn as mentioned above.

The same specimen popped up in 1956 in the Chi-ANA Convention sale (James F. Kelly, lot 1571), with no mention of its connection to the Roach sale. The coin dropped in grade to just Extremely Fine to About Uncirculated:

> 1849 Charlotte Mint with Open Wreath. Extremely Fine to About Uncirculated. From the Newcomer and later the Williams Collection, but discovered and first published by Mr. Schermerhorn. The above picture, which is double size, shows the distinctiveness of this type. Certainly no collection could be called complete without it. It is very difficult to set a valuation on this unique coin. Mr. Schermerhorn values it at $7,500. This seems justified when we compare it to what numerous rare coins, not unique, have brought at recent sales. This coin is mounted in a large plastic holder, approximately fifteen by ten inches, with blown up photos of the 1849 Philadelphia Open and Closed Wreaths, and 1849 Charlotte Open and Closed Wreaths for comparison. Certainly a prized possession for some fortunate collector.

Years later, in Auction '79 (Stack's, lot 749), the same coin was re-offered:

> 1849-C Open Wreath. Extremely Fine . . . David Akers in his book on U.S. gold dollars has clearly traced all of the known specimens, including prior ownership. In addition, since the publication of that book, one other specimen has come to light. The known specimens are as follows: 1. Waldo C. Newcomer-Belden Roach, Charles M. Williams-Robert Schermerhorn—Last sold in the 1956 A.N.A. Auction. This coin. 2. The specimen in the G.E.N.A. Auction, 1974. 3. Sale by private treaty to New Netherlands Coin Co. 4. Sale by private treaty by NERCG recently, reportedly at a figure in the high five-figure area. It is interesting to note that there were three auction appearances representing only two coins . . . It is our opinion that this specimen, the 'finest known' and which also has the best pedigree of all, should realize a bid close to the six-figure mark."

Note that the grade of the coin has slid further, down to Extremely Fine. Now the pedigree is given as Newcomer to Roach to Williams to Schermerhorn. However, Williams did not sell his collection until 1950, and in 1951 Schermerhorn stated in *The Numismatist* that he had owned this coin for about eight years.

By the 1982 Orchard Hill Collection sale (New England Rare Coin Auctions, lot 1350), the grade of this piece had revived to a low About Uncirculated category, now with hairlines and a mark carefully noted:

> 1849-C $1 Type One, Open Wreath, AU-53, lightly circulated, with a few minor hairlines and tiny lint mark near the chin, a characteristic that may be used to identify this piece in the future. This is the Newcomer-Roach-Williams-Schermerhorn specimen, the finest of the three known examples . . . Truly this coin ranks as one of the 'aristocrats' of all U.S. coinage, and fully deserves being labeled as 'The King' of all Charlotte gold coins.

In 1999 it reappeared in the FUN sale (Heritage, lot 7722), now graded AU-58 and with an especially detailed description of the dies. The "lightly circulated" aspect of the preceding description was viewed as incorrect, it seems, since in the new description the coin had "no real wear visible on either side,"

> 1849-C Open Wreath AU-58 (PCGS). One of just four known . . . As on the other relatively high grade 1849-C Open Wreath gold dollar, this piece has a distinctive quality of strike. The obverse is slightly concave, giving the portrait an almost three-dimensional appearance. At the same time, there is some weakness on the dentils and the star at 9 o'clock shows pronounced weakness. The reverse is not as sharp as the obverse but the leaves and lettering are bold; the 4 and the bottom of the 8 are a bit weak while the mintmark is very sharp. There are some obvious diagnostic features that are seen on all genuine examples. The star opposite the tip of Liberty's nose, in addition to being weak, has a short right point. The leaf below the 1 in the date is hollow while the tip of the leaf below the 9 is partly detached. The ribbons are incomplete due to die lapping and there is a tiny die file mark above RI in AMERICA. In terms of its overall appearance, this is a pleasing coin. It has light green-gold color and original surfaces with no real wear visible on either side.

The preceding illustration is informative on several levels. First, it shows how the interpretations of grades can differ among experts, since these descriptions are from some of the best-known names in the business. As to whether the coin is Very Fine (as described in an article by Walter Breen, not quoted here), Extremely Fine (as Stack's listed it in 1979), or Uncirculated (per the Mehl offering of 1944) is a matter of opinion.

To add to the narrative on the 1849-C Open Wreath, the following is a listing of known specimens:

1. Newcomer specimen, so called. Discussed above. Variously described all the way from Mint State down to Very Fine, currently AU-58.
2. New Netherlands specimen. Variously graded from Extremely Fine to AU-58 (PCGS), then, in 2004, this was publicized as Mint State and added to the sale of the Richmond Collection as MS-63; sold for a record $690,000.
3. McReynolds specimen. Pine Tree Auction Company's Great Eastern Numismatic Association sale, 1974, lot 1952, Very Fine, mounted at one time and used as jewelry. Currently graded Fine-15 (NGC), cf. Douglas Winter, *Gold Coins of the Charlotte Mint, 1838–1861*, p. 40.
4. Lumadue specimen. Discovered by Connecticut dealer Donald Lumadue and offered for sale to the dealer community including to the present writer. Extremely Fine.
5. "Private Collection" specimen. Another specimen discovered in 1988 (cf. Breen, *Encyclopedia*, 1988). Grade not stated. This may or may not be a coin reported to the author in 2004, which was called a new discovery, and to this day has not appeared on the market.

The 1849-C Open Wreath gold dollar situation is somewhat parallel to the scenario for the 1817/4 half dollar in that a coin once thought to be unique in collectors' hands is now known to the extent of a half dozen or so pieces. Because three of these are recent discoveries, it is possible that close examination of other 1849-C gold dollars will reveal others. No matter, the variety will always remain a rarity.

1849-C, Close Wreath

Circulation-Strike Mintage
11,638 (less about 200 Open Wreath coins)

Enlarged 2x
(actual size 13 mm)

Whitman Coin Guide (WCG™)

VF-20	EF-40	AU-50	AU-55	MS-60	MS-63	MS-65
$1,500	$2,350	$3,250	$4,250	$9,500	$19,500	$17,500

CERTIFIED POPULATIONS

G-4–VF-35	EF-40–AU-58	MS-60–62	MS-63	MS-64	MS-65	MS-66	MS-67	MS-68–70
38	154	33	11	2	0	0	0	0

Key to Collecting. The 1849-C is a key issue in the series. Examples are scarce to rare in any grade and very rare in Mint State. The 1849-C gold dollars were placed quietly into circulation, apparently without any ceremony or special notice. Not a single example was set aside for the Mint Cabinet. In 1988 in his *Encyclopedia*, Walter Breen wrote that the 1849-C gold dollars in numismatic hands are "usually Very Fine or worse, prohibitively rare choice." Today, with grading being more liberal, many coins are classified Extremely Fine and About Uncirculated. The elusive nature of 1849-C is unchanged.

Estimated Total Population (Mint State). 10 to 15. Only a few Mint State coins exist, although the precise number will never be determined. Most are MS-60 or close to it and likely would be called About Uncirculated by old-time dealers and collectors. An MS-63 coin is a notable rarity. Douglas Winter suggested a population of only six true Mint State examples in his study, *Charlotte Mint Gold Coins*, 1987 edition, with perhaps the finest being the Dr. Alfred Globus specimen, ex Kagin's sale of July 1974, lot 1327, possibly ex Mehl's Atwater sale of 1946. On the other hand, more than 40 certification *events* have taken place in the Mint State level, but this includes resubmissions of the same coins and pieces that have enjoyed (or suffered from?) "gradeflation." We agree with Winter, that only a few *really* Mint State coins exist. *Certified population MS-63 and higher:* 13.

Estimated Total Population (Circulated Grades). 150 to 225. Usually seen in Very Fine grade. Scarce in Extremely Fine, rare in About Uncirculated.

Characteristics of Striking and Die Notes. Die striae are seen on early impressions. Often seen with some lightness of strike at the obverse center. The reverse, from the heavy wreath and lettering used on all branch mint coins of the Close Wreath type, is usually well defined. On some the obverse is slightly prooflike.[23] Per conventional wisdom, the obverse field is deeply basined or concave on most. However, some have the field flattened or planed, by taking the regularly basined obverse die and relapping the center on a flat grinding surface to remove the basining.

Note, for example, this description of a specimen from a New Jersey collection examined in October 1999: Obverse: Center of die is planed (flat) and somewhat prooflike; field curves upward (basined) beginning at the stars; the basined part is frosty. Reverse: Centers are filled on certain figures: A (DOLLAR) and 849 (1849). The reverse die was heavily striated at an orientation of about 10° to the right of vertical.

Numismatic Notes

Die Data. On June 10 and 13, die pairs for 1849-C gold dollars were shipped from the Philadelphia Mint (where dies for branch mints were made) to Charlotte. On July 10, two more reverses were sent. Most probably, the shipments of June 10 and 13 had the "old" reverses with Open Wreath, as used on Philadelphia Mint coins earlier in the year; the reverses of July 10 were probably the Close Wreath type as discussed here. The mintmark C is rather small. Some pieces are highly prooflike.

Auction Information. Hundreds of examples have crossed the auction block from the late 19th century onward. In the early years, nearly all were described as being in Circulated grades, typically Fine or so. An interesting exception is provided by the *Catalog and Price List* published by Alvin J. Fink of Dayton in March, 1910, listed as lot 52, "1849-C Uncirculated." Fink, whose main business was fireworks, was a fraudster who sold counterfeit, altered, and polished coins, and who remained a nuisance to the hobby well into the 1950s. Very little about him has ever appeared in print.

In November 1939 in the William B. Hale Collection, B. Max Mehl offered lot 699, described as "Uncirculated, with bright mint lustre. Scarce in any condition, very rare so choice. Not even listed in the *Standard Catalogue.*" This is one of the earliest true Uncirculated listings the writers have encountered. Afterwards, pieces described as Uncirculated or, later, more popularly as Mint State, began appearing with frequency, although usually at lower levels.

In June 1946 the William Cutler Atwater Collection, sold by B. Max Mehl, included lot 2141, described as "a beautiful sharp Uncirculated specimen semi-Proof surface. The reverse is about equal to a Proof. Raised borders." A January 1999, Heritage listing gives this information:

> *1999: North Georgia Collection* (Heritage), lot 7721: "1849-C Closed Wreath MS-63 (PCGS). Very sharply struck and frosty with a slightly prooflike reverse. Both sides show superb yellow-gold color that deepens to orange-gold at the borders. The surfaces have a few small, unobtrusive marks but this is a remarkably fresh coin that clearly has never been dipped. There are 8 to 10 Mint State 1849-C Closed Wreath gold dollars known. The finest is the ex: Globus Collection coin (earlier in the Atwater Collection) that is probably in the Harry Bass Collection. The North Georgia Collection coin is the second finest known; it was earlier sold as lot 752 in Stack's October, 1994 James Stack Collection . . . We sold the only other example ever graded MS-63 by PCGS as lot 8097 in the 1996 ANA sale."

1849-D, Open Wreath

Circulation-Strike Mintage
21,588

Enlarged 2x
(actual size 13 mm)

Whitman Coin Guide (WCG™)

VF-20	EF-40	AU-50	AU-55	MS-60	MS-63	MS-65
$1,400	$2,250	$2,850	$3,400	$5,500	$13,500	$40,000

Certified Populations

G-4–VF-35	EF-40–AU-58	MS-60–62	MS-63	MS-64	MS-65	MS-66	MS-67	MS-68–70
31	360	125	23	11	1	0	0	0

Key to Collecting. The 1849-D is scarce, but among gold dollars of the Dahlonega Mint, it is the date most often seen.

Estimated Total Population (Mint State). 120 to 160 (certification data, less an estimate for duplicate submissions, plus an estimate for pieces not submitted). Very scarce. Most are in the range of MS-60 to MS-62 and include examples graded About Uncirculated a generation ago, although some notably choice examples have been described in the literature. As to the 160 different certification listings for MS-60 and higher, Douglas Winter (by correspondence) suggests that there is "no way!" this represents even close to that number of true Mint State coins. As is true of many branch mint gold dollars, population reports are bloated at the lower end and likely include coins a connoisseur would call About Uncirculated. *Certified population MS-63 and higher:* 36.

Estimated Total Population (Circulated Grades). 400 to 700. Grades are usually Very Fine or Extremely Fine, less often About Uncirculated.

Characteristics of Striking and Die Notes. Many if not most 1849-D gold dollars are irregularly struck, with lightness at the center, particularly in the hair details of the portrait, making high-grade examples appear as if they have sustained some wear. Here, indeed, is a variety ideal for cherrypicking, because many sharply struck coins exist as well. Some pieces are prooflike, which on a higher grade coin can be a positive aspect. Lower grade prooflike coins tend to accent the visibility of contact marks. On some examples, the die was ground away at the center, resulting in a flat area (rather than the normal lightly basined characteristic) around the portrait, with prooflike surface—a phenomenon sometimes called an "aura" or "halo" by catalogers. Some coins seen today have the reverse slightly off-center and must have been early impressions.[24] Lightness of O (DOLLAR) may be explained by relapping.

Numismatic Notes

Die Data. One obverse and one reverse die were sent from Philadelphia on June 6, 1849, and another pair on June 7; all four dies arrived in Dahlonega on June 16, 1849.[25] Apparently, it was felt that there would be little call for large quantities of this new federal denomination in that district—although Bechtler gold dollars privately minted in North Carolina circulated extensively in the area. Further, by June the year was nearly half over. On January 3, 1850, one undated obverse and two dated reverse dies were defaced. It is a certainty that the reported mintage for 1849-D gold dollars is correct, since no reverses remained on hand in 1850.

Only the Open Wreath or early configuration was used for the 1849-D issues. Among Type I gold dollars, the D mintmark is small on 1849 through 1851 and 1854 issues, and large on 1852 and 1853 coins.

The Commencement of Coinage. A milling machine used to make planchets for small-diameter *half dimes* was sent to Dahlonega from Philadelphia to prepare blank planchets for coining gold dollars, the machine giving each disc a raised rim. In addition, a device was sent to make collars—the vertically grooved retaining rings outside the dies in the coining press.

The coinage of 1849-D gold dollars probably commenced, on a test basis, on July 11. Two specimens were sent on July 12 to Philadelphia for inspection, with Superintendent James F. Cooper commenting, "I am enabled to report to you the first coinage of gold dollars at this Mint and to send you two specimens of our coin . . . All [of the mint employees] were desirous of giving me the honor of uttering the first gold dollar in Georgia before the arrival of my successor in this office."

Mint Director Robert M. Patterson replied upon receipt of the sample gold dollars: "The milling was too slight, the reverse is blurred due to polishing of the die before hardening; and the reverse is off center." This was hardly an auspicious beginning!

Regular coinage for circulation began on July 15. In August, the irregularities in alignment, die quality, etc., were corrected.

An evaluation of the earlier quoted mintages for the year, totaling 21,588 coins (1,622 on July 15 and 4,971 on July 17, followed by additional pieces on August 21 and later times), suggests that the 6,593 pieces made in July, amounting to about a third of the year's coinage, probably were from overly lapped and misaligned dies.

The coinage of the first Dahlonega Mint gold dollars took place in the waning period of Superintendent James F. Cooper's tenure. His successor, Col. Anderson W. Redding, was officially appointed on September 3, nearly two months after Cooper had been advised of the change. However, Cooper was not in a hurry to leave. On October 1, Superintendent Redding moved into his office at the mint.

Mintage. Mintage commenced on July 15, 1849, at which time 1,622 coins were struck for circulation plus 4 reserved for assay (assay coins were not included in the year-end totals). On July 17, a further 4,971 (+10) coins were struck. Then followed 3,430 (+7) on August 21; 4,146 (+9) on September 25; and 3,959 (plus ? for assay) in October. The last coinage was on December 12 and involved 3,462 (+7). For the year, the circulating coinage was 21,588 plus at least 37 assay coins (records are not complete for assay pieces).

Auction Information. These verbatim listings of the 1849-D include notes about rarity, with modern comments added.

1880–11: Catalog of American Coins, Medals, Etc., 15th Sale (S.K. Harzfeld), lot 641: "1849 Dahlonega Mint. Very good, very rare." Realized $2. This was a very strong price for the time.

1882–03: Property of J. Colvin Randall (George W. Cogan), lot 597: "1849-D Good and scarce. (R.6)" Realized $1.10. "R.6" referred to Randall's own schedule of die varieties. As noted earlier, this was never published in monograph form, and today we can only speculate as to the varieties it contained.

1939–06: Alex. J. Rosborough Collection (B. Max Mehl), lot 753: "1849-D, Rarest gold dollar of this date. Uncirculated, sharp, with mint luster. Struck a trifle off center. The first I have ever seen. Rare, especially so choice."

1943–04: David Proskey Estate (Stack's), lot 1312: "1849-D Brilliant Uncirculated Gem." Lot 1313: "1849-D Brilliant Uncirculated Gem." Lot 1314: "1849-D Brilliant Uncirculated Gem." Lot 1315: "1849-D Brilliant Uncirculated Gem." Lot 1316: "1849-D Brilliant Uncirculated Gem." No information is known regarding the location today of coins from this remarkable hoard, a cache of unequalled size. Proskey had been in the rare coin trade in New York City (later, New Jersey) since the 1870s and at one time was a well-known figure. His competitor, Ed. Frossard, also of New York, had this to say about him (with a swipe at E.B. Mason Jr. as well), in the January 1881 issue of his house organ, *Numisma:* "Bro. Mason believes that the expression 'rare thus' which has lately crept into coin catalogs, originated with Mr. S.K. Harzfeld. He is mistaken. Scott & Co.'s catalogs, generally ascribed to Mr. David Proskey, a nice looking young man, with a level head and a big India rubber conscience, have frequently contained the expression, and if any credit of originality is due in the use of the term it belongs to Mr. David Proskey."

1849-O, Open Wreath

Circulation-Strike Mintage
215,000

Enlarged 2x
(actual size 13 mm)

Whitman Coin Guide (WCG™)

VF-20	EF-40	AU-50	AU-55	MS-60	MS-63	MS-65
$200	$300	$425	$625	$1,200	$4,000	$9,250

CERTIFIED POPULATIONS

G-4–VF-35	EF-40–AU-58	MS-60–62	MS-63	MS-64	MS-65	MS-66	MS-67	MS-68–70
46	492	252	88	33	9	3	0	0

Key to Collecting. The 1849-O gold dollar is easily enough available in the marketplace, but is scarce in comparison to the much higher mintage Philadelphia issue. Striking varies from weak to (rarely) sharp, that is, showing full design details. Careful buying is highly recommended.

Estimated Total Population (Mint State). 200 to 300. Very scarce, a low number in comparison to the mintage. Most are in lower levels such as MS-60 to MS-63, although a few gems exist up to and including MS-66 and are true treasures. *Certified population MS-63 and higher:* 129.

Estimated Total Population (Circulated Grades). 1,500 to 3,000. Most are in the grade of Very Fine. Coins are occasionally found in Extremely Fine, but are quite scarce in About Uncirculated.

Characteristics of Striking and Die Notes. Generally fairly well struck at the centers, but often with weakness at the dentils. Sometimes with prooflike surfaces. A few show die cracks on both sides.

Numismatic Notes

Die Data. Three pairs of dies were shipped from the Philadelphia Mint to New Orleans on June 2, 1849. All known 1849-O gold dollars are of the Open Wreath configuration.

Auction Information.

> *1882–03: Property of J. Colvin Randall* (George W. Cogan), lot 596: "1849-O Very Good. R5." This was another use of Randall's scheme of die varieties.
>
> *1929–08: George W. Fash, Joseph F. Atkinson and Carrie E. Perkins Collection* (Thomas L. Elder) "1849-O. Die break wreath to border. Mint bloom." This must have been a very nice coin. By this time, anyone following auction listings would have concluded that any Mint State 1849-O was a rarity.
>
> *1975–02: Davies and Niewoehner Collections* (Paramount [Akers]), lot 408: "1849-O, Unc.-65. An absolutely gorgeous coin. Boldly struck on an excellent planchet. The coin is a beautiful deep greenish-gold color and the surfaces are virtually flawless. The 1849-O is much more scarce than most people realize. Only 215,000 were minted and most available specimens are in the Very Fine to Extremely Fine range, This frosty gem is as choice as any that I have ever of this date and I would not be surprised to see it bring close to four figures." Since that time quite a few Uncirculated 1849-O gold dollars have crossed the auction block, but not many that have been classified as gems.

2005–05: Harry W. Bass Jr. Collection, Part III (Bowers and Merena Galleries), lot 6: "1849-O MS-62. Satiny deep yellow lustre with a few minor marks. The obverse and reverse edges are rounded . . . Some light die rust is noted, otherwise perfect dies. Obverse with heavy, bold rim framing the portrait more dramatically than on Philadelphia Mint coins. Fields gently basined. Reverse with heavy berries, not relapped, and with stems present (the reverse of this year seems come in two different styles—delicate berries and heavy berries) . . . Purchased from [William] Mitkoff, December 19, 1972." The reverse, not being relapped (ground down slightly), showed heavier details.

AMERICA AND NUMISMATICS IN 1850

The Gold Rush continued. On May 31 it was reported that in the harbor of San Francisco there were 623 sailing vessels mostly from the eastern United States, but some from foreign ports, many of them abandoned. Twelve steamships were also in port, these being especially active in connecting to Panama, and smaller vessels served the inland waterway to Sacramento. The Act of September 30, 1850, provided for a contract between Moffat & Co., the leading private coiner of gold in San Francisco, and the Treasury Department, from which the United States Assay Office of Gold emerged. In the meantime, the unofficial coinage issues of Baldwin & Co., Pacific Company, J.S. Ormsby, and others were common in circulation on the West Coast, along with Spanish-American gold and silver. Federal coins were scarce. Six new furnaces were put into operation at the Philadelphia Mint to process incoming bullion. Gold became abundant, and in relation to this, silver became undervalued. It now took slightly over $1.01 in silver to make a dollar. That would increase to $1.04 in 1851.

Silver coins disappeared from circulation, into the hands of hoarders and speculators. Remaining in use were millions of Mexican and other Spanish-American silver coins, most familiarly the two-real or "two bit" pieces valued at 25¢, most of which were well worn. One-real and half-real (medio) coins were also seen. The shortage of federal silver paved the way for the success of the gold dollar, which was becoming increasingly popular. The silver three-cent piece or trime was introduced, with just 75% silver content instead of the normal 90%, to permit them to be made for a cost less than face value, and to circulate effectively. The new double eagle denomination appeared in circulation.

The decennial federal census showed that 23,191,876 people lived in the United States. Nearly a million had arrived from European countries since 1846 (including 370,000 from Ireland between 1847 and 1849). Only two million citizens lived west of the Mississippi River. In Congress, the Compromise of 1850—largely engineered by Henry Clay—permitted California to be admitted to the Union (on September 9) as a free state. It did not forbid slavery in other territorial areas acquired from Mexico (nor did it condone the practice).

P.T. Barnum, recognized by now as America's most famous showman, signed Swedish singer "Jenny" Lind, age 30, for a two-year tour in America. From the outset, Lind captured the fancy of Americans, and her opening concert at Castle Garden in New York City exceeded expectations and brought in $17,864.05. At the time, many Americans earned fifty cents to a dollar per day. As railroads expanded, the growth of canals slowed. High tariffs warded off many foreign imports, and factories hummed with activity along the Eastern Seaboard.

1850

Enlarged 2x
(actual size 13 mm)

Circulation-Strike Mintage
481,953

Proof Mintage
Small, if any

Whitman Coin Guide (WCG™)

VF-20	EF-40	AU-50	AU-55	MS-60	MS-63	MS-65
$155	$210	$235	$265	$400	$1,600	$4,950

CERTIFIED POPULATIONS

G-4–VF-35	EF-40–AU-58	MS-60–62	MS-63	MS-64	MS-65	MS-66	MS-67	MS-68–70
21	310	273	121	59	24	4	5	1
PF-50–58	PF-60–62	PF-63	PF-64	PF-65	PF-66	PF-67	PF-68–70	
0	1	0	0	0	0	0	0	

Key to Collecting. While today there is abundant information attesting to the scarce nature of the 1850 Philadelphia Mint gold dollar, especially in Mint State, it was not always so. It seems that a century ago many specialists acquired examples in Fine or Very Fine grade, with the expectation that they would easily find a Mint State coin as a replacement—but they never did. Today, finding an 1850 gold dollar in any desired grade through about MS-62 or MS-63 can be done with some patience. True gem MS-65 or finer coins are few and far between.

Estimated Total Population (Mint State). 300 to 400. The 1850 is *far more elusive* than the second-scarcest Philadelphia coin of the Type I design, the 1854. Most examples are clustered in grades MS-61 to MS-63—although a few gems exist—with a solo entry in the MS-68 slot. Because this is a Philadelphia Mint coin with a mintage of close to half a million, its rare nature in Mint State is generally overlooked. In fact, in the late 20th century the *Guide Book of United States Coins*, the most widely circulated of all price guides, listed an MS-60 1850 at only slightly more than the very common 1853! The publication of population reports has made all of us wiser! In today's market, most Mint State 1850 gold dollars are certified. Because the popular penchant is often to buy a coin today, tire of it tomorrow, and sell it on the following day, auction offerings are much more extensive than they were a century ago. However, the 1850 remains as rare as ever in absolute terms. *Certified population MS-63 and higher:* 194. This figure is large and impressive. One cannot help but wonder how many *different* coins are involved.

Estimated Total Population (Circulated Grades). 5,000 to 7,000. Grades such as Very Fine and Extremely Fine are easy enough to find. About Uncirculated examples are somewhat scarce.

Characteristics of Striking and Die Notes. Generally sharply struck. Early impressions are apt to show extensive parallel raised die striae.

Numismatic Notes

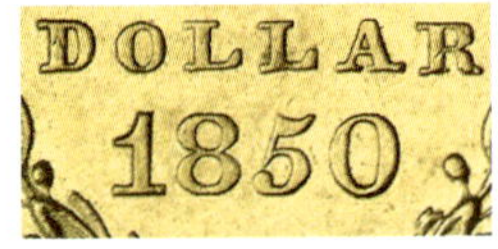

Die Data. 1850 four-digit date logotype: Numerals 185 spaced slightly wide apart, 50 slightly wider still. Italic or slanting 5 with large ball close to upright (can vary in distance based on die finish and relapping); 0 with large open center, left and right interior sides nearly parallel but slightly curved. This logotype was used on all dies of all mints.

Notes About "Proofs." Proof *may have been* included in a set produced for the Congressional Committee on the Library (a letter by Mint Director Robert Maskell Patterson, September 26, 1850, mentions coins were sent; Walter Breen has assumed these were Proofs). This set is not traced today. No example was retained for the Mint Cabinet. In his 1989 revision to his Proof coin reference, Breen states: "This set may be in the Bibliothèque Nationale" (Paris). In actuality, the gold dollar and double eagle are still there. The other Proofs have been traded away over the years. In the early 21st century a prooflike example was bandied around the market in the hope it would be certified as a Proof. It finally was certified (as a Proof-60), but its true status remains in question, according to some experts (Douglas Winter and the writer among them).

Auction Information. Most early catalogers had no clue that the 1850 gold dollar was extremely rare in high quality, but knew it was elusive in lower grades. While the Col. Mendes I. Cohen Collection (sold by Edward Cogan in 1875) had an Uncirculated 1850, as did the Rev. W. Foster Ely Collection (Scott Stamp & Coin Co., 1888), many other famous cabinets did not, even though they were often laden with Proofs and other rarities. The Robert Coulton Davis coin (New York Coin & Stamp Co., 1890) was cataloged as "1850 Very Fine and sharp." The Richard B. Winsor Collection (S.H. and Henry Chapman, 1895) offered an "1850 dollar. Very Fine." The Harlan P. Smith Collection (S.H. and Henry Chapman, 1906) had an "1850 Extremely Fine." In 1912, Henry Chapman cataloged the George H. Earle Jr. Collection with an "1850 Very Fine. Scarce." This little Very Fine coin kept company with many Mint State and Proof dollars of other dates in the same cabinet. The Malcolm N. Jackson Collection (U.S. Coin Co., 1913) "Fine" specimen is noteworthy for not being in a higher grade, and the same can be said of the "Very Fine" coin in the John Story Jenks Collection (Henry Chapman, 1921).

In contrast, in his 1939 offering of the William B. Hale Collection, B. Max Mehl said this of lot 657: "1850 Small stars, finely cut. Brilliant semi-proof, nearly equal to a Proof. Rare variety in rare state." This coin was probably from a relapped die, giving the surface a prooflike characteristic while reducing the size of the stars—a situation that constantly recurred in the many years this denomination was issued.

Beginning in the 1940s and continuing ever since, Uncirculated pieces have turned up fairly regularly at auctions, such as in Stack's sale of the David W. Proskey Estate, April 1943, which included as lot 1319, a "brilliant Uncirculated gem." In the next year, B. Max Mehl's Belden E. Roach Collection included a "beautiful Uncirculated specimen, sharp with mint lustre," while Stack's offering of the J.F. Bell Collection included a piece described as "Uncirculated, with hair not struck up sharp." J.F. Bell was actually Jake Shapiro, a Chicago financier. He bought many of his own coins back at the Stack's offering, only to try again by consigning them to Numismatic Gallery (Abe Kosoff and Abner Kreisberg), who billed the offering as the Memorable Collection in Beverly Hills in 1948. That was a dreary time in the market, and action was slow. Kreisberg later related the anecdote that upon Bell's arrival in California, he spent time showing him the tourist sights and restaurants around town—in order to keep Bell away from the office and prevent him from noticing that hardly anyone was showing up to look at the lots. The sale flopped, and Bell bought many items back for the second time. Later, his son, David Shapiro (who at one time was president of the Professional Numismatists Guild), sold many of them, sometimes as consignments to RARCOA, of which he was once a principal.

1850-C

Enlarged 2x
(actual size 13 mm)

Circulation-Strike Mintage
6,966

Whitman Coin Guide (WCG™)

VF-20	EF-40	AU-50	AU-55	MS-60	MS-63	MS-65
$1,500	$1,800	$2,750	$5,000	$10,000	$30,000	

CERTIFIED POPULATIONS

G-4–VF-35	EF-40–AU-58	MS-60–62	MS-63	MS-64	MS-65	MS-66	MS-67	MS-68–70
14	136	30	5	0	0	0	0	0

Key to Collecting. The 1850-C registered the lowest production figure of any gold dollar in the span of 1849 to 1853 and the second smallest Charlotte Mint gold dollar quantity overall (the 5,235 for 1859-C being the only lower number). Not unexpectedly, it is a key issue today, a true rarity in terms of the demand for it. Nearly all are in circulated grades. Mint State coins have been certified, but it is the writer's view that more than just a few of these suffer from "gradeflation" and are more likely About Uncirculated in grade. See the Heritage comment quoted below.

Estimated Total Population (Mint State). 20 to 30. In Mint State the 1850-C is a notable rarity, with the top of the certified line being just MS-63. Most are at or close to MS-60 and would have been graded About Uncirculated a generation ago. Historically, the rarity of the 1850-D has been recited many times. In modern times, about three dozen certification events have occurred—including duplicate submissions of the same coins. Perhaps a reality check is offered by David W. Akers (1975): "This is the rarest collectible C Mint gold dollar from the standpoint of total number of pieces available. Although there are nine auction records for this date in Uncirculated condition, I have never seen one that I would call full Mint State, and even strict About Uncirculateds are very rare." In 1986, Paul F. Taglione commented that grading 1850-C gold dollars was one of the most controversial aspects of the gold dollar series, and that "even the most experienced individuals often fail to agree on particular examples of the issue," and "at least two examples which I consider Mint State are AU-55 in the opinion of one of my most respected colleagues."[26] Such examples of "gradeflation" could be given for many other varieties of gold dollars. Probably the best option for the well-financed specialist is to seek out an MS-63 and inspect it for striking, planchet, and visual quality. *Certified population MS-63 and higher:* 5.

Estimated Total Population (Circulated Grades). 200 to 300. This is a front-row center coin for the specialist. Enough exist in circulated grades that they are quite collectible, and yet they are sufficiently elusive that some patience is needed to find one that is just right.

Characteristics of Striking and Die Notes. Usually seen somewhat lightly struck on the highest hair details and with some lightness at the dentils at the borders. Some are struck on defective planchets.

Numismatic Notes

Die Data. All known specimens are from a single die pair, Douglas Winter's combination 3-C.[27] On later strikings, the reverse die was evidently relapped, causing the lowering of relief of the date and certain details. In comparison to Philadelphia Mint coins, the typical 1850-C has the star points closer to the dentils, and on the reverse, the letters are heavier and more closely spaced.

Auction Information. Various adjectives describing rarity have been the rule in auction offerings for many years.

1905–09: Public Auction Sale (Thomas L. Elder), lot 134: "1850 C Mint. Excessively rare. Uncirculated. Limited coinage." This was part of an extensive run of gold dollars in Elder's initial foray into the public auction business in New York City.

1944–02 Belden E. Roach Collection (B. Max Mehl), lot 1085: "1850-C The rarest date of this Mint. And this specimen is practically Uncirculated with mint luster. The rarity of this coin was not recognized until just a few years ago when it was listed at only $10. The 1942 catalog *[Standard Catalog of United States Coins]* lists it at $35 and a Very Fine specimen in my last sale brought its full listed price. But this coin is far superior. In fact it is the most beautiful specimen of this date and mint gold dollar I have ever seen and should bring a much higher price that it is now cataloged for, $40 in only Very Fine condition. (This specimen cost $50.) Recent record, $95." Realized $105.

1981–08: Auction '81 (Paramount [Akers]), lot 1319: "1850-C, Choice Uncirculated 63. Boldly struck with razor sharp hair detail on Liberty and every star fully defined. Lustrous, semi-prooflike surfaces and uniform light golden toning. An area of planchet roughness below the bust (resulting from something adhering to the die when the coin was struck; many specimens of this date have it) but the surfaces are very clean and unmarked. This is the finest 1850-C gold dollar that we have ever seen. In fact, it is the only strictly Uncirculated 1850-C that we have ever encountered. This date is rare in all grades and is a major rarity in high grade, *i.e.*, AU or better. From the standpoint of total number of pieces available, it is the rarest C-Mint gold dollar with the exception of the 'impossible' 1849-C Open Wreath. A very important coin and one of the many highlights of this remarkable selection of gold dollars."

1999–02: William Miller et al. Collections (Heritage), lot 6090: "1850-C MS-62 NGC . . . Only 3–5 pieces are believed known in strict Mint State in spite of several times that many pieces having been certified as such by the combined staffs of the grading services. The striking details on this coin are uncommonly well defined with strong definition on the hair of Liberty as well as peripheral stars . . . Tied with several other pieces as finest known." The remarks about Mint State coins are telling.

1850-D

Circulation-Strike Mintage
8,382

Enlarged 2x
(actual size 13 mm)

Whitman Coin Guide (WCG™)

VF-20	EF-40	AU-50	AU-55	MS-60	MS-63	MS-65
$1,600	$2,350	$3,250	$5,500	$11,000	$28,500	

CERTIFIED POPULATIONS

G-4–VF-35	EF-40–AU-58	MS-60–62	MS-63	MS-64	MS-65	MS-66	MS-67	MS-68–70
22	143	20	6	2	0	0	0	0

Key to Collecting. The 1850-D gold dollar is a key issue in any grade. *True* Mint State coins are so rare as to be virtually unobtainable (see auction information below).

Estimated Total Population (Mint State). 15 to 22. Typically seen in grades from MS-60 or MS-62. Eight certification events have taken place at the MS-63 and MS-64 levels, these representing an unknown number of *different* coins. A true Mint State 1850-D is a great rarity by any measure. Examples graded as low level Mint State today are likely to have been classified as About Uncirculated a generation ago. *Certified population MS-63 and higher:* 8.

Estimated Total Population (Circulated Grades). 125 to 200. Rare. Most are Very Fine, occasionally Extremely Fine, and rarely About Uncirculated. David Akers (1975) commented that this variety has "the third lowest average grade of any gold dollar in the entire series." Some cabinets—the North Georgia Collection is an example—that had many Mint State and other high-level coins lacked a Mint State 1850-D.

Characteristics of Striking and Die Notes. Usually seen weakly struck at the obverse and reverse centers, although a few sharp specimens exist. The 5 (1850) is often light. Some specimens have die clashes, especially on the reverse. Excessive relapping, a problem with the 1849-D gold dollars, was not a factor with the 1850-D.

Numismatic Notes

Die Data. Three obverse and three reverse dies were sent from Philadelphia at an unknown time, and arrived in Dahlonega by January 3, 1850. One obverse and one reverse die were sent by mistake from Philadelphia to Charlotte, then forwarded from Charlotte to Dahlonega, and arrived in Dahlonega on April 3, 1850. On January 13, 1851, the four dated reverse dies were defaced. Reported to be still on hand were five usable obverse dies. Among Type I gold dollars, the D mintmark is small on 1849 through 1851 and 1854; large on 1852 and 1853.

Mintage. Coinage took place in May (3,345), August (1,714), October (2,099), and December (1,224). The number of extra coins minted for the Assay Commission is not known.

Auction Information. Many 1850-D gold dollars have crossed the auction block, but from early times to present, very few have been called Uncirculated. The latter are usually certified at MS-60 to MS-62 and likely are among some that were called Extremely Fine or About Uncirculated in earlier times. The elusive nature of the variety was showcased in this 1985 description:

> *1985–05: Dr. Jasper L. Robertson Collection* (Mid-American), lot 1109: "1850-D Choice Uncirculated (63/63). An amazing example of this date, with completely frosted devices, and semi-prooflike fields. There is a small, mint-caused defect on the obverse rim; otherwise, this is a completely problem-free example. The strike is as sharp as we have seen on any Dahlonega Mint gold dollar! We could find no offering of a specimen which even approached the quality of this example. The Montgomery specimen (sold by Stack's in 1984) graded About Uncirculated, and the Eliasberg coin graded only Very Fine! It is not often that collectors have the chance to purchase a coin which offers the unique combination of quality and rarity."

1850-O

Circulation-Strike Mintage
14,000

Enlarged 2x
(actual size 13 mm)

Whitman Coin Guide (WCG™)

VF-20	EF-40	AU-50	AU-55	MS-60	MS-63	MS-65
$285	$500	$1,000	$1,600	$3,600	$8,000	$15,000

CERTIFIED POPULATIONS

G-4–VF-35	EF-40–AU-58	MS-60–62	MS-63	MS-64	MS-65	MS-66	MS-67	MS-68–70
6	177	71	11	3	0	0	0	0

Key to Collecting. The 1850-O gold dollar is the rarest New Orleans coin of this denomination—in all grades from well worn to Mint State. The anomalous low mintage of just 14,000 coins—far below any other New Orleans gold dollar of the Type I design—is not explained, but was probably due to lack of requests for the denomination by depositors of bullion. A survey of thousands of auction listings revealed that Mint State 1850-O gold dollars were virtually unheard of in collections of the 19th and early 20th centuries. Beginning in a significant way in the late 20th century, Mint State coins were regularly included in auctions. Inspection of many of these revealed that most were coins that would have been more properly graded as About Uncirculated.

Estimated Total Population (Mint State). 50 to 70. The 1850-O is very scarce in Mint State. Normally, a higher rate of survival would be expected. Most Mint State coins are in lower grades, at or near MS-60, some if not most of which have moved up from earlier About Uncirculated evaluations. Only 14 certification events have occurred at MS-63 or MS-64, including duplicate submissions. The elusive character of the 1850-O in Mint State is not recognized, and thus catalog values do not reflect it. *Certified population MS-63 and higher:* 14.

Estimated Total Population (Circulated Grades). 300 to 400. Very scarce, even fewer than might be expected from the low mintage. Of all New Orleans Mint gold dollars, the 1850-O is the rarest by far. Grades are mostly Very Fine, Extremely Fine, or About Uncirculated.

Characteristics of Striking and Die Notes. Generally, the 1850-O is well struck. Some show evidence of die rust, including on the portrait of Miss Liberty.

Numismatic Notes

Die Data. Only one die variety is known from six pairs of dies sent to New Orleans for this coinage.

Auction Information. Over a long period of years many 1850-O dollars have been described in auction catalogs, but the vast majority bore grades ranging from VG to Extremely Fine, rarely About Uncirculated. Many *years* would often pass between appearances of Uncirculated coins. In recent decades this has changed, due to a combination of more liberal grading interpretations and the tendency of many buyers to hold coins for just a short time. In 2003, for example, several certified Mint State coins were offered, the highest being Heritage's Ashland City Collection coin, MS-64 (PCGS), from the Harry W. Bass Jr. Collection Part II sale in 1999, at the same grade. It had been in the Bass Collection since 1972, reflective of a dedicated specialist buying a coin, appreciating it, and holding it for a long time.

AMERICA AND NUMISMATICS IN 1851

The Gold Rush continued to infuse prosperity into the economy. Liberty Seated silver coins were minted only in reduced numbers, since they cost more than face value to produce. Accordingly, they were sold at a premium at banks and brokerages, with none in circulation. The clipper ship *Flying Cloud* raced around Cape Horn at the tip of South America to make the trip from New York City to San Francisco in a record 89 days. Most California gold was converted into double eagles, for it was more efficient to make a single $20 coin than two of $10, four of $5, eight of $2.50, or 20 gold dollars. Still, gold dollars were produced in quantity and were widely used. Historian Neil Carothers described money in circulation at the time:

> Trade was being carried on with gold dollars, three-cent pieces and underweight dimes and half dimes and badly worn Spanish reals and medios. The gold dollars were too small in size and too large in value. The dimes and half dimes were the few survivors of a systematic culling out of good-weight coins. The adverse ratio had long since stopped the importation of Spanish [Mexican] coins of good condition, but badly worn pieces were still brought in.
>
> No United States or Spanish silver coin could circulate unless it was reduced by wear as much as 3%. The average depreciation was much larger, possibly as great as 15%. Copper coins, if they had been in general circulation, might have been very useful, but they were very large, were unattractive in use, and had an uncertain legal status. The coinage of one cent pieces showed a marked increase in 1851, but the total coinage from 1851 to 1853, inclusive, was only one piece for each person in the country. The total [supply of coins] of all kinds was quite inadequate.
>
> Railways, hotels, and stores, which required small change as a business necessity, were buying small coins at a premium, first gold dollars, then three-cent pieces, and finally any sort of United States or foreign silver coins whatever. A customer who offered a gold dollar in payment for a small article would receive in exchange perhaps 10 or 15 three-cent pieces and a half dozen almost unrecognizable reals and medios. A Philadelphia paper referred derisively to shopkeepers scooping up three-cent pieces with a ladle to make change for a $5 bank note.[28]

The first American numismatic auction sale of importance was held this year on February 20, under title of *Executors' Sale. Valuable Collection of Gold and Silver Coins and Medals, Etc., Catalogue of the Entire Collection of Rare and Valuable Coins, Medals, Autographs, Mahogany Coins Case, Etc., Late of Doctor Lewis Roper, deceased.* The 24-page catalog described 698 lots, the last 45 of which were autographs. The sale realized $1,172.47, making it the first American coin sale definitely known to have crossed the $1,000 level.[29]

The New York Times made its debut in 1851, and would evolve to become one of the nation's most important newspapers. In major cities it was not uncommon for a dozen or more papers to be printed, including some in foreign languages, and with morning and afternoon editions. Nathaniel Hawthorne's *The House of the Seven Gables* and Herman Melville's *Moby Dick* were published, the latter achieving more fame among professors of English literature than with the general public, since it was a difficult "read."

Steam power proliferated, permitting textile and other factories to be located in places other than along rivers.

New Varieties of Gold and Silver Coins, a slim book written by Mint Cabinet Directors Jacob R. Eckfeldt and William E. Dubois, enjoyed a wide sale. Particularly informative were illustrations and descriptions of privately minted coins received from California. However, other than pieces fortuitously saved for the Mint Cabinet, no others are known to have been deliberately preserved by numismatists of the era.

1851

Circulation-Strike Mintage
3,317,671

Proof Mintage
None verified

Enlarged 2x
(actual size 13 mm)

Whitman Coin Guide (WCG™)

VF-20	EF-40	AU-50	AU-55	MS-60	MS-63	MS-65
$155	$210	$235	$265	$400	$1,450	$4,500

CERTIFIED POPULATIONS

G-4–VF-35	EF-40–AU-58	MS-60–62	MS-63	MS-64	MS-65	MS-66	MS-67	MS-68–70
111	1,791	2,608	921	574	139	40	11	5

Key to Collecting. This high-mintage issue is easy to find in any grade desired. In Mint State the 1851 gold dollar is very plentiful. There will be no problem whatever in acquiring a piece from MS-62 to MS-64 grade and, of course, lower levels of Mint State are more plentiful yet. True gems at the MS-65 level or higher are a bit elusive in comparison to demand for them, but enough exist that you will have no difficulty obtaining an example. Since many dies were used, some for a long time, surface quality and sharpness vary widely.

Estimated Total Population (Mint State). 5,000 to 7,000. Most are very lustrous. Trophy hunters can snare very high grade examples of this otherwise common gold dollar, with certification reaching all the way to MS-68. *Certified population MS-63 and higher:* 1,714.

Estimated Total Population (Circulated Grades). 60,000 to 90,000. Very common in just about any circulated grade desired, especially Very Fine, Extremely Fine, and About Uncirculated.

Characteristics of Striking and Die Notes. Usually sharply struck. However, some are lightly struck at the hair curl above Miss Liberty's ear and at the central part of the date.

NUMISMATIC NOTES

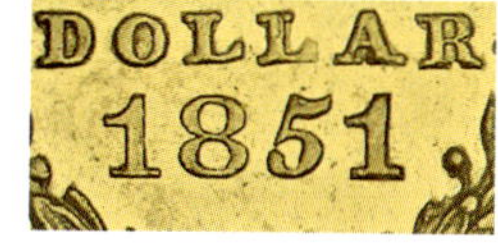

Die Data. 1851 four-digit date logotype: The numerals 185 are spaced wide apart, and the 51 slightly closer together. The 8 has large top and bottom loops, with the bottom loop slightly larger. The 5 is Italic or slanting, with a small ball. This logotype was used on all dies of all mints.

This item in the personal diary of James B. Longacre indicates that, presumably, five different sizes of date logotypes for the 1851 coinage were prepared by an outside engraver, Dougherty, who had done other work for the Mint[30] "*Saturday, August 31, 1850:* Certified W. Dougherty's bill to Mint U.S. for 5 date punches for 1851, $4 each,

$20." For this coinage, 28 pairs of dies were made, and probably most were used, thus minute variations exist.

Notes About "Proofs." On Friday afternoon, January 21, 1870, the numismatic items in James B. Longacre's estate were sold by Philadelphia auctioneer, Thomas & Sons, 139 and 141 South Street. Lots 175 and176 were each described: "1851 One dollar piece, Proof, rare." They realized $1.45 each. This would seem to indicate that, indeed, they were special strikings, for an Uncirculated 1851 would have been worth scarcely more than face value. Knowledge of what was a "Proof" and what was a prooflike circulation strike was slight in 1870, and the situation is not enhanced by the auctioneer of the Longacre estate being well known in art and antiques, but not recognized as an expert in coinage (although one or more local numismatists may have helped). Thus, unless a specimen is located from the offering, it will remain unknown whether these are true Proofs.

Auction Information. If we were to recite selections from the hundreds of auction offerings of gold dollars of this date, we would waste your time. The coin was and is common, and few catalogers had much to say about it. In recent times, certified coins in high grades have evoked breathless prose of the sort that is appealing to buyers who find, for example, an MS-67 or MS-68 example of this common date to be more desirable that an MS-63 Charlotte or Dahlonega coin. A seasoned numismatist would likely feel the opposite.

1851-C

Circulation-Strike Mintage
41,267

Enlarged 2x
(actual size 13 mm)

Whitman Coin Guide (WCG™)

VF-20	EF-40	AU-50	AU-55	MS-60	MS-63	MS-65
$155	$210	$235	$265	$400	$1,450	$4,500

CERTIFIED POPULATIONS

G-4–VF-35	EF-40–AU-58	MS-60–62	MS-63	MS-64	MS-65	MS-66	MS-67	MS-68–70
50	537	251	27	18	9	3	0	0

Key to Collecting. The 1851-C has the largest production figure for any Charlotte Mint gold dollar. Examples are easy enough to find, even in Mint State, although surface quality and eye appeal can be a problem. The 1851-C gold dollar is the only Charlotte coin of this denomination that comes to market in Mint State with some frequency. The number of such pieces extant can only be estimated. Among these are a few high-level coins graded MS-65 or even finer. Douglas Winter, who is recognized as an expert in the gold series, suggested in 1987 that only 10 to 15 Mint State coins survive (today, he advises that the number has been revised upward). Compare this to a whopping 251 certification events in grades from MS-60 to MS-62, with dozens more at higher levels! Because overgrading and optimism prevail in the evaluation of Charlotte Mint coins, the number of true Mint State coins is very difficult to determine. One person's AU-58 can be another's MS-62.

Estimated Total Population (Mint State). 40 to 55. This range is probably in the ballpark, although published estimates vary widely (see above). On this one, theories come aplenty, the truth is unknown, and it seems that anything goes with regard to making estimates! I tend to be conservative. As to how many coins are really and truly Mint State, by conservative standards and without hyperbole, Doug Winter's estimate is probably closer to the mark than mine. *Certified population MS-63 and higher:* 57. Again, this is a very generous figure that probably includes a measure of "gradeflation."

Estimated Total Population (Circulated Grades). 600 to 900. Typical grades run from Very Fine to About Uncirculated, with the latter appearing with frequency. From the standpoint of surviving examples, the 1851-C is far and away the most available Charlotte Mint gold dollar of the Type I design. In fact, the production of 41,267 is greater than for all other Type I Charlotte varieties *combined.*

Characteristics of Striking and Die Notes. Sharp striking is the rule, a very unusual situation for Charlotte Mint gold dollars. As time went on, quality control deteriorated, and later Charlotte gold dollars are usually softly struck or even *miserably* struck.

Due to multiple production runs, no single rule fits all coins. Some pieces are light at the obverse center. Some show clashmarks. Some show up to four sets of clashmarks on the reverse (*e.g.*, New Netherlands 54th Sale, lot 930, and others); this same die was relapped to remove the clashmarks, after which a crack developed at the tops of the letters in OF and AM(ERICA). For those with an inclination, the study of die progressions can be fascinating!

Some have a die crack at F (OF), connecting to AM (AMERICA). Others have a die crack connecting the border with the left side of the final S in STATES. The relapping of a die caused the relief to be lowered on letters and devices. Thus, such designations as "small stars," "thin letters," etc., for various gold dollar date and mintmark varieties usually refer to late die states, not as deliberately created varieties.

NUMISMATIC NOTES

Die Data. Three pairs of dies were shipped from Philadelphia to Charlotte. By this time serviceable obverses from earlier times could have been used. Douglas Winter states that three different obverses and three different reverses were used to produce the coinage.

Auction Information. While late 19th and early 20th century offerings of Uncirculated coins are few and far between for some Charlotte gold dollars, this is not so for 1851-C, as these representative listings reflect (modern comment added for some):

> *1893–05: Nicholas Petry Collection* (S.H. and Henry Chapman), lot 324: "1851-C dollar. Uncirculated. Mint luster."
>
> *1895–12: Richard B. Winsor Collection* (S.H. and Henry Chapman), lot 339: "1851-C dollar. Uncirculated. Rare."
>
> *1897–04: M.A. Brown Collection* (S.H. and Henry Chapman), lot 188: "1851-C Uncirculated. Brilliant Luster. Rare." Realized $1.60.
>
> *1903–06: John Hurd Comstock Collection* (Lyman H. Low), lot 420: "1851-C Mint. Uncirculated, scarce." Realized $2.60.
>
> *1906–05: Harlan P. Smith Collection* (S.H. and Henry Chapman), lot 335: "1851-C Uncirculated."
>
> *1908–10: $25,000 Collection, revised October 1908* (Charles Steigerwalt) No lot #: "1851-C Uncirculated."
>
> *1912–06: 64th Public Sale* (Thomas L. Elder), lot 341: "1851. Charlotte. Uncirculated, scarce." Lot 342: "1851. Charlotte. Uncirculated, scarce." Unusual offering of a *pair* of Mint State coins.

1913–05: Malcolm N. Jackson Collection (U.S. Coin Co.), lot 370: "1851-C Uncirculated." Realized $2.50. Lot 371: "1851-C Very Fine." Realized $2.35. In 1913, there was not much price differential between Mint State and Very Fine.

1851-D

Circulation-Strike Mintage
9,882

Enlarged 2x
(actual size 13 mm)

Whitman Coin Guide (WCG™)

VF-20	EF-40	AU-50	AU-55	MS-60	MS-63	MS-65
$1,500	$2,000	$2,500	$3,000	$6,000	$16,500	$35,000

CERTIFIED POPULATIONS

G-4–VF-35	EF-40–AU-58	MS-60–62	MS-63	MS-64	MS-65	MS-66	MS-67	MS-68–70
15	181	55	8	7	1	0	0	0

Key to Collecting. Although the 1851-D has a remarkably low mintage, the survival ratio of this variety is higher than normal for Dahlonega coins of this era. The circumstances of distribution of the 1851-D are not known, but there must have been an unusual circumstance to account for the availability today of more About Uncirculated and Mint State coins than expected.

Estimated Total Population (Mint State). 45 to 60. Most range from MS-60 to MS-62, and some might be more properly called About Uncirculated (gradeflation, you know). A generous handful at the MS-64 line and a stand-alone MS-65 are at the top of the line in certification events and certainly must be the crème de la crème of the crop. The 1851-D is a rarity, but within the context of Dahlonega Mint gold dollars, this is nevertheless one of the more available issues in Mint State. *Certified population MS-63 and higher:* 16.

Estimated Total Population (Circulated Grades). 225 to 325. Included are a surprising number of Extremely Fine and About Uncirculated coins, with Very Fine examples being fewer than expected.

Characteristics of Striking and Die Notes. So far as is known, just two pairs of dies were pressed (literally) into service, both eventually cracking. Light striking at the center of the obverse is typical, and some have light striking on the reverse as well. Many show evidence of die clashing.

Numismatic Notes

Die Data. Three dated reverse dies were sent from Philadelphia from December 9 to 13, 1850, and arrived in Dahlonega between December 18, 1850, and January 4, 1851. Two dated reverse dies were sent from Philadelphia on July 2, 1851, and arrived in Dahlonega on July 11, 1851. No new obverse dies were sent to Dahlonega for the 1851 gold dollar coinage, those on hand being sufficient. On January 3, 1852, two obverse and five reverse dies were defaced. Three obverse dies remained on hand for further use.

In June 1851, Dahlonega Mint Director Anderson W. Redding sent a report stating that all but one of the reverse dies on hand had been broken, and the remaining reverse die was defective, having "hard and soft streaks."[31] This accounts for the two additional reverse dies being shipped in July (see above). However, there seems to have been no further coinage of 1851-D gold dollars after the new dies arrived. It seems evident that three reverse dies were actually used, although the characteristics of these have not been differentiated in numismatic literature.

1851 four-digit date logotype: The numerals 185 are spaced wide apart, while the digits 51 are slightly closer. The 8 leans right; the 5 is italic or slanting, with a small ball distant from the upright. This logotype was used on all dies of all mints.

Among Type I gold dollars, the D mintmark is small on 1849 through 1851 and 1854 issues; large on 1852 and 1853 coins.

Mintage. Coinage took place in February (3,147) and June (6,735). The number of additional pieces made for assay is not known.

Auction Information. The 1851-D gold dollar has been well respected by catalogers over the years. Most auction offerings have been of worn examples. Some listings are hard to decipher, such as Lyman H. Low's December 1898 offering of the James T. Callender Collection coin: "1851 Dahlonega Mint. Slight nick on obv. edge, another above 1 on reverse, otherwise Uncirculated. Brilliant, rare." Might this coin be called About Uncirculated today? Perhaps more curious is this listing for lot 881 by Chicago dealer Ben G. Green in his January 1913 sale of the Morris and Johnston Collections: "1851-D About Fine. Revers die crackt. Rare." Green was employing phonetic spelling; this pervaded many of his catalogs of the era. A few decades earlier in 1870, William P. Brown, the New York City dealer, did the same, with the result that his *Kuriositi Kabinet* magazines were painful to read.

Not many buyers in 1913 or today are concerned with the rarity, or lack thereof, of coins with die cracks—but they are interesting to mention, as was done by the U.S. Coin Co. (Wayte Raymond as operating partner, Elmer S. Sears as financial backer) for lot 356 in the sale of the Malcolm N. Jackson Collection: "1851-D Perfect die, Extremely Fine, mint luster. Much rarer than the broken die." At this time there were no regularly issued books listing coin mintages, rarity, and prices, and information had to be gathered here and there, mainly by reading auction catalogs.

1851-O

Circulation-Strike Mintage
290,000

Enlarged 2x
(actual size 13 mm)

Whitman Coin Guide (WCG™)

VF-20	EF-40	AU-50	AU-55	MS-60	MS-63	MS-65
$200	$250	$325	$450	$900	$2,750	$9,500

CERTIFIED POPULATIONS

G-4–VF-35	EF-40–AU-58	MS-60–62	MS-63	MS-64	MS-65	MS-66	MS-67	MS-68–70
37	1,120	295	92	76	42	3	0	0

Key to Collecting. The 1851-O is readily available today, with most examples being in circulated grades. Mint State coins are plentiful, but are mostly at lower levels.

Estimated Total Population (Mint State). 250 to 400. Most are MS-60 or MS-62, occasionally MS-63, less often MS-64, and not often higher. The forty-two MS-65 and three MS-66 certification events reveal that gems can be found. In the context of New Orleans gold dollars, 1851-O is plentiful, although not quite so available as the 1853-O of identical mintage. *Certified population MS-63 and higher:* 223.

Estimated Total Population (Circulated Grades). 2,500 to 4,500. Most are in Very Fine or Extremely Fine grade, although About Uncirculated coins are plentiful. A realistic goal for the typical numismatist is to acquire an About Uncirculated coin.

Characteristics of Striking and Die Notes. Some are lightly struck at the centers, but most are fairly sharp. Several auction listings describe pieces that closely resemble a full Proof.

Numismatic Notes

Die Data. Multiple die pairs were used, and thus minor die varieties exist.

Counterfeits. The March 1960 and January 1964 issues of *The Numismatist* discussed die-struck counterfeits of the 1851-O and 1854-O gold dollars (the 1854-O being nonexistent in original form; none was ever coined), the latter article (by John J. Ford Jr., and Don Taxay under the aegis of the Professional Numismatists Guild) reporting "the apprehension, trial and conviction of the notorious distributor of the fake gold dollars" that had taken place since the 1960 article appeared.

Auction Information. Many examples of this date and mintmark have appeared in auction sales over the years, dating back to the 19th century. A representative example is lot 338 from Ed. Frossard's personal collection, offered by dealer Frossard in October 1884: "1851 Orleans [*sic*] Mint. Uncirculated. Very scarce." It was the practice of many dealers then, continuing to today, to take a fancy to a series, build a collection and gain knowledge in the process, and then put it up for sale.

AMERICA AND NUMISMATICS IN 1852

Gold, gold, and more gold! In 1852, $45,506,177 worth was sent by steamer from San Francisco. Of this amount, $39,007,367 was destined for New York City, $470,783 for New Orleans, $6,020,027 for London, $46,000 for Panama, and $15,000 for San Juan. Large quantities of American gold coins were exported. A letter from George Peabody & Company, London, to the Bank of England, February 19, 1852, stated in part: "We have received and sent in to your institution, subject to our further orders, a parcel of gold bullion, melted from $250,000 American eagles, and by next steamer expect another large shipment . . ." Gold dollars remained popular, although there were complaints about their small size. Federal silver coins, excepting trimes, were nowhere to be seen.

In June, *Banker's Magazine* printed this:

> One way of forming an idea of the state of our currency is to observe the count of a church collection. Such a one, taken last Sunday, in which the contributions varied from a twenty-dollar note to a dark-brown cent, gave the following details (I omit the cents, as we know there are enough of them). The bank-notes reckoned $99, the gold $57, the silver $37, in all, $193. The gold consisted chiefly of quarter-eagles and dollars; the silver of Spanish quarters, and our own smaller pieces. As far as this census goes, it shows a very good share of the metallic element in Philadelphia currency. I suppose that a similar sum-total in any of the paper-dollar states would have shown $156 in paper, the rest in small silver. Nummularius.

And, in the same issue:

> Split gold dollar pieces are rapidly multiplying, and the caution cannot be too often repeated to be on the look-out for them. The piece, by some fine and ingenious

> machinery, is split in two, about one half of the coin abstracted, and the plundered sides stuck together again, the face of the piece not the least scarred or injured. A little care will readily detect the fraud. The milling around the edge will be found broken, and very generally a pewter-colored cement may be observed protruding from it. The coin, too, is thin in the middle.

From the Boston Traveler, May 20:

> *New Pattern for a Gold Dollar.* Mr. M.A. Stickney of Salem, who by the way is a perfect *dilettante* in coinage as well as other 'curious matters,' having, as is believed, a larger collection of American coins than can anywhere else, in private hands, be found, has shown us a specimen, just received by him from the Mint, of the new pattern which is proposed for the gold dollar, only a very few of which have been struck. It is in the form of a ring, being as large and thick as a ninepence, with a hole in the center sufficiently large to make the pieces of the requisite weight. It is a very handsome coin, and much more tangible and convenient than the little bit now in use, and which is found to be practically unfit for currency, so much so that it is already almost entirely out of circulation. Congress would do well to adopt this new pattern as a substitute.

In the presidential contest in November, Democratic candidate Franklin Pierce of New Hampshire defeated the Whig entry, Mexican War hero Winfield Scott. Divided over the issue of slavery, the Whig party became increasingly weak. Harriet Beecher Stowe's narrative of "life among the lowly" (actually its subtitle), *Uncle Tom's Cabin*, was published in serial form in a magazine in 1851 and in book form in Boston in 1852. The first printing of 5,000 copies sold out in a week, and seven weeks later, 50,000 copies had reached buyers. Within a year the total climbed to 300,000. The text set more Northerners against slavery and widened the gap of understanding between the North and the South.

Railroads continued to expand apace, with their stocks creating a lot of attention in the market. New lines were constructed in many different places, often using different track widths and styles of equipment. Some were speculations or frauds. Others such as the Baltimore & Ohio, Pennsylvania, and Erie became increasingly important to commerce. The National Road, begun as the Cumberland Road in 1811, extended from Maryland to Illinois, and was a well-used route for passenger coaches and freight wagons. Commerce on the Ohio and Mississippi rivers was very active, with leading ports including Cincinnati, St. Louis, and New Orleans.

Slavery continued to be the number one social issue in America. The number two social movement, temperance, saw prohibition adopted by Louisiana and Vermont, following Maine's lead. Temperance meetings, newspapers, books, and even medals abounded.

1852

Circulation-Strike Mintage
2,045,351

Proof Mintage
None

Enlarged 2x
(actual size 13 mm)

Whitman Coin Guide (WCG™)

VF-20	EF-40	AU-50	AU-55	MS-60	MS-63	MS-65
$155	$210	$235	$265	$400	$1,450	$4,500

CERTIFIED POPULATIONS

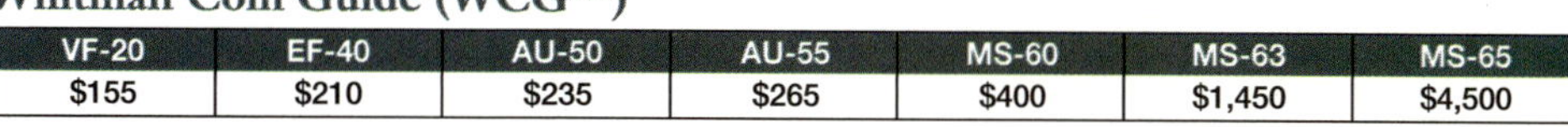

G-4–VF-35	EF-40–AU-58	MS-60–62	MS-63	MS-64	MS-65	MS-66	MS-67	MS-68–70
39	1,629	2,370	754	427	98	26	11	5

Key to Collecting. Made in large quantity, the 1852 is one of the most common gold dollars in the marketplace today. Because many die pairs were used, sharpness and striking quality vary, but most coins are very nice.

Estimated Total Population (Mint State). 4,000 to 6,000, with most being in the MS-60 to MS-63 range, although choice and gem coins are easily enough available. The certification service data are of no help, and most lower range Mint State coins have not been submitted for grading. In Mint State this issue is a bit scarcer than the 1851, as a comparison of the respective mintages might indicate. However, enough were minted that the date can be called plentiful in the context of the series. Those competing for the highly popular Registry Set listings can contemplate four MS-68 certification events and a solitary MS-69. *Certified population MS-63 and higher:* 1,376.

Estimated Total Population (Circulated Grades). 40,000 to 60,000. A very common gold dollar. Very Fine is a typical grade, but Extremely Fine coins are common, and About Uncirculated coins are readily available as well.

Characteristics of Striking and Die Notes. Usually these are sharply struck and very attractive. Some have nearly full prooflike surfaces (e.g., the Virgil M. Brand Collection coin sold by Bowers and Merena Galleries, November 1983, lot 4, called "choice BU" at that time—but earlier called "semi-proof" by B. Max Mehl in his sale of the H.E. Rawson and A. deYoanna collections, December 12, 1922, lot 9).

As is the case with other high-mintage Philadelphia Mint gold dollars of Type I, many interesting die variations can be found, because so many die pairs had been used for coinage. Possibilities include die cracks on obverse and reverse, die lumps, clashmarks, evidence of relapping, etc. One reverse die has curious raised dots inside the wreath: one below the upright of the D, and the other below the tail of the R.

Numismatic Notes

Die Data. 1852 four-digit date logotype: The digits are spaced fairly closely together, the 185 at about the same distance, the 52 ever so slightly farther apart. The 1 is small and leans slightly right. The 8 leans slightly left, and its upper interior is slightly smaller than its bottom interior. The 5 is italic with its ball distinctly separated from its upright. A fancy 2 is used, with a ball at the top and a curved base. This logotype was used on dies for all mints.

Eighteen obverse and 13 reverse dies were made, and leftover obverses may have been used as well.

Notes About "Proofs." It is not known whether Proofs were made. None have been recognized by the leading certification services. David W. Akers noted in his 1975 book: "Reportedly one Proof was struck, but its present whereabouts is unknown." Perhaps this was a reference to lot 9 in B. Max Mehl's 1922 sale of H.E. Rawson, Dr. A. de Yoanna, and David Strasser Collection: "1852 Brilliant Proof." In November 1983 this same coin was auctioned as lot 4 of the Virgil Brand estate, with this description:

> 1852 Choice Brilliant Uncirculated, prooflike. A superb, glittering showpiece which was designated as a 'Proof' by B. Max Mehl over a half century ago. Perhaps the finest business strike in existence; certainly we have never seen a finer one . . . The present coin is sharply and exquisitely struck on both the obverse and reverse and possesses a prooflike surface intermingled with tiny hints of mint frost. As typical business strikes

possess deeply frosted mint lustre, it is logical to presume that this coin was a presentation piece of some type, probably for an occasion whose significance has been lost in the sands of time . . . From B. Max Mehl's sale of the H.E. Rawson and A. deYoanna collections, December 12, 1922, lot 9 . . . Brand inventory No. 125,162.

Auction Information. Because this is a very common gold dollar, auction catalogs had little to say about the variety until recent times, when all sorts of superlatives have been trotted out to describe coins certified in high grades. Among hundreds of citations, we might mention lot 1143 from Edward Cogan's December 1879 sale of the Theodore W. Riley Collection: "1852 Good and scarce." This is an excellent example of a meaningless description—pure Cogan—probably prompting his more educated peers to raise their eyebrows. If an 1852 was "scarce," then how could *really* scarce and rare varieties be described?

1852-C

Circulation-Strike Mintage
9,434

Enlarged 2x
(actual size 13 mm)

Whitman Coin Guide (WCG™)

VF-20	EF-40	AU-50	AU-55	MS-60	MS-63	MS-65
$1,400	$1,800	$2,250	$2,750	$5,000	$13,500	$25,000

CERTIFIED POPULATIONS

G-4–VF-35	EF-40–AU-58	MS-60–62	MS-63	MS-64	MS-65	MS-66	MS-67	MS-68–70
25	142	48	14	10	4	1	0	0

Key to Collecting. The low mintage of this issue contributed to its rarity today. The 1852-C is elusive in all grade levels. More than just a few are overgraded, with practitioners of "gradeflation" seemingly concentrating more on Charlotte and Dahlonega coins than on Philadelphia issues. This can be readily observed by comparing, say, a certified MS-62 1852-C with an MS-62 Philadelphia coin. In fact, in the interest of awareness, I suggest you do this.

Estimated Total Population (Mint State). 70 to 90, most of which hover in the MS-60 or MS-61 range, but which are often graded higher, though nod is made to the five certification listings at MS-65 and the sole occupant of the MS-66 slot. Relevant to the number of *real* Mint State coins, Douglas Winter noted: "Like most Charlotte gold dollars, the 1852-C is often overgraded; many of its 32 or more 'Uncirculated' auction appearances from 1944 to 1986 can be discounted." I mention now and again in this book that numerical grading can be one thing, and quality can be another. *Certified population MS-63 and higher:* 33.

Estimated Total Population (Circulated Grades). 150 to 250. Most are in such grades as Very Fine or Extremely Fine, not often About Uncirculated.

Characteristics of Striking and Die Notes. Douglas Winter noted: "A number of examples show weakness from the bases of LA in DOLLAR up to the base of 1 (*i.e.*, the denomination). This was caused by the adherence of some foreign matter to the dies at the time of striking. Because this was mint-induced, and is frequently seen on surviving examples, this 'imperfection' should not adversely affect the value of the coin." This is Winter's die pair 7-H. Many show areas raised from die rust.

Numismatic Notes

Die Data. Three pairs of dies were shipped to Charlotte for this coinage, but not all were used. One reverse die has a repunched 1 (1851), this being evident below the base of the 1; this is Douglas Winter's variety 7-H and is the most often seen. The other variety listed by Winter, 7-G, has a perfect 1.

Auction Information. Many examples of the 1852-C have appeared in catalogs over the years. Perhaps the finest is the following, cataloged by David W. Akers and sold in July 1981 in Paramount's section of Auction '81 (lot 1328):

> 1852-C, Superb Gem Uncirculated 67. An incredible one-of-a-kind coin that must be seen to be fully appreciated. It is very sharply struck and has the richest natural orange gold toning imaginable. There is a prooflike "halo" around Liberty's head and the surfaces are pristine. Not only is this the finest 1852-C gold dollar we have ever seen or heard of, but it is also the choicest C-Mint coin of any date or denomination that we have encountered. This coin is one of the many highlights of this unprecedented offering of gold dollars and it is our guess that many viewers will consider it to be the most beautiful coin in the entire collection.

1852-D

Circulation-Strike Mintage
6,360

Enlarged 2x
(actual size 13 mm)

Whitman Coin Guide (WCG™)

VF-20	EF-40	AU-50	AU-55	MS-60	MS-63	MS-65
$1,500	$2,000	$2,750	$3,750	$9,000	$28,500	

CERTIFIED POPULATIONS

G-4–VF-35	EF-40–AU-58	MS-60–62	MS-63	MS-64	MS-65	MS-66	MS-67	MS-68–70
17	143	38	4	0	0	0	0	0

Key to Collecting. The 1852-D gold dollar is rare in any grade. Most were casually struck from a single die pair that clashed early in its life. Extensive overgrading complicates the search for a "nice" 1852-D, usually ending in a compromise.

Estimated Total Population (Mint State). 25 to 35. Most are around the MS-60 to MS-62 level, about the same situation as with the lower mintage 1854-D, also a rarity. Some of the "Mint State" coins on the market are the same coins that years ago were graded at the About Uncirculated level (in case the student of old-time collections and catalogs wonders why years ago there were hardly any Mint State coins around, while today multiple examples are included in grading service reports). Mint State "listings" have multiplied like rabbits. In 1986, Paul F. Taglione ventured the opinion that "fewer than 10 Mint State examples are extant, and the actual number could quite possibly be as few as a half-dozen."[32] I don't mean to overemphasize this, but it is important for you to realize that branch mint gold dollars have suffered from "gradeflation" as much as, if not more than, most other series. The top four certification events are at the MS-63 level. *Certified population MS-63 and higher:* 4.

Estimated Total Population (Circulated Grades). 120 to 200. The 1852-D is very elusive in worn grades, even more difficult to find than the low mintage suggests. Today, the typically encountered grade is Very Fine.

Characteristics of Striking and Die Notes. Most have die "markers" of one sort or another, including clashmarks, relapping (especially at the bridge of Miss Liberty's nose), etc.

NUMISMATIC NOTES

Die Data. One obverse and one 1852-dated reverse die were sent from Philadelphia December 9, 1851; two more pairs were sent in the same month; four dies arrived in Dahlonega by January 1, 1852, and two more arrived on January 3, 1852. These shipments totaled three obverse and three reverse dies. On January 17, 1853, the three 1852-dated reverse dies were defaced at the mint. Six usable obverses remained on hand.

At least two of the reverse dies were used for coinage. Some 1852-D gold dollars have misaligned reverse dies: the Harry W. Bass Collection, Part II, lot 63, coin was described as rotated nearly 180° from the normal position. Among Type I gold dollars, the D mintmark is small on 1849 through 1851 and 1854 issues; large on 1852 and 1853 coins.

Mintage. Gold dollars were minted in January (1,946), April (1,727), and December (1,029). (The total of these numbers is different from the summary total of 6,360.) The number of additional pieces made for assay is not known.

Auction Information. Many 1852-D gold dollars have crossed the auction block from the late 19th century to the present, usually in circulated grades. Here is a sampling of higher grade listings from the 1940s:

> *1944–02: Belden E. Roach Collection* (B. Max Mehl), lot 1095: "1852-D Brilliant Uncirculated with Proof surface. The reverse is almost equal to a Proof. Very rare so choice. Recent record for only a Very Fine specimen, $34." Realized $62.50.
>
> *1944–12: J.F. Bell Collection* (Stack's), lot 56: "1852-D Uncirculated, does not have the full mint luster." Realized $75.
>
> *1945–05: George H. Hall Collection* (Stack's), lot 1669: "1852-D Uncirculated." Realized $60.
>
> *1946–06: William Cutler Atwater Collection* (B. Max Mehl), lot 2152: "1852-D Extremely Fine, near Uncirculated, with considerable mint luster. Record for a similar specimen, $75."
>
> *1946–08: ANA Convention Sale* (Numismatic Gallery), lot 1225: "1852-D Extremely Fine and scarce." Realized $65.
>
> *1947–06: Will W. Neil Collection* (B. Max Mehl), lot 2351: "1852-D. Variety with light die breaks on reverse. Practically Uncirculated with mint luster. Record $75." Realized $55.

1852-O

Circulation-Strike Mintage
140,000

Enlarged 2x
(actual size 13 mm)

Whitman Coin Guide (WCG™)

VF-20	EF-40	AU-50	AU-55	MS-60	MS-63	MS-65
$200	$250	$425	$750	$1,550	$6,000	$10,000

CERTIFIED POPULATIONS

G-4–VF-35	EF-40–AU-58	MS-60–62	MS-63	MS-64	MS-65	MS-66	MS-67	MS-68–70
33	406	150	33	15	1	2	0	0

Key to Collecting. Although the 1852-O gold dollar is often encountered in circulated grades, true Mint State coins are surprisingly rare. Across all grades, most have satisfactory eye appeal. Striking quality varies, with most showing weakness in areas.

Estimated Total Population (Mint State). 100 to 150. Most are in the range of MS-60 to MS-62. Examples at the MS-63 level are rare, and anything above that is very rare. At the top of the population reports are one at MS-65 and two at MS-66. The population of Mint State 1852-O gold dollars is surprisingly smaller than one might expect for a mintage of 140,000 coins. *Certified population MS-63 and higher:* 54.

Estimated Total Population (Circulated Grades). 900 to 1,200. The 1852-O is ranked as slightly scarce, but is hardly a rarity. However, one might think that with a mintage of 140,000 coins, more would be encountered. The typical distribution of circulated grades is centered at the Extremely Fine range, with About Uncirculated above and Very Fine below.

Characteristics of Striking and Die Notes. The typical 1852-O is lightly struck at the centers, particular on the obverse portrait. The dentils at the border are usually soft. Some pieces have interesting, often extensive die cracks, particularly on the obverse. One variety shows evidence of repunching on the base of the 1 in the date.

Numismatic Notes

Die Data. Six pairs of dies were shipped to New Orleans, and at least four pairs were used.

Auction Information. The 1853-O has never attracted much attention. Most coming on the market have been in worn grades or, if Mint State, at lower levels.

AMERICA AND NUMISMATICS IN 1853

In California, Gold Rush production achieved its all-time peak this year. The Coinage Act of February 21, 1853, reduced the weight of silver coins from the half dime to the half dollar (but not the dollar), thus enabling them to circulate once again. This became effective on July 1. To note the difference in weight, arrowheads were placed next to the dates of the new coins. For the first time, excepting for the 1851 trime, American silver coins did not contain full value of metal. Accordingly, from this point onward, the United States was on the gold standard, *de facto* (the country did not officially go on the standard until years later in 1900). Earlier silver coins remained worth a premium and could be sold to bullion and exchange dealers. Liberty Seated dollars, made at the old standard, continued to be produced, but cost more than face value to produce. They were valued as bullion coins, did not circulated, and were mostly exported to China.

In time, the new silver coins became plentiful in circulation, and would remain so until spring 1862 (see listing for that year). Spanish-American silver coins still predominated, but were gradually diminishing in use. Large copper cents were produced in large numbers. Because the Mint made a profit on the difference between copper content and the face value, and since the price of copper was rising, pattern cents of lighter weight were struck for consideration. However, the large copper versions remained the standard through January 1857.

The Director of the Mint was George N. Eckert, who took office in July 1851 and served until April 1853. In April 1853 he was succeeded by Thomas M. Pettit, who served only a few weeks—explaining why so little is heard of Pettit in numismatic chronicles. In June 1853 he was replaced by James Ross Snowden, who held the office until 1861. Snowden was quite interested in numismatics and wrote two books on the subject.

The New York Central Railroad, formed from ten smaller companies, became the first large-scale U.S. rail combine. However, the continuing problem of track gauges changing at state borders seemed to make truly long railroad lines an impossibility, at least in the Northeast. At Cape May, New Jersey, the Mount Vernon Hotel, the first in the world with private baths, opened its doors to visitors. For the majority of American citizens, bathing was done only at infrequent intervals, and often not at all during the winter.

Prosperity continued, with strong protective tariffs creating unprecedented demand for domestically made goods. Now, fewer than 50% of Americans were engaged in agriculture (compared to 80% in farming in 1820). The Crystal Palace opened in New York City, a focal point for industrial and trade exhibits, a private "world's fair" so to speak. In charge of publicity was P.T. Barnum, who in the same year published the *Illustrated News*, a weekly filled with engravings. Pictures became all the rage, and during the 1850s, publishers issued many illustrated books on history, music, geography, and other subjects.

1853

Circulation-Strike Mintage
4,076,051

Proof Mintage
None

Enlarged 2x
(actual size 13 mm)

Whitman Coin Guide (WCG™)

VF-20	EF-40	AU-50	AU-55	MS-60	MS-63	MS-65
$155	$210	$235	$265	$400	$1,450	$4,500

CERTIFIED POPULATIONS

G-4–VF-35	EF-40–AU-58	MS-60–62	MS-63	MS-64	MS-65	MS-66	MS-67	MS-68–70
115	3,950	6,222	1,900	1,182	261	81	19	4

Key to Collecting. The mintage of the 1853 Philadelphia Mint gold dollar, 4,076,051 pieces, represents the largest quantity of any issue of the denomination. Accordingly, it is not surprising that this is the most common gold dollar today. Examples are available in virtually any grade desired—from well worn to gem Mint State. The 1934 "Baltimore Find" included 976 gold dollars of this date, by far the largest quantity of any gold dollar date in the hoard. Most of these were Mint State and were acquired by Thomas L. Elder, who included selected examples in his auctions in ensuing years.

Estimated Total Population (Mint State). 15,000 to 20,000. With a super-generous mintage figure crossing 4,000,000 (the only gold dollar to do so), the 1853 is the most plentiful of all gold dollars at the Mint State level. Thousands exist, with populations spiking at MS-60 and MS-61 (by far the most plentiful grades), plenty at MS-65 and even higher, and three population events at MS-69. When will we see our first MS-70 graded? Certification-service data do not reflect this true distribution, because lower level Mint State pieces are typically not sent in for grading because the grading cost vs. retail price ratio is not satisfactory. By way of explanation, the gold dollars of the 1880s, all of which have fairly low mintages and are expensive in *any* grade, are certified frequently—even if in low Mint State levels. In contrast, few low-level Mint State 1853 coins ever get certified. *Certified population MS-63 and higher:* 3,541.

Estimated Total Population (Circulated Grades). 70,000 to 110,000. This is a ballpark estimate; the figure is anybody's guess. Walter Breen suggested a 0.9% survival rate as a rule of thumb; this calculation yields about 37,000 remaining coins. Perhaps 2% would be more likely. We do know that certain *branch mint* gold dollars have a survival rate of well over 2%. Suffice it to say that when even a small handful of gold dollars is found in some long-forgotten cache, the date 1853 is usually the mostly plentiful. Available grades are usually Very Fine or Extremely Fine, but About Uncirculated coins are common, and there are thousands of lower grade and impaired coins around.

Characteristics of Striking and Die Notes. Sharp striking from perfect dies is the rule. Some coins are lightly impressed at the centers, these being the exception. Because dozens of dies were used in the coinage, the collector interested in die varieties can find pieces with clashmarks, die bulges, obverse and/or reverse cracks, or combinations thereof.

NUMISMATIC NOTES

Die Data. 1853 four-digit date logotype: Digits are about the same distance apart. The 1 leans slightly right. The 8 leans slightly right, and its upper interior is slightly smaller than its bottom interior; and italic style 5, with the ball close to and sometimes touching the upright, is used. The 3 is large and its lower ball is positioned slightly more to the left than its upper ball. This logotype was used on all dies of all mints.

Auction Information. With its record high mintage figure, the 1853 did not raise the blood pressure of dealers or catalogers until recent decades, when coins certified in high Mint State grades prompted catalogers to trot out copies of *Roget's Thesaurus* in the search for superlatives. After a while, their descriptions became cloying, except to newcomers and buyers of "trophy coins."

1853-C

Circulation-Strike Mintage
11,515

Enlarged 2x
(actual size 13 mm)

Whitman Coin Guide (WCG™)

VF-20	EF-40	AU-50	AU-55	MS-60	MS-63	MS-65
$1,500	$1,750	$2,350	$2,750	$6,000	$13,000	$35,000

CERTIFIED POPULATIONS

G-4–VF-35	EF-40–AU-58	MS-60–62	MS-63	MS-64	MS-65	MS-66	MS-67	MS-68–70
31	139	43	16	3	1	0	0	0

Key to Collecting. The 1853-C is another rarity in the lineup of Charlotte Mint gold dollars. Most are poorly struck and lack eye appeal. The survival of examples was strictly a matter of chance, because there was no numismatic interest in them at the time. Nearly all are in circulated grades. Some have been graded MS-60 or slightly above. The finest known to Douglas Winter, in his survey, was MS-63. Grading these pieces is somewhat of a sport or game, since poor striking and planchet quality introduce variables that are hard to evaluate. From any perspective, a Mint State 1853-C gold dollar is a highly important coin. Finding a nice example will be a challenge.

Estimated Total Population (Mint State). 40 to 55. Nearly all are barely Mint State, although a handful are choice. There are *dozens* of auction listings of Uncirculated coins, nearly all without mention of striking or planchet quality. *Certified population MS-63 and higher:* 20.

Estimated Total Population (Circulated Grades). 200 to 250. Most are in the range of Very Fine to Extremely Fine. About Uncirculated coins are very scarce.

Characteristics of Striking and Die Notes. Usually lightly struck at the center at the high area of the portrait on the obverse, or at OLLA and at 18 of the date on the reverse, or on both sides. Some show evidence of die rust on the obverse. Planchet quality is usually very poor. The citations given below demonstrate this vividly. Among Type I gold dollars struck at the Charlotte Mint, this is the most "rustic" in appearance.

NUMISMATIC NOTES

Die Data. Three reverse dies were shipped to Charlotte, and at least two were used. Leftover dies were used from the preceding year. Exists with two sizes of C mintmark, large and "normal" (Breen, *Encylopedia*, 1988). One reverse die has a repunched C mintmark.

Auction Information. As was the case for virtually all Charlotte (and Dahlonega) gold dollars, early auction offerings for the 1853-C were nearly always for well-worn coins. Only in modern decades have high grade coins appeared with frequency. Until recent times, when labels on holders are all that have been needed to sell coins, mentions of weak striking and poor planchets were avoided like the plague. It would be interesting to see how these coins would be viewed today.

> *1922–12: H.E. Rawson, Dr. A. de Yoanna, and David Strasser Collections* (B. Max Mehl), lot 77: "1853-C Brilliant Uncirculated, sharp and perfect in every respect, with entire surface covered with brilliancy. Nearly equal to a Proof."
>
> *1943–04: David Proskey Estate* (Stack's), lot 1304: "1853-C Brilliant Uncirculated Gem." Lot 1305: "1853-C Uncirculated Recut 'C,' very scarce, discovered in 1922 by Mr. Proskey." Lot 1300: "1853-C Uncirculated." Proskey (he of India rubber conscience—as noted in entry under 1849-D) had laid in a fine inventory of gold dollars, and Stack's presented a marvelous selection of dates and mintmarks in Mint State.
>
> *1945–06: No. 56 Auction Sale* (Walter F. Webb), lot 191: "1853-C Uncirculated." Webb, for years a seller of seashells by the seashore in St. Petersburg, Florida, was also active in the rare coin profession. Later, he moved to Rochester, New York, and concentrated on numismatics. From 1935 to 1951 he issued at least 81 auction catalogs, interesting in their time but little remembered today. These sales often included rare Mint State gold dollars, often with the same description carried forward through two or more sales. It is not known whether these represented multiple specimens, or the same coin unsold and reoffered, nor is it known how they would grade today. He seems to have graded coins rather loosely, for some of his "Uncirculated" pieces, with pedigree intact into recent times, have been classified as About Uncirculated.

1853-D

Circulation-Strike Mintage
6,583

Enlarged 2x
(actual size 13 mm)

Whitman Coin Guide (WCG™)

VF-20	EF-40	AU-50	AU-55	MS-60	MS-63	MS-65
$1,500	$1,900	$2,850	$4,250	$9,500	$29,500	$57,500

CERTIFIED POPULATIONS

G-4–VF-35	EF-40–AU-58	MS-60–62	MS-63	MS-64	MS-65	MS-66	MS-67	MS-68–70
10	159	30	9	2	2	1	0	0

Key to Collecting. The 1853-D gold dollar is nearly always lightly struck or has other problems. This situation, combined with the rarity of the variety in all grades, makes finding a nice example a challenge. The "rustic" nature of certain C and D mint coins of this era imparts to them a certain fascination, making them very popular with numismatists.

Estimated Total Population (Mint State). 25 to 35. True Mint State coins are very rare. Most are in the range of MS-60 to MS-62 and, repeating a familiar comment, would have been called About Uncirculated years ago. Although the number of different coins involved is not known, marvelous exceptions include the handful certified from MS-64 up to a single MS-66. The latter came from a Jackson, Tennessee, dealer who handled quite a few coins from a hoard of gold unearthed in that town in 1986—suggesting it may have been from that source. *Certified population MS-63 and higher:* 14.

Estimated Total Population (Circulated Grades). 150 to 225. As its mintage suggests, the 1853-D is quite scarce. Most specimens are in higher circulated grades, Extremely Fine being a general rule, although About Uncirculated coins are seen now and then.

Characteristics of Striking and Die Notes. The 1853-D is nearly always seen poorly struck, especially on the hair details of the obverse portrait. All authentic examples have prominent raised die scratches, as made, including a raised line from the border to a star at the left obverse. Many have die clashes, although these are not usually mentioned in descriptions. On a few, the reverse die is misaligned from the normal orientation. A specimen in the Elliott Collection (described by Birdsall, *Dahlonega*, p. 61; not cited below) "has several die cracks on the obverse."

Numismatic Notes

Die Data. One 1853-dated reverse die was sent from Philadelphia on December 4, 1852, and arrived in Dahlonega on December 14, 1852. Another two 1853-dated reverse dies left Philadelphia on December 14, 1852, and arrived in Dahlonega by December 24, 1852. No meaningful records exist to reveal the number of dies defaced and/or carried over for further use at Dahlonega for the coinages of 1853 and later years. Only one die pair is known to have been used. Among Type I gold dollars, the D mintmark is small on 1849 through 1851 and 1854 issues; large on 1852 and 1853 coins.

Mintage. Coinage included February (1,643), July (2,143), and September (2,792). (The total of these is different than the summary total of 6,583.) The number of additional pieces made for assay is not known. Although California gold bullion had been shipped to Dahlonega for coinage since 1850, in 1853 the high mark was achieved when 79.4% of the metal used for coinage at Dahlonega came from California.

Auction Information. Until recent decades, planchet quality and eye appeal of the 1853-D were rarely mentioned, paralleling the situation for other Dahlonega and also Charlotte coins that today we describe as poorly struck. Accordingly, it is difficult to tell how early listings would be viewed by leading certification services today. A few samples:

> *1903–11: American Coins* (New York Coin & Stamp Co.), lot 312: "1853-D, Minute nick on cheek, sharp; Uncirculated." An early offering of a seemingly splendid coin.
>
> *1913–05: Malcolm N. Jackson Collection* (U.S. Coin Co.), lot 358: "1853-D, Uncirculated, mint luster, rare." Realized $7.25. Lot 359: "1853-D, Uncirculated, mint luster, rare."
>
> *1939–10: 45th Catalog Sale* (Barney Bluestone), lot 954: "1853-D, Unc. Considerable luster. Rare, so choice."
>
> *1939–11: William B. Hale Collection* (B. Max Mehl), lot 710: "1853-D Uncirculated, with semi-proof surface; highest portion of Liberty head shows slight cabinet friction. One of the best I have seen of this rarity." "Cabinet friction" was a popular term indicating rubbing on the high points of a coin. Such pieces were really About Uncirculated.

We *do* know how this listing fared:

> *1943–12: Auction Catalog No. 47* (Walter F. Webb), lot 1401: "1853-D Unc." *Later offering, 1982–10: Eliasberg Collection (U.S. Gold Coin Collection)* (Bowers and Ruddy Galleries) lot 20: "1853-D . . . AU-50. Although the obverse displays some weakness, overall the piece is quite sharp and is far above normal . . . The obverse die shows numerous minute traces of clashmarks. A needle-like die break extends diagonally from the bottom of the third star to the border. A few scattered light marks are to be observed including one on the chin and another on the neck. *From Walter F. Webb, December 1943.*"

1853-O

Circulation-Strike Mintage
290,000

Enlarged 2x
(actual size 13 mm)

Whitman Coin Guide (WCG™)

VF-20	EF-40	AU-50	AU-55	MS-60	MS-63	MS-65
$1,500	$1,900	$2,850	$4,250	$9,500	$29,500	$57,500

CERTIFIED POPULATIONS

G-4–VF-35	EF-40–AU-58	MS-60–62	MS-63	MS-64	MS-65	MS-66	MS-67	MS-68–70
20	710	586	147	59	14	3	1	0

Key to Collecting. The 1853-O gold dollar can be compared to the 1851-O, also with a mintage of 290,000, except that the latter coin is more available in all grades. Striking is usually satisfactory, and eye appeal is good. The typical high-grade coin is a joy to behold.

Estimated Total Population (Mint State). 400 to 600. Most are MS-60 to MS-63, although higher grades come on the market every now and then, with the population charts topped out with three MS-66 listings and a single MS-67. This is the most available New Orleans Mint gold dollar in any and all grades, including Mint State. *Certified population MS-63 and higher:* 233.

Estimated Total Population (Circulated Grades). 2,500 to 4,000. This is a very popular and easily obtainable coin. Most are in Very Fine or Extremely Fine grade, although About Uncirculated coins are plentiful.

Characteristics of Striking and Die Notes. Nearly always seen well struck. A few show evidence of die rust, probably from the damp climate of New Orleans; these rust indications are in the form of tiny *raised* lumps and dots on the finished coin.

Numismatic Notes

Die Data. Six reverse dies were shipped to New Orleans. Undated obverse dies were employed from preceding years.

Auction Information. Many listings for Uncirculated coins have appeared over a long span of years. Among New Orleans gold dollars there has never been a lack of opportunity to buy a nice example of the 1853-O, most of which are very attractive.

AMERICA AND NUMISMATICS IN 1854

This year saw the end of the silver crisis. New lightweight half dimes, dimes, quarters, and half dollars became common, at which time demand (and mintages) for the silver three-cent piece and the gold dollar plummeted. Both of these denominations had helped fill the needs of commerce when federal silver coins were hoarded or melted. Many of the older silver coins came out of hiding and were turned in at banks and at the Mints, yielding a premium over face value to the depositors.

The $3 gold denomination was minted for the first time. Its utility was uncertain from the start, because $2.50 and $5 coins were in circulation aplenty. Mintages declined. The San Francisco Mint opened for business in March, and coined gold $1, $2.50, $5, $10, and $20 coins, but no $3 pieces and no silver. In the same city, Wass, Molitor & Co. and Kellogg & Co. did a good business in the private minting of gold coins, mostly of the $20 denomination. On the West Coast there were not enough coins to go around, and the Mint did not mind the competition.

Prosperous America was a magnet for disadvantaged Europeans, who continued to arrive in large numbers. Immigrants often lived in clusters and settlements in larger cities, where they could enjoy the company of their countrymen while learning the English language. In the Midwest there was great land speculation, fueled by inexpensive acreage, a flood of paper money (often of uncertain value) in circulation, and the excitement of the expansion of the railroad network. Amidst this, there were some problems—including the uncertain value of some railroad stocks and bonds—and in the autumn, scattered bank failures were reported. On November 27, monetary scholar William M. Gouge reported to Secretary of the Treasury James Guthrie that it was only the steady influx of gold from California to the East that was preventing economic disaster.

Walden, by Henry David Thoreau, was published and went on to become a literary sensation. From it such quotations as "The mass of men lead lives of quiet desperation," and "If a man does not keep pace with his companions, perhaps it is because he hears a different drummer," are familiar today. Entertainment in public places often consisted of minstrel shows, vaudeville acts, and musical numbers.

1854, Type I

Enlarged 2x
(actual size 13 mm)

Circulation-Strike Mintage
855,502

Proof Mintage
Very few

Whitman Coin Guide (WCG™)

VF-20	EF-40	AU-50	AU-55	MS-60	MS-63	MS-65
$155	$210	$235	$265	$400	$1,450	$4,500

CERTIFIED POPULATIONS

G-4–VF-35	EF-40–AU-58	MS-60–62	MS-63	MS-64	MS-65	MS-66	MS-67	MS-68–70
21	1,268	2,385	702	396	85	36	10	0

Key to Collecting. The 1854 Type I Philadelphia Mint gold dollar is usually a "poster example" of a nice coin. Nearly all are well struck and have good eye appeal. Finding a choice coin in any grade desired will be no problem.

Estimated Total Population (Mint State). 4,000 to 5,500. Among Type I gold dollars, Mint State 1854 specimens are scarcer than any other Philadelphia Mint date except the seldom-seen 1850 (which outdistances it by a country mile). The 1854 is usually seen at grades MS-60 through MS-63, not often MS-64, and less often MS-65, with a nod to a few dozen MS-66 and MS-67 certification events. *Certified population MS-63 and higher:* 1,258.

Estimated Total Population (Circulated Grades). 12,000 to 16,000. Plentiful. Usually seen in Very Fine and Extremely Fine grades.

Characteristics of Striking and Die Notes. Sharp striking is the rule. One often-seen die pair has a bulge at the upper left obverse in front of the forehead, and clashmarks on the reverse within the wreath. Another has an *interior* piece out of the die, on the left below I (UNITED) and attached to that letter; this later expands to create the variety with a prominent die crack connecting the left side of a wreath with the bottom of IT, a very unusual location for such a feature (normally a die break involves a crack or a chip extending from the edge; the present break is actually a piece out of the die, without a crack).

Numismatic Notes

Die Data. 1854 four-digit date logotype: The 18 and 54 appear close together; while 85 appears more widely separated. The top serif of the 1 ends in a point. The top and bottom interior of the 8 are about the same size, and the 8 leans slightly right. The 5 is italic, with a large ball close to but separated from upright; the larger bottom right part of the 5 is thicker and more substantial than the top part. The 4 is crosslet style. This logotype was used on all dies of all mints, for Types I and II. The relative size of the 1854 on Type I is larger than on Type II because the coin is smaller.

Mintage. In 1854, gold dollars were made of two styles at the Philadelphia Mint, the Type I and Type II designs. The division of the total mintage figure for the year into 855,502 pieces for the Type I and 783,943 for the Type II is per Breen (*Encyclopedia,*

1988) and the *Guide Book of U.S. Coins*. Certain other estimates of the relative numbers have differed. Most probably, the *precise* figures will never be known.

Auction Information. A listing of the hundreds of auction offerings would fill many pages, even if condensed to basic seller and grade information. The Abe Kosoff sale in April 1956 of the Thomas G. Melish and Clinton W. Hester Collections is exceedingly unusual for its detailed die descriptions (given below), something that Kosoff rarely did in other sales and which, in any event, did not play to a wide audience of collectors interested in such features. Indeed, in my perusal of more than 5,000 auction catalogs, no other comparable listing was found.

> Lot 1731: 1854. Small size. Die crack from point of bust to rim between first and second stars; another crack from rim through 4th star. Roughness behind neck and hair. Uncirculated.
>
> Lot 1732: 1854. Small size. Outline of Liberty head on reverse. In original envelope from S.H. Chapman's famous sale of the Gable Collection in 1914. (Cost $3!). Uncirculated.
>
> Lot 1733: 1854. Small. Double outline to stars, several touching rim. Double outline to most of reverse letters in legend. Uncirculated.
>
> Lot 1734: 1854. Small. Faint crack at 3rd, 6th, 11th and 12th stars connect them to rim. Uncirculated.
>
> Lot 1735: 1854. Small. The 2nd, 4th, 8th and 12th stars are connected to rim by faint cracks. Uncirculated.
>
> Lot 1736: 1854. Small. Irregular stars, several connected to rim. Extremely Fine.
>
> Lot 1737: 1854. Small. A crack from bust to rim is broken; heavy reverse crack rim through wreath to 1 in date. Uncirculated.
>
> Lot 1738: 1854. Small. Heavier crack at 2nd star, crack between 1st and 2nd stars, diagonal crack through 3rd star, 4th connected to rim by one crack and to 5th star by another; arc-like crack through 6th, crack from rim to head between 8th and 9th, crack from rim through 12th to hair back of neck. Uncirculated.
>
> Lot 1739: 1854. Small. Straight crack between 1st and 2nd; 5th is connected to rim by small crack. Uncirculated.

Proofs

Estimated Total Population and Key to Collecting. One or two, perhaps. Only a single Proof has been seen by modern scholars. The number struck must have been very small. None have been recognized by the leading certification services. A Proof is said to have been in a set shipped to Bremen, Germany, in 1854. Walter Breen says this was "liberated" during World War II, later surfacing at the 1975 ANA convention. He also reported that Wayte Raymond had seen an additional specimen "before 1951." If this information is correct, it would yield a Proof mintage of at least 2. The "Bremen specimen" is now (2008) part of the Bass "core" collection. Stack's cataloged it as follows for Auction '85, lot 1874:

> 1854 Type I. Choice Brilliant Proof. Sharply struck, with glittering surfaces. This is the only known specimen of this die variety. In July of 1854, a complete Proof Set in

gold, silver and copper, was struck for presentation to the city fathers of Bremen, Germany in exchange for a set of coins of Bremen. Several specimens exist in each denomination from the half cent to the silver dollar. The gold coins, however, seem to be limited to the single set give to Bremen, along with a few Type II gold dollars and about a half dozen three dollar gold pieces. The quarter eagle we sold in the 1976 A.N.A. and this gold dollar are unique. The whereabouts of the half eagle, eagle, and double eagle is unknown. The 1854 Type I Proof gold dollar has never before been offered at public auction. Therefore, this is perhaps a once-in-a-lifetime opportunity. A remarkable specimen of the highest rarity.

Die Data and Notes. Obverse has raised rust marks on the head. There are die file marks at the left rim, opposite stars 2 to 4. On the reverse, the left side of the 1 (1854) and right side of the 4 virtually touch the wreath.

1854-D, Type I

Circulation-Strike Mintage
2,935

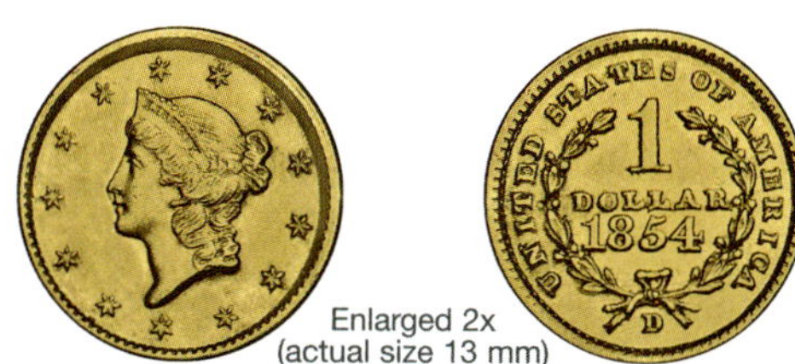

Enlarged 2x
(actual size 13 mm)

Whitman Coin Guide (WCG™)

VF-20	EF-40	AU-50	AU-55	MS-60	MS-63	MS-65
$1,700	$2,400	$5,750	$7,250	$12,500	$35,000	

CERTIFIED POPULATIONS

G-4–VF-35	EF-40–AU-58	MS-60–62	MS-63	MS-64	MS-65	MS-66	MS-67	MS-68–70
7	101	40	1	0	0	0	0	0

Key to Collecting. The 1854-D gold dollar is one of the very rarest issues in the series and has been highly prized ever since its rarity was first recognized. Most are in circulated grades, although a few Mint State coins exist. Nearly all have areas of light striking (see notes).

Estimated Total Population (Mint State). 20 to 30. Mint State specimens are very rare. Those that exist are nearly all around the MS-60 to MS-62 level. In 1986, Paul F. Taglione suggested just four coins qualified as Mint State.[33] In his reference on Dahlonega gold, Douglas Winter listed only four Mint State examples of this date, with another small group of AU-58 coins. On the other hand, the leading services have certified 39 coins. What do *you* make of this? Significantly, just one is certified as MS-63, and none higher. *Certified population MS-63 and higher:* One.

Estimated Total Population (Circulated Grades). 80 to 110. A survival ratio of 2% to 3% would suggest about 60 to 90 pieces, which, indeed, is probably quite close to the mark. (Deducting the Mint State coins noted above yields perhaps 50 to 80 circulated coins, the figure used here.) The 1854-D is far and away the rarest Type I gold dollar from the Dahlonega Mint.

A review of historical auction listings reveals that the typically encountered grade of an 1854-D, including in "name" collections, was apt to be Very Fine, Extremely Fine, or, very occasionally, About Uncirculated.

Characteristics of Striking and Die Notes. The quality varies. The U (UNITED) is often light or weak. Some 1854-D gold dollars have been described as well struck, while

Breen (*Major Varieties of U.S. Gold Dollars*, 1964) comments, "The specimens . . . are always unevenly struck and generally show severe die injuries. These are clashmarks—heavy traces of profile within wreath." The center of the word DOLLAR is often lightly impressed.

Some have raised die scratches as struck (see above); sometimes these have been confused with scratches acquired after minting. As is the case with all Dahlonega (and also Charlotte) gold coins, an understanding of the minting process and die state is necessary before endeavoring to assign a grade.

NUMISMATIC NOTES

Die Data. Three 1854-dated reverse dies were sent from Philadelphia on December 20, 1853, and arrived in Dahlonega on December 29, 1853. It is believed that all coins were struck from one reverse die (the obverse has not been as closely studied) with raised die lines at the lower left. Eight obverse and five reverse dies were shipped to New Orleans in anticipation of an 1854-O gold dollar coinage, but none were used, and apparently, these were later discarded since the design was changed after 1854.

Among Type I gold dollars, the D mintmark is small on 1849 through 1851 and 1854 issues; large on 1852 and 1853 coins.

Mintage. Coinage of 2,935 took place in August. The number of additional pieces made for assay is not known.

Auction Information. A small selection of offerings:

> *1890–01: Robert Coulton Davis Collection* (New York Coin & Stamp Co.), lot 985: "1854-D Very Good."
>
> *1905–09: XVIII Mail Auction Sale* (Ben G. Green), lot 110: "1854-D Small type. Very Fine. Very rare." Realized $8.65. Very few 1854-D gold dollars had appeared on the market by this time.
>
> *1911–03: 48th Public Sale, William H. Woodin Collection* (Thomas L. Elder), lot 849: "1854-D. Entire coinage only 2,935 pieces, making it one of the rarest of the branch mint gold dollars. About Fine . . ." By this time the 1854-D was emerging in the literature as a rarity.
>
> *1913–05: Malcolm N. Jackson Collection* (U.S. Coin Co.), lot 360: "1854-D Extremely Fine, mint luster, extremely rare."

Then a later listing of a truly memorable coin:

> *1981–07: Auction '81* (Paramount), lot 1335: "1854-D, Gem Uncirculated 65. The finest known example of this very rare and desirable date. It is very sharply struck on an excellent planchet and has lustrous light gold and rose toning. There are some raised die scratches at several obverse stars and at the lower reverse that are free of hairlines or contact marks. Even if this were not such a rare date, it would be highly desirable because of its excellent quality. This is the McNally specimen that was sold as lot 577 of NASCA's December 1976 Sale. Although there are several other specimens of this rare date that can legitimately be called 'Uncirculated,' to the best of our knowledge, this is the only known specimen in gem condition. As such, it is one of the most important gold dollars in this collection."

1854-S, TYPE I

Circulation-Strike Mintage
14,632

Enlarged 2x
(actual size 13 mm)

Whitman Coin Guide (WCG™)

VF-20	EF-40	AU-50	AU-55	MS-60	MS-63	MS-65
$350	$475	$875	$1,250	$2,500	$6,750	$18,000

CERTIFIED POPULATIONS

G-4–VF-35	EF-40–AU-58	MS-60–62	MS-63	MS-64	MS-65	MS-66	MS-67	MS-68–70
9	188	67	10	14	4	0	0	0

Key to Collecting. Among Type I gold dollars the 1854-S is one of the most interesting. It is the first coin of this denomination to be struck at the San Francisco Mint. Examples are scarce today in all grades and rare in Mint State. Nearly all are well struck and have excellent eye appeal.

Except for a few pieces which may have been saved as souvenirs, examples of the 1854-S dollar quietly slipped into commerce, where they soon became worn. At the same time, privately minted gold dollars were beginning to become popular, along with related 25¢ and 50¢ gold coins. There must have been a special reason for the production of 14,632 1854-S gold dollars, in view of the fact that the other lower denominations—the quarter eagle and half eagle—were produced only in minuscule amounts, while primary coinage attention was focused upon the $10 and, especially, the $20 denomination. In the early 20th century the 1854-S was considered to be an extreme rarity. As time went on, more examples appeared on the market.

Estimated Total Population (Mint State). 60 to 80. Mint State coins cover a range of grades from basic MS-60 to gem MS-65, but only a handful are known at the upper range. (Lower range coins are not as "stretched" in grade as are low-range C and D mint coins.) A trophy hunter would walk a mile to capture an MS-65, for which only four are recorded at ANACS, NGC, and PCGS combined. Nearly all Mint State coins are very attractive, higher range pieces being particularly so. The Pittman coin (cited below) seems to be *the* prize 1854-S known today. *Certified population MS-63 and higher:* 28.

Estimated Total Population (Circulated Grades). 300 to 500. In worn grades, most 1854-S gold dollars seen today are in such grades as Very Fine and Extremely Fine, with About Uncirculated coins being in the distinct minority. Examples always find a ready market with collectors due to the status of the variety as the first San Francisco gold dollar and the only S-Mint gold dollar of the Type I design.

Characteristics of Striking and Die Notes. Sharp striking is the rule. Early strikes show die striae from the die preparation process. Some show clashmarks. A number of high-grade pieces show prooflike surfaces. Paul F. Taglione commented on a coin sold from one dealer to another in 1980:[34] "This coin is really a sight to behold with reflective fields, an exceptional strike, and pristine surfaces. Although the coin is clearly not a Proof, a strong case could be marshaled for its status as a presentation striking."

Numismatic Notes

Die Data. Five pairs of dies were shipped to the San Francisco Mint for the initial coinage of gold dollars, but it is not certain that all were used. In any event, unused dies were of no lasting utility, because the next mintage of San Francisco gold dollars was in 1856, by which time the design had been changed to the Type II. At least two reverse die varieties are known, with slightly different placements of the S mintmark.

Auction Information. The following are selected early offerings of a gold dollar viewed as rare at the dawn of collecting coins by mintmark varieties:

> *1901–11: C.S. Wilcox Collection* (S.H. and Henry Chapman), lot 250: "1854-S Uncirculated. Excessively rare."
>
> *1906–05: XXIII Public Auction Sale, A.L. Schuyler Collection* (Ben G. Green), lot 310: "1854-S Mint. Loop removed, still Very Fine. Very rare."
>
> *1906–11: R.B. Leeds Collection* (Henry Chapman), lot 72: "1854-S Uncirculated. Extremely rare."
>
> *1910–11: 45th Sale* (Thomas L. Elder), lot 916: "1854-S Uncirculated. Excessively rare. In over 50 sales cataloged by Mr. Elder, he has not had one of the above to offer, while he has offered three of the dollars 1861 D Mint, and two of the 1870 dollars S Mint, indicating that the rarity of this piece is considerably greater than heretofore supposed. This is undoubtedly the finest specimen known." Elder often wrote in the third person.
>
> *1922–12: H.E. Rawson, Dr. A. de Yoanna, and David Strasser Collections* (B. Max Mehl), lot 85: "1854-S First year of issue. Beautiful Uncirculated specimen, with full mint brilliancy. As perfect a specimen of this rare coin as undoubtedly exists."
>
> *1940–10: Fred W. Burton and G.B. High Collections* (B. Max Mehl), lot 576: "San Francisco Mint. 1854-S looks like a Proof, but has been polished. Was purchased as a brilliant Proof, which of course were not even minted at this mint. Rare." From about this time onward the 1854-S was not showcased as a great rarity in auction listings.

In 1997 this memorable specimen created a lot of attention:

> *1997–04: John J. Pittman Collection Part I* (David W. Akers Numismatics, Inc.), lot 863: 1854-S, Gem Uncirculated. This is an amazing coin that is one of the highlights of JJP's collection of gold dollars. It is fully struck with fabulous satiny luster and superb rich orange gold toning. The surfaces on the reverse are exceedingly choice, virtually perfect in fact, but the obverse has a few light hairlines in the field and one tiny mark on the neck. Normally, these might be enough to remove a coin from the Gem category, but the overall appearance of this coin is so superior that to call it less than a Gem would be doing it an injustice. In all my years of both collecting and selling Gold Dollars, I can say that this is one of the two or three finest examples of this date that I have ever seen, possibly even the finest. JJP purchased it from Numismatic Gallery's 1949 ANA sale, lot 653, for $37, where it was succinctly described as "Perfect Brilliant Uncirculated with mint luster. A superb Gem. Rare." The reaction to this coin when it was on display at coin shows (obverse up) was very interesting; no one could believe that it was an S Mint coin!

8

Type II Gold Dollars (1854–1856)

Indian Princess

A New Design

In 1854 James B. Longacre restyled the gold dollar to an increased diameter from 1/2 inch (12.7 mm) to a new standard of 9/16 inch (14.3 mm), a move intended to make the gold dollar easier to handle in commerce. This diameter was retained for the rest of the life of the denomination. The first pieces of "the new gold dollar" were struck on September 1, 1854, on Press No. 3.[35] This information from the records of the Medal Department and probably describes Proof strikings, since the first circulation strikes were made on August 19 (see below).

In *Description of Ancient and Modern Coins, in the Cabinet Collection at the Mint of the United States, 1860,* Mint Director James Ross Snowden described the shift to the Type II gold dollar: "This dollar, after a few years' trial, was found to be rather small in diameter, and many complaints were made against it on that account. Consequently, in 1854 an alternative in the size was determined upon. The enlarged dollar of this year (1854) has as its emblem of Liberty a beautiful Indian head crowned with feathers. The band in which the feathers are confined is inscribed with the 'LIBERTY.' Legend. 'UNITED STATES OF AMERICA.' On the reverse is inscribed '1 DOLLAR 1854' within a wreath of cereals. This dollar being considerably larger in diameter than the old piece, has a proportionate decrease in thickness. The new motif was approved by Secretary of the Treasury James Guthrie on August 18, 1854, after which no time was lost in implementing the design. Dies were already made, and on August 19 the first circulating coins were struck."

As Snowden noted, the obverse motif was changed to the head of an Indian princess wearing a feather headdress. The band is inscribed LIBERTY in incuse (recessed) letters, facing left, with UNITED STATES OF AMERICA surrounding (the master hub has the L first punched too far to the left, then corrected; this is seen on many 1854 Type II examples). The reverse shows a wreath of corn, cotton, wheat, and tobacco, similar to that used on the $3 coin of the same year (and the Flying Eagle cent minted later, beginning in 1856).

In 1906 the *American Journal of Numismatics,* printed this commentary by J.C.F.: "In 1854 the 'bonnet,' as it was often called—always suggestive of the excesses of the French Revolution, and which had given place to a simple fillet or band in 1838—was abandoned on some of the smaller gold coins [$1 and $3] and an Indian head with a feathered head-dress, sometimes called a panache, was substituted. An Indian head had appeared on the octagonal quarter dollars, struck by private parties in California in 1852,[36] but these pieces were never in general circulation. The use of the panache in place of the Liberty cap was continued on the gold dollars struck from 1854 to 1889, when the coinage of those pieces was discontinued. It was placed on the three-dollar coins of gold, struck from 1854 to 1889, when they also were discontinued, but was never used on the silver coins."[37]

From the very outset, difficulties in striking ensued. The high relief of the head of Miss Liberty on the obverse caused a situation in which metal flowing into the deep die recess for the obverse prevented the relief areas on the corresponding part of the reverse, particularly the central two digits of the date, from striking up properly, unless the dies were spaced unusually close together. However, very close spacing resulted in extreme die damage, creating a lose–lose situation. Also there were problems with the striking up of the wreath on the reverse. Longacre moved the stars to correct the reverse striking problems with the Type I; to eliminate the weakness in the wreath on the Type II, he moved the lettering closer to the edge, as well as enlarging and reducing the relief of the head.

Some dies deteriorated either from use or from rust, with the result that certain Type II gold dollars have irregularities such as raised areas and ridges.

Mints and Mintages

After coinage of Type II dollars in 1854 at the Philadelphia Mint, expanded coinage took place in 1855 at the Philadelphia, Charlotte, Dahlonega, and New Orleans mints, followed by restricted coinage in 1856 at the San Francisco Mint only. In the latter year, at mints other than San Francisco, the obverse motif was modified to the Type III design.

Total circulation-strike mintage for the Type II design, combining all dates and mints, amounted to a paltry 1,633,426 coins. No wonder the term *scarce* is applicable to even the most available varieties, these being the 1854 and 1855 Philadelphia Mint coins. Walter Breen (*Encyclopedia*, 1988) suggests that 0.9% of the original Type II mintages survive; to calculate his estimates, just do the math: *e.g.*, for the 1854 Type II with a mintage of 783,943, his estimate is 7,055 coins; for the rare 1855-D with a mintage of 1,811, his estimate is 16 coins. The present writer's estimates are higher, as given in the narrative under each variety.

A handful of Proofs were also struck and were not recorded.

Type II circulation strikes were made as follows:

Philadelphia (1854 and 1855): 1,542,212

Charlotte (1855-C): 9,803

Dahlonega (1855-D): 1,811

New Orleans (1855-O): 55,000

San Francisco (1856-S): 24,600

Total all mints: 1,658,026

Collecting Considerations

Although the 1854 through 1856 Type II is the scarcest of the gold dollar designs and is the key to a gold dollar type set, you will have no difficulty in finding one. Most frequently seen are Philadelphia Mint coins of 1854 and 1855, these being available in any desired grade from Very Fine through Mint State. Choice Uncirculated pieces (MS-63) are scarce, and superb Uncirculated coins are seldom encountered. Many are weak at the obverse center (check the letters in LIBERTY and the hair and feather details). Nearly all pieces are lightly struck at the center of the date on the reverse; this is to be expected (not that you have to be satisfied with the situation). Indeed, this is the reason the design was changed in 1856. It is common for coins to have extensive clashmarks on the obverse and reverse—caused by the dies coming together without an intervening planchet. Overall eye appeal is often mediocre for Type II gold dollars, especially the Charlotte and Dahlonega issues.

The foregoing stated, there is hope for the connoisseur to find an exceptional specimen to illustrate the type. The very occasional specimen seen on the market is sharply struck and from perfect dies. Because certification service holders do not mention sharpness or weakness of strike or eye appeal, sometimes it is possible to acquire an attractive and sharp coin for only a small additional amount of money. All things considered, many if not most sophisticated buyers would rather have a sharply struck MS-64 than a lightly struck MS-65 or MS-66. As to buyers who are not sophisticated—and these are the majority—a number such as MS-66 is a siren call that is far more alluring than a technical mention of a sharp strike on an MS-64. More than for either of the other two designs, cherrypicking for a really choice, well-struck Type II can be a worthwhile pursuit.

Of all gold dollars of all three years, the sweepstakes for rarity is won handily—with no close contenders—by the 1855-D, of which just 1,811 were struck. The runner-up is the 1855-C, with 9,803, or more than five times as many. Both varieties are in further special demand due to the popularity of Charlotte and Dahlonega coins.

The 1855-O and 1856-S Type II dollars are the only branch mint issues for which there is a decent chance of locating a nice MS-60 coin. The 1856-S is anachronistic, a numismatic fossil so to speak, because other gold dollar varieties of this date are of the new Type III design.

1854

Circulation-Strike Mintage
783,943

Proof Mintage
5 to 10 (estimate)

Enlarged 2x
(actual size 15 mm)

Whitman Coin Guide (WCG™)

VF-20	EF-40	AU-50	AU-55	MS-60	MS-63	MS-65	PF-63	PF-65
$350	$475	$700	$1,050	$2,750	$11,500	$30,000	$275,000	$425,000

CERTIFIED POPULATIONS

G-4–VF-35	EF-40–AU-58	MS-60–62	MS-63	MS-64	MS-65	MS-66	MS-67	MS-68–70
246	5,931	1,689	369	323	79	17	3	0
PF-50–58	PF-60–62	PF-63	PF-64	PF-65	PF-66	PF-67	PF-68–70	
0	0	0	5	3	0	0	0	

Key to Collecting. The 1854 and 1855 Type II gold dollars are in strong demand for inclusion in type sets, this being far and away the scarcest of the three designs. Enough are on the market, however, that finding one will be no problem. The demand for them is sufficiently intense and widespread that when a single piece in a high certified grade such as MS-65 or MS-66 comes on the market, it typically is given a nice play in an auction catalog and attracts a lot of attention. Considerably more elusive are coins with high grades that are also sharply struck and from perfect dies. The last is particularly challenging, since probably 90% of the gold dollars of 1854 have clashmarks. Take your time when buying.

Estimated Total Population (Mint State). 2,500 to 3,200. In Mint State the 1854 Type II is slightly more available than the 1855 of comparable mintage. In terms of certification events, in the context of gold dollars it is downright common, or nearly so. Most pieces, including those classified as gems, are lightly struck on one or both of the central date digits on the reverse. Grading is highly subjective, and one person's "About Uncirculated" is sometimes another's "Mint State." In terms of sharply struck coins, on excellent planchets, and with "Buy me!" eye appeal, you can probably divide the population reports by 5 or 10. *Certified population, MS-63 and higher:* 830.

The 1934 "Baltimore Find" included 215 pieces of this variety, virtually all of which were Uncirculated. Curiously, the 1854 Type I, 1854 Type II, and 1855 gold dollars were each listed as having been found in a quantity of 215—perhaps suggesting the inventory was very approximate. Perry Fuller, the auctioneer, lacked a numismatic consultant.

Estimated Total Population (Circulated Grades). 6,000 to 8,000. This estimate is equal to about 1% of the original mintage. Typical grades are Very Fine, Extremely Fine, and About Uncirculated.

Characteristics of Striking and Die Notes. Nearly all are lightly struck at the centers, with the central date figures, 85, lightly defined to one degree or another (upon examination in person or even by looking at catalog illustrations, many pieces cataloged as "sharply struck" are, in fact, seen to have at least *some* lightness at the date, especially on the central 85 digits). Other areas of weakness often include the high points of the portrait on the obverse and the wreath on the reverse, these not being as noticeable. The dentils can also be run together or mushy in appearance.

Extreme wear and attrition occurred on some dies, giving a grainy appearance to certain areas of the field, especially toward the dentils (which are often mushy). Evidence of clashed dies is seen on many pieces. A curious coin in the Bass Collection displayed an obverse from an extremely rusted die, with raised rust marks and indistinct areas around the rim and lettering, and a raised rusted outline to the portrait, but not as well defined above the plumes at the top of the headdress. The reverse was struck from a normal die.

Numismatic Notes

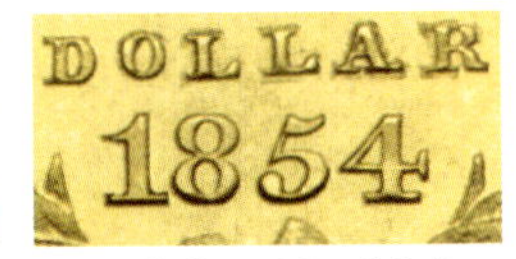

Die Data. 1854 four-digit date logotype: The 18 and 54 are closely spaced; the 85 wider. The top serif of the 1 ends in a point. The top and bottom interior of the 8 are about the same size, and the 8 leans slightly right. The 5 is italic, with a large ball close to but separated from the upright; the larger bottom right part of the 5 is thicker and more substantial than the top part. A crosslet 4 is used. This logotype was used on all dies of all mints, Types I and II. The *relative* size of the 1854 on the Type II is smaller than on the Type I, since the coin is larger.

Circulation-strikes, not widely collected by die varieties *per se* (nearly everyone is satisfied with one to illustrate the date or type), include double-punched dates—one variety with traces of an earlier date slanting up to the right, and another showing the date slanting down to the right. Yet another variety has a doubled obverse die.[38] There is a more common form of "doubling" seen on many gold dollars that sometimes is confused with doubled dies: on some examples, there is an extra outline to the letters, and sometimes to the devices, that is called "Longacre doubling." This is caused by the lettering being impressed too deeply into the master die, which transfers to the working dies. This "doubling" is seen on all sides of the lettering, while true die doubling has the lettering shifted in one direction.

Auction Information. Catalog listings are legion. A few selected examples are given below.

> *1882–03: 40th Auction Sale, John W. Scott Collection* (Scott & Co.), lot 130: "1854 Indian Head; Very Good." Realized $2. It is seen that "Indian Head" was a standard term for the new motif. On other occasions the Chapman brothers were chastised for using the term "Indian Princess" (which was also used by others).
>
> *1921–12: John Story Jenks Collection* (Henry Chapman), lot 5821: "1854. Head of Liberty as an Indian Queen to left, diadem inscribed LIBERTY, around UNITED STATES OF AMERICA. R, Tobacco wreath enclosing 1 DOLLAR 1854. Both obverse and reverse show suction marks in center. Uncirculated. Mint luster. Type 1854–1889." "Suction marks" was the term widely used for what today are called clashmarks. Chapman mis-identified the date range of the type.
>
> *1958–12: 52nd Sale, Eliot Landau Collection* (New Netherlands Coin Co.) lot 688: "1854 Type 2. Large size; small, or narrow, Indian Princess head. Slender obverse letters. Superb. Brilliant, sharp and flawless . . . Struck from badly injured dies, the reverse showing some striations or die scratches (like many cents of the time) . . . Ex Brand."
>
> *1970–06: 61st Sale, Jesse M. Taylor and Dr. Angus C. Black Collections* (New Netherlands Coin Co.) lot 431: "1854. Second design (narrow Indian Princess head). Variety of B. II-4, undusted obv. die. More or less Uncirculated; brilliant . . . The head shows a double row of beads above LIBERTY as usual. The other and rarer obv. die with this reverse has a triple row. When Walter Breen revises his monograph, that variety will probably be called No. II-8."
>
> *1986–07: Auction '86* (RARCOA) lot 883: "1854 Type II. Nicely struck Choice brilliant Uncirculated . . . Struck with clashed dies that were breaking apart, as evidenced by the two reverse 'cuds' on right rims. The date and value are bold and complete."

Proofs

Estimated Total Population and Key to Collecting. 4. Only four different Proofs have been confirmed by modern scholars (see Akers/Pittman auction listing below). More are certified, these representing events or submissions, not different coins.

Die Data and Notes. Proofs have die striations on the obverse border including at OF AM (AMERICA). David W. Akers' guidelines (per the Pittman coin description, 1997):

> The Proof 1854 Type II gold dollar was struck from an obverse die prepared and used only for 1854 Proofs . . .
>
> (a) On the Proof 1854, the incused LIBERTY on the headband is larger and higher on the band than on any other Type II obverse; it is also more deeply impressed. The left upright of the L is midway between beads two and three. LIBERTY slants down noticeably to the right with Y much farther from the beads than L. On business strikes of 1854 and 1855, and Proofs of 1855, LIBERTY is smaller and centered,

more weakly impressed, and the left side of L is under the left edge of bead three. L and Y are approximately equidistant from the beads.

(b) On the Proof 1854, the beads in the bottom row are much larger than the beads in the top row. On business strikes and the 1855 Proofs, however, the beads in the top row are more nearly equal in size to those in the bottom row, perhaps even slightly larger.

(c) The feathers of the headdress are quite different on the Proofs of 1854 as compared to any business strike Type II gold dollars or the 1855 Proofs. On the Proof 1854, there is a distinct notch on both sides of the second feather, and a slightly smaller notch on the right side of the third feather. These serve to make the first three feathers, especially the second, stand out. Also, the feathers are rectangular in shape and distinct from one another. On business strikes of 1854 and 1855, and the Proof 1855, the described notches are not present; the feathers blend together and are not clearly defined and separated. The differences in the feathers do not sound very significant when reduced to a written description, but visually the differences are quite striking and allow instant identification.

David Akers gave this trial roster of known pieces:

> Four of these Proofs can be accounted for totally and are as follows. 1. Smithsonian Institution. 2. ANS; J.P. Morgan. 3. John Jay Pittman, the specimen offered here; Thomas Melish: 1742; William H. Woodin: 851; Lorin G. Parmelee: 1244; Mendes Cohen: 240. 4. Auction '83: 761; John W. Garrett: 403; Harold P. Newlin (1884) . . . JJP purchased this coin at the 1956 Melish sale, which was held in conjunction with the CSNS Convention in Indianapolis, Indiana.

AMERICA AND NUMISMATICS IN 1855

Silver half dimes, dimes, quarters, and half dollars of the lighter standard were plentiful in circulation, so much so that Mint Director James Ross Snowden insisted that those who deposited silver bullion at the Philadelphia Mint had to receive silver coins in exchange, and could not opt for gold. (No such restriction was made at the other mints.) Some merchants and banks refused to accept silver coins for any part of a transaction over $5; per the law of the time, this was the maximum legal-tender amount allowed—it prevented disgruntled debtors from dumping massive sacks of small coins to pay large bills. In the meantime, pre-1853 silver coins of heavier weight were trading at exchange offices and bullion dealers at a 5% premium over face value.

In the 1820s, Peter (a.k.a. Pierre) Flandin had been an active numismatist in New York City. Apparently, his interest continued for many years thereafter. Finally, he tired of the pursuit, and on June 6, 1855, his collection was auctioned by Bangs, Brother & Co., of the same city, in the first truly notable numismatic sale held by what would become, in various forms, a very long-lived auction house. The Flandin Collection offering comprised 230 lots with a total of 1,195 pieces, and sold for the aggregate sum of $736.02.[39] Although it was smaller than the Roper sale of 1851, it attracted wider attention, since the numismatic hobby was expanding rapidly. Now, perhaps, 200 to 300 active collectors were involved.

Prosperity continued apace. Land speculation and railroad building flourished along with the demand for agricultural products and domestic goods. Short-lived "runs" on banks took place in Cincinnati and soon extended to Louisville, Chicago, Cleveland, Columbus, and Pittsburgh. Stock frauds contributed to the uncertainty. A few naysayers suggested that too much was being built on credit, but not much attention was paid to such comments. Congress voted funds to construct a telegraph line from the Mississippi River to the West Coast, expanding the most popular form of long-distance communication. In an article in the *New York Herald* on April 1, a judge expressed the opinion that crimes could be attributed to people of various national backgrounds. For example, murders, riots, and other violence were the forte of Irishmen, while Englishmen specialized in highway robberies and daring burglaries. Germans were said to excel in theft. Established American citizens were apt to engage in more passive crimes such as forgery and obtaining goods under false pretenses. In the meantime, immigrants from Europe continued to arrive in large numbers.

1855

Circulation-Strike Mintage
758,269

Proof Mintage
Fewer than 15 (estimate)

Enlarged 2x
(actual size 15 mm)

Whitman Coin Guide (WCG™)

VF-20	EF-40	AU-50	AU-55	MS-60	MS-63	MS-65	PF-63	PF-65
$350	$475	$700	$1,050	$2,750	$11,500	$30,000	$200,000	$375,000

CERTIFIED POPULATIONS

G-4–VF-35	EF-40–AU-58	MS-60–62	MS-63	MS-64	MS-65	MS-66	MS-67	MS-68–70
242	5,083	1,600	448	312	63	23	14	0
PF-50–58	PF-60–62	PF-63	PF-64	PF-65	PF-66	PF-67	PF-68–70	
0	1	0	1	4	5	1	0	

Key to Collecting. Comments for the 1855 closely parallel those for the 1854 Type II, except the 1855 is slightly scarcer. Nearly all are weakly struck in areas. Clashmarks are common. Needle-sharp coins exist, but finding one will be a challenge. The good news is that since certification services take no notice of sharpness, die quality, or eye appeal, when you do find one, it is apt to cost little more than the typical weak example. This comment is, of course, appropriate to all gold dollars.

Estimated Total Population (Mint State). 2,200 to 2,800. This statistic ranks the Mint State 1855 as slightly scarcer than the 1854 Type II, although in ultra-high grades, the 1855 edges into the lead. As with the 1854 issue, the 1855 is often optimistically graded. Most are poorly struck, more so than for 1854. Breen (*Encyclopedia*, 1988) reported that a "hoard" of Uncirculated pieces was discovered circa 1972; if so, the present writer has no details. The "Baltimore find" had 215 coins, nearly all Uncirculated. *Certified population, MS-63 and higher:* 870.

Estimated Total Population (Circulated Grades). 5,000 to 7,500. This estimate is about the same as for 1854 Type II, a figure equal to less than 1% of the original mintage of the 1855. Typical grades are Very Fine, Extremely Fine, and About Uncirculated.

Characteristics of Striking and Die Notes. Nearly all examples are weak at the centers, including at the 85 of the date and the LL (DOLLAR). The weak 8 may have been caused on *some* specimens by die deterioration, but as many die pairs were used, most often the weakness was due to striking. In general, the 1855 gold dollars tend to be more poorly struck than the 1854s (which win no prizes). Evidence of clashed dies is seen on most pieces.

Numismatic Notes

Die Data. 1855 four-digit date logotype: Digits are very closely spaced. The 1 has a very thick upright, and leans slightly to the right. The interior top of the 8 is about the same size as the bottom of the 8; the base of the 8 is flattened. The 5s are italic, the second more deeply punched into the *matrix* than the first, giving it a somewhat heavier appearance and with its ball virtually touching the upright, as opposed to being slightly farther away as on the first 5. On working dies, if the logotype is not driven straight into the die, the last digit can be heavier, and the ball can be closer to the upright or even touching it. This logotype was used on all dies of all mints.

Auction Information. A few selections from hundreds of citations:

> *1932–06: W.L. Stetson, E.H. Adams, B.L. Belden, Miss Sayre, F.F. Fletcher, Mrs. R.S. Maloney, Wesley Hayes, and Gustav Senft Collections* (Thomas L. Elder) lot 2099: "1855 Cracked die, obv. & rev. Rare. Uncirculated." Elder auctions were often a potpourri or *omnia gatherum* of consignments, sometimes listed in the title as here.
>
> *1935–06: Wendell C Foster Collection* (Thomas L. Elder) lot 2741: "1855 Large type. Very small word Liberty. Brilliant Unc. (Gold found in Baltimore)." Lot 2742: "1855 Large. Double cut letters and figures. Mint bloom. (Gold found in Baltimore)." Lot 2752: "1855 Brilliant Unc. (Gold found in Baltimore)." Lot 2754: "1855 red gold. Brilliant Uncirculated, uncommon. (Gold found in Baltimore)."
>
> *1958–12: 52nd Sale, Eliot Landau Collection* (New Netherlands Coin Co.) lot 689: "1855 Partly recut legend, triple cutting on U and final A. Frosty, choice Uncirculated, though not quite on the level of the last. The 8 weak as usual; likewise struck from injured dies." In its day, New Netherlands was essentially alone among major auctioneers who gave negative but true comments about coins being sold, as appropriate. However, rarity information was often wildly incorrect.
>
> *1992–08: Orlando Sale* (Superior) lot 533: "1855. Type 2. PCGS MS-66 . . . A superb example of the elusive Type 2 gold dollar. There have been only four graded so far in MS-66 condition. This one, too, is an outstanding specimen; fully struck in the centers except for the 8 in date which is characteristically weak. The lustre is fabulous!" This is an interesting reflection of the expansion of certification service numbers, since by 2007 there were 23 certified as MS-66 (by the leading services) plus 14 as MS-67.

Proofs

Estimated Total Population and Key to Collecting. 8 to 10. By any evaluation, a Proof is a great rarity, although market appearances have been more frequent than for the 1854 of this type.

Die Data and Notes. On the Proof die, the top of the 1 (1855) is below the O (DOLLAR) and the adjacent L. Because multiple dies were made for *circulation-strike* coinage, this positioning is not necessarily unique for Proofs.

Proofs are usually weakly struck at the 8 (1855) due to metal flow requirements, this point in the reverse die being opposite the deepest recess of the obverse die.

Auction Information (Proofs). In lieu giving multiple listings, the 1999 description, by David Akers, of the 1911 Woodin coin covers numerous offerings.

1911–03: 48th Public Sale, William H. Woodin Collection (Thomas L. Elder), lot 852: "1855. Brilliant Proof. The only record of a Proof piece having been sold I find in the Stickney Sale, where it sold for $33, and as gold has advanced considerably since then, it should bring much more in this almost unique state." Realized $35.

1956–04: Thomas G. Melish and Clinton W. Hester Collections (A. Kosoff), lot 1743: "1855. Brilliant Proof. Rare."

1997–10: John Jay Pittman Collection, Part I (David W. Akers), lot 866: "1855, Type II, Choice Proof. Very sharply struck with brilliant, deep mirror fields and only a few light hairlines on both the obverse and reverse . . . Following is a complete roster of the known Proof 1855 Type II gold dollars. I have personally examined each of the eight specimens listed, and am therefore certain that they are distinct examples. 1. Smithsonian Institution. 2. ANS; J.P. Morgan. 3. John Jay Pittman, the specimen offered here; Thomas Melish: 1743; William H. Woodin: 852; Lorin G. Parmelee: 1255. 4. Harold Bareford: 29; 'Memorable': 9; 'World's Greatest Collection': 9; John Story Jenks: 5822. 5. Norman Stack. Sold with his type set in 1990. In the Stack Collection since at least 1971, per Harvey Stack. 6. Ed Trompeter: 1; Louis Eliasberg Sr.: 26; John H. Clapp; Elmer S. Sears (1909). 7. Mocatta Metals. Purchased privately in 1975. 8. Floyd T. Starr: 1084; Probably George H. Hall: 1678; J.F.Bell: 9. Not from 'W.G.C.' as stated in the Starr catalog. See No. 4 above. One Proof 1855 Type II gold dollar was auctioned in the 1940s by B. Max Mehl on two occasions, first as Belden E. Roach: 1041 and then as Will W. Neil: 2303. It is likely that this is the same coin as either No. 5 or No. 7 above; if not, it is a ninth known specimen. I have also not accounted for the Matthew A. Stickney: 766 specimen in the above list. I believe it to be either No. 4 or No. 6, but cannot be sure of this; however, I am reasonably certain that it is one of the specimens in this listing, and thus not an additional example."

1855-C

Circulation-Strike Mintage
9,803

Enlarged 2x
(actual size 15 mm)

Whitman Coin Guide (WCG™)

VF-20	EF-40	AU-50	AU-55	MS-60	MS-63	MS-65
$1,750	$4,250	$10,500	$15,000	$27,500		

CERTIFIED POPULATIONS

G-4–VF-35	EF-40–AU-58	MS-60–62	MS-63	MS-64	MS-65	MS-66	MS-67	MS-68–70
77	249	15	0	0	0	0	0	0

Key to Collecting. The 1855-C, the only Charlotte Mint gold dollar of the Type II design, is rare in all grades, exceedingly so in Mint State. It is *always weakly struck* in some areas. David W. Akers (1975) commented: "Invariably the planchets and the quality of striking are extremely poor, and the date and word DOLLAR are almost always weak. In fact, the 8 is almost missing on some specimens. Many pieces also show distinct clashmarks. Because of the pòor planchets and equally poor quality of striking, grading is difficult." Douglas Winter (1998) commented: "There might not be a single example currently known which has truly good eye appeal. The quality conscious collector will have to relax his standards when it comes to this issue." In the foregoing respects, the 1855-C is a kissing cousin to the 1857-C Type III gold dollar. Misery rules! Just as "folk art" is popular with collectors of paintings, the rustic nature of certain Charlotte and Dahlonega coins *increases* their appeal to collectors. This has been true for many years. That said, within a given date and mintmark, a sharper one is always more desirable than a weaker example.

Estimated Total Population (Mint State). 8 to 12 per grading interpretations, with a liberal dose of "gradeflation." Discard this, and you have an *incredible rarity.* In his study of the series, Winter stated that only *one* Mint State coin was known to him. In 1975 (the early period in the context of modern market research), Akers was not aware of even a single Mint State coin. Perhaps the finest to come to market since was in Auction '89, lot 1343, described by Akers as Uncirculated, "planchet and strike are good and the lustre in particular is unusually excellent." This coin had been sold by Mid-American in May 1986 with the Skiles Collection. Today, as the grading interpretations change and seem to continue to do so, a seasoned expert's About Uncirculated seems to be another's Mint State—perhaps explaining the 15 certification events from MS-60 to MS-62. *Certified population, MS-63 and higher:* 0.

Estimated Total Population (Circulated Grades). 140 to 190. The typical specimen is Very Fine, very occasionally Extremely Fine, and almost never About Uncirculated—as a survey of "name" collection sales will quickly demonstrate.

Characteristics of Striking and Die Notes. The 8 (1855) is always weak, and sometimes other features are lightly defined as well, including the OLL (DOLLAR) and the 8 (1855).

NUMISMATIC NOTES

Die Data. Three pairs of dies were shipped from Philadelphia to Charlotte in anticipation of the coinage. After 1854, any undated obverse dies on hand were useless, because the design had changed. Apparently, two obverse dies were employed and but a single reverse, that having the mintmark C as a very small letter.

Auction Information. Selected offerings featured coins that must have been rather miserable from an eye-appeal viewpoint, but until recent times this aspect was hardly ever mentioned. The varied comments bring to the fore the sometimes widely differing opinions of experts as to grade and rarity within a grade, such as Mint State. The detailed listings of Type II and III Charlotte and Dahlonega coins in the present book will be enlightening to many readers who have not been aware that for such coins a single grading number can have little meaning with regard to their desirability. After you read these listings, plus the above text about the 1855-C, you will have a greater awareness of what exists and what does not, and what to look for, than do 90% of the buyers of certified 1855-C gold dollars in the marketplace. At present, experts can differ, and differ widely—but once a coin is encapsulated, all questions seem to stop! We won't address the logic of this.

1943–04: David Proskey Estate (Stack's), lot 1308: "1855-C Recut obverse die all letters and profile. Brilliant Uncirculated."

1944–12: J.F. Bell Collection (Stack's), lot 50: "1855-C Uncirculated gem." Realized $35. This coin later went into the Josiah K. Lilly Collection and is now in the Smithsonian Institution.

1975–02: Fixed Price List Catalogue, Volume 4 (New England Rare Coin Galleries): "1855-C EF-AU, a sharp example of this scarce issue. Choice AU, very close to Mint State. A few normal planchet imperfections, characteristic of this date. Still one of the finest known examples, since this date is unknown in Mint State!" New England Galleries owner Jim Halperin (later a partner in Heritage) was aware of no Mint State coins by 1975.

1976–03: John Work Garrett Collection (Stack's), lot 379: "1855-C Brilliant Uncirculated, with some proof-like surface although it is mostly frosty. A superb strike and deserving of the term 'gem' in spite of a few minute bagmarks. From the Wilharm Collection, lot 307, and by far the finest branch mint coin sold in that sale."

1978–12: Harold S. Bareford Collection (Stack's), lot 30: "1855-C Brilliant Uncirculated. Frosty mint bloom with delicate coppery overtones. The reverse, as usual, is better struck than the obverse but it is by far, better than normally encountered. The clashmarks are lightly in evidence. The planchet is excellent and overall it is a very attractive coin. The date is fully struck-up. Of the four Mint State specimens recorded by Akers, we've sold three of them. This is the best of all and it could probably be the 'finest known' From David Bullowa, October 10, 1951." *Later offering: 1999–10: Harry W. Bass Jr. Collection, Part II* (Bowers and Merena Galleries), lot 98: "1855-C AU-58 (PCGS) . . . This is an exceptional example and is listed as second finest known by Douglas Winter in his reference on Charlotte gold coinage. Winter noted that only seven or eight examples from the original mintage of 9,803 coins grade better than EF . . . It is interesting to note that Harold Bareford was enamored by the strike exhibited, for on his original collection envelope that accompanies this lot is the notation 'numerous die lines or suction marks.' PCGS Population: 3; 2 finer (MS-61 finest). Light obverse and reverse clashmarks." Here we have the probable "finest known" Uncirculated coin to the expert at Stack's, called AU-58 by PCGS. This is another "poster example" of the eccentricities of grading branch mint gold dollars. Don't look for any logic when studying comments and market descriptions relating to 1855-C gold dollars.

1986–05: Wayne J. Skiles Collection, GNA Sale (Mid-American), lot 1816: "1855-C About Uncirculated (50/50). Struck from clashed dies and on a somewhat inferior planchet (as are most all known specimens). This is a very difficult coin on which to place an accurate grade. Close examination shows a near total absence of wear but the fields are a bit disturbed from poor preparation of the planchet (this is particularly evident on the obverse, where the fields are granular). Where struck, the coin is quite sharp, with a full date and LL in DOLLAR; the surfaces have acquired a lovely orange-gold coloration and show considerable luster . . . Approximately 70–75 1855-C

Charlotte gold dollars are known, with most of these grading VF and characterized by wretched planchets and/strikes. Approximately 6–7 AU's are known. The following is a revised Condition Census for this date. 1. Elrod Collection, ex Stack's 10/83 lot 11, Stack's 12/72, lot 48. Mint State-60 and the only example of this date which is graded Uncirculated by most specialists. 2. Bareford 12/78, lot 30, ex Bullowa 10/10/51 and, possibly, Roach, lot 1089. Nice AU-55. 3. Quality Sales 9/73, lot 1006. AU-55 and nearly as nice as the last. 4. Stack's 2/80. Lot 35, ex Stack's 2/78 lot 980 and Stack's 3/73 lot 743. AU-55; similar to the last but on a slightly less attractive flan. 5. The presently offered example." The experts at Mid-American, these being Ron Guth and Jeff Garrett, considered the true population of Uncirculated coins to be just a single coin in 1986, but not this one. *Later appearance: 1989–07: Auction '89* (David W. Akers), lot 1343: "1855-C Uncirculated 60 (NGC) or better. This is the only Mint State 1855-C Gold dollar to have been graded by either grading service, hardly surprising in view of the issue's great rarity in high grade. Although called 'MS-60' by NGC, we feel this coin is a bit better than that in terms of what has happened to it since it was struck (not much). But the planchet and caliber of striking leave a lot to be desired, as they invariably do for an 1855-C, and that was undoubtedly taken into consideration by NGC when grading this piece. Actually, by 1855-C standards, the planchet and strike are quite good and the lustre in particular is unusually excellent. We have never seen a finer or even equal quality example of this issue. Even the Bareford piece . . . way back in 1978 was not fully Mint State in our opinion (it has long been considered the finest known) and so this piece may well be unique in this grade. With today's race for quality, this coin may get overlooked in the rush but it is actually one of the rarest coins in this entire sale." Now, the same coin has leapfrogged from AU-50, past AU-53, AU-55, and AU-58, to be labeled MS-60.

1988–05: Georgia Numismatic Association Sale (Mid-American), lot 1849: "1855-C Uncirculated (60). An extraordinary example of this important rarity! . . . Quite lustrous and definitely a superior specimen of this rarity which is considered extremely rare in all grades above VF. Mint State examples are practically unheard of."

1993–10: Reed Hawn Collection (Stack's), lot 884: "1855-C Brilliant Uncirculated. Outstanding condition for this date. This is the only Type II gold dollar from the Charlotte Mint, one of only 9,803 struck. Pale yellow gold. Typically softly struck, particularly under the tips of the feathers. Several obverse planchet flaws, one through UN. Struck from clashed dies. The 1855-C is famous for poor planchet quality . . . Struck from the obverse with clear die file marks slanting down from rim through UNIT."

1994–03: Whitney P. Sunderland Collection (Bowers and Merena Galleries), lot 1557: "1855-C MS-62 (NGC). A prized rarity at the Uncirculated grade level. The only specimen called MS-62 by NGC, with none certified higher. Lightly struck from rusted and heavily clashed dies. Several planchet flaws are noted, typical for this date."

1999–01: North Georgia Collection (Heritage), lot 7732: "1855-C MS 60 PCGS. A much better struck example than is typical for this issue with very sharp central detail in spite of a number of clashmarks around the portrait.

Very lustrous with attractive light yellow-gold and rose color; the surfaces are choice with the exception of a fine hairline scratch that runs from the throat to the T in UNITED. The reverse is as nice as we can recall having seen on an 1855-C gold dollar. This is the rarest collectible gold dollar from the Charlotte Mint in higher grades. A dozen or so accurately graded AUs are known as well as between one and four Mint State coins; the appearance and poor manufacture of this date make it extremely difficult for even experts to grade . . . This is certainly the finest 1855-C gold dollar that has been made available to collectors in many years." Here we have a wide estimate of between one and four true Mint State coins known.

1855-D

Circulation-Strike Mintage
1,811

Enlarged 2x
(actual size 15 mm)

Whitman Coin Guide (WCG™)

VF-20	EF-40	AU-50	AU-55	MS-60	MS-63	MS-65
$5,500	$13,500	$23,000	$28,500	$50,000	$95,000	

CERTIFIED POPULATIONS

G-4–VF-35	EF-40–AU-58	MS-60–62	MS-63	MS-64	MS-65	MS-66	MS-67	MS-68–70
10	83	5	2	4	0	0	0	0

Key to Collecting. The 1855-D is at once the rarest Type II gold dollar and the rarest coin of this denomination from the Dahlonega Mint. An example in *any* grade is a memorable item, never mind that many (but not all) are rustic in appearance—with striking and/or planchet problems. As to how many Mint State coins are known, that depends on interpretation—and, as with the 1855-C, experts often disagree. Lest there be any doubt, check the description of the coin in the Heritage Platinum Night Sale, January 2004, quoted below. Expert descriptions in auction presentations have ranged from AU-50 to the present MS-62. Wonder how many other low-grade About Uncirculated coins would be classified as Mint State now, if sent to the certification services? Grading aside, any coin that has decent strike and eye appeal is a prize.

Estimated Total Population (Mint State). 8 to 12. The number of different Mint State specimens is very low. Breen (*Encyclopedia*, 1988) suggested three. The two finest may be the Bass Collection, Part II and the North Georgia Collection coins, each certified as MS-62 by PCGS (or perhaps one of the four MS-64 coins certified is better). Of course, that total might not equate to that many different coins. An 1855-D is sufficiently valuable that an entrepreneur, in the hope of gaining an extra grade point or two, might not mind paying to submit it for certification—multiple times.

In 1986, Paul F. Taglione remarked that an 1855-D described as "Gem Uncirculated" in an auction was graded as "AU by a highly respected gold specialist."[40] Such differences of opinion have existed for a long time and are normal in the context of gold coins, especially those with wide variations in strike sharpness, die state, and planchet quality. Such remarks serve as a reality check for the uninitiated numismatist who may think that a number on a certification holder represents an unequivocal scientific evaluation. *Certified population, MS-63 and higher: 6.*

Estimated Total Population (Circulated Grades). 60 to 80. Most are in lower grades. Interestingly, in *Major Varieties of U.S. Gold Dollars* (1964), Walter Breen commented: "I know of eight specimens of this coin, though possibly others exist." Breen's work was often very myopic, based on relatively few catalogs.

David Akers commented (1975): "This is one of the rarest of all gold dollars and is extremely difficult to find in high grades. Because of its rarity, it is generally grossly overgraded, and most specimens that I have seen, including those called AU or even Uncirculated, would barely make EF if they had been the more common 1854 Type II or 1855. Most specimens have an extremely weak 8 in the date, and exhibit severe clashmarks on both obverse and reverse."

The same writer stated that certain numismatists had claimed that only a dozen specimens are known in all grades combined, but he suggested that "at least twice that many exist, most of them are very low grade."

Characteristics of Striking and Die Notes. With a handful of exceptions, known specimens are imperfectly struck in one or more areas, most often near the center of the date, 8 or 85, but also often on the high points of the portrait on the obverse and the wreath on the reverse. Most have clashmarks, often heavy. The planchets used were very poor in quality. The auction citations given below demonstrate this.

NUMISMATIC NOTES

Die Data. Three obverse and three 1855-dated reverse dies were sent from Philadelphia on November 24, 1854. The shipment, comprising three pairs of each of the gold $1, $2.50, and $5 denominations, was sent in one box and forwarded by Adams' Express from Philadelphia, but was lost for a time in Savannah, Georgia; after it was found, it was forwarded to Dahlonega and arrived there on December 27, 1854. It seems that only a single pair of dies was used for coinage.

Mintage. The mintage of 1,811 pieces was accomplished in February. The number of additional pieces made for assay is not known.

In anticipation of the new Type III standard to be adopted the following year, the Philadelphia Mint furnished sample Type III planchets and a new gauge for measuring strip thickness to the Dahlonega Mint.[41]

Auction Information. Again, a listing of specific sale descriptions is enlightening and reflects the views of many experts over a span of years.

> *1905–12: Philip D. Hoch Collection, Part II* (Lyman H. Low), lot 368: "1855-D Only the outline of 8 in date is visible, the other figures and mint letter are full and strong, otherwise Very Good, approaching Fine. This peculiarity of imperfection is not uncommon in issues from the mints of Charlotte and Dahlonega. While the dies were cut at Philadelphia, the branch mints rolled and cut the blanks to strike their coins, and the machinery being less perfected than at the chief mint, the impressions varied and in few if any instances, equal those of the Philadelphia Mint. Whether good, bad, or indifferent, I find but a single record since 1886, and I challenge the announcement of a duplicate." This reflects that in 1905 Lyman H. Low was not aware of a single other specimen in numismatic hands! Low's expanded description of minting is extremely unusual for a catalog of this early era.

1907: Superb Collection of United States and Foreign Gold, Silver and Copper Coins, Fractional Currency, Etc., Fixed price list (Elmer S. Sears), lot 515: "1855 Dahlonega Mint. VF and excessively rare. Probably less than a dozen are known and this is one of the best I have seen."

1907–10: XIII Public Auction Sale (Thomas L. Elder), lot 1351: "1855 D Mint. Slight flake in obverse field due to a die crack. Fine. Excessively rare. Has only been offered twice at auction in recent years."

1935–04: E.H. Adams and F.Y. Parker Collection (Thomas L. Elder), lot 1806: "1855-D Extremely Fine. Extremely rare. The figure 8 in date is not as strong as the other figures which are very fine. The mintmark D. is very bold. We have not had one in many years."

1944–12: J.F. Bell Collection (Stack's), lot 59: "1855-D One of the rarest in this series. Uncirculated, numeral '8' in date not as sharp as the other figures. Rarely seen in this state of preservation" This must have been an incredible coin.

1950–06: Menjou Collection (Numismatic Gallery), lot 472: "1855-D Large size and one of the rarest of the Dahlonega Mint dollars. Characteristic of this coin, the LL and 8 on reverse are weakly struck. We haven't seen a much better specimen than this one which is about Extremely Fine." (Adolph Menjou was a character actor in "B" movies who collected coins, but the auction mainly consisted of the cabinet of Charles Williams, of Cincinnati, which had been purchased outright by Abe Kosoff and Abner Kreisberg.)

1961–06: June Sale (Stack's), lot 237: "1855-D . . . A superb Uncirculated specimen, with characteristic weak strike on '8' of date. The mint mark 'D' is very bold. A specimen of this quality has not been offered at public auction for almost a decade. This is within the top half dozen best specimens."

1965–05: Grant Pierce & Sons Collection (Stack's), lot 1016: "1855-D Brilliant Uncirculated Gem. A superb specimen, sharply struck all over with the exception of the '8' which always comes weak. The coin has a prooflike surface obverse and reverse. The only comparable coin we know of we sold in our June 1961 Sale . . . Since that time we sold many fine collections and none had a specimen even close to this." *Later offering: 1993–10: Reed Hawn Collection* (Stack's), lot 885: "1855-D Choice Brilliant Uncirculated, with fully reflective surfaces . . . This example must be among the finest known. Ex Grant Pierce & Sons Sale."

1986–05: Wayne J. Skiles Collection, GNA Sale (Mid-American), lot 1817: "1855-D Uncirculated (60/60). Struck from clashed dies, as are all known examples of this date. Fully struck except for the often seen weakness on the 8 in the date. Semi-prooflike, with some areas of frost within the surfaces. The reverse is truly exceptional. This is one of the true rarities in the gold dollar series, with an estimated total population of only 30–40 specimens . . . There are only two specimens of this date which might exceed the quality of the specimen here offered, the Ullmer, lot 340 (ex Miles) example and the Stack's 11/74 coin. This newly discovered coin is definitely superior to the Montgomery, lot 1301, Auction '81, lot 1340 and James Carter, lot 32 coins and, as such, represents the finest example of this date currently available."

Another, more recent offering is given in chapter 5 (on page 36). That listing also reflects how coins play musical chairs as they move around from one buyer to another, often without landing in a serious specialized collection that the owner intends to keep for a long time. This particular coin had well over a dozen owners from 1968 to 2004. This "buy-and-soon-sell" philosophy is a godsend to auction houses!

1855-O

Circulation-Strike Mintage
55,000

Enlarged 2x
(actual size 15 mm)

Whitman Coin Guide (WCG™)

VF-20	EF-40	AU-50	AU-55	MS-60	MS-63	MS-65
$550	$950	$1,850	$2,750	$8,000	$26,500	

CERTIFIED POPULATIONS

G-4–VF-35	EF-40–AU-58	MS-60–62	MS-63	MS-64	MS-65	MS-66	MS-67	MS-68–70
62	670	72	19	11	0	0	0	0

Key to Collecting. The 1855-O, the final gold dollar coined at the New Orleans Mint, is slightly scarce in any grade and moderately rare in Mint State. Most are well struck (except for the 8 in the date) and have excellent eye appeal.

Estimated Total Population (Mint State). 60 to 80. By any accounting a Mint State specimen is difficult to find. Happily, among these are quite a few graded MS-63 or finer. This and the 1856-S Type II are the only branch mint gold dollars of the design that are reasonably available in Mint State. In the 1950s John J. Ford Jr. had a group of ten 1855-O gold dollars, "each one a gem, which I sold to Harry Forman." [42] *Certified population, MS-63 and higher:* 30.

Estimated Total Population (Circulated Grades). 900 to 1,200. Scarce, but not rare. In everlasting demand as the only New Orleans dollar of the Type II design.

Characteristics of Striking and Die Notes. Most 1855-O gold dollars are decently struck, including the central date figures, *except for the 8.* There are exceptions to the overall quality, but in no way can the 1855-O be compared to the other branch mint dollars of this year, which are miserable. A few are highly prooflike.

Numismatic Notes

Die Data. Six pairs of dies were shipped from Philadelphia to New Orleans for this coinage, but not all were used.

Auction Information. Dozens of Mint State coins have crossed the auction block, mostly beginning in the late 20th century. A few selections of various grade pieces are given here, from a wide span of years. One of the finest offered in early times was the David S. Wilson coin, March 1907, described by S.H. Chapman (on his own, after dissolving the Chapman brothers partnership in 1906), simply as "Uncirculated." An exceptional specimen (but who knows?) may have been the coin sold by B. Max Mehl in December 1922 in his catalog of the H.E. Rawson, Dr. A. de Yoanna, and David Strasser Collections, lot 84, described as: "1855-O The rarest date of this mint. The 8 of date not as boldly struck as the balance of date. Brilliant semi-proof, nearly equal to a perfect Proof, and as such very rare and valuable." This coin later resurfaced in Mehl's November 1939 sale of the William B. Hale Collection. A similar description befit lot 1598 in James F. Kelly's Chi-ANA Convention Sale: "1855 O Mint, a gem. If they struck Proof Gold at New Orleans, this is one."

Remarkably, the team of John J. Ford Jr. and Walter Breen, catalogers of lot 690 in New Netherlands Coin Company's December 1958 sale of the Eliot Landau Collection, had never seen an Uncirculated coin before: "1855-O Extra brilliant 'gem' Uncirculated; almost but not quite Superb. Head and 8 rather weak as always. Exceptionally rare condition for this mint-mark, which is a type coin—the only Type 2 gold dollar from New Orleans. This specimen is the first strictly Mint State impression we have seen, as fine as the day it left the press." Because quite a few had crossed the auction block by this time, we can only surmise that Ford and Breen were either collectively forgetful, or had not spent much time in the real world marketplace. Listings such as this are stimulating to numismatic researchers who enjoy deciphering the thought processes of catalogers.

AMERICA AND NUMISMATICS IN 1856

Professor E.D. Groux announced the forthcoming publication of *A Numismatical History of the United States. Banker's Magazine* reported:

> The work will consist of three volumes. The first volume will contain a narrative of a journey, undertaken by the author throughout the United States, for the purpose of visiting the principal collections (both public and private) of medals and coins, and also paintings, statuary, relics and mementoes of former times, &c. to be described in the book. The second volume is designed to contain 350 wood cuts, being accurate representations of coins; and the third volume is designed to contain sixty or seventy copperplates, representing 600 medals. Prof. Groux has, in his own collection, representations of nearly all the medals and coins that have been struck in America, and also those that have been struck elsewhere for America. It is stated that about the middle of the sixteenth century, Hubertus Golzius traveled over a great part of Europe, in search of coins and medals, and published a list of the principal collections then existing. Prof. Groux designs to make a similar tour throughout this country, and he solicits the assistance of possessors of coins and other objects falling within his plan, to give him their aid in carrying out his enterprise. The work will be issued in numbers. The first number of the first volume will shortly be issued, and will contain a short description of the collections in Massachusetts.

This project never came to be, and in time Groux was exposed as a phony promoter.

In his *Annual Report of the Director of the Mint*, James Ross Snowden related that silver coins were circulating effectively and that the benefits of the Coinage Act of February 21, 1853, were continuing. He felt, however, that if the government would step in and prevent state-chartered banks from issuing bills under the denomination of $20, gold and silver coins would be more popular. Metal poured into the Mint. In July, *Banker's Magazine* reported: "Adams & Co.'s Express at Louisville, May 16th, received by the *Niagara* from New-Orleans, 38 tons of silver, in bars and coin, the property of the United States, in charge of J.D. Colmesnil, to be forwarded to the Mint at Philadelphia. The precious stuff was in 153 huge boxes, which were drayed . . . to the mail-boat landing under the care of the trusty messengers of the express company. The *Jacob Strader* delayed her departure until after two o'clock in the afternoon for the money, but only about half of it was received up to that time, and she left without waiting for the balance. The total value of the specie was $1,120,000."

Seeking still more silver, and endeavoring to remove Spanish-American coins from circulation, the Mint posted these buying prices for delivery at Philadelphia:

> French five franc pieces, 99¢ each. Mexican and South-American dollars, 106-1/4¢ each. Old Spanish dollars, 105¢ each. Revolutionary or "hammered" dollars, often mistaken for the true Spanish dollar, 101¢ each. Half dollars of the United States coined before 1837, 52-1/4¢ each. The same since 1837 to the last change of standard in 1853, 52-1/2¢ each. Quarter dollars are proportionally less productive of premium, while dimes and half dimes coined before 1837 have lost rather more by wear, on an average, than the premium would make up; those coined since 1837, to 1853, will average a premium of 3-1/2% on their nominal value. German, Swedish, Danish and Norwegian crowns, 114¢ each. Old French crowns, 114¢ each. German florins 41-1/2¢ each. Prussian and Hanoverian thalers, 72¢ each. American plate, best manufacture, 120 to 122¢ per ounce. Genuine British plate, 125¢ per ounce.

Experiments to reduce the size of the one-cent piece culminated in a new-format coin by Chief Engraver James B. Longacre. Made of a copper-nickel alloy (88% copper, 12% nickel) the new coin weighed 72 grains. The obverse depicted a Flying Eagle borrowed from Christian Gobrecht's silver dollar of 1836, while the reverse incorporated Longacre's "agricultural wreath" first used on the 1854 three-dollar gold piece. In the meantime, while double eagles continued to be produced in quantity, demand for gold dollars diminished, in view of the abundance of silver coins in circulation.

In November the presidential election pitted James Buchanan, a Democrat from Pennsylvania, against John C. Fremont, of the recently formed Republican Party. Buchanan won. His presidency, commencing with his inauguration on March 4, 1857, was ineffective because he was overwhelmed by bickering and squabbles between senators and representatives from the North, advocating abolition, and the South, insisting that slavery be maintained.

Economic prosperity continued, fueled by the usual catalysts: continuing speculation in western lands, extensive building of railroads, incoming gold from California, and extensive paper money issued by state-chartered banks. Nothing could go wrong. Or could it?

1856-S, Type II

Circulation-Strike Mintage
24,600

Enlarged 2x
(actual size 15 mm)

Whitman Coin Guide (WCG™)

VF-20	EF-40	AU-50	AU-55	MS-60	MS-63	MS-65
$950	$1,350	$2,250	$3,000	$8,000	$32,500	

CERTIFIED POPULATIONS

G-4–VF-35	EF-40–AU-58	MS-60–62	MS-63	MS-64	MS-65	MS-66	MS-67	MS-68–70
30	349	65	8	4	0	0	0	0

Key to Collecting. The 1856-S gold dollar is very curious, since it is of the Type II design, but struck in a year when the other mints were using the new Type III motif. There are few enough 1856-S dollars to make the issue scarce, but a sufficient number that examples are always available for a price. In Mint State this issue is quite scarce, especially if truly choice, such as MS-64 (its highest certification level). *Nearly all* show repunching of the mintmark S, so catalog comments about the rarity of this feature can be ignored—as can separate listings in some published population reports.

Estimated Total Population (Mint State). 40 to 60. Most are in the range of MS-60 to MS-62, occasionally MS-63. Opinions are often optimistic, and it is likely that some lower level Mint State coins might be more properly called About Uncirculated. There are a few marvelous exceptions, and several memorable gems are cited in the listings below. *Certified population, MS-63 and higher:* 12.

Estimated Total Population (Circulated Grades). 600 to 800. Most are Very Fine or Extremely Fine, less often About Uncirculated. Nearly all of the "name" collections brought to the auction forum in recent decades have had Very Fine or Extremely Fine specimens, as even a cursory perusal of leading auctioneers' catalogs will ascertain.

Characteristics of Striking and Die Notes. All known specimens have an upright 5 in the date. Striking quality varies, although sharp examples exist.

NUMISMATIC NOTES

Die Data. 1856 Upright 5 date logotype: There is medium separation of the 185; the 6 is spaced farther away and leans slightly right, is slightly low, and is heavy. The base of the 1 is high and the 1 leans slightly right. The 8 leans slightly right. The 5 is upright; its ball extends to the left of the upright. This logotype was used on all 1856-S Type II, 1856 Upright 5 Type III, and 1856-C and D dies, as well as on 1856 *half dime* dies.

Die pairs for this coinage seem to have been made in late 1855 with the 1856 date, and perhaps some were shipped then. Who knows? Walter Breen relates that six pairs of dies were shipped in March 1856, but were probably made in 1855 before the decision to change the design was implemented. At the time there was no easy overland communication from Philadelphia to San Francisco, and coinage materials were sent by sea through Panama (overland by the Panama Railroad across the isthmus), causing round-trip communications to take about a month. Curiously, the new Type III design was adopted at the Philadelphia Mint on January 1, 1856. How this reconciles with Type II dies being shipped to San Francisco *later* is not known. It could have been that the dies, made in 1855, were shipped West rather than waste them. However, at the other mints (Charlotte, Dahlonega, and New Orleans) the serviceable (obverse) dies on hand were discarded, and no new 1856 dies of the *Type II* format were made.

The Harry Bass Jr. collection had two reverse varieties:

1. Normal S, Repunched 6 in date. The lower left serif of the mintmark aligns with the center of a dentil. Normal S, normal 6 in date. The lower left serif of mintmark over space between dentils. This variety is very scarce.
2. Doubled S. Lower left serif of mintmark aligns with a space between the dentils. Popular wisdom is that it was discovered by Walter Breen in 1959 and published in 1960, and at that time was thought to be a great rarity.

However, it was known earlier (see 1947 Neil Collection below). Later, it was found that most 1856-S gold dollars have this feature, after which it was realized that the earlier rarity hoopla was much ado about nothing—die states exist from relapping. Included were coins with all signs of the doubling removed, these being plentiful. At least two obverse dies were combined with this reverse, one of which shattered. Also see listings below.

Auction Information. These listings culled from hundreds of auction offerings are interesting to contemplate:

1887–05: Frank McCoye Collection (S.H. and Henry Chapman), lot 871: "1856 Gold dollar. San Francisco Mint. Uncirculated."

1943–04: David Proskey Estate (Stack's), lot 1346: "1856-S Perfect Brilliant Uncirculated Gem."

1947–06: Will W. Neil Collection (B. Max Mehl), lot 2368: "1856-S. Upright 5, as all are. Interesting and rare variety with double-struck S. Extremely Fine with frosty mint surface." A fairly early mention of the doubled-S feature.

1960–04: 54th Sale, Jonathan Glogower Consignment, Etc. (New Netherlands Coin Co.), lot 944: "1856-S. Double S. First punched far too high and to right, then corrected. Brilliant Uncirculated. Sharp, somewhat frosty; choice, despite microscopic traces of handling. Very rare, only the third we have handled, fourth we have seen."

1964–08: ANA Convention Sale (Federal Brand Enterprises), lot 2395: "1856-S Variety with a double S (a blundered die). The die sinker set his punch much too high and too far to the right and on a slight bias. He then noticed his error and re-set the punch in the proper position to correct this first S. However, without too much concern as to correcting the first wrong placed S. We carefully noted that the first S, in part, is virtually as sharp as the other coin features. Another fact of interest is also called to your attention, which is also mentioned in a letter from Walter Breen, which goes with this coin, who examined the coin on March 22, 1964. This coin was struck with a badly broken die—both obverse and reverse is so indicated, and by its looks, the die could not have lasted too much longer and must have rendered itself useless by this time. Extremely Fine and, of course, a rare variety." At the time Walter Breen was widely used as an authenticator and commentator on unusual die varieties. Typically, he would prepare a typed letter describing the coin and sign his name to it. Today, some but hardly all such documents are viewed as correct. It seems that on occasion his opinion could be "bought."

1981–07: Auction '81 (Paramount), lot 1341: "1856-S, Gem Uncirculated 65 . . . All things considered (technical grade, strike, color and luster), this is the finest 1856-S gold dollar we have seen . . . It is the variety with the double punched mintmark where the first S was punched high and to the right and then only partially effaced before the mintmark was punched into the correct position directly below the bow. An exciting and important coin."

1997–04: John J. Pittman Collection, Part I (David W. Akers Numismatics, Inc.), lot 871: "1856-S, Type II, Choice Almost Uncirculated . . . This coin has a double mintmark as seen on most, if not all, known specimens. The first mintmark was punched very high and right, and was only partially effaced before the mintmark was punched into the proper position. Personally, I have never seen an 1856-S gold dollar without the double punched mintmark. It is just that on some late die state specimens, like this one, it is very faint to the point of near invisibility; on earlier die state examples, the original misplaced mintmark is very prominent." Here we have emerging information that, after all, the repunched S is not rare.

9

Type III Gold Dollars (1856–1889)

Indian Princess (Modified)

The Design Improved

In an effort to create a motif that would strike up sharply and properly (the Type II being an utter failure in this regard), in 1856 Chief Engraver James B. Longacre moved the lettering closer to the edge and redesigned the head of the obverse of the gold dollar. The Indian Princess style of Miss Liberty was continued, but in the new version, the relief was lower and the details were different. The portrait on the Type III gold dollar was a copy of the image Longacre had created for use on $3 gold coins beginning in 1854.

With its shallow portrait, the Type III did not require as much metal flow and thus did not disturb the resolution of the reverse elements. The reverse remained the same as used for the Type II.

Striking Peculiarities

The restyled obverse created a coin which indeed could be struck properly, with the result that gold dollars of the Type III design usually (but with many exceptions) are well struck in most areas, including at the central two digits of the date, this being the area which caused the greatest problem on the preceding type. For a Type III coin to be well struck, the dies in the coining press had to be spaced closely together to permit the metal to flow into the deepest die recesses. A planchet had to be annealed (softened) properly prior to striking, so that the metal flowed properly.

As will be seen from the following listings, at the Charlotte and Dahlonega mints the dies were usually spaced too far apart in the coining press, and it is the rule, not the exception, that "C" and "D" mint gold dollars were poorly struck—some being abysmally so. Incorrect annealing may have been a factor as well. Peculiarities are noted under the descriptions.

Mints and Mintages

Four mints were used to strike Type III gold dollars. At Philadelphia, coinage was continuous and all dates were struck, although mintages dipped to low levels after 1862 (exceptions being 1873 and 1874). The low point was reached in 1875 when only 400 circulation strikes and a few dozen Proofs were made. In general, Philadelphia Mint coins are well struck. Today, Mint State specimens of such years as 1856 (Slanting 5 variety), 1858, 1859, 1861, and 1862 are generally available among the early dates. In Mint State, dates from 1863 to 1878 range from scarce to exceedingly rare—save for the plentiful 1873 and 1874 issues.

The Charlotte, Dahlonega, and San Francisco mints each struck a few varieties in the Type III series. All are rare, and some are extremely so, if in high grades such as AU or

Mint State. Most C and D coin are poorly struck, often with weaknesses at the centers and other areas. In addition, planchets tended to be poor, this being especially true at the Charlotte Mint. Thus, "C" and "D" mint gold dollars are very rustic—or crude—or naïve—in comparison to those of other mints. This is similar to the situation for the 1855-C and D Type II gold dollars described earlier. Today, this gives them a special charm, and many collectors have made a specialty of acquiring Charlotte and Dahlonega Mint coins, but ignoring the others. The 1861-D is in a class by itself—a product of the Confederate States of America, struck after Southern forces took over the Dahlonega Mint.

The San Francisco Mint struck Type III gold dollars from 1857 through 1860 and again in 1870. The dies were well finished in the machine shop there, and most coins were well struck, nearly always on excellent planchets. These were strictly utilitarian coins, and little or no thought was given to saving them for numismatic purposes. Today, the earlier "S" mint issues are scarce in any grade and incredible rarities in Mint State. The 1870-S gold dollar is the only branch mint coin after 1860, and is recognized as a rarity today.

Type III circulation strikes (plus Proofs at the Philadelphia Mint) were made as follows:

Philadelphia: 5,242,965 circulation strikes, 8,700 (estimate) Proofs

Charlotte: 18,515

Dahlonega: 14,988

New Orleans: None

San Francisco: 51,000

Total all mints: 5,327,468

Production Over the Years

The Type III or Large Head motif was produced continuously from 1856 through 1889, although during and after the Civil War, mintages were exceedingly low for all years except a few. Gold dollars were not circulated in the East or Midwest from 1862 to 1878, and saw only limited use after that time. On the West Coast, gold dollars were occasionally seen in circulation during and after the Civil War, but never in quantity because the mintage figures were small. The 1870-S marked the end of branch mint coinage.

In December 1873, *Banker's Magazine* printed this: "We understand the U.S. Mint is now employed in melting up one million one-dollar pieces, for the purpose of converting the product into pieces of larger denominations, principally into double eagles. It is reported that twenty millions of these smallest gold coins are to be melted up. This is an indication most unfavorable to a return to coin circulation. The double eagles to be made are to be used as counters for the exchange of large sums between bankers and bullion dealers. They would scarcely at all enter into circulation, even if paper was at par with coin. The movement at the Mint is one directly away from a resumption of specie payments.—*Philadelphia Ledger.*"

At the time, $1 and $3 denominations were being made only in tiny quantities and served no useful purpose in commerce. The *Ledger's* figure of 20 million gold dollars was equal to the vast majority of the mintage of this denomination dating back to 1849!

Production of gold dollars at the Philadelphia Mint was discontinued in 1889. The Act of September 25, 1890, officially abolished the denomination.

Along the way, the total mintage for circulation strikes of the Type III design amounted to an estimated 5,327,468 coins. Proofs were made to the extent of an estimated 8,700 or so, spread over all of the dates (although records are incomplete). Complicating the Proof situation is that today, for certain issues struck between 1879 and 1889, there is no unequivocal distinction between a Proof and a mirrorlike circulation strike.

PROOFS

Proofs were minted of each of the Philadelphia Mint dates in the Type III series, with those struck from 1884 through 1889 being produced in relatively large quantities. As noted, most seem to have gone to the jewelry trade. The highest mintage of them all—the 1889 with 1,779 Proofs struck—is today the rarest Proof after the early 1880s. It is also the highest mintage Proof gold coin of all the pre-1915 United States issues. The rare coin market was in a quiet period at the time, and collectors and dealers seem to have reduced their orders for Proofs.

Today, Proofs made before 1881 are great rarities, and later Proofs range from scarce to rare. Most famous of all is the 1875, for which a mintage figure of just 20 Proofs has been published for many years. However, this year fell within with the era of numismatic shenanigans behind the walls of the Mint—and the number of Proof 1875 dollars known today suggests that a few more than 20 were struck. However, the issue remains very important.

As is related under the various descriptions for certain dates of the 1880s, experts often differ as to what is a Proof versus a prooflike circulation strike.

COLLECTING CONSIDERATIONS

If you desire an example for a type set you can easily locate a choice example dated in the 1880s. Examples of the more plentiful circulation-strike dates, in desired grades from Very Fine to AU, as well as Mint State specimens of certain dates are plentiful.

If you aspire to form a collection by dates and mintmarks you will be challenged on several varieties—which, of course, is what numismatics is all about. Without such an effort, you will be reduced simply to the mindless writing of checks—no fun at all.

The rarest of all Mint State Philadelphia dollars seems to be the 1863, although the lower mintage 1875 (of which only 400 are said to have been made) is better known. Generally, all gold dollars from 1863 through 1872 are scarce to rare in Mint State. Years ago, 1864 was considered to be the be-all and end-all rare date of the 1860s, but as noted, the palm has been passed to the 1863.

A flurry of investment and speculative activity among jewelers and numismatists between 1879 and 1889 resulted in the survival of more Uncirculated specimens of these dates than would otherwise have been the case. Thus, while all dates in the last 11 years of mintage have low production figures, Mint State examples, including superb gems, are readily available of most. For the low-mintage (1,600) year of 1880, *most* coins still survive in Mint State! Differences from year to year are explained under the listings. Proofs from 1884 to 1889 were made in very large quantities, more than 1,000 each year, and seem to have been bought by jewelers who had difficulty obtaining circulation strikes from the Mint, banks, or other sources. The gold dollar was a favorite for use in charms, brooches, bracelets, and other ornaments—much to the frustration of Mint officials.

All Charlotte and Dahlonega coins range from scarce to rare at any grade level, but enough exist that none are "impossible." Garnering the lion's share of fame is the aforementioned curious and very historical 1861-D minted under the auspices of the Confederate States of America at a time when the South was at war with the North. Among San Francisco gold dollars, all are scarce, and in Mint State or close to it, all are very rare. The spotlight has fallen on the 1870-S for a long time, quite possibly because it is the only gold dollar from any branch mint to be struck after the Civil War. However, in terms of the rarity of extant specimens in Mint State, several other San Francisco gold dollars outrank it.

Auction descriptions of branch mint gold dollars make interesting reading, and a perusal of the citations in the following text will demonstrate how basic listings such as "Very Good" and "Fine," used in the late 19th and early 20th centuries, have given way to very detailed descriptions in recent times. Often these are mere recitals of sales appearances, but sometimes they delineate various striking and planchet peculiarities. More than just a little hype—everyone seems to like a bit of P.T. Barnum–style ballyhoo—is often found when offered coins are among the finest certified of their date or mint.

1856, Upright 5

Circulation-Strike Mintage
176,294 (estimate)

Proof Mintage
None

Enlarged 2x
(actual size 15 mm)

Whitman Coin Guide (WCG™)

VF-20	EF-40	AU-50	AU-55	MS-60	MS-63	MS-65
$175	$250	$300	$500	$550	$1,750	$5,000

CERTIFIED POPULATIONS

G-4–VF-35	EF-40–AU-58	MS-60–62	MS-63	MS-64	MS-65	MS-66	MS-67	MS-68–70
26	331	97	35	25	6	0	0	0

Note: An unknown but no doubt proportional quantity of other pieces were classified simply as "1856"; those quantities are not given here.

Key to Collecting. The upright 5 is far and away the rarer of the two date styles of this year, at an estimated ratio of 1 to 10. There are only two reverse dies that used the Upright 5, while there are numerous Slanting 5 reverse dies. In some old accounts this is called the "Small Date." Examples are elusive at all grade levels, with Mint State being particularly so. Published market prices do not reflect the true differential, nor do population reports (as a given high-grade Upright 5 is more likely to be submitted for certification than is one of the Slanting 5 style).

Estimated Total Population (Mint State). 130 to 160. Choice and gem coins are in the minority, with just five certification events at the MS-65 level and none higher. This issue has been recognized as scarce for a long time. Most of the "name" collections that have been auctioned have had circulated examples. *Caveat:* In the early years, certain certification services did not attribute 1856 dollars by Upright and Slanting 5 varieties; accordingly, current data is partly corrupted. *Certified population, MS-63 and higher:* 66.

Estimated Total Population (Circulated Grades). 600 to 900. Somewhat scarce. Typical grades are VF or EF, with an occasional AU. The elusive quality of the 1856 Upright 5 is overlooked by most modern collectors and catalogers. Interestingly, it was recognized as rare in the late 19th century.

Characteristics of Striking and Die Notes. Some have the obverse die with an R clashmark behind the head of Miss Liberty, transferred from the R in DOLLAR on the reverse.

Numismatic Notes

Die Data. 1856 Upright 5 date logotype: Medium separation is seen on the 185; the 6 is farther away, leans slightly right, is slightly low, and is heavy. The base of 1 is high; the 1 leans slightly right. The 8 also leans slightly right. The 5 is upright and its ball extends to the left of the upright. Used on all 1856-S Type II, 1856 Upright 5 Type III, and 1856-C and D dies. This punch was also used on 1856 *half dime* dies.

Mintage. The mintage of the Upright 5 is unknown. For both the Upright 5 as well as the Slanting 5 the total is 1,762,936. Assuming the Upright 5 to be ten times rarer than the Slanting 5, and assuming that both were distributed into circulation the same way (no special hoards, export shipments, meltings, etc.), this would suggest that 1/10 of the mintage, or, 176,294 consisted of the Upright 5 and 1,586,642 were of the Slanting 5. Both of these figures appear precise, but, as explained, are simply estimates. Years ago Walter Breen suggested 33,600 Upright 5s were struck, stating, without any proof, that a delivery of coins on February 17, 1856 of this amount constituted all that were made. Today that can be dismissed in view of the population of the Upright 5. Since there were only two reverse dies that had the Upright 5 feature, the 176,294 estimate likely is closer to the truth.

Auction Information. Selected citations dramatically reflect the rarity of the variety.

> *1880–11: American Coins, Medals, Etc., 15th Sale* (S.K. Harzfeld), lot 647: "1856 Small date, straight 5. Fine, rare variety." Realized $2.10, a very strong price for the time. In this year a Proof 1875 rarity was valued at $4.
>
> *1911–03: 48th Public Sale, William H. Woodin Collection* (Thomas L. Elder), lot 857: "1856. Straight 5. Uncirculated. Very scarce variety." Realized $2.75. Woodin was a consummate scholar of the gold series at the time, and the comments in the Woodin catalog—as brief as they are—remain authoritative to this day.
>
> *1922–12: H.E. Rawson, Dr. A. de Yoanna, and David Strasser Collections* (B. Max Mehl), lot 17: "1856 The scarcer type with 5 in date upright. Brilliant Uncirculated, as though it was made today."
>
> *1935–06: Wendell C Foster Collection* (Thomas L. Elder), lot 2745: "1856 Straight 5 Red gold. Brilliant Unc, scarce. (Gold found in Baltimore)." Realized $3.25. Lot 2748: "1856 Straight 5. Yellow gold, very brilliant. (Gold found in Baltimore)." Realized $2.50. Lot 2749: "1856 Straight 5. Yellow gold, brilliant Unc (Gold found in Baltimore)." Realized $2.50. Lot 2750: "1856 Straight 5. Red gold. Brilliant gem, Unc (Gold found in Baltimore)." Realized $3.35. Lot 2755: "1856 Straight 5. Brilliant Mint State. Yellow gold. (Gold found in Baltimore)." Realized $2.70. An unusual offering from an unusual hoard.

1935–10: John G. Townsend Collection (Thomas L. Elder), lot 246: "1856 Straight 5. Brilliant Unc. (Baltimore Find)." Lot 247: "1856 Straight 5. Brilliant Unc. (Baltimore Find)." Lot 248: "1856 Straight 5. Brilliant Unc. (Baltimore Find)." Lot 249: "1856 Straight 5. Brilliant Unc. (Baltimore Find)." Same comment as preceding.

1940–09: 54th Catalog Sale (Barney Bluestone), lot 714: "1856 Upright 5, Semi-Proof. A beautiful specimen from the Brand collection. Rare condition."

1957–06: 49th Sale, Eliasberg Duplicates (New Netherlands Coin Co.), lot 712: "1856. The much rarer type with Upright 5. Brilliant Unc. Comparable to the Melish example which displayed strength in the right direction at $25. Atwater, Dr. Green, Kern, Menjou and Graves had only VF specimens. This is just beginning to come into its own, even though the Red Book continues to list it at the same price Unc. as the far commoner Slanting 5."

1960–04: 54th Sale, Jonathan Glogower Consignment, Etc. (New Netherlands Coin Co.), lot 945: "Large Indian Princess Head design: Type 3. 1856. Upright 5. First Variety: Serration-like defects within ribbon bows. Brilliant Uncirculated, frosty and choice; deserves this rating despite its few bag marks. Softly struck on curls . . ." Lot 946: "Similar. Upright 5. Second Variety: The narrow leaves left and right of date and left of D and their opposite numbers outside wreath as all strong (in contrast to the third variety, below). Brilliant Uncirculated, like the last, a little more strongly struck . . ." Lot 948: "Similar. Upright 5. Third Variety: Weak wreath, with the above mentioned leaves very faint, one or two nearly invisible. Inverted R of DOLLAR visible behind head on obverse. Extremely Fine plus . . . 33,660 of the Upright 5 type were coined, Feb 17, 1856."

1963–04: CSNS/J.F. Bell Sale (RARCOA), lot 32: "1856 Upright 5, Brilliant Uncirculated Gem. This variety is approximately ten times scarcer than the Slanting 5, and is seldom seen."

1984–07: Auction '84 (Paramount), lot 811: "1856, Upright 5, Choice Uncirculated 63+. A borderline gem of one of the scarcest, yet most unappreciated Philadelphia Mint Type III gold dollars . . . This was one of the few issues missing from our superb gold dollar offering in Auction '81. During the seven year period that collection was being assembled, we never had the opportunity to buy an 1856 Upright 5 gold dollar as nice as this one!"

Notes about "Proofs." I believe that no Proofs were made intentionally as such. None have been certified by the leading services. However, it seems that a pair of circulation-strike dies was relapped and given high polish at the time, creating a *de facto* or *inadvertent* Proof. This is a theoretical comment based upon the Breen description given below, since I have not examined the coin in person.

This coin first appeared in Ira S. Reed's August 1941 ANA sale as lot 586, described as "1856 Upright 5 Proof." In Stack's October 1992 sale of the Floyd T. Starr Collection, it reappeared as lot 1085. Stack's description reflects an element of uncertainty (a more careful procedure than followed by Breen, who was well known for making factual-appearing statements based on guesses).

> 1856 Upright 5 in date. Brilliant Proof. Unique. First auction appearance of this rarity in over half a century. The only known Proof specimen from this obverse and believed to be among the first struck from this die on February 17, 1856. Specifically mentioned and described by Breen on page 102 of his *Encyclopedia of United States Proof Coins* as " . . . thought to be the first of the new design . . . No duplicate reported." The obverse and reverse surfaces are brightly reflective, while Liberty's bust is lightly frosty. Some faint hairlines are visible but these are insignificant compared to the numismatic importance of this rarity. As described by Breen, struck from lapped dies . . . From Ira S. Reed's ANA Convention sale, August 19, 1941, lot 586. Breen has speculated that the Upright 5 variety was coined first, using the Half Dime date logotype, and that the Slanting 5 variety followed, using the quarter eagle date logotype. The former is known from only one or two obverse dies while the latter accounts for 24 dies. It is equally possible that the Upright 5 variety was the last to be struck, and not the first . . . In this scenario, the 1856 Upright 5 Proof gold dollar was struck as an example of the new date design adopted for the denomination late in 1856.

After examining this coin carefully, the late Harry W. Bass Jr. did not consider this to be a true Proof. John Dannreuther also examined the coin and came to the same conclusion. Several additional listings of "Proofs" can be found in auction catalogs issued by Florida dealer Walter F. Webb, for sales 53 to 56, as "1856 Upright 5 Brilliant Proof." Likely the Webb listings represent the same coin reoffered. In any event, Webb was a notorious overgrader, and today such listings have no meaning without modern confirmation.

1856, Slanting 5 (a.k.a. Italic 5), Large Date

Circulation-Strike Mintage
1,586,642 (estimate)

Proof Mintage
Fewer than 15 (estimate)

Enlarged 2x
(actual size 15 mm)

Whitman Coin Guide (WCG™)

VF-20	EF-40	AU-50	AU-55	MS-60	MS-63	MS-65	PF-63	PF-65
$165	$210	$235	$265	$325	$1,350	$2,500	$27,500	$65,000

CERTIFIED POPULATIONS

G-4–VF-35	EF-40–AU-58	MS-60–62	MS-63	MS-64	MS-65	MS-66	MS-67	MS-68–70
44	1,009	480	201	92	22	10	2	2
PF-50–58	**PF-60–62**	**PF-63**	**PF-64**	**PF-65**	**PF-66**	**PF-67**	**PF-68–70**	
0	0	0	2	3	1	1	0	

Note: An unknown but no doubt proportional quantity of other pieces were classified simply as "1856"; those quantities are not given here.

Key to Collecting. The 1856 Slanting 5 gold is readily available in nearly any grade desired. Most have excellent eye appeal.

Estimated Total Population (Mint State). 1,200 to 2,000. Among these are many choice and gem pieces. Unlike Mint State coins of the 1880s, of which many are in numismatic hands, many of the 1856 pieces are owned by the general, non-collecting public. This is a date that is sometimes seen in old-time groups. Since lower range MS coins are not of great value, there has not been a rush to certify them. *Certified population, MS-63 and higher:* 342.

Estimated Total Population (Circulated Grades). 20,000 to 30,000. The date is very common, and there are enough to supply the numismatic demand and then some.

Characteristics of Striking and Die Notes. Many are well struck. Others have weakness at the ribbon knot and/or the 5 of the date. Early strikes from a given die typically show tiny striae, which eventually wore away as more coins were made. Some pieces show clashmarks.

Numismatic Notes

Die Data. 1856 Slanting 5 four-digit date logotype: The numerals 18 are separated the widest, the 56 about the same width, but slightly closer, and the 85 slightly closer yet. The 1 leans slightly right. The top interior of the 8 is slightly smaller than the bottom interior, and the 8 leans right. The 5 is italic, with its bottom ball very close to its upright, and touching it on some impressions. The 6 is heavy to the left and the right on the ball, but somewhat lightly defined at the top of the curve and at the base. This logotype was used on some Philadelphia Mint coins.

Walter Breen (*Major Varieties of U.S. Gold Dollars*, 1964) reported examples with either a "thin" or "heavy" 6 in the date, the former probably either from a light impression of the four-digit logotype into the working die, or from relapping. Breen (*Encyclopedia*, 1988) mentioned a curious issue: "At least one variety has the date too low in the wreath (from the Beck estate), with the numeral 5 touching the bow."

Several dozen dies were prepared for this coinage, and many, if not most, were used. Thus, minute die varieties are numerous. The same Slanting 5 logotype date punch was also used to make *quarter eagle* dies.

Mintage. The mintage of the Slanting 5 is unknown. I estimate that these consisted of 90% of the total mintage of 1,762,936 for Philadelphia Mint dollars, or net 1,586,642. This is simply an educated guess, although without explanation the number seems precise.

Auction Information. Hundreds have appeared at auctions over the years, usually without much in the way of added commentary. In modern times, high-grade coins have commanded a lot of attention.

Proofs

Estimated Total Population and Key to Collecting. 8 to 10. Proofs are very rare and used to appear only when important collections were dispersed. In modern times, some have been bought and sold as "trophy coins" by other than gold dollar specialists. Such coins are often bought, and then when the passion fades (not being backed up by a serious numismatic interest in the series), the pieces are consigned to an auction house and appear on the market again.

As to how many Proofs are known today, perhaps 8 to 10 is a good estimate, although the certification data show only a few. For this year and other Proof issues, institutional holdings are not included in population reports, eliminating specimens held by the American Numismatic Society, the Smithsonian Institution, and others. In his offering of lot 872 of the Pittman Collection, Part I, 1997, David W. Akers gave a roster of eight different, including institutional holdings that would not have been certified.

Die Data and Notes. Several Proofs have on the reverse a pronounced outline of clash from the obverse Liberty head. Could these have been made as inadvertent Proofs by relapping the dies to remove what might have been even deeper clashmarks?

Auction Information (Proofs). Many listings have been found, of which a few samples are given here:

> *1864–05: John F. McCoy Collection* (W. Elliot Woodward), lot 2001: "1856 dollar. Brilliant Proof."
>
> *1865–03: Bache, Bertsch, Lightbody, Lilliendahl, Vinton, and Watson Collections* (W. Elliot Woodward), lot 2830: "1856 Dollar; brilliant Proof." Sold to M.I. Cohen. *Later offering: 1875–10: Col. Mendes I. Cohen Collection* (Edward Cogan), lot 242: "1856 Fine Proof." Realized $1.63.
>
> *1956–04: Thomas G. Melish and Clinton W. Hester Collections* (A. Kosoff), lot 1750: "1856. Slanting 5. Brilliant Proof . . ." *Later offering: 1997–10: John Jay Pittman Collection, Part I* (David W. Akers), lot 872: "1856, Slanting 5, Gem Proof. A magnificent example of this rarity, with a full strike, deep mirror fields, and superb medium orange gold toning . . . It was purchased by JJP as lot 1750 from the famous Melish Collection sale conducted by Abe Kosoff in 1956." *Later offering: 2003–03: Smith and Youngman Collections* (Bowers and Merena), lot 2043: "1856 Slant 5. Proof-66 Cameo (NGC). Light yellow gold. Offered as Gem proof not numerically graded, by David W. Akers, as lot 872 in Part I of the John Jay Pittman Collection." *Later offering: 2004–05: Pre-Long Beach Elite Coin Auction* (Superior Galleries), lot 2252: "1856 Proof-65 Ultra Cameo (NGC) . . . Characteristics of the 1856 Proofs include a low date slanting up to right, as on the other Proof gold dollars of this date; faint clashmarks, as on the ANS coin . . . Eight are traceable today, including: (1) Bowers 5/2000 Bass III: 28 Proof-64 PCGS $23,000; (2) Smithsonian; (3) Matthew Adams Stickney, John H. Clapp, Eliasberg: 31, $10,450 (1982, as "Choice Brilliant Proof-65"), "Connoisseur": 259 (1/31/89, also as Proof-65), $14,300, Ed Trompeter 2/92: 2, $18.700; (4) Woodin: 856, Newcomer, Boyd, WGC: 11, J.F. Bell, "Memorable": 11. Ill. in Breen's Proofs book; (5) Brock, Univ. of Pennsylvania, P.H. Ward. Possibly later to Lenox R. Lohr and/or Auction '85: 1367 at $12,650; (6) Naftzger, Melish: 1750, Pittman; (7) Superior's 2/93: 1266, $16,500. NGC Proof-64 Cameo; (8) Stack's 11/94: 1162, "Very Choice Proof"; (9) Heritage 8/96: 8125, PCGS Proof-64, unsold."

1856-D

Circulation-Strike Mintage
1,460

Enlarged 2x
(actual size 15 mm)

Whitman Coin Guide (WCG™)

VF-20	EF-40	AU-50	AU-55	MS-60	MS-63	MS-65
$4,000	$6,500	$9,500	$12,500	$32,500	$75,000	

CERTIFIED POPULATIONS

G-4–VF-35	EF-40–AU-58	MS-60–62	MS-63	MS-64	MS-65	MS-66	MS-67	MS-68–70
6	73	12	1	0	0	0	0	0

Key to Collecting. The 1856-D is a key coin on several counts. In terms of absolute rarity it is one of the most important in the gold dollar series, this being true of all grades. In Mint State the coin approaches the impossible. In any grade the 1856-D usually (but not always) has planchet or striking problems.

Estimated Total Population (Mint State). 10 to 14. *An extreme rarity.* In Mint State the 1856-D is more elusive than the much publicized 1861-D of approximately the same mintage. Only one has been certified above MS-62, that being an MS-63. Defying earlier comments by experts, there are 12 certification instances at the MS-60 to MS-62 level. Assuming that some of these might better be called AU, and that others are duplicate listings, I give the estimate above. At the time the 1856-D gold dollar was issued, not a single specimen is known to have been added to a numismatic collection. *Certified population, MS-63 and higher:* 1.

Estimated Total Population (Circulated Grades). 70 to 90. The precise figure will never be known. Most grade in the range of VF to EF, with an occasional AU. By any standard, here is a major American rarity, and yet the 1856-D has received very little publicity. This may be its own fault, simply from the lack of available specimens in any grade coming onto the market. When they do, the typical piece, showing extensive wear, is not apt to cause a great deal of excitement to anyone except a knowledgeable buyer. An AU 1856-D, prized by a specialist, is probably the very antithesis of a "trophy coin"!

Characteristics of Striking and Die Notes. The 1856-D usually has a mushy strike, with the U (UNITED) weak or even missing. Examples are usually weak at both obverse and reverse centers. On the reverse, the O (DOLLAR) is filled at the center. The two central date digits, 85, are usually weakly defined, or sometimes just the 5 is weak. Planchets sometimes show flaking or laminations. However, occasionally a sharply struck coin is seen.

NUMISMATIC NOTES

Die Data. Three obverse and three reverse dies were sent from Philadelphia on March 17, 1856, and arrived in Dahlonega on April 5, 1856.[43] These all bore the 1856 Upright 5 logotype punch.

Mintage. In May, 1,460 coins were struck for circulation plus three for assay. The mintage figure of the 1856-D is second lowest in the gold dollar series (the lowest being the 1875, with 400 circulation strikes plus 20 Proofs).

Assay Commission Finding. At the Assay Commission evaluation of 1856-D gold dollars held in Philadelphia in early 1857, examples were found above and below the authorized standard weight range.[44] Apparently, even with the new gauge, the facility had problems with rolling gold strip to the proper thickness for cutting planchets.

Regarding the gold denominations in general, it was found that several Dahlonega Mint gold coins were below the legal limit in weight. This was startling news to Dahlonega Mint Superintendent Julius M. Patton, who informed Mint Director James Ross Snowden that the person adjusting the planchet weights in 1856 was the same employee who had been doing this since the first gold coinage in 1838. Moreover, although a few stray single pieces may have been of low weight, the deviation of Dahlonega Mint gold coins, when weighed in quantity and averaged, was within statutory limits. Apparently, more care was given to planchet adjusting at Dahlonega after that time, for the subject did not arise again.[45]

Auction Information. This is one Dahlonega Mint rarity that has been consistently recognized as such, since the early 20th century. A few samples from many listings surveyed:

1903–07: A.C. Muma, Thomas Adam, George Giffen, and E.M. Turner Collections (Lyman H. Low), lot 348: "1856-D Fine. Excessively rare. Two auction records in 7 years, $75 and $65." Realized $43.50.

1905–09: XVIII Mail Auction Sale (Ben G. Green), lot 117: "1856-D Very Fine. Extremely rare." Realized $77. This is among the higher prices realized for *any* gold dollar in the first decade of the 20th century. The same amount of money would have bought nearly ten Proof 1856 Flying Eagle cents!

1907: Superb Collection of United States and Foreign Gold, Silver and Copper Coins, Fractional Currency, Etc., Fixed price list (Elmer S. Sears), lot 520: "1856 Dahlonega Mint. Extremely Fine, with some original lustre. I have never seen a finer specimen. Excessively rare and less than a dozen known. $110." Sears' comments generally reflected the state of the level of research at the time.

1910–10: Major Richard Lambert Collection (S.H. Chapman), lot 117: "1856-D Vertical 5. Fine. Excessively rare, no specimen sold since our Eavanson Sale, 1903, which fetched $65 then before the greatly increased attention to the gold series. Not in the Wilson sale."

1938–03: Samuel H. McVitty Collection (B. Max Mehl), lot 180: "1856-D Practically Uncirculated, with full brilliant mint luster. Can almost be classed as a semi-proof. Extremely rare in any condition especially when so choice. One of the rarest gold coins of our entire series. Listed up to $125 in Very Fine condition. This specimen is one of the finest, if not the finest known." Realized $55. The anomalous low price is not explained as the market for gold coins was very strong at the time.

1946–05: Collection of U.S. Gold and Silver Coins (Stack's), lot 598: "1856-D Uncirculated Gem. Rarely offered in so choice a condition."

1946–06: William Cutler Atwater Collection (B. Max Mehl), lot 2156: "1856-D. Mr. Atwater purchased this coin as Uncirculated. Even through a strong glass it fails to show the slightest evidence of circulation. It has an even brilliant mint luster, proof-like appearance. Undoubtedly one of the finest specimens of this rarity in existence. Recent record for a specimen not as choice, $230." Realized $250. *Later offering: 1947–06: Will W. Neil Collection* (B. Max Mehl), lot 2355: "1856-D. Practically Uncirculated with brilliant mint luster. This is the identical coin from the great Atwater Collection where it was described as undoubtedly one of the finest specimens of this rarity in existence, and it brought $250. It now catalogs for $275." Realized $282. *Later offering: 1956–08: Chi-ANA Convention Sale* (James F. Kelly), lot 1602: "1856 D mint. Extremely Fine to About Uncirculated. From the Neil Sale . . . One of the finest specimens known. Auction records over $500." It seems that with each offering the grade was described at a lower level! Usually, the opposite is true.

1986–01: James Walter Carter and Margaret Woolfolk Carter Collections (Stack's), lot 37: "1856-D Brilliant Uncirculated. Wholly prooflike, with faint hairlines magnified by the surface, some frosty luster. The obverse is fully struck, with the U in UNITED weak (a hallmark of authenticity). The reverse is also fully struck, with only the 8 of date a trifle weak. The kernels are fully in evidence. Without question, a major rarity. This is the first Mint State example offered at auction since our Charles Jay specimen in 1967, and is a better example because the Jay coin had an obverse planchet defect."

1993–10: Reed Hawn Collection (Stack's), lot 890: "1856-D Brilliant Uncirculated. Rare Rims and denticles mostly fully formed and struck up. Typically soft on U in UNITED and the 5 in the date. Struck from lightly clashed dies . . . Die file marks on reverse from lower left rim up through wreath. Ex Philip H. Ward Jr. Sale (Stack's, April 30, 1964, lot 1605)."

2003–01: FUN 2003, Ashland City Collection (Heritage), lot 4636: "1856-D MS-61 NGC . . . Only two other Mint State examples have appeared at auction over the past ten years.

2004–01: Platinum Night Sale (Heritage, January 2004), lot 1009: "1856-D MS-62 (PCGS). Variety 8-K. The strike is typical for the issue with some diagnostic peculiarities seen on the obverse and the reverse. The obverse has an almost illegible U in UNITED and some weakness on the curls around the face but does show exceptional definition on the denticles. On the reverse, the O in DOLLAR is somewhat blurry and the 5 in the date is weak. The denticles are weak at the top but are very sharp on the lower reverse, especially from 4 to 9 o'clock. A set of clashmarks in front of Liberty's nose suggests that this is a late die state and this is further evidenced by the fact that the surfaces show fewer raised die lines than normally seen . . . This is the plate coin in the second edition of Doug Winter's book on Dahlonega gold and it is cited in the revised Condition Census as the single finest 1856-D gold dollar."

AMERICA AND NUMISMATICS IN 1857

The Coinage Act of February 21, 1857, discontinued the copper half cent and cent and provided for the new Flying Eagle cent, small and of copper-nickel. It abolished the legal tender status of Spanish-American coins, giving a deadline of two years from the date of the act (later extended by six months). On May 25, the new cents were made available in quantity to the public, in exchange for old copper coins as well as Spanish-American silver. This precipitated a wave of sentiment for the soon-to-be-absent copper cents of childhood. Many citizens hurried to form collections of different dates. Thus was born numismatic fever. Interest in collecting coins expanded, articles about scarce and rare issues appeared in magazines and newspapers, and the number of devotees increased to the thousands. Historical Magazine was launched and included features on rare coins. Jeremiah Colburn (of Boston) and Augustus B. Sage (New York City) contributed numismatic articles to newspapers. In the eastern cities, several professional numismatists enjoyed good business. In time, societies were formed, books and catalogs were issued, and a dynamic market arose.

In one of the darkest moments in American judicial history, the Supreme Court handed down the Dred Scott decision, ruling that Scott, a fugitive slave who lived in freedom in the Minnesota Territory, and who brought suit to defend that right, was in fact still a slave. It was decreed that black people had no right to bring suit in federal court, and, further, Congress had no license to ban slavery in any territory. Southerners were jubilant, and cash rewards were offered to Northerners who could capture runaways to be hauled back into captivity. To its credit, in April the entire New York State Legislature resolved that through this decision the Supreme Court had impaired the respect and confidence of the American people.

The economy continued its boom, and in New York City and other money centers, bankers and others were delighted to make loans at the current strong interest rates to finance speculation in land and railroads. As the months went on, some financiers became apprehensive of the future. Then on August 24, the Ohio Life Insurance & Trust Co., based in Cincinnati and with offices in New York City, abruptly failed, sending a wave of shock throughout the financial community. All of a sudden, money became scarce. Bankers and others attempted to call in their loans, but debtors could not pay. Advances made on collateral such as bank stocks were found to be unsecured as the market took a sharp downturn. Several brokerage houses and exchange offices collapsed, causing further distress. The Panic of 1857, as it came to be called, erupted into a fury. Nearly everyone was affected by the financial contagion.

On September 12, 1857, on its way to New York City from Panama, the steamship S.S. *Central America* foundered in a hurricane, taking to the bottom of the sea several hundred hapless souls and an estimated $1,600,000 in gold treasure. The news of the tragedy precipitated further gloom in the eastern cities, since for a long time California gold had helped sustain prosperity. Soon, every financial institution in New York City except the Chemical Bank stopped paying out coins in exchange for bills. Most other eastern banks took the same course. The business boom was completely dead by October, and the lingering effects of the panic caused thousands of businesses and banks to close their doors.

1857

Circulation-Strike Mintage
774,789

Proof Mintage
Fewer than 16 (estimate)

Enlarged 2x
(actual size 15 mm)

Whitman Coin Guide (WCG™)

VF-20	EF-40	AU-50	AU-55	MS-60	MS-63	MS-65	PF-63	PF-65
$165	$210	$235	$265	$325	$1,350	$2,500	$15,000	$26,000

CERTIFIED POPULATIONS

G-4–VF-35	EF-40–AU-58	MS-60–62	MS-63	MS-64	MS-65	MS-66	MS-67	MS-68–70
18	805	663	148	56	20	16	5	1
PF-50–58	**PF-60–62**	**PF-63**	**PF-64**	**PF-65**	**PF-66**	**PF-67**	**PF-68–70**	
0	0	2	5	3	1	0	0	

Key to Collecting. The 1857 gold dollar is very common, although in Mint State it is scarce at the MS-65 level or higher. Most have good eye appeal.

Estimated Total Population (Mint State). 1,000 to 1,500. Mint State specimens of the 1857 are somewhat scarce, and represent but a tiny fraction surviving from the generous mintage. Most of these are in grades from MS-60 through MS-63, although enough populate the higher slots through MS-66 that finding one will not be a problem. Any graded MS-67 and MS-68 are in the Registry Set category. Such coins must be regarded as rare, especially if well struck—the last to be determined only upon close inspection. *Certified population, MS-63 and higher:* 273.

Estimated Total Population (Circulated Grades). 7,000 to 12,000 or more. Very plentiful. If only 2% exist, this would indicate a population of more than 15,000 coins.

Characteristics of Striking and Die Notes. Sometimes the 1857 is well struck, but usually it is not. Some coins show evidence of clashed dies. Dentils are "fuzzy" on some pieces, and a few are lightly struck on the high points of the portrait and near the center of the reverse, from the dies being spaced slightly too far apart. Others have been cataloged as struck from rusted dies.

NUMISMATIC NOTES

Die Data. 1857 four-digit date logotype: The numerals are fairly widely and evenly spaced. The 1 leans slightly right. The top interior of the 8 is smaller than the bottom interior. The 5 is of the upright type, slanting ever so slightly, not enough to be called italic or slanting; its ball is large. The 7 has a delicate top, the upper left serif being large and slanting down to left. This logotype was used on all dies of all mints.

Auction Information. As might be expected from the generous mintage, 1857 gold dollars have appeared hundreds of times in the sale room. One of the earlier citations is lot 1214 in Augustus B. Sage's sale of the Henry Bogert Collection, February 1859, "1857 Dollar. *Very Fine.*" The coin realized $1.12½, selling to New York City dealer John Curtis, a young man who was one of America's first full-time coin dealers. Since the coin was scarcely more than a year old by that time, the 1857 was probably what we would call AU or Mint State today. From then to the present time, listings have generally been brief, save in recent decades when an ultra-high Mint State coin has been offered.

PROOFS

Estimated Total Population and Key to Collecting. 10 to 12. David W. Akers (Pittman I sale, 1997 lot 876) suggests 10 to 12 are known. Several dozen auction appearances over the years do not reflect the number of *different* specimens involved. Proof 1857 gold dollars were probably struck individually in one or more short press runs. These were furnished to numismatists for face value plus a small charge. So far as is known, no full Proof sets (all denominations $1 through $20) were made this year.

Auction Information (Proofs). Several dozen Proof listings have appeared in catalogs from the 19th century to the present. Most simply emphasize the rarity.

1857-C

Circulation-Strike Mintage
13,280

Enlarged 2x (actual size 15 mm)

Whitman Coin Guide (WCG™)

VF-20	EF-40	AU-50	AU-55	MS-60	MS-63	MS-65
$1,150	$1,750	$3,500	$5,500	$12,000	$30,000	

CERTIFIED POPULATIONS

G-4–VF-35	EF-40–AU-58	MS-60–62	MS-63	MS-64	MS-65	MS-66	MS-67	MS-68–70
48	244	10	0	0	0	0	0	0

Key to Collecting. In terms of poor striking and planchet quality, this may be the *worst* of all gold dollars. As noted earlier, such rustic aspects add to the appeal of the issues and make challenging the search for one that is above average.

Estimated Total Population (Mint State). 7 or 10. An extreme rarity. It is likely that some of these among the ten Mint State coins in the population reports would be called AU by certain seasoned observers. Thus, the 1857-C is a great *sleeper* in Mint State, but because the aesthetic appeal of high-grade pieces is very low, there has never been much excitement about them. David W. Akers (1975): "Because even Uncirculated specimens generally have such a poor appearance, they rarely bring prices that are commensurate with their true rarity." *Certified population, MS-63 and higher:* 0.

Estimated Total Population (Circulated Grades). 200 to 250. This figure may be optimistic. Douglas Winter in his excellent study of Charlotte gold coins suggests that only about 100 to 110 are known. Virtually all observers agree that 1857-C is much rarer than its mintage suggests. We wonder why?

Characteristics of Striking and Die Notes. The 1857-C gold dollar gets the cellar award for the poor quality of striking. Except for a few early impressions, which are slightly better than the others, this issue is usually wretched. The striking is poor, the dentils are poorly defined, and the planchets defective.

David W. Akers (1975): "The planchets used for striking 1857-C gold dollars were downright atrocious, as was the quality of minting. Even the best available specimens look terrible, and are very difficult to grade." Walter Breen (*Encyclopedia*, 1988): "Planchets are virtually always defective, and striking is irregular." Douglas Winter (1998): "The 1857-C gold dollar generally shows a very poor strike . . . This date is almost always found with severe mint-made planchet defects. The obverse fields have an irregular almost 'wavy' look, while the reverse is frequently very rough at the center." Winter noted that there are a few coins of better quality.

Numismatic Notes

Die Data. Walter Breen (*Encyclopedia*, 1988) states that there are "three minor varieties" of the 1857-C, while Douglas Winter (1998) states that just one pair of dies was employed. The 1857-C dollars have a significantly larger mintmark than seen on the next earlier issue, the 1855-C (there being no 1856-C coins).

Auction Information. Selected offerings hold interesting information. As a rule, early auctioneers completely ignored the poor quality of these coins and simply assigned them lower grades.

1890–01: Robert Coulton Davis Collection (New York Coin & Stamp Co.), lot 989: "1857-C Very Good."

1895–12: Richard B. Winsor Collection (S.H. and Henry Chapman), lot 353: "1857-C dollar. Fine. Charlotte Mint. Rare."

1897–04: M.A. Brown Collection (S.H. and Henry Chapman), lot 202: "1857-C Charlotte Mint. Very Good. Rare."

1905–10: XVIII Mail Auction Sale (Ben G. Green), lot 120: "1857-C Slight edge nicks. Fine. Rare."

1905–11: Philip D. Hoch Collection (Lyman H. Low), lot 522: "1857-C Mint. Good; rare." Realized $2.60.

1911–03: 49th Public Sale, E.J. Woodgate Collection (Thomas L. Elder), lot 1324: "1857-C. Uncirculated. Very rare, especially in this state." This must have been an incredible coin.

1922–12: H.E. Rawson, Dr. A. de Yoanna, and David Strasser Collections (B. Max Mehl), lot 78: "1857-C The 18 of date not as bold as the balance of date. Uncirculated, with broad borders, the obverse edge of which is very slightly nicked, this defect is only mentioned for the sake of accuracy, but it is hardly noticeable to the naked eye. I do not recollect of ever handling as choice a specimen of this gold dollar. Its surface is a frosty mint luster."

1936–01: Charles W. Sloane and Frank Lenz Collections (Thomas L. Elder), lot 2700: "1857-C Uncirculated. Very rare."

1939–11: William B. Hale Collection (B. Max Mehl), lot 704: "1857-C Uncirculated, sharp, with frosty mint surface. Very rare."

1943–04: David Proskey Estate (Stack's), lot 1310: "1857-C Brilliant Uncirculated."

1944–12: J.F. Bell Collection (Stack's), lot 51: "1857-C Uncirculated gem, with '18' in date struck weak, as all are."

1967–10: Charles Jay Collection (Stack's), lot 221: "1857-C Brilliant Uncirculated, mint lustre, deep yellow gold. As with the specimen sold at the Pierce auction, the coin was struck on a planchet which was somewhat rough both obverse and reverse. (It must be a common characteristic.) Superior to Walton, Ward and Wolfson."

1975–02: Davies and Niewoehner Collections (Paramount), lot 443: "1857-C, MS-60. Softly struck at the denticles but with full original mint lustre and partially proof-like surfaces that are remarkably free of handling marks. One of the finest 1857-C gold dollars ever offered at public auction and unmatched by any of the few offered in recent years."

1999–01: North Georgia Collection (Heritage), lot 7737. "1857-C MS 61 PCGS. Very well detailed, despite having been struck from clashed and somewhat swollen dies. The quality of the planchet is outstanding for the issue with none of the Mint-made defects that are often seen. There is quite a lot of luster present while both the obverse and reverse show light to medium orange-gold and greenish hues. This is the finest known 1857-C gold dollar. The 1857-C is the fifth rarest Charlotte gold dollar in high grades. Approximately two dozen are known in AU but there are only two unequivocal Mint State specimens currently accounted for: the North Georgia Collection coin and an NGC MS 61 that is owned by a New York collector. The presently offered 1857-C gold dollar is the plate coin in the forthcoming version of Doug Winter's book on Charlotte gold coinage and it was last sold as lot 1164 in Stack's December, 1994 auction." Note this estimate of two Mint State coins existing, vis-à-vis later population reports.

1857-D

Circulation-Strike Mintage
3,533

Enlarged 2x
(actual size 15 mm)

Whitman Coin Guide (WCG™)

VF-20	EF-40	AU-50	AU-55	MS-60	MS-63	MS-65
$1,400	$2,600	$4,250	$5,500	$11,000	$35,000	$70,000

CERTIFIED POPULATIONS

G-4–VF-35	EF-40–AU-58	MS-60–62	MS-63	MS-64	MS-65	MS-66	MS-67	MS-68–70
10	155	26	0	0	0	0	0	0

Key to Collecting. The 1857-D is, in a way, déjà vu—a reiteration of what is usual for Dahlonega gold dollars of this era—scarce in all grades, chronically overgraded, very rare in Mint State, and usually seen with problems of striking, planchet, and eye appeal. That said, the 1857-D, like its cousins, is high on the "must have!" lists of numismatists. These coins have had a particular charm for collectors for a long time.

Estimated Total Population (Mint State). 25 to 35, based on certification service figures, plus an allowance for resubmissions and a further allowance for coins not sent in. Very rare. All known pieces are poorly struck—this based upon the collected observations of modern catalogers. Certain high-grade 1857-D coins, including Mint State, were blithely listed years ago without any information concerning striking. It is presumed that these were also poorly struck. Although 26 certification events have taken place at low Mint State levels, to come to any better estimate than that given above, the author would need to see all of them and study them carefully. In Superior Galleries' February 1999 auction, lot 1685 was described: "This is the finest certified Mint State 1857-D gold dollar to be sold at public auction in many years . . . There are only three or four known in Mint State." There is no real reason to suggest that more *really* Mint State coins have popped out of hiding since then. Calling yesterday's AU coin a Mint State coin today does not make it one. Still, today we deal with the fact that the certification services have listed more than two dozen in this grade. *Certified population, MS-63 and higher:* 0.

Estimated Total Population (Circulated Grades). 150 to 200. The 1857-D is often compared to the 1858-D of somewhat comparable mintage, as well as to other Dahlonega issues. In 1975 David W. Akers commented: "In my opinion, this date is one of the most underrated Type III gold dollars. In the 192 auction catalogs surveyed, the 1857-D was offered *10 times less* than the highly regarded 1860-D."

Characteristics of Striking and Die Notes. The 1857-D is always seen poorly struck, especially on the higher features. Miss Liberty's headdress typically lacks detail. In fact, the striking is *so poor*, that catalogers of auction sales, who often overlook such aspects, mention this feature with frequency (of course, certification services always overlook the quality of striking and assign just a single number for grade, although it would be nice if this feature could also be noted).

A number of pieces, perhaps the majority, show evidence of die clashing, and some show a die crack above the wreath. The reverse is usually weak at the border (clockwise from ten o'clock to two o'clock) and at 85 (1857). On some, the reverse is relapped with the heavy hand used by the machinists at the Dahlonega Mint.

NUMISMATIC NOTES

Die Data. Two obverse and two 1857-dated reverse dies were sent from Philadelphia on November 26, 1856, and arrived in Dahlonega on January 4, 1857 (the dies had been sent by Adams' Express; delays in delivering 1855-dated dies had occurred two years earlier; Adams' Express was also involved). The date logotype is as described above, under the 1857 Philadelphia issue.

Mintage. Mintage took place in April (1,896) and November (1,637). The number of additional pieces made for assay is not known.

Auction Information. Quite a few 1857-D gold dollars have appeared at auction and in fixed-price catalogs over the years, often designated as rare or very rare. Most early listings did not mention surface descriptions, as with this 1907 offering by Elmer S. Sears: "1857 Dahlonega Mint. Practically Uncirculated, with mint lustre, and the finest specimen I have ever seen. Very rare. $15."

> *1922–12: H.E. Rawson, Dr. A. de Yoanna, and David Strasser Collections* (B. Max Mehl), lot 67: "1857-D Brilliant Uncirculated, with an unusually bold impression on obverse. Very rare and valuable. Considered a great rarity in this wonderful condition." This particular coin eventually found its way into the fabled Eliasberg Collection, sold in 1982, and was described, in part, as: "Brilliant Uncirculated, MS-60, with some features of Select Brilliant Uncirculated, MS-63. More sharply struck than average for this issue (which usually occurs with very weak definition). Satin surfaces as made. Microscopic planchet chip, also as made, on the reverse at the highest point of the wreath on the right side."
>
> *1956–08: Chi-ANA Convention Sale* (James F. Kelly), lot 1605: "1857 D Mint. Fine with mint luster. The reverse is weak struck as usual though all letters and figures are readable. This is better than average." Normally, coins in Fine grade do not have mint luster. Probably, this coin, if run through a certification service today, would be AU or even Mint State. In earlier times catalogers often compensated for the miserable appearance of these coins by simply assigning them lower grades—a "market grading" concept.
>
> *1968–05: The Alex Shuford Collection* (A. Kosoff), "1857 EF-45. Incusations on obverse and reverse create a most interesting example of this rare date.

> Seldom offered so nice." This coin sold in November 2000 in the Harry W. Bass Jr. Collection, Part IV, graded ten points higher: "1857-D AU-55 (PCGS) . . . Typical weakness is displayed on both obverse and reverse, with upper obverse and lower reverse very poorly defined . . . Moderate to heavy clashmarks are visible both on obverse and reverse. The reverse, especially toward the bottom, is covered with intriguing coarse die lines, perhaps resulting from die finishing or polishing at the Dahlonega Mint. An interesting numismatic puzzle for the researcher."
>
> *1985–07: Auction '85* (Paramount [Akers]), lot 1371: "1857-D, Almost Uncirculated (55/55). Extremely well struck for the issue; in fact, this is at least as sharp as any 1857-D we've seen. The planchet and lustre are also outstanding and the coin shows just a hint of friction in the fields and on the highest points of the design. Overall, this specimen is one of the best, if not the very best, 1857-D gold dollars that we have ever seen or handled . . . We have never seen an unequivocal Unc. of this date and feel that it is one of the most underrated of all gold dollars. Actually, one is more likely to encounter an AU or Unc. 1861-D than one is an 1857-D in comparable condition!" Akers, whose auction descriptions were remarkably free of hyperbole and exaggeration, were viewed as authoritative at the time he conducted various sales. New information may later have come to light, but any contemporary comment could be taken to the bank, so to speak.

This coin later appeared in the Harry W. Bass Jr. Collection, Part II sale as AU-58 (PCGS).

> *1986–05: Wayne J. Skiles Collection* (Mid-American), lot 1820: "1857-D About Uncirculated (50/50). Very lustrous and quite minimally worn, but showing the usual poor strike for which this date is notorious. The top of the headdress and the corresponding portion of the reverse are faint. The surfaces are very pleasing and the overall quality is exceptional for the date . . . Most of the survivors are in Very Fine or Extremely Fine condition, and strict AU's easily rate an R-7. We are, in fact, not aware of a single true Mint State example of this date."

Informed comments such as these are interesting to read in view of the *many* "Uncirculated" and "Mint State" coins listed in various other sales. The preceding is ample evidence of the value of a numismatic library in connection with forming a collection of gold dollars. A comprehensive group of reference books and significant auction catalogs of the past 50 years would likely cost less than $500 to assemble—pocket change in relation to the cost of gold dollars themselves.

1857-S

Circulation-Strike Mintage
10,000

Enlarged 2x
(actual size 15 mm)

Whitman Coin Guide (WCG™)

VF-20	EF-40	AU-50	AU-55	MS-60	MS-63	MS-65
$500	$750	$1,250	$1,900	$6,500	$21,000	

CERTIFIED POPULATIONS

G-4–VF-35	EF-40–AU-58	MS-60–62	MS-63	MS-64	MS-65	MS-66	MS-67	MS-68–70
16	210	18	3	2	0	0	0	0

Key to Collecting. The 1857-S gold dollar is scarce in all grades, and in true Mint State it is a formidable rarity. While Charlotte and Dahlonega gold coins each have a wide group of fans who specialize in these two mints, the same cannot be said for San Francisco (or New Orleans) issues. Accordingly, the 1857-S has attracted comparatively less ink in auction catalogs over the years. Striking can vary. Most have good eye appeal.

Estimated Total Population (Mint State). 15 to 20. The 1857-S is a major rarity in Mint State. In the 1999 Pittman sale David Akers commented, "I would be surprised if more than 15 to 20 Uncirculated examples are known." Only five have been graded MS-63 or MS-64, and this might include duplicate submissions. None were found in the S.S. *Central America* treasure. *Certified population, MS-63 and higher:* 5.

Estimated Total Population (Circulated Grades). 220 to 270. Virtually all of the famous collections over the years have had EF or AU specimens, sometimes VF, but rarely Mint State. Today, a quality AU coin is ranked as a rarity.

Characteristics of Striking and Die Notes. Striking varies. Some have areas of lightness, while others are very sharp.

NUMISMATIC NOTES

Die Data. Two minor die varieties are known, both with a medium-sized S mintmark.

Auction Information. There have been many listings for the 1857-S over the years, including quite a few described as Uncirculated before 1950. Among these were the pieces in M.H. Bolender's 66th Sale (April 1931), J.C. Morgenthau & Co.'s Sale 401 (June 1949), several in Walter F. Webb catalogs (generally useless for research, due to exploitative grading) of the mid-1940s, the Bell Collection coin (Stack's, December 1944), the so-called "World's Greatest Collection" (F.C.C. Boyd Collection; Numismatic Gallery, January 1946), and the H.R. Lee Collection (Stack's, October 1947, later in the Bareford Collection, October 1947). There is no way to equate these with the numerical grade designations of today. Probably some would live up to expectations, and others would fall short.

AMERICA AND NUMISMATICS IN 1858

The coin hobby continued to grow by leaps and bounds. The Philadelphia Numismatic Society, organized in December 1857, became the first organization within the specialty, quickly followed in March 1858 by the American Numismatic Society. Proof coins attracted widespread attention for the first time. During the year an estimated 210 silver sets were sold, plus even more single copper-nickel Flying Eagle cents, and dozens of Proof gold coins. The silver coins were available for face value to interested collectors (except for the dollar, which cost $1.08, since it contained more bullion than its face value indicated).

J.H. Hickcox, of Albany, published *An Historical Account of American Coinage*, the first general information guide of value to coin collectors, but since only 200 regular copies were printed, it had little impact on the hobby. In New York City on April 29, the American Bank Note Company was formed by consolidating eight firms, the largest of which was Rawdon, Wright, Hatch & Edson. The new company went on to monopolize the industry.

Gold was discovered near the Front Range of the Rocky Mountains at Cherry Creek, near what would become the city of Denver. In the mountains Central City, Black Hawk, and other communities sprang up. Next year in 1859, "Pikes Peak or Bust" would be the rallying cry for a new group of fortune seekers headed west. By this time the California Gold Rush had peaked, and most industry was conducted by large firms, not individuals or small partnerships. The Atlantic telegraph cable between America and England was completed, signals were received, and celebrations were held. Jubilation was short-lived because the connection soon failed—not to be resumed until after the Civil War. In New York City the Crystal Palace burned to the ground. Augustus B. Sage issued a small medal to memorialize the event.

1858

Circulation-Strike Mintage
117,995

Proof Mintage
25 to 40 (estimate)

Enlarged 2x
(actual size 15 mm)

Whitman Coin Guide (WCG™)

VF-20	EF-40	AU-50	AU-55	MS-60	MS-63	MS-65	PF-63	PF-65
$165	$210	$235	$265	$325	$1,350	$3,500	$12,000	$22,500

CERTIFIED POPULATIONS

G-4–VF-35	EF-40–AU-58	MS-60–62	MS-63	MS-64	MS-65	MS-66	MS-67	MS-68–70
3	201	133	38	21	7	2	2	7
PF-50–58	PF-60–62	PF-63	PF-64	PF-65	PF-66	PF-67	PF-68–70	
0	4	4	14	8	5	0	0	

Key to Collecting. Likely, most 1858 dollars were paid out at the time of issue, after which they were seen in circulation for the next several years. Relatively few Mint State coins were saved by intent or chance. In fact, among old-time collections, choice and gem *Proof* 1858 dollars have appeared more often than have equivalent-quality circulation strikes—and Proofs are rarities. Circulated examples are seen with frequency and can be easily acquired.

Estimated Total Population (Mint State). 140 to 180. This is a gold dollar that should be plentiful in Mint State, but is not. At this grade level any 1858 dollar is scarce, and choice and gem pieces are extremely rare. The several certified on the long side of MS-67 must be "wonder coins." *Certified population, MS-63 and higher:* 79.

Estimated Total Population (Circulated Grades). 1,200 to 1,800. Most are in grades of VF and EF.

Characteristics of Striking and Die Notes. Usually seen well struck except for the first 8 (1858) which is often lightly impressed. There are exceptions, and these are worth seeking out because they cost no more when found.

Numismatic Notes

Die Data. 1858 four-digit date logotype: The numerals 18 are spaced closest, but barely, the 85 slightly farther apart, and the 58 even farther, although the differences in each instance are not great. The 1 leans slightly to the right. The top interior of the 8 is slightly smaller than the bottom interior. The is 5 about the same style as preceding, upright, but leaning slightly to the right, not enough to be called slanting or italic. Its ball is very heavy and close to upright above it, sometimes touching it. The second 8 is from the same punch as the first 8, and also leaning slightly right; its interior spaces appear smaller than on the first 8. This logotype was used on all dies of all mints.

"1858/7" Overdate. The "1858/7 overdate" listed by Breen (*Encyclopedia*, 1988) as Breen-6055 was described by Breen as follows: "1858/7 Serif and tiny part of cross bar of 7 shown at upper left of final 8; interiors of loops of this eight irregular right. Date low and heavy." Modern scholars do not consider this to be an overdate.

Auction Information. Over a long period of years, hundreds of 1858 dollars have crossed the auction block. In early times they were accompanied by little or no comment except the grade. Recently, catalogers have pulled out all the stops when high-grade certified coins are offered.

Proofs

Estimated Total Population and Key to Collecting. 15 to 20. Most examples are quite attractive and are choice or gem quality. Although nearly 100 auction appearances of Proofs have occurred from 1860 to the present, the number of *different* examples in existence today is much smaller. Harry W. Bass Jr. was able to obtain three Proofs in some 30+ years of collecting. The 1858 represents the earliest-dated Proof gold dollar for which there is a reasonable chance of acquiring a specimen, given several years of searching. Proofs were recognized as being scarce soon after they were minted, although over the years more of this date have been sold at auction than have certain others of the ensuing decade or so.

Die Data. The 5 (1858) is close to and centered over the highest point of the ribbon bow.

1858-D

Circulation-Strike Mintage
3,477

Enlarged 2x
(actual size 15 mm)

Whitman Coin Guide (WCG™)

VF-20	EF-40	AU-50	AU-55	MS-60	MS-63	MS-65
$1,550	$2,500	$4,000	$5,500	$10,500	$27,500	$55,000

CERTIFIED POPULATIONS

G-4–VF-35	EF-40–AU-58	MS-60–62	MS-63	MS-64	MS-65	MS-66	MS-67	MS-68–70
12	159	39	13	3	2	2	0	0

Key to Collecting. Although the mintage of the 1858-D (3,477) can be compared to that of the 1857-D (3,533), there all similarity ends. The 1857-D is a prime rarity in any and all grades. While the 1858-D is elusive, over the years at least two have appeared in the marketplace for every one of 1857-D. The strike is usually sub-par (see below).

Estimated Total Population (Mint State). 35 to 55. The number of *true* Mint State 1858-D gold dollars is very low, population reports of grading services notwithstanding. Most survivors are in lower levels, although this issue is a favorite for overgrading. Sometimes old wisdom is the best wisdom, and we quote David W. Akers' commentary from 1975: "It is almost impossible to obtain an 1858-D in full Mint State (I have seen only two or three), VF and EF examples are reasonably obtainable." Once again, it is nearly impossible to sift out facts from rarity estimates made by well-respected experts and old timers as opposed to more plentiful catalog listings and certification data. A handful of coins have been certified as MS-64 or higher, these being remarkable. *Certified population, MS-63 and higher:* 20.

Estimated Total Population (Circulated Grades). 200 to 260. This suggests a fairly high population for a branch mint gold dollar with a mintage of only 3,477 pieces.

Characteristics of Striking and Die Notes. Weakly struck, especially at the centers of both obverse and reverse, especially at the two central figures of the date on the latter. The dies were spaced slightly too far apart, with the result that the metal did not flow into the deepest recesses of the portrait on the obverse die, or into certain reverse details. On the obverse, the U (UNITED) is light on some specimens. The R (AMERICA) is sometimes light or defective. Usually the two central date numerals, 85, are shallow or almost invisible, or at least the 5 is—although an occasional exception is encountered. The OLL (DOLLAR) is usually weak.

Some impressions are from clashed dies. Some have a depressed area in the field below ED (UNITED) from a foreign substance clinging to the die at the time of striking [see Breen's *Encyclopedia* (1988) comment under B-6057].

Numismatic Notes

Die Data. Two obverse and two 1858-dated reverse dies were sent from Philadelphia on November 14 or 16, 1857, by Adams' Express, and arrived in Dahlonega on January 6, 1858.[46]

Mintage. In the third quarter of the year 2,197 were struck; in the fourth quarter, 1,280. The number of additional pieces made for assay is not known.

Auction Information. A few citations were selected from many studied.

> *1911–03: 48th Public Sale, William H. Woodin Collection* (Thomas L. Elder), lot 865: "1858-D. Part of date weak as is usually so with this piece. Practically Uncirculated. Only 3,477 pieces coined. Rarely ever comes better than Very Good condition." Realized $7.
>
> *1911–08: LXIII Public Auction Sale* (Ben G. Green), lot 595: "1858-D Extremely Fine. DOLLAR poorly engraved or die worn. Very rare." At the time the causes of weakness on gold coins (die spacing and/or poor annealing of the planchet) were not well known by numismatists.
>
> *1916–06–02: George N. Olcott, N. Homsey, and A. Knowles Collections* (Thomas L. Elder), lot 269: "1858-D The figures 5 and 8 weak as usual, otherwise the coin is Uncirculated. Extremely rare, coinage about 3,000." Elder, who does

not assign a grade to this coin, implies that the coin is not Uncirculated, or at least not worth an Uncirculated price, since it has weakness.

1939–11: William B. Hale Collection (B. Max Mehl), lot 713: "1858-D The most remarkable specimen of this gold dollar I have ever seen; First of all, it is Uncirculated, then the date is boldly struck up. I do not recall of ever having seen the 1858 D gold dollar with the first 8 and 5 struck up; they are always found weak. This specimen is undoubtedly from an early impression of the die, as it is struck sharp, well centered, with full raised borders and full mint luster. In this remarkable condition I consider it one of the greatest rarities of the entire series."

1943–04: David Proskey Estate (Stack's), lot 1328: "1858-D Perfect Brilliant Uncirculated Gem." Lot 1329: "1858-D Perfect Brilliant Uncirculated Gem."

1963–08: ANA Convention (A.C. Overton), lot 260: "1858-D a coin with little wear, everything sharp and boldly struck, but signs near reverse rim of having been skillfully removed from a pin, plus slight buffing on both obv. and rev. however a most attractive coin with date, mintmark, etc. all sharp and bold. A very rare coin, only 3277 struck." A valiant effort at describing a real dog.

1989–07: Auction '89 (David W. Akers), lot 1345: "1858-D Gem Uncirculated 65. An amazing example of this very rare and underrated issue, hands down the finest example we have ever seen or heard of. Except for a slight softness on the tops of several feathers, the strike is excellent with full denticles all around and every major design detail sharp and clear. The planchet is also outstanding with no problems whatsoever. The surfaces are semi-prooflike and just radiating mint lustre and the color of the coin is superb, a rich orange gold . . . Although the 1858-D is slightly more available than the 1857-D in the circulated grades, in full Mint State they are equally rare. We have seen no more than a few other Mint State 1858-D gold dollars, none better than MS-63, and so we feel that this outstanding specimen is in class all its own as the finest known 1858-D gold dollar." *Later offering: 1990–08: Auction '90* (David W. Akers), lot 1825: "1858-D Very Choice Uncirculated 64 (PCGS) . . ." Now graded by PCGS. *Later offering: 1999–02: William Miller et al. Collections* (Heritage), lot 6121: "1858-D MS-65 NGC." Now graded by NGC.

1858-S

Circulation-Strike Mintage
10,000

Enlarged 2x
(actual size 15 mm)

Whitman Coin Guide (WCG™)

VF-20	EF-40	AU-50	AU-55	MS-60	MS-63	MS-65
$375	$700	$1,450	$1,900	$6,250	$16,500	$25,000

CERTIFIED POPULATIONS

G-4–VF-35	EF-40–AU-58	MS-60–62	MS-63	MS-64	MS-65	MS-66	MS-67	MS-68–70
17	156	17	2	0	1	0	0	0

Key to Collecting. The 1858-S is scarce in any grade and is a rarity in Mint State. Most are well struck and have nice eye appeal. Because San Francisco gold dollars are not as widely sought as are those of the Charlotte and Dahlonega mints, average market prices are lower for coins of comparable rarity.

Estimated Total Population (Mint State). 12 to 18. Most are in lower numerical levels, and this estimate no doubt includes quite a few that would have been graded as AU a generation ago. The 1858-S gold dollar is an important rarity in Mint State, joining the several earlier Type III S-Mint dollars in this regard. Writing in 1975, David W. Akers commented: "As is the case with the 1857-S, strictly Uncirculated examples of the 1858-S are all but nonexistent. In my estimation, all three of the 1857-S, 1858-S, and 1859-S are extremely underrated compared to other more glamorous dates in this popular series." *Certified population, MS-63 and higher:* 3.

Estimated Total Population (Circulated Grades). 170 to 250. Typically encountered in VF grade, sometimes EF, but rarely AU.

Characteristics of Striking and Die Notes. Usually sharply struck.

Numismatic Notes

Die Data. Three obverse and ten reverse dies were shipped to San Francisco, but only two reverse varieties are known, these differing only slightly.

Auction Information. When the occasional Uncirculated example was offered in the early days, the reaction was one of enthusiasm and sometimes surprise. This was recognized as a rarity from the outset, even before Heaton's *Treatise on Mint Marks* was published in 1893. Dr. George W. Massamore's 39th Sale, September 1890, of the Maj. William J. Thomsen coin reflects this: "Lot 793: 1858-S Uncirculated. Very rare." In December 1910, Thomas L. Elder, in his 46th Sale, the Joseph Barnet Collection, offered this: "Lot 447: 1858-S Very Fine and very rare. I doubt if I have ever offered one." This is a telling statement from Elder, who by 1910 had bought and sold more gold dollars than any other rare coin dealer. It seems that he had not handled even a worn one!

In November 1939, B. Max Mehl presented the William B. Hale Collection, including lot 726: "1858-S Uncirculated; as perfect as the day it was minted. I do not recall of ever having seen an equal and certainly not a better specimen of this coin. It is superb, and as such, very rare and valuable."

The Uncirculated coin in the Bell Collection (Stack's, 1944) belonged to Jake Shapiro, did not sell, and was reoffered in the same grade by Numismatic Gallery in the "Memorable Collection" in March 1948. Again, Shapiro bought many items back. The piece resurfaced in Stack's December 1978 offering of the Harold S. Bareford Collection lot 36: "1858-S Brilliant Uncirculated and a gem. Full blazing lustre with delicate toning. In overall strike, color, and appearance, we do not believe this coin has its equal. It is also one of the most underrated coins in Mint State in the entire series." The buyer was Harry W. Bass Jr. When his coins were sold in November 2000, this was certified as MS-65 (PCGS), the finest graded by that service, far ahead of the runner-up, an MS-63.

Another notable coin crossed the block in October 1989 as part of the Jascha Heifetz Collection offered by Superior, lot 3907: "1858-S Mint State-64. Boldly struck . . . It is estimated by students of the of the series that only 3 or 4 pieces are known in Mint State. Because the only finer example of 1858-S known is the piece which sold in the Bareford Sale of 1978, we unhesitatingly rate this the second finest known. That places it squarely in the Condition Census. Formerly sold in NASCA's McNally Sale, December 1976 lot 592."

AMERICA AND NUMISMATICS IN 1859

The numismatic hobby continued to grow, with excitement everywhere. In New York City, teenager Augustus B. Sage, leading founder of the American Numismatic Society, was the lead auction cataloger, with several public sales—more than the hobby had seen in any earlier year. The making of tokens and medalets for numismatic sale caught on like wildfire, and several dealers and die shops turned out dozens of varieties. Tokens and medals featuring George Washington were hottest in the marketplace, because Mint Director James Ross Snowden made it known that he wanted to vastly expand this section of the Mint Cabinet. In the meantime, Snowden and other Mint personnel commenced making restrikes of 1856 Flying Eagle cents, Gobrecht dollars, and other items, for secret sale to dealers and collectors. The hobby benefited from all of this, as otherwise unobtainable varieties became readily available, thus increasing collecting interest. The *American Numismatical Manual*, by Montroville W. Dickeson, M.D., reached print, a large and lavishly illustrated volume that was subsequently produced in editions of 1860 and 1865. It was the first widely sold numismatic book published in the United States. The Indian Head cent made its debut, in time to become a favorite of just about everyone. For reasons not known today, the American Numismatic Society ran out of steam, and held its final meeting this year.

The seemingly unsolvable dispute between the North and South involving slavery continued to dominate the American scene. On October 16, John Brown led a group of more than a dozen white men and five blacks on a raid of Harper's Ferry, Virginia. Soon, the town and federal arsenal were under their control. This was intended to be the beginning of an uprising of blacks against their masters. However, the hoped-for widespread insurrection did not materialize, President James Buchanan ordered troops to search out those involved in the raid, and on December 2, John Brown was hanged. Meanwhile, Southerners became increasingly resentful toward Northerners who were intruding into the institution of slavery. In Richmond, a newspaper offered a $25,000 reward for the heads of Northerners considered to be particularly offensive.

In Nevada the Comstock Lode was discovered, soon to become a bonanza yielding untold millions in silver (an estimated 60% of the lode's value) and gold (40%). In Titusville, Pennsylvania, Col. E.L. Drake struck oil, setting off a boom that would spawn many things, including the formation of the Standard Oil Company and (numismatically) the business fortunes of John M. Clapp, who would become one of the most important early collectors of gold coins.

1859

Circulation-Strike Mintage
168,164

Proof Mintage
Fewer than 30 (estimate)

Enlarged 2x
(actual size 15 mm)

Whitman Coin Guide (WCG™)

VF-20	EF-40	AU-50	AU-55	MS-60	MS-63	MS-65	PF-63	PF-65
$165	$210	$235	$265	$325	$1,350	$2,500	$9,500	$14,000

CERTIFIED POPULATIONS

G-4–VF-35	EF-40–AU-58	MS-60–62	MS-63	MS-64	MS-65	MS-66	MS-67	MS-68–70
10	222	254	70	36	28	8	9	3
PF-50–58	**PF-60–62**	**PF-63**	**PF-64**	**PF-65**	**PF-66**	**PF-67**	**PF-68–70**	
0	0	5	9	12	2	1	0	

Key to Collecting. Examples are readily available today in nearly any grade desired. Most are sharply struck. Clashmarks are the rule, not the exception. Most have excellent eye appeal.

Estimated Total Population (Mint State). 300 to 450. For reasons unexplained—and unexplained situations add to the charm of the gold dollar series—pieces of this date seem to have survived in Mint State at a higher ratio than expected for a Type III gold dollar of the late 1850s. When encountered in higher grades, the 1859 is apt to be a lovely, frosty gem. Certified coins reach all the way to MS-68. *Certified population, MS-63 and higher:* 155.

Estimated Total Population (Circulated Grades). 1,200 to 2,000. VF, EF, and AU coins are easy enough to locate. Approximately comparable in availability to the 1858 Philadelphia Mint gold dollar.

Characteristics of Striking and Die Notes. Sharpness of strike is the rule for the 1859 Philadelphia Mint gold dollar, although a few have weakness at U (of UNITED) or at the 5 (1859). Many if not most have clashmarks, including a lesser number with the raised word LIBERTY transferred from the incuse obverse letters in the headband. This LIBERTY anomaly is seen on certain other gold dollars as well (see expanded commentary under 1859-C). Many high-grade coins display prominent die striae from incomplete polishing of the dies.

Numismatic Notes

Die Data. 1859 *Philadelphia* four-digit date logotype. The numerals 18 are spaced closer together than other pairs. The bottoms of 1 and 8 are on the same level. The 1 has a thick upright. The 5 is wide, slants very slightly right, but not enough to be designated italic; the flag on the 5 is thick, curved at the top, and its tip extends as far to the right as does the curve below it. The 9 is widely separated from the 5, its top is on about the same level as the 5; its ball is close to its curve and sometimes touches it. This logotype may be by Anthony C. Paquet, an assistant engraver at the Mint, who earlier on private contract supplied letter and number punches to the Mint. The depth of punching the logotype into working dies can create optical illusions. On the Proof die the impression was deep.

Auction Information. Many 1859 gold dollars have appeared at auction over the years, mostly with a minimum of information, until "high-grade coins!" became the rallying cry. An illustration is nicely provided by David W. Akers' offering in Auction '88 (July): "1859 Superb Uncirculated 67. It is hard to imagine how a Type Three gold dollar could be much, if any, nicer than this one, and a grade of 'MS-68' could probably be applied to this coin with little fear of contradiction. The coin is very sharply struck although, as on all business strikes of 1859 that we have seen, the planchet is lightly striated and there is some indistinctness (due to the dies) at the borders. Essentially this coin is 'as struck' and it has truly superb lustre and color. In this high grade, an 1859 gold dollar is a major rarity. How many could possibly exist like this? Ten? Five? Probably somewhere in the single digits, that's for sure."

By 1988, assigning numbers to coin grades had become widely popular. Certification had not yet caught on in a large way, but PCGS (established in 1986) and NGC (1987) were growing rapidly.

Proofs

Estimated Total Population and Key to Collecting. 15 to 20. Although there have been many auction appearances, the number of *different* specimens of the Proof 1859 gold dollar is very small. Those seen are very attractive. Certification service data for this or any other Proof gold dollar are largely irrelevant, due to resubmissions of the same coins.

Die Data and Notes. 1859 *Philadelphia* four-digit date logotype for the *Proof* gold dollar: The four digits are small and differently styled from anything seen to this point. The 1 is short and with a particularly thick upright, not at all delicate; the 8 is heavy with very small pieces, its top interior being about the same size as the bottom interior. The 5 is very curiously shaped, with its flag being as wide as, or slightly wider than, the curve below it, heavy, and sharply pointed. Its ball is large and close to upright, touching it on most, if not all, impressions. The 9 is thick to the left and right, somewhat small at the bottom, and has a small ball close to or touching the curve above. This distinctive set of numeral punches, bearing no relation to anything used earlier in the series, is popularly attributed to Anthony C. Paquet. This logotype was used on the Proofs of the Philadelphia Mint, but not on circulation strikes or at any other mint.

Two reverse dies are known:

Reverse Die 1: Perfect die. The 1 (1859) is about centered between O (DOLLAR) and the ribbon below. This seems to be the "normal" die seen on Proof dollars of this year.

Reverse Die 2: Repunched date. Light repunching is seen at the date. The 1 (1859) is distant from the O (DOLLAR) and closer to the ribbon below. A few Proofs have a lightly clashed outline from the obverse Liberty Head visible on the reverse; the proportion of coins with this characteristic is unknown, since clashmarks are rarely described in catalog listings. Harry W. Bass Jr. had one (offered in Part III of his sale, certified as Proof-64 PCGS). While this variety has all of the characteristics of a Proof coin, it may have been made as an *inadvertent* or *unintentional* Proof by relapping clashed dies (and in the process, giving them a Proof finish). The obverse die has light clashmarks as well and has been resurfaced, making the first feather incomplete (see notes below). This is a different die than that used to strike certain Proofs of 1862 and later dates.

Breen (*Proof*, 1989) states, "first feather incomplete," a description indicating a die similar or identical to that used to strike 1862 (which see) and certain later Proofs; while the first feather on the Proof 1859 dollar is, indeed, incomplete, it is definitely a different die from that used to make 1862 and certain later Proofs.[47]

The Pittman Collection Sale, Part I and Bass Collection Sale, Part II Proofs both had a complete first feather, these being struck from Reverse Die 1 as given above.

1859-C

Circulation-Strike Mintage

5,235

Enlarged 2x
(actual size 15 mm)

Whitman Coin Guide (WCG™)

VF-20	EF-40	AU-50	AU-55	MS-60	MS-63	MS-65
$1,300	$1,900	$3,750	$7,000	$14,000	$34,500	

CERTIFIED POPULATIONS

G-4–VF-35	EF-40–AU-58	MS-60–62	MS-63	MS-64	MS-65	MS-66	MS-67	MS-68–70
15	123	32	3	0	0	0	0	0

Key to Collecting. The 1859-C is the final Charlotte gold dollar and also the issue with the lowest mintage figure. While circulated examples are often seen today, conservatively graded Mint State coins are great rarities. Most coins have problems with sharpness and/or eye appeal, which adds to the desire for them. Charlotte and Dahlonega gold dollars have always played to a wide audience. The date logotype on the 1859-C is distinctive, a fact not widely known (see details below; also see 1859-D).

Estimated Total Population (Mint State). 24 to 30. *True* Mint State coins are exceedingly rare. Most are in the MS-60 or MS-61 level and would be called AU by seasoned experts. However, the elements of grading and poor striking come together to cause a muddled situation, and what one person might call AU or even EF, another might designate as Mint State, a comment that applies to other gold dollar varieties as well. *Certified population, MS-63 and higher:* 3.

Estimated Total Population (Circulated Grades). 180 to 270. VF and EF are typical grades, although AU coins are available with searching. Douglas Winter described the 1859-C as a "sleeper" among Charlotte Mint gold dollars.

Characteristics of Striking and Die Notes. Lightly and irregularly struck in areas. Breen (*Encyclopedia*, 1988): "Typically weak at the center, usually at two numerals, 18 or 85; O (DOLLAR) is usually flat. The planchets are miserable." Dentils mostly indistinct at borders, in some areas blending into the flat border making the border appear to be very wide.

David W. Akers' commentary (1975) amplifies the situation: "Along with the 1857-C, the 1859-C ranks as the most consistently poorly struck gold dollar. The quality of the planchets used was also remarkably bad, and as a result, an 1859-C gold dollar, even one in high grade, always has a relatively unattractive appearance. Grading is difficult and one must take into consideration such factors as surface characteristics, mint lustre, etc. in order to accurately determine a grade. Even then, a certain amount of guesswork goes into the grading since it is difficult for even the expert to be able to say with assurance exactly what is wear and what is the result of a weak strike."

Numismatic Notes

Die Data. 1859 Charlotte (and San Francisco) Mint four-digit date logotype: All figures are widely spaced, but the 18 is slightly closer that other pairs. The base of the 1 is significantly higher than the base of the 8. The bottom left serif of the 1 is much longer than the bottom right serif. The 5 is upright; its flag is smaller than on the Philadelphia logotype, and is shorter than the curve below it. The top of the 9 is low; its ball is close to, but usually does not touch, the curve above it. This logotype was used on Charlotte and San Francisco dies.

Making Planchets at the Charlotte Mint. Planchets were produced at the Charlotte Mint by casting gold into ingots, then running the ingots through a rolling mill, reducing the spacing between the rollers several times until the acquired thinness was obtained. It would be interesting to study a number of Charlotte Mint gold dollars to see if any of the planchet defects are repetitive; that is, if they are found in the same pattern on more than one coin. If so, this would indicate rust or problems on the steel rollers. Otherwise, the problems were probably mainly due to annealing and lamination.

Auction Information. Due to generally poor striking and planchets, 1859-C gold dollars are hard to evaluate from the many listings, indeed the majority, that simply give a grade. A small sample from a wide field:

> *1943–04: David Proskey Estate* (Stack's), lot 1311: "1859-C Brilliant Uncirculated Gem."
>
> *1944–02: Belden E. Roach Collection* (B. Max Mehl), lot 1091: "1859-C Beautiful Uncirculated specimen. The obverse is of the same type die as that of the Dahlonega Mint gold dollars, with broad border. Extremely rare so choice. A specimen not as choice as this one brought $26 in my last sale."
>
> *1950–05: Golden Jubilee Sale / Jerome Kern Collection* (B. Max Mehl), lot 291: "1859 C Mint. The coin is strictly Fine but can be classed as 'Very Fine for coin,' a description I do not like to use. Last year of issue of the gold dollars at this Mint."
>
> *1975–02: Davies and Niewoehner Collections* (Paramount), lot 450: "1859-C, MS-60. The usual weak strike but on a better than average planchet. No indications of actual wear, but sometimes it is difficult to determine exactly what is wear and what is the result of weak striking. The 1859-C is even more rare as a date than the 1857-C, and is all but unobtainable in the choice condition. This is the finest 1859-C gold dollar that we have handled and certainly one of the best to appear at auction in recent years."

1978–08: N.M. Kaufman Collection (RARCOA), lot 603: "1859-C . . . This date is probably equaled only by the 1857-C as the most consistently poorly struck and unattractive-appearing of all gold dollars. The poor quality of the planchet makes grading very difficult to determine accurately. This specimen is a strong Very Fine with considerable luster. However, it has rim marks at both the top and bottom and is bent at both spots."

1994–10: James A. Stack, Sr. Collection (Stack's), lot 792: "1859-C Choice About Uncirculated. Only 5,325 struck. This coin displays the usual crude strike known for this date, but has heavy luster, with a wealth of detail and exceptional visual appeal . . ." *Later offering: 1999–01: North Georgia Collection, FUN Sale* (Heritage), lot 7739: "1859-C MS-61 (PCGS) . . . This is the finest known 1859-C gold dollar. While PCGS has graded an MS-62 1859-C gold dollar, we feel that the North Georgia coin is easily the finest known. A few average quality Uncirculated pieces have been encapsulated but none of these are remotely comparable to the present specimen. It was last offered for sale as lot 792 in Stack's October, 1994 James Stack Collection . . . In addition, it is the plate coin in the new edition of Douglas Winter's *Charlotte Mint Gold Coins, 1838–1861*." Now, this coin has marvelously graduated from being a lightly worn AU coin to one in Mint State, plus, now, "the finest known." Situations such as this are common with gold dollars and are exceedingly confusing to newcomers and experienced numismatists alike, since rankings can change quickly, and, it seems, anything goes.

1859-D

Circulation-Strike Mintage
4,952

Enlarged 2x
(actual size 15 mm)

Whitman Coin Guide (WCG™)

VF-20	EF-40	AU-50	AU-55	MS-60	MS-63	MS-65
$1,400	$1,950	$3,250	$5,500	$11,500	$25,000	

CERTIFIED POPULATIONS

G-4–VF-35	EF-40–AU-58	MS-60–62	MS-63	MS-64	MS-65	MS-66	MS-67	MS-68–70
11	183	42	11	6	1	0	0	0

Key to Collecting. The low-mintage 1859-D is scarce today. Most are in circulated grades, although Mint State examples appear on the market with frequency. In 1861 and 18622, in the early years of the Civil War, many Southerners hid gold coins, thus accounting today for the survival of many of the higher grade Charlotte, Dahlonega, and New Orleans gold coins dated in the late 1850s onward. The date logotype on the 1859-D is distinctive, a fact not widely known (see details below; also see 1859-C).

Estimated Total Population (Mint State). 45 to 55. Over the years several dozen 1859-D gold dollars have been certified or described as Mint State. Among gold dollars of the Type II design, this is the only Dahlonega Mint variety that appears on the market with some frequency. However, in an absolute sense, they are rare. *Certified population, MS-63 and higher:* 18.

Estimated Total Population (Circulated Grades). 150 to 225. If this estimate has validity, the 1859-D is fairly plentiful in terms of Dahlonega Mint gold dollars of the Type III style, but on an absolute basis, especially in comparison to other United States coins of the era, it is still a rarity.

Characteristics of Striking and Die Notes. Perhaps more than any other Dahlonega Mint gold dollar, the poor striking of the 1859-D varies from one specimen to another in the degree of weakness and even the motifs and inscriptions affected; three or four 1859-D gold dollars can have as many different "personalities." The poor striking of the 1859-D gold dollar is not reflected in grades assigned by the certification services (nor should it be, since striking is a separate situation). In the absence of reading a specialized text, such as David W. Akers' excellent 1975 study or Breen's 1988 *Encyclopedia*, the casual collector would have no way of knowing about the characteristics of striking.

The typical 1859-D is lightly and irregularly struck including at the two central figures of the date. Usually the headdress and hair strands of Miss Liberty are weak, as are reverse wreath details. Nearly all have light striking at 85 of the date, but a very few pieces are weak only at the 5. The center letters of DOLLAR are weak. Some pieces are lightly struck at the lower area of the obverse, and at the corresponding position on the opposite die—the upper area of the reverse (possibly due to non-parallel alignment of die faces). Many, if not most, have numerous raised die finish lines within the wreath.

Numismatic Notes

Die Data. 1859 Dahlonega Mint four-digit date logotype (presumably; since just one die is known, there is a possibility the numerals may have been punched in by hand): The numeral pair 18 is closely spaced; 85 and 59 are wider apart. The base of the 1 is significantly higher than the base of the 8. The bottom left serif of the 1 is slightly longer than bottom right serif. The top space of the 8 is smaller than the bottom space. The 5 is upright and leans slightly left; its flag is smaller than on the Philadelphia logotype and is shorter than the curve below it. The top of the 9 is on the same level as the top of the 5; the ball of the 5 is close to the bottom curve of the flag above it.

Two 1859-dated reverse dies were sent from Philadelphia on or after September 15, 1858 (this being the date of a note by Chief Engraver J.B. Longacre stating that the request for dies had been complied with), and arrived in Dahlonega in early January 1859. Only one die is known to have been used.

Mintage. In the second quarter 3,480 were struck; in the fourth quarter, 1,472. The number of additional pieces made for assay is not known.

Auction Information. Listings mirror those for other C and D gold dollars of the late 1850s, sometimes mentioning sharpness of strike, other times not.

> *1911–11: W. B. Guy Collection* (Henry Chapman), lot 992: "1859 Dahlonega Mint. Strong impression. The design and letters, with the exception of the mint mark D, are all double cut, and remarkably so, as they appear to have been resunk, as if the die was too shallow. Very rare."
>
> *1927–12: Dr. Daniel W. Valentine Collection* (Thomas L. Elder), lot 123: "1859-D Extremely Fine, sharp, almost Uncirculated. Very rare gem. Coinage very small." Today's student of grading will puzzle over the grade of this description!

1944–12: Auction Catalog No. 53 (Walter F. Webb), lot 239: "1859-D Unc." *Later offering: 1982–10: Eliasberg Collection* (U.S. Gold Coin Collection) (Bowers and Ruddy Galleries), lot 43: 1859-D . . . AU-50 with some features of Choice AU-55. Far above average strike, with the only weakness being a trace of lightness on the third digit of the date . . . *From Walter F. Webb, December 1944.*"

1947–10: H.R. Lee Collection (Stack's), lot 959: "1859-D Brilliant Uncirculated. Full mint luster, really a choice piece, rarely seen so sharp." This was an Eliasberg Collection duplicate, perhaps better than the one retained—which supposition could only be proven by comparing them side by side today.

1960–04: 54th Sale, Jonathan Glogower Consignment, Etc. (New Netherlands Coin Co.), lot 958: "1859-D. Obverse just barely short of full Uncirculated. Reverse full Mint State, beyond any possible question. Much original frost; an excellent even strike, exceptionally sharp for this mint . . . We have seen three or four that could possibly approximate this, none more sharply struck and none with a finer reverse. This may be the Baldenhofer coin, 'Unc.' . . ."[48] Interesting description—with the obverse less than Uncirculated (*i.e.*, worn or circulated) and the reverse Uncirculated.

1975–02: Davies and Niewoehner Collections (Paramount), lot 451: "1859-D, AU-55. Partially prooflike surfaces with lovely orange toning in the letters and around the wreath and mintmark. The 5 in the date is a bit weak but certainly much sharper than on many specimens I have seen. There is one tiny reverse rim cut at ten o'clock that has been partially ground away. The overall strike on this coin is distinctly above average as is the planchet. The surfaces are suggestive of a strictly Uncirculated coin, and actually the coin very well may be Uncirculated."

1859-S

Circulation-Strike Mintage
15,000

Enlarged 2x
(actual size 15 mm)

Whitman Coin Guide (WCG™)

VF-20	EF-40	AU-50	AU-55	MS-60	MS-63	MS-65
$1,400	$1,950	$3,250	$5,500	$11,500	$25,000	

CERTIFIED POPULATIONS

G-4–VF-35	EF-40–AU-58	MS-60–62	MS-63	MS-64	MS-65	MS-66	MS-67	MS-68–70
33	204	17	3	2	0	0	0	0

Key to Collecting. The 1859-S is somewhat scarce in worn grades, but easily obtainable. True Mint State coins are great rarities. As is true of other San Francisco Mint gold dollars of the Type III design, this variety is under-appreciated in the marketplace.

Estimated Total Population (Mint State). 12 to 18. This is one of the rarest gold dollars in Mint State, population reports notwithstanding. In more than 55 years of numismatics, I recall handling no Mint State 1859-S until 1999 when the Bass Collection coin was sold. Today, any coin grading even a minimum of MS-60 by old-time standards would be a find. Of course, old time standards are dead, and today finding one in a certified holder marked as Mint State is an opportunity that occurs with some frequency. *Certified population, MS-63 and higher:* 5.

It is relevant to mention David W. Akers' comment (1975): "Reasonably scarce as a date (on a par with the 1857-S and 1858-S) but extraordinarily difficult to find better than EF as the data clearly shows. Out of 70 total offerings in the 192 auctions tallied, only 10 pieces grade AU or better! I personally have never seen a Choice Uncirculated specimen, and only two or three that could even really be called 'sliders' [high-level AU]. Possibly the most underrated date in high grade in the entire gold dollar series."

Today, the grading data seem to indicate that more exist, but I believe that this is due in large part to overly optimistic grading and the resubmission of the same specimens. Modern data concerning the availability of the 1859-S in Mint State should be taken with a grain of salt.

Estimated Total Population (Circulated Grades). 250 to 400. VF and EF grades are typical of what you will find in the marketplace. AU coins are extremely rare. It is significant to note that David Akers know of only two or three at this level. (The Eliasberg specimen was graded VF-30.) These coins were quickly put into circulation and became worn. So far as is known, not a single coin was saved, at the time of issue, by a numismatist.

Characteristics of Striking and Die Notes. The 1859-S is usually seen well struck, but there are a few exceptions. Particularly high-grade pieces may have prooflike surfaces.

Numismatic Notes

Die Data. 1859 San Francisco (and Charlotte) Mint four-digit date logotype: All figures are widely spaced, but the numerals 18 are slightly closer together than the other pairs. The base of the 1 is significantly higher than the base of the 8. The bottom left serif of the 1 is much longer than its bottom right serif. The 5 is upright; its flag is smaller than on the Philadelphia logotype and is shorter than the curve below it. The top of the 9 is low; its ball is close to, but usually does not touch, the curve above it.

Ten 1859-dated reverses were shipped to San Francisco in November 1858.[49] Leftover obverses, undated, were employed. The S mintmark is medium sized.

Auction Information. A few selected citations from a wide field of offerings are given.

> *1911–03: 48th Public Sale, William H. Woodin Collection* (Thomas L. Elder), lot 867: "1859-S. Uncirculated; rare state." Realized $6.50. A remarkable quality early listing. Woodin became President Franklin D. Roosevelt's first secretary of the Treasury in 1933.
>
> *1927–12: Dr. Daniel W. Valentine Collection* (Thomas L. Elder), lot 123: "1859-D Extremely Fine, sharp, almost Uncirculated. Very rare gem. Coinage very small." Elder was known for is ambiguous grading descriptions.
>
> *1945–02: Auction Catalog No. 54* (Walter F. Webb), lot 249: "1859-S Proof." Based on items from him that can be traced today, Webb was a chronic overgrader, a charlatan. He is cited occasionally in the present text to alert scholars who may not be aware of his dishonest practices. In the mid-1940s he listed Uncirculated 1859-S dollars in multiple sales. In any event, no "Proof" impressions have been confirmed. Perhaps the coin was polished or buffed.

1979–07: Auction '79 (RARCOA), lot 1164: "1859-S Choice Brilliant Uncirculated with lovely mint luster. Some light reverse surface marks and tiny obverse rim bruises. The finest example of this date that we have ever seen . . . Only four appearances in auctions that were ever cataloged as Uncirculated since 1944." The "four appearances" is from David Akers' survey, limited to catalogs of leading firms. If obscure catalogs are included, the number more than doubles.

1985–07: Auction '85 (Paramount), lot 1379: "1859-S AU (58/58). Light orange toning and only a few light hairlines, and minimal marks. Sharply struck with considerable lustre." *Later offering: 1999–10: Harry W. Bass Jr. Collection, Part II* (Bowers and Merena Galleries), lot 134: "MS-61 (PCGS). Lustrous brilliant yellow gold with very pleasing, choice surfaces . . . In 1985 (Auction '85 sale lot 1379) Paramount described this as the best example they had seen. We tend to agree with this assessment. We do not recall having previously handled a strictly Mint State example of this issue." This listing is a documented instance of two well respected graders—David W. Akers at Paramount and the Professional Coin Grading Service—differing, and of a coin earlier described as AU being described later as Mint State. Generally, veteran dealers such as Akers are more traditional and conservative.

2000–10: California Sale (Ira & Larry Goldberg Coins & Collectibles), lot 647: "1859-S. PCGS MS-63 . . . There are some very faint lines in the fields, probably from handling, and we note a bit of copper toning starting to form in the fields. Identifiable by a tiny tick mark on Liberty's nose, near her eye. PCGS has only graded 2 coins this high, with a single coin graded higher, similar at NGC, which has graded 2 this high, with 2 higher."

AMERICA AND NUMISMATICS IN 1860

At the Mint, the Washington Cabinet was dedicated in a special ceremony on Washington's Birthday, February 22. This was the pride and joy of Mint Director James Ross Snowden, who had spent nearly a year adding dozens of specimens to what had been a meager holding. In this year a highly important book of 412 pages was published under Snowden's name, *A Description of Ancient and Modern Coins in the Cabinet of the Mint of the United States.* The volume was primarily researched and written by William Ewing Dubois and George Bull, the latter being nominally the latest curator of the Mint Cabinet, although DuBois made most of the decisions. The auction scene expanded, with W. Elliot Woodward conducting his first event—and issuing the precursor of what would become one of the most illustrious strings of catalogs in American numismatic history. Coin shops sprung up in many cities. *Boyd's Directory* listed these in Philadelphia: Edward Cogan, 48 North 10th Street; William Idler, 111 North 9th Street; A.C. Kline, 824 Walnut Street; E. Mason Jr., 453 North 2nd Street, "Coins bought, sold, and exchanged"; and Alfred W. Newton, northwest corner of 20th and Spruce streets. Idler had close connections to Mint Director Snowden and profited immensely. Cogan, for one, was shut out and could not acquire restrikes and other delicacies.

Gold dollars piled up in banks. The Mint took in three million of them, to be melted and the metal used to make double eagles.

On the national scene, 1860 was a year of decision, a year of change. For a long time the North and South had been at odds over many issues, the most important of which was slavery, not to overlook the great controversy that surrounded the protective tariff schedule of the 1820s. The last had brought great prosperity to Northern factories, while at the same time dampening exports of cotton from the South. President James Buchanan continued his incompetent bungling, and during the year the tense political situation went from bad to worse as he tried to please both sides, but alienated each.

In the presidential election of November, Abraham Lincoln carried the day with 40% of the popular vote and 180 electoral votes, while his main opponent, John C. Breckenridge, got 18% of the popular vote and 72 electoral votes. Stephen A. Douglas, who had challenged Lincoln in debates, had 30% of the popular votes but just 12 electoral votes. John Bell gained 12% of the popular votes and 39 electoral votes. All of these candidates were featured on campaign tokens during the summer and autumn.

On December 20, the Legislature of South Carolina voted an overwhelming 169 to 0 to secede from the Union, not an unexpected end to threats that had been made since 1830. Government finances were in crisis in 1860. John Sherman in his *Recollections* noted: "On the meeting of Congress in December 1860, the Treasury was empty. There was not enough money even to pay members of Congress. The revenues were not sufficient to meet the demands for ordinary expenditures in time of peace. Since 1857 money had been borrowed by the sale of bonds and the issue of Treasury notes bearing interest, to meet deficiencies. The public debt had increased during the administration of Mr. Buchanan about $70,000,000. The Secretary of the Treasury, Howell Cobb, resigned on the December 10, 1860, declaring that his duty to Georgia required such action. He had aided in every possible way to cripple the department while in charge of it . . ."[50] Clearly, problems lay ahead.

1860

Circulation-Strike Mintage
36,514

Proof Mintage
154

Enlarged 2x
(actual size 15 mm)

Whitman Coin Guide (WCG™)

VF-20	EF-40	AU-50	AU-55	MS-60	MS-63	MS-65	PF-63	PF-65
$165	$225	$250	$285	$475	$1,450	$4,500	$7,750	$13,000

CERTIFIED POPULATIONS

G-4–VF-35	EF-40–AU-58	MS-60–62	MS-63	MS-64	MS-65	MS-66	MS-67	MS-68–70
1	89	118	36	22	16	5	1	0
PF-50–58	PF-60–62	PF-63	PF-64	PF-65	PF-66	PF-67	PF-68–70	
0	1	9	13	10	5	0	0	

Key to Collecting. There were sufficient gold dollars on hand in 1860 that the call for new ones was modest. Today, circulated examples are common (but years ago were described as scarce or rare), while Mint State coins are indeed scarce, actually rare at the gem level. Most are well struck, and the typical high-grade piece has nice eye appeal.

In the *Annual Report of the Director of the Mint*, covering the fiscal year ended June 30, 1860, Director James Ross Snowden mentioned that *since* June 1860 many of the old-style (1849 to 1854) "thick" gold dollars had been melted down (presumably at the New York City Assay Office and at the Philadelphia Mint), and had been recoined into the newer, thinner versions (Type III design instituted in 1856). However, most of this reclaimed metal was used for larger denominations, particularly in 1861.

Estimated Total Population (Mint State). 175 to 225. Most are in grades from MS-60 to MS-63. Decent pieces graded MS-65 or higher are very seldom encountered. In the late 19th and early 20th centuries there were more auction appearances of *Proofs* than of choice and gem Mint State coins! In modern times, the true net number of *different* Mint State specimens in existence has been rendered nearly impossible to ascertain, except in a relative sense, by multiple submissions of coins to grading services and also by grade inflation. Some of yesteryear's AU coins are today's Mint State pieces. That said, perhaps a small hoard of Mint State 1860 dollars was discovered but not publicized. *Certified population, MS-63 and higher:* 84.

Estimated Total Population (Circulated Grades). 400 to 700. The 1860 is very scarce in circulated grades. When seen, the coins are mostly in such grades as VF and EF. This is a small number relative to the mintage of 36,514 pieces, indicating that there must have been wholesale melting of this date, or a large number of pieces met an unknown fate.

Characteristics of Striking and Die Notes. Sharpness of strike is the rule for the 1860 gold dollar, as noted above.

Numismatic Notes

Die Data. 1860 four-digit date logotype: Digits are very small, as in the following year (1861). The 18 and 60 are spaced wider apart than the 86. The 1 has prominent bottom serifs but a delicate upper left serif. The 8 has an upper space slightly smaller than the lower space. The 6 is rather "squashed" in appearance, with top curve close to the curve below it, and with the ball usually touching the curve. The 0 is large with a large center space, its base significantly lower than the other digits. This logotype was used on dies for all mints.

Beginning this year the date numerals were in much smaller fonts than used earlier; small figures were used through and including 1865.

Auction Information. A few of many listings are given here.

> *1907–03: David S. Wilson Collection* (S.H. Chapman), lot 303: "1860 Uncirculated." Realized $13.
>
> *1907–11: Rev. J. Zimmerman, James Bindon and Charles G. Zug Collections* (S.H. Chapman), lot 339: "1860 Uncirculated. Scarce." Realized $3.50. Compare to the above Wilson listing and note the dramatic price differential between two coins in the same grade, offered by the same dealer, in the same year.
>
> *1914–05: Public Sale* (Thomas L. Elder), lot 552: "1860. Extremely Fine. A rare dollar, which seldom appears and should bring as much as some later dates in the '60s."
>
> *1970–06: 61st Sale, Jesse M. Taylor and Dr. Angus C. Black Collections* (New Netherlands Coin Co.), lot 437: "1860. Extremely Fine. An early impression from dies retaining much original prooflike polish. This date rare and underrated; it represents the lowest pre-Civil War Philadelphia mintage."
>
> *1981–07: Auction '81* (Paramount), lot 1351: "1860, Superb Gem Uncirculated 67 . . . This is the finest example of this very scarce date that we have ever seen . . ." Lot 1352: "1860. Gem Uncirculated 65. Were it not for the

preceding lot, we would describe this coin as the finest 1860 gold dollar that we had ever seen. In its own right, it is an outstanding coin . . . In our opinion, it is one of the most underrated dates of the series in choice condition."

Proofs

Estimated Total Population and Key to Collecting. 25 to 30. Proofs are rare in an absolute sense, but in the context of the early gold dollar, are among the most often-seen date. The production figure of 154 is a high number for any Proof gold dollar of the decade of the 1860s.

In this era—during a rapidly rising tide of numismatics in America—the Mint was optimistic that many Proofs would be sold. When Proofs were struck, all on April 15, hopes were high that they would sell out. In actuality, probably no more than several dozen found buyers in the numismatic community. Perhaps Proofs were also distributed elsewhere, such as when the Japanese ambassador visited the Mint and received a full Proof set of the year, and others in his retinue possibly received single Proofs. (That event, widely covered in newspapers and in *Harper's Weekly*, was a sensation at the time, a validation of Japanese acceptance of the Commodore Perry expedition a few years earlier, that had opened that country to world trade.)

Die Data and Notes. Proofs usually (always?) have lint marks in the field due to tiny pieces of lint and fiber adhering to the die (this is also true of silver Proofs of the year).

Auction Information (Proofs). Most of the located listings gave little numismatic information beside the grade and a call for bidding.

1860-D

Circulation-Strike Mintage
1,566

Enlarged 2x
(actual size 15 mm)

Whitman Coin Guide (WCG™)

VF-20	EF-40	AU-50	AU-55	MS-60	MS-63	MS-65
$3,000	$4,350	$7,750	$11,500	$22,500	$47,500	

CERTIFIED POPULATIONS

G-4–VF-35	EF-40–AU-58	MS-60–62	MS-63	MS-64	MS-65	MS-66	MS-67	MS-68–70
16	108	18	1	2	0	0	0	0

Key to Collecting. The low mintage of just 1,566 coins has made the 1860-D gold dollar a landmark for many years. Examples are eagerly sought whenever offered for sale. Produced on the eve of the Civil War, many 1860-D coins were carefully hoarded and hidden by citizens as, beginning in 1861, paper money rapidly depreciated. Accordingly, the survival rate is proportionately higher than might be expected, and the average grade is fairly high for circulated issues. This coin shares the same obverse die with the 1861-D.

For one reason or another, an aura has surrounded the 1860-D for a long time. Most probably this has to do with auction catalog descriptions and other notations in print, many of which have lauded this variety to the skies. In comparison, the far rarer 1857-D has attracted relatively little notice!

In the cradle days of gold dollar research, in *Major Varieties of U.S. Gold Dollars* (1964), Walter Breen commented: "Probably less than a dozen known." People tend to believe what they see in print, and the more they see it, the more they believe it. Lewis Carroll in "The Hunting of the Snark" said "Whatever I tell you three times is true." That remark notwithstanding, certainly at least *part* of the 1861-D's mantle of fame is deserved—for on an absolute basis, any issue of which only 85 to 120 (or so) specimens are known is, indeed, rare.

This coin is often ranked alongside the 1860-D as one of two great rarities among Dahlonega Mint gold dollars. At one time the latter was considered by some to be the rarer, but now the 1861-D has that honor.

Estimated Total Population (Mint State). 20 to 25. Grading tends to be a bit liberal on these and other rare Dahlonega gold dollars, and because of this, the 1860-D, once thought to be a great rarity, is now seen with some frequency. This is due to "gradeflation," a situation that pleases the owners of coins and adds to the bottom line results of certification services, but makes correlation of current "rarity" with old-line more conservative studies (such as Akers' seminal 1975 study), impossible. *Certified population, MS-63 and higher:* 3.

Estimated Total Population (Circulated Grades). 80 to 110. The number remaining from the small original production of 1,566 can only be estimated, but is higher than the mintage figure might suggest, probably somewhere in the range of 100 to 130 surviving pieces as noted (including Mint State examples), although some estimates have ranged higher.

Characteristics of Striking and Die Notes. All authentic specimens seen have the U (UNITED) ranging from slightly weak to completely absent; the N is often weak as well; this same die was used to strike 1861-D gold dollars which have the same weakness. Certain other areas are lightly struck. Die clashmarks are usually prominent. Planchets are of very poor quality.

NUMISMATIC NOTES

Die Data. Two obverse and two reverse dies were sent from Philadelphia for the 1860-D coinage, but shipment dates are not known.

Mintage. In the third quarter 906 were coined; in the fourth quarter, 660. The number of additional pieces made for assay is not known.

Auction Information. Most of the hundreds of auction listings surveyed have commentary attached, in addition to the grade. Several citations are given here.

> *1907: Superb Collection of United States and Foreign Gold, Silver and Copper Coins, Fractional Currency, Etc.*, Fixed price list (Elmer S. Sears), lot 541: "1860 Dahlonega Mint. Extremely fine and one of the rarest gold dollars in the Dahlonega coinage. Rarer than any of the preceding coins, and probably not more than 7 are known. The finest specimen I have ever seen, either at auction sales or in private collections. $135."
>
> *1909–04: 29th Public Sale, F.W. Doughty Collection, Part III* (Thomas L. Elder), lot 466: "1860 Dahlonega Mint. Slightest rubbing on highest part of

hair. Fine specimen. This coin has not been offered for years, while the 1861-D seems to have been offered several times in the last two years, indicating that it is of nearly equal, if not equal rarity." Doughty was especially well known as a collector of large copper cents. He was a writer of fiction stories for boys and movie scenarios.

1932–11: R. Taylor Collection (B. Max Mehl), lot 238: "1860-D Strictly Fine, especially for this coin. Excessively rare. At one time considered next in rarity to the 1861-D, but in the past several years several specimens of the 1861-D mint have been discovered, where I believe that today there are far more of 1861 than there are of 1860. Certainly there are far fewer 1860-D Mint gold dollars offered at auction or private sale than those of 1861 . . ."

1944–02: Belden E. Roach Collection (B. Max Mehl), lot 1103: "1860-D Uncirculated with brilliant luster. Probably the rarest gold dollar of the entire series . . ."

1947–10: H.R. Lee Collection (Stack's), lot 960: "1860-D Brilliant Uncirculated with deep wide border. Part of UN in United did not strike up evidently due to worn die. Rarely seen in this condition. One of the outstanding rarities in the gold dollar series." Realized $225 per a printed list. Actually, the coin did not sell. *Later offering: 1957–06: 49th Sale, Eliasberg Duplicates* (New Netherlands Coin Co.), lot 721: "1860-D. Extremely Fine or better. Softly struck at the lower left side of the obv., and corresponding area of the reverse, but showing much original luster. With only the faintest touch of rubbing on the high spots; a minute reverse rim nick . . . This example from the 'Lee' sale, lot 960, where it was called 'Brilliant Uncirculated with deep wide border.' We have seen fewer of this mintmark than of the 1861-D . . . The weakness at lower l. obverse and upper l. reverse border is seen on all specimens of this date and mint . . ."

1948–03: Memorable Collection (Numismatic Gallery), lot 64: "1860-D. Second rarest of the Dahlonega dollars. Usual weak left obverse. Very Fine and highly desirable example." Note that Abe Kosoff, cataloger for the Numismatic Gallery, ranked the 1860-D second to the 1861-D in rarity.

1950–05: Golden Jubilee Sale / Jerome Kern Collection (B. Max Mehl), lot 296: "1860-D. Practically Uncirculated with mint lustre. I doubt if this coin was ever in circulation. Unusually bold date for this rarity. Considered the second rarest gold dollar of this mint. Personally, I think this coin is as rare as any gold dollar . . ." Mehl waffles a bit about the rarity.

2004–01: Platinum Night Sale (Heritage, January 2004), lot 1013: "1860-D MS-62 (PCGS). The 1860-D has the reputation of being the worst struck gold dollar from the Dahlonega Mint. This example, while certainly not boldly detailed, is actually quite a bit better struck than usually seen. The U in UNITED is, as on all known pieces, very weak but the rest of the obverse shows acceptable detail including full denticles from 11:00 to 4:00. The reverse is not as well struck with weakness at the left border and the bottom of the right side of the wreath. The 1 and the 0 in the date are full and the mintmark is sharp . . . Tied with one other piece as the second finest known."

1860-S

Circulation-Strike Mintage
13,000

Enlarged 2x
(actual size 15 mm)

Whitman Coin Guide (WCG™)

VF-20	EF-40	AU-50	AU-55	MS-60	MS-63	MS-65
$325	$450	$750	$1,150	$2,500	$6,500	$17,000

CERTIFIED POPULATIONS

G-4–VF-35	EF-40–AU-58	MS-60–62	MS-63	MS-64	MS-65	MS-66	MS-67	MS-68–70
6	188	36	10	8	1	0	0	0

Key to Collecting. The 1860-S is slightly scarce in circulated grades and rare in Mint State. Gems (MS-65 and higher) are exceedingly rare. The typical coin is well struck and very attractive.

Estimated Total Population (Mint State). 35 to 45. Minted toward the end of the glory days of the Gold Rush, these pieces were put into circulation without any thought of their future numismatic desirability. Accordingly, relatively few Mint State pieces exist today, and these only as a matter of chance. In 1986, Paul F. Taglione gave the opinion that no more than a dozen Mint State coins existed.[51] However, among Type III San Francisco Mint gold dollars, the 1860-S is more likely to be found in Mint State than any other. In 1975 David Akers commented: "I have seen a fair number that would qualify as gems." Today, most Mint State coins are less than gem (MS-65, with just one certified at this level), but perhaps some surprises await all of us. *Certified population, MS-63 and higher:* 19.

Estimated Total Population (Circulated Grades). 250 to 400. Most of these are in higher levels such as EF and AU. A survey of auction catalogs indicates that these are the typical grades encountered, including in "name" cabinets.

Characteristics of Striking and Die Notes. Usually well struck, including at the high details of Miss Liberty and the wreath. Some are slightly prooflike.

Numismatic Notes

Die Data. Four pairs of dies for the 1860-S coinage were shipped on December 2, 1859, from the die shop at the Philadelphia Mint, to San Francisco. Coins struck from one obverse die sometimes show rust on the portrait. One reverse die has what has been described as an inverted "S" mintmark, with the upper curve larger than the bottom curve. (New Netherlands' 51st Sale lot 787; later designated as Breen 6068); this variety is not widely collected or noticed today.

Auction Information. Several offerings from over a wide span of years:

> *1890–01: Robert Coulton Davis Collection* (New York Coin & Stamp Co.), lot 991: "1860-S Very Fine; rare."
>
> *1904–01: Auction Sale* (Joseph Barnet), lot 311: "1860-S Extremely Fine. Sharp. Seldom found in this condition. Very rare."

1909–10: Charles Gordon Zug Collection (S.H. Chapman), lot 329: " 1860-S Uncirculated. Rare."

1911–03: 48th Public Sale, William H. Woodin Collection (Thomas L. Elder), lot 871: "1860-S. Coinage limited, and rarer than generally supposed, as very few of the largest sales had it. Very Fine. Present record stands at $13 (Wilson Sale)." Realized $9.50.

1913–07: 82nd Public Sale (Thomas L. Elder), lot 694: "1860-S! Uncirculated. Very rare." An enthusiastic (with exclamation point) early offering of a high-grade specimen.

1946–06: William Cutler Atwater Collection (B. Max Mehl), lot 2173: "1860-S Brilliant semi-Proof; almost equal to a Proof. Pin-point nick on upper reverse edge. Scarce so choice. Record over $25." Realized $22.50.

1963–05: Emerson Gaylord Collection (Mayflower Coin Auctions), lot 41: "1860-S Brilliant Gem Uncirculated. Full bold strike with much prooflike lustre. A real gem."

1975–02: Dr. Charles L. Ruby Collection, Part III (Superior), lot 956: "1860-S. Inverted S mint mark. Easily identifiable by lower curve of S being smaller than upper curve. Choice Extra Fine with traces of mint lustre still evident. This is the finest specimen we have handled. Rare."

AMERICA AND NUMISMATICS IN 1861

On February 4, 1861, the Confederate States of America (CSA) was established, with Montgomery, Alabama, as its capital. This was the culmination of the secession of several states from the Union, beginning with South Carolina in December 1860, and continuing to include Mississippi, Florida, Alabama, Georgia, Louisiana, Texas, Virginia, Tennessee, Arkansas, and North Carolina. The formation and rise of the Confederacy resulted in the closing of the branch mints at Charlotte, Dahlonega, and New Orleans, although some limited coinage took place early in the year at Dahlonega and New Orleans—including the notable production of 1861-D gold dollars.

President Abraham Lincoln was inaugurated on March 4. In the second week of April, Confederate forces bombarded Fort Sumter in the harbor of Charleston, South Carolina, and soon afterward the War of the Rebellion, later called the Civil War, was in progress. Commercial interests envisioned disaster as large parts of their markets were cut off. It was expected to be a short affair, after which normal relations would surely be restored. Lincoln called for three-month enlistments by volunteers. It was widely thought that the South had a poor industrial and technological basis, and would be no match for the forces of the North. Parties and parades were held as soldiers marched off to settle the matter.

Reality proved to be different—far different. On July 21 the Battle of Bull Run carried the day for the CSA. On July 22, the Union called for 500,000 volunteers. Soon the nation settled into protracted conflict. After other Union setbacks, Lincoln appointed General George B. McClellan in charge of the federal forces. By year's end the outcome of the war had become increasingly uncertain. As the war commenced, a chill enveloped the country. *Banker's Magazine* later stated that 5,935 businesses failed in the North and 1,058 in the South. On December 28, certain banks stopped paying out gold coins at par in exchange for paper money, and by December 30, many other institutions had joined in the suspension.

The Union issued currency in the form of Demand Notes, payable in gold. In Montgomery, the Confederate States of America issued its own paper money early in the year, printed by the National Bank Note Co. in New York City, then, after the war began, by Southern printers. *Medals and Seals, Ancient and Modern*, by W.C. Prime, 202 pages, copyright 1860, was published in New York City in 1861 and was intended for beginners.

1861

Circulation-Strike Mintage
527,150

Proof Mintage
349 (official), likely about 30 to numismatists

Enlarged 2x
(actual size 15 mm)

Whitman Coin Guide (WCG™)

VF-20	EF-40	AU-50	AU-55	MS-60	MS-63	MS-65	PF-63	PF-65
$165	$210	$235	$265	$375	$1,350	$2,200	$6,750	$12,000

CERTIFIED POPULATIONS

G-4–EF-45	AU-50–58	MS-60–62	MS-63	MS-64	MS-65	MS-66	MS-67	MS-68–70
25	464	909	385	197	59	14	14	0
PF-50–58	PF-60–62	PF-63	PF-64	PF-65	PF-66	PF-67	PF-68–70	
0	2	0	8	18	5	2	0	

Key to Collecting. The 1861 gold dollar is readily available in choice and gem Mint State grade. The typical example is well struck, lustrous, and with good eye appeal, although there are many exceptions.

Estimated Total Population (Mint State). 1,500 to 2,500. Mint State examples of this date were saved in some quantity (relatively speaking). Most of these are choice or gem quality with frosty and lustrous surfaces. No doubt these were innocently reposing in banks when the economic situation tightened in the East, and banks stopped paying out gold coins (beginning on December 28, 1861). Any supplies on hand were quickly squirreled away by bank officers, favored patrons, and others. Numismatists are the beneficiaries—for among early-date gold dollars of the Type III design, this issue is third only to the 1862 and 1874 in terms of availability. *Certified population, MS-63 and higher:* 665.

Estimated Total Population (Circulated Grades). 4,000 to 7,000. Rare in *low* circulated grades (the same can be said for all later-dated gold dollars from this point). Grades such as EF and AU (in particular) are the norm.

Characteristics of Striking and Die Notes. Usually seen well struck, with sharp details in all areas. Many coins are from clashed dies, or those which came together without an intervening planchet, causing details of the obverse die to be impressed into the reverse die and vice-versa. Occasionally an example is seen with the reverse die rotated 180° from normal orientation.

Numismatic Notes

Die Data. 1861 four-digit date logotype: Small numerals were used, as in 1860. The digits 18 are close together, 86 are wide, and 61 are close. The 1 leans slightly right; its base is slightly higher than the base of the 8. The top space of the 8 is slightly smaller than the lower space. The 6 appears "squashed," with its top curve and ball very close to curve below (as in 1860). This logotype was used on all dies including 1861-D.

For the anticipated coinage, 31 obverse and 36 reverse dies were prepared, not all of which were used. There are numerous minor die varieties.

Misaligned Dies. A press run was made with the obverse and reverse dies aligned in the same direction, rather than the usual 180° apart. Today perhaps 1 in 20 coins shows this feature. An early offering of such a coin was in Thomas L. Elder's June 1932 sale of the W.L. Stetson, E.H. Adams, B.L. Belden, Miss Sayre, F.F. Fletcher, Mrs. R.S. Maloney, Wesley Hayes, and Gustav Senft Collections (what a title line-up!), lot 2106: "1861 Upset die. Rare. Uncirculated." Another appeared in the January 1936 J.C. Morgenthau & Co. Sale No. 359 (cataloged by Wayte Raymond and John G. Macallister), lot 16: "1861 Upset reverse. Very Fine and rare. We do not remember seeing another." Related is this coin sold in December 1960 by New Netherlands Coin Co. in Collection Cicero, lot 394: "1861 . . . Struck from heavily injured and rather sloppily polished dies (thousands of striae on both sides). Reverse "upset" (180° away from normal); unusual. An exceptionally clear example of 'blanked' dies.[52] This coin has DOLLAR recut and reversed LIBERTY showing twice left of denomination."

Source of Gold Metal. Bullion from melted-down gold coins of earlier times, including eight million earlier small-diameter gold dollars, supplied much of the metal to strike gold dollars, \$2.50 pieces, and \$20 coins of 1861 and 1862 (Breen *Encyclopedia*, 1988).

Auction Information. Many listings have been found among the more than 5,000 catalogs examined. Most give little information other than grade and surface appearance.

Proofs

Estimated Total Population and Key to Collecting. 18 to 22. Rarer than the Proof 1860 gold dollar. The widely quoted figure of 349 Proofs seems to bear no relation to the number actually *issued to numismatists*, which was probably fewer than 30.

Die Data and Notes. Proofs were well made, and the lint problem (see 1860) was mostly history. All Proofs show frosted devices, giving the pieces a cameo-like appearance. The four-digit date logotype was punched very deeply into the Proof die, making the numerals on the coins appear heavier and closer together than on the typical circulation strike.

Mintage. The reason for producing 349 Proof coins is not stated in Mint records, and if in 1861 a quantity such as this was indeed produced, this might have been for a special occasion—what occasion? The inauguration of President Abraham Lincoln comes to mind—what a nice souvenir an 1861 Proof dollar (the smallest gold denomination), would have made. The concept of an extra number of Proof coins or special strikes being made for presidential inauguration is not new, and may have originated with Michael Hodder in an essay in Stack's catalog for the James A. Stack Collection, in which he noted that certain early (pre-1858) Proofs tend to exist in larger numbers for inaugural years. The cataloger of the Floyd T. Starr Collection (Stack's, October 1992 lot 1093) states forthrightly that the official mintage figure is correct, but most were never distributed: "Although 349 Proofs were struck the vast majority remained unsold and were melted in 1862."

Auction Information (Proofs). Many listings can be found from the 19th century to date, most imparting little information other than grade and surface appearance.

1861-D

Circulation-Strike Mintage
1,000 to 1,500 (estimate)

Enlarged 2x
(actual size 15 mm)

Whitman Coin Guide (WCG™)

VF-20	EF-40	AU-50	AU-55	MS-60	MS-63	MS-65
$9,500	$15,500	$26,500	$35,000	$50,000	$95,000	$125,000

CERTIFIED POPULATIONS

G-4–EF-45	AU-50–58	MS-60–62	MS-63	MS-64	MS-65	MS-66	MS-67	MS-68–70
15	48	16	6	3	1	0	0	0

Key to Collecting. The popularity of the 1861-D gold dollar knows no bounds. It is believed that the mintage took place in May, by which time the mint was under the control of the Confederate States of America—this aspect being unknown to early catalogers, but widely publicized from the 1970s to date. The mintage figure was not reported by the Confederacy. Estimates in numismatic publications have ranged from below 1,000 to "between 2,750 and 3,250 pieces," the latter being the range given by Clair M. Birdsall.[53] David Akers suggests 1,200 to 1,500 pieces.

Most known specimens are in AU grades, certified as 53, 55, or 58. Some that have been called "Mint State" are coins that show wear or rubbing and are more properly AU. There are several that truly merit the choice or gem designation (see auction citations below), and these are special prizes. Any auction or other offering of an 1861-D gold dollar invariably stirs up a lot of attention. Few American gold coins in any series have a richer history.

Estimated Total Population (Mint State). 12 to 20. A handful of pieces can be described as truly Mint State. Perhaps more than any other single gold dollar, many 1861-D coins formerly called EF and AU are now bought and sold as Mint State. *Certified population, MS-63 and higher:* 10.

Estimated Total Population (Circulated Grades). 45 to 60. Most are EF or AU.

Characteristics of Striking and Die Notes. The U (UNITED) is always weak or absent on authentic coins. ICA (AMERICA) is often weak as are the hair details. The obverse die is the same as used to coin 1860-D gold dollars, those also having the weak or absent U. The entire coin appears somewhat "mushy" in details. The reverse die is relapped, most evidently below the wreath with a disconnected ribbon. Thus, the *personality* of an authentic 1861-D gold dollar is defined.

Numismatic Notes

History of the 1861-D Gold Dollar. Of all gold coins in the American series, there are few if any that have more history and romance than the 1861-D gold dollar. Its story is marvelous to contemplate.

To begin with, two pairs of dies were sent from the Philadelphia Mint to Dahlonega on December 10, 1860, mint officials not realizing that Georgia would be seceding from the Union within the month. The package arrived on January 7. Soon thereafter, following instructions from the governor of Georgia, insurgent troops seized the federal Mint. What happened after that can only be conjectured, since no unequivocal records are known to have survived. Apparently a small quantity of gold bullion was on hand, or perhaps some new deposits were made.

Clair Birdsall stated that near the end of the Dahlonega Mint's operations, in May 1861, about $3,000 face value in gold coins was minted under Confederate auspices. These could have been entirely gold dollars (as Birdsall suggests) or a combination of $1 and $5 coins (a possibility he also mentions). Assay coins with a face value of $6 were sent to Montgomery, Alabama, then the capital of the Confederate States of America (later moved to Richmond). It was not stated whether this consisted of six $1 coins or one $1 coin and one $5 coin. Nothing has been found concerning any Assay Commission the Confederacy may have had, or contemplated having, in early 1861.

In any event, dies for the 1861-D gold dollar were put into a coining press, and some pieces were run off. Because there had been no 1861-D coinage prior to the occupation of the mint by Georgia forces, *de facto* all 1861-D gold dollars are really 1861-D *Confederate States of America* gold dollars. The pieces are believed to have been struck in April, the same month that Confederate troops took over from their brethren, the troops of Georgia, or early in May. Shortly thereafter, the Dahlonega Mint ceased coinage operations, never to be reopened for this purpose.

Die Data. The same four-digit date logotype was used on Philadelphia and Dahlonega dies.

Other Branch Mint Coinage Contemplated. Two reverse dies were shipped to Charlotte, two to New Orleans, and four to San Francisco, but none of these were used for 1861 coinage.

Early Commentaries. In 1893 in his *Mint Marks* treatise, Augustus G. Heaton commented about Dahlonega Mint gold dollars in general and the 1861-D in particular: "The precious Dahlonega or 'D' mint issues are 13, of the years 1849, '50, '51, '52, '53, '54, '55, '56, '57, '58, '59, '60, and '61. Of these the 1852 and '53 are rare, 1854, '57 and '58 are very rare; 1860 exceedingly rare; 1855 and '56 excessively rare, and of 1861, which is not in the *Mint Report*, but two pieces are known, one being in our possession."

In *The Numismatist*, January 1896, it was reported that a Detroit member of the American Numismatic Association (Isaac M. Bates, although his name was not given) had bought an 1861-D gold dollar from an Ohio collector, then sold it to John M. Clapp, of Tidioute, Pennsylvania, for $100, who came to Detroit to pick it up. Generations later, this coin was described as Mint State by the present writer and was sold in the Eliasberg U.S. Gold Coin Collection sale, October 1982.

In August 1903, Augustus G. Heaton contributed an article to *The Numismatist*, "Eccentricities of Coin Valuation," which stated that, among other coins, such gold rarities as "the S mint dollar of 1870, and the D mint dollars of 1855, 1856, and 1861, would raise the numismatic temperature of an auction room to fever heat."

In *The Numismatist*, May 1904, The St. Louis Stamp & Coin Company advertised the availability of the collection of H.C. Beerman, of Atlanta, Georgia, "costing over $1,100. It is rich in rarities of all the U.S. series. Send us your want list and we will quote you low prices. P.S.: The 1792 Birch Cent, 1861-D U.S. gold dollar and 1798 over 7 eagle are in stock today. Let us hear from you."

Auction Information. Selected auction offerings reflect different opinions of rarity. Although 1861-D gold dollars appear only infrequently in comparison to many other date and mintmark issues, they are given a lot of "play" when offered. In view of the interest in the 1861-D and the die characteristics, more citations than usual are given here, including one in which B. Max Mehl states this is his favorite coin. No mention has been located of the Confederate States of America connection for the 1861-D until toward the end of the 20th century.

1907–03: David S. Wilson Collection (S.H. Chapman), lot 305: "1861-D Extremely Fine. Only four specimens known. The first time a specimen has been offered at auction."

1911–03: 48th Public Sale, William H. Woodin Collection (Thomas L. Elder), lot 874: "1861-D. The rarest of gold dollars! Coinage not given in Mint record, so it can only be guessed at, but judging by the number of pieces which have been offered at public sale the piece is several times rarer than the 1875, or even the 1870-S. This is one of the finest examples extant, being Extremely Fine."

1920–07: Public Auction Sale (Thomas L. Elder), lot 482: "1861-D Mint. Two slight test cuts on edge otherwise Uncirculated and sharp. Extremely rare. Probably not over 12 or 15 known."

1922–12: H.E. Rawson, Dr. A. de Yoanna, and David Strasser Collections (B. Max Mehl), lot 72: "1861-D The rarest known gold dollar. As near Uncirculated as this great rarity is undoubtedly known. A pin point, hardly noticeable nick above 1 on reverse. In order to 'play safe' I catalog this specimen as Extremely Fine, but I'm quite certain that it will readily be accepted as Uncirculated. The obverse is strongly struck, with full mint luster, only the highest portions show the barest touch of circulation. The reverse is evenly well struck up, with a nice even mint luster surface. Undoubtedly one of the finest, if not the finest, specimen of this excessively rare coin . . ." This early listing by Mehl reflects a great deal of the cataloger's personality and describes the coin in a manner that is very appealing, this being quite different from the normal basic notations of the era.

1946–06: William Cutler Atwater Collection (B. Max Mehl), lot 2161. "1861-D. This date and mint gold dollar has always been considered the rarest known of the series. This specimen is strictly Uncirculated with full brilliant mint luster. As is characteristic of all known specimens of this rarity, the U in UNITED STATES is not struck up, and the ICA in AMERICA is not as bold as the balance of the legend. The entire legend, UNITED STATES OF AMERICA, is double-struck. I consider this the gem gold dollar of the collection. I do not recall handling or having seen an equal, and certainly not a better, specimen. Of the greatest rarity . . . The Mint report does not give a coinage record of it. Apparently, being the last year of mintage, so few specimens were struck that no record was made of it. The 1861-D gold dollars always give me a great thrill, as it recalls to my mind my first 'great discovery' and, incidentally, my first 'big sale.' Upon examination of the coin [bought as a regular 1861 gold dollar], I found it to be the 1861-D. Fortunately, I had a copy of Heaton's work on *Mint Marks*, and lo and behold I noted that only two specimens were known. I offered the coin to Mr. H.O. Granberg, who was then one of the leading, if not the leading collector in the country, and received an offer of no less than $350, which, of course, I immediately accepted. It does not take a great deal of imagination to realize what that amount meant to me in those days and I might say, struggles. Since that incident I have made sales privately where the remittance ran into figures close to the six-figure mark, but I am yet to receive a remittance which would give me the thrill of that first $350 check. So you can hardly blame me if I still consider the 1861-D gold dollar my favorite coin."

1984–07: Auction '84 (Stack's), lot 1307: "1861-D . . . More than likely no more than 1,500 were coined and of that figure no more than two dozen are extant in all conditions . . . This coin is Gem Brilliant Uncirculated, full lustre and prooflike obverse and reverse. An incredible coin with virtually a full U in UNITED and a full 6. Suffice it to say that this coin is one of the keynotes of this entire collection. Ex Grant Pierce Collection (Stack's), May 1965; R.L. Miles Jr. Collection (Stack's), October 1968; Theodore Ullmer Collection (Stack's), lot 343, May 1974. From the Arthur R. Montgomery Collection." This coin was "bought in" by consignor Montgomery and later sold to George Elliot via dealer Jack Hancock. In January 1987 it appeared in Mid-American's FUN Convention sale lot 1810, graded as MS-65. Apparently, it was bought in again, for in March 2000 it reappeared as Lot 455 in Stack's sale of the George Elliot Collection, as "1861-D Choice Brilliant Uncirculated, nearly Gem quality. A simply amazing example of this great, historical rarity in the gold dollar series. We have come across no other specimen as nice as this one. In fact, this is the coin that branch mint gold specialist Winter classified as the finest known to him. Dave Akers described this coin as 'the incredible Ullmer coin (purchased by Stanley Kesselman) being the finest that I have seen.'"

AMERICA AND NUMISMATICS IN 1862

On January 15, the *London Post* commented: "The monetary intelligence from America is of the most important kind. National bankruptcy is not an agreeable prospect, but it is the only one presented by the existing state of American finance. What a strange tale does not the history of the United States for the past twelve months unfold? What a striking moral does it not point? Never before was the world dazzled by a career of more reckless extravagance. Never before did a flourishing and prosperous state make such gigantic strides towards effecting its own ruin."

The single most hectic year in American monetary history may well be 1862. A *book* could be written about what happened. In brief, gold coins disappeared from circulation in the East and Midwest early in the year, silver coins were gone by early Summer, and in the second week of July, even one-cent pieces were nowhere to be seen. A flood of substitutes arose, including privately-printed scrip bills, bronze tokens, regular postage stamps put in paper envelopes, and, beginning in August, federal Postage Currency with designs printed to resemble stamps.

Legal Tender paper money made its debut in March, was not widely trusted, and such bills traded at a discount in terms of gold and silver coins. Many American coins went to Canada, where, in Montreal, more than two dozen bullion brokers were in business, mostly trading in silver. Copper "large" cents of the 1850s and earlier were in abundance in circulation there.

In May the William A. Lilliendahl Collection, cataloged by W.H. Strobridge, crossed the auction block—the first truly great holding to be sold in this manner, handily eclipsing all earlier sales. Meanwhile, the rare coin hobby continued to prosper, with Washington items leading the market.

The Civil War continued, with victories, defeats, and heavy losses for each side. In Hampton Roads, at the base of Chesapeake Bay, the Confederate ironclad *Merrimack* engaged the Union ironclad *Monitor*, this after the rebel ship had wreaked havoc in the area. The contest was a draw, but forever changed the way military vessels were constructed. General George B. McClellan, with a case of the "slows," was relieved of his command by President Lincoln, and General Ambrose E. Burnside was named as commander of the Army of the Potomac.

On September 22, Lincoln issued the Emancipation Proclamation, to be effective on January 1. It was moot at the time, since slaves held in the South had no practical way to escape. In the meantime, the West was largely unaffected by the conflict. Business continued apace in California. Congress offered 100 million acres of federal land to the Union Pacific, Central Pacific, and other railroad lines, to promote construction of links from coast to coast.

1862

Circulation-Strike Mintage
1,361,355

Proof Mintage
35

Enlarged 2x
(actual size 15 mm)

Whitman Coin Guide (WCG™)

VF-20	EF-40	AU-50	AU-55	MS-60	MS-63	MS-65	PF-63	PF-65
$165	$210	$245	$275	$400	$1,400	$2,200	$6,750	$12,000

CERTIFIED POPULATIONS

G-4–EF-45	AU-50–58	MS-60–62	MS-63	MS-64	MS-65	MS-66	MS-67	MS-68–70
39	80	869	430	241	72	24	4	0
PF-50–58	**PF-60–62**	**PF-63**	**PF-64**	**PF-65**	**PF-66**	**PF-67**	**PF-68–70**	
0	1	6	6	16	7	0	0	

Key to Collecting. While the vast majority of 1862-dated gold dollars are frosty and lustrous, a few are prooflike. As the most plentiful date in Mint State within the Type III design, and also as a coin which is usually very well struck and quite lustrous, the 1862 is an ideal candidate for a high-grade type set. When offered for sale, most are so nice that they figuratively say, "Buy me!"

Estimated Total Population (Mint State). 3,000 to 4,000. Many if not most of these are lustrous, frosty, and very beautiful. These were probably hoarded early on, in the early days of 1862, after banks stopped paying out gold coins at face value, but when the premium was nominal. *Certified population, MS-63 and higher:* 1,546.

Estimated Total Population (Circulated Grades). 4,000 to 7,000. Most are in higher ranges such as EF and, especially, AU. Beginning this year, gold dollars no longer circulated in the East or Midwest. Such coins were seen in commerce on the West Coast, but traded at a premium in comparison to Legal Tender Notes and other paper money.

Characteristics of Striking and Die Notes. The 1862 gold dollar is usually seen very well struck in all areas. Some have clashmarks, but these are much less often seen than on the coinage of 1861. A very few pieces are highly prooflike and closely resemble full Proof strikings. Die striae in the form of tiny parallel raised lines are common, as they are on many silver and gold coins of the Civil War era.

Numismatic Notes

Die Data. 1862 four-digit date logotype: Small numerals were used, but slightly larger than for 1860 and 1861. The 18 and 86 are about the same distance apart, with the 62 slightly farther apart. The lower left serif of the 1 is longer than its lower right serif. The interior top of the 8 appears slightly smaller than its interior bottom, and the 8 leans slightly right; the base of the 1 is higher than the base of the 8. The 6 has a small ball separated from curve below, but close to it. These may touch on some deep die impressions. An ornate digit 2 has a small ball at upper left and a curved base. A tiny horizontal projection is noted at about the center outside right of the 2. This logotype was used on all dies.

For the coinage of this year, 53 obverse and 47 reverse dies were made, most of which were probably used. Thus, there are many minute die variations to study—but these have never been delineated. Among these varieties, not widely collected, are those with Doubled Date, Doubled Die obverse, and a repunched 1. Likely, the Doubled Die obverse is the most significant of these.

Thomas L. Elder's June 1932 sale of the W.L. Stetson, E.H. Adams, B.L. Belden, Miss Sayre, F.F. Fletcher, Mrs. R.S. Maloney, Wesley Hayes, and Gustav Senft Collections included: lot 2108: "1862 Wreath closed at top. Uncirculated." Lot 2109: "1862 Wreath open at top. Uncirculated." The descriptions *may have* indicated that the first coin had the wreath apex elements touching, or nearly so, while the second coin may have been from a relapped die that showed the elements farther apart.

Metal From Melted Earlier Gold Dollars. Bullion from melted-down gold coins of earlier times, including eight million earlier small-diameter gold dollars, supplied much of the metal to strike gold dollars, $2.50 pieces, and $20 coins of 1861 and 1862 (Breen *Encyclopedia*, 1988).

Not Paid Out at Face Value. The 1862 gold dollar is the first date (of the later range in the gold dollar series) in which most coins were kept by the Treasury Department and not paid out at face value. However, upon application, and by paying a sharp premium in terms of Legal Tender notes or other federal paper money, such pieces could be obtained. Also, citizens could order them through banks, again paying a premium. The double standard of different prices for gold coins and paper money did not end until December 17, 1878, when for the first time since late 1861, gold coins and paper became on par with each other. This was slightly in advance of the par date mandated by Congress, January 1, 1879.

Auction Information. With few exceptions, auction listings dating back to the 1860s include little information other than the grade. In recent times, "trophy coins" in ultra grades have been showcased with extensive commentary.

Proofs

Estimated Total Population and Key to Collecting. 18 to 22. Proofs were struck on February 16, 1862, to the extent of 35 coins. Most likely, some remained unsold. Most remaining pieces are very attractive. Gems are of great rarity.

Die Data and Notes. The 2 (1862) is more prominent in the four-digit logotype than are the other numerals.

The key identification feature for Proof obverses is that the vertical element of the leftmost feather in the headdress plume is mostly polished away, giving Proof field in this area. This die was used to strike Proof gold dollars from 1862 through 1873, 1875, and some of 1876. The area of polish was increased as the years went by. This same die was employed for some circulation strikes (not Proofs) of 1879, and, relapped and now with polish areas also in the headband, to make certain circulation strikes (not Proofs) of gold dollars in 1888 and 1889. (This is a different "incomplete feather" obverse die than that used to strike certain 1859 Proof dollars.)

On the Proof reverse die of 1862 the O (DOLLAR) is mostly frosty rather than Proof finish at the center. The date is closer to the ribbon point than the point above it, with the 6 centered slightly to the left of the peak of the ribbon (not definitive, because certain circulation strikes have the same position).

Auction Information. As a general rule, most auction listings of Proof gold dollars from this point onward include very little numismatic information beyond grade and rarity estimates.

AMERICA AND NUMISMATICS IN 1863

Silver and gold coins remained out of sight, and copper-nickel cents were scarce in circulation. This year saw an unprecedented flood of copper Civil War tokens and privately printed scrip paper bills, the last mostly in denominations of 3¢ to 50¢, to which federal Fractional Currency was added. On February 25, it took $172.37 in federal paper to buy $100 in gold coins (this being the high for the year). By August 26, the differential had dropped sharply due to the North repulsing the Southern advance at the Battle of Gettysburg, and it took just $122.50 in paper to buy $100 in gold coins (this being the low point, after which the gap widened once again). Gold dollars were made only in small quantities, and could be obtained at the Mint in exchange for depositing bullion, or paying a premium in terms of paper. Meanwhile, the Civil War continued, with heavy casualties on both sides. No end was in sight.

The National Banking Act of February 25, 1863, authorized state-chartered banks, in sound condition, to reorganize ("convert" in Treasury terms) as National Banks, under which authority they could issue paper money against bonds posted as security. In the Treasury Building in Washington, D.C., Spencer M. Clark supervised a large staff in the preparation of paper money, including, by year's end, the imprinting of serial numbers and the Treasury Seal on National Bank notes. Fractional Currency formed the thrust of most activity of the National Currency Bureau, as it was called. Much federal paper money was printed by the American, National, and Continental Bank Note companies in New York City, with American taking the lion's share of contracts. Meanwhile, these firms continued to turn out paper money for more than a thousand state-chartered banks and other issuers.

In terms of importance in the field of numismatic auctions, W.H. Strobridge's catalogs were notable on the coin auction scene in 1863, including gems from the George

F. Seavey Collection offered in September and more coins from the William Lilliendahl Collection in December. W. Elliot Woodward's April sale of the Brooks, Finotti, and Colburn Collections and his October presentation of more Colburn coins were likewise laden with rarities. Edward Cogan's untitled sale of April also attracted attention. Among gold coins, Proofs of all denominations, any and all issues from 1795 to early 1834, and gold dollars were popular and attracted many bids.

1863

Circulation-Strike Mintage
6,200

Proof Mintage
50

Enlarged 2x
(actual size 15 mm)

Whitman Coin Guide (WCG™)

VF-20	EF-40	AU-50	AU-55	MS-60	MS-63	MS-65	PF-63	PF-65
$600	$1,150	$2,300	$3,250	$4,500	$8,500	$18,500	$7,500	$12,000

CERTIFIED POPULATIONS

G-4–EF-45	AU-50–58	MS-60–62	MS-63	MS-64	MS-65	MS-66	MS-67	MS-68–70
2	22	21	10	18	4	2	1	1
PF-50–58	**PF-60–62**	**PF-63**	**PF-64**	**PF-65**	**PF-66**	**PF-67**	**PF-68–70**	
0	2	4	18	7	7	1	0	

Key to Collecting. The 1863 gold dollar is one of the key rarities in the series, and in Mint State is the most difficult-to-find Philadelphia Mint coin other than 1875. Today, the true significance of this elusive coin is nearly completely overlooked, although, to be sure, the Guide Book singles out its only Mint State listing, MS-60, to assign the 1863 a price higher than any other Philadelphia Mint gold dollar except 1875. However, in casual conversation about scarce gold dollars, focus is apt to be on Charlotte and Dahlonega coins, or on the 1875, or on the low-mintage issues of the 1880s—rarely on the 1863.

This was not always the case. A generation or so ago the 1863 was recognized one of the great classics of the gold dollar series. Reflective of the traditional view, David Akers commented in 1975: "This is the rarest Philadelphia Mint gold dollar of the 1860s and also the rarest gold dollar in Uncirculated after 1861. As a date, it is only marginally less rare than the 1875 but, it is actually more difficult to obtain in full Mint State than the highly regarded 1875." Among auction offerings of most "name collections" of yesteryear, gold dollars of this date are usually seen either in worn grades or Proof. In recent years, Mint State coins have outnumbered Proofs, possibly due in part to recycling of the same coins through the marketplace.

Estimated Total Population (Mint State). 50 to 80. Most are in lower Mint State levels. Any coin with legitimate claim to MS-63 or finer status is a first-class rarity and outclasses a Proof in this regard. *Certified population, MS-63 and higher:* 36.

Estimated Total Population (Circulated Grades). 100 to 140. As noted, some few pieces are Mint State, but most are in higher circulated grades such as EF and AU. For reasons unexplained, the number surviving from this mintage is smaller, percentagewise, than for later dates in the decade. Thus, in rarity the 1863 outclasses the lower mintage 1864 made the following year.

Characteristics of Striking and Die Notes. All authentic circulation strikes have many parallel die striae visible under magnification, this feature being visible only on higher grade pieces (AU or above). The dies of most gold and silver denominations of the Civil War era were quickly prepared, and across all denominations, the majority show many parallel striae resulting from grinding the fields.

Occasionally, a gold dollar of this date will show a minor planchet lamination or a carbon (black fleck) inclusion. Some high-grade pieces show doubling of lettering and features at the center of the reverse—a minor doubled-die effect.

Numismatic Notes

Die Data. 1863 four-digit date logotype: The punch employed small numerals, but larger than for 1860 and 1861. The digits 18 were spaced very close together, the 86 wider, and the 63 about the same width as the 86. The 1 has an overly long lower left serif; its base is higher than the base of the 8. The 8 is somewhat flattened at the top and bottom, chunky or angular rather than smoothly rounded on the outside. The 6 has a rather straight upright at left, its top part extending horizontally with a small ball at the end. The 3 is rather crude, with little interior space at the top or bottom; the base of the 3 is slightly lower than that of other figures. This logotype was used on all dies.

Mintage. The mintage was delivered from June 24 to November 30.

Auction Information. Several selected listings contain interesting information:

> *1890–01: Robert Coulton Davis Collection* (New York Coin & Stamp Co.), lot 947: "1863 Barely touched by circulation; very rare."
>
> *1892–04: Colin E. King Collection* (S.H. and Henry Chapman), lot 662: "1863 Uncirculated. Mint luster. Extremely rare."
>
> *1897–04: M.A. Brown Collection* (S.H. and Henry Chapman), lot 210: "1863 Extremely Fine. Excessively rare." Realized $20. Use of the "excessively rare" term to describe a worn circulation-strike specimen is indicative of the esteem in which the 1863 was held by the Chapman brothers, who by 1897 were esteemed in turn, as the best auctioneers in the business.
>
> *1898–03: New Jersey Collection* (Ed. Frossard), lot 1034: "1863 Mint State. Very rare."
>
> *1921–11: L. Langfelder and August Jaedicke Jr. Collections* (B. Max Mehl), lot 1180: "1863 Practically Uncirculated, with brilliant luster. Excessively rare. One of our rarest gold dollars."
>
> *1929–04: George W. Fash, Joseph F. Atkinson, and Carrie E. Perkins Collections* (Thomas L. Elder), lot 1343: "1863. A very rare date. Obv. Unc. Rev. Proof."
>
> *1932–01: Stevens and Zolotzeff Collections* (Thomas L. Elder), lot 462: "1863 A very precious date. Worth $35 to $40. Uncirculated."
>
> *1955–04: 45th Sale* (New Netherlands Coin Co.), lot 769: "1863 Brilliant Uncirculated. A flawless little 'gem,' the reverse rather proof-like. Many times rarer than a Proof in this preservation, like so many other coins bearing this date."
>
> *1983–11: Virgil M. Brand Collection, Part I* (Bowers and Merena Galleries), lot 29: "1863 Choice Brilliant Uncirculated, MS-65. A superb specimen of

this great rarity. A virtually flawless coin which probably could even merit the Gem Uncirculated, MS-67 designation. Sharply struck and with frosty fields. Numerous minute parallel *die* striae are visible as on all genuine specimens (the dies were not completely treated prior to use). Examination . . . reveals a wealth of recutting of letters, especially at the center of the reverse . . . We believe it is no exaggeration to state that fewer than a half dozen specimens equal to the present coin exist in all of numismatics. A rare, rare prize and certainly one of the highlights of the present gold dollars from the Brand Collection." This may be the finest known example.

Proofs

Estimated Total Population and Key to Collecting. 18 to 24. The Proof 1863 gold dollar has been popular for a long time, due in no small part to the nearly impossible challenge of locating gem Mint State coins. Most are well struck and very attractive.

Mintage. Proofs were struck on March 23, 1863, apparently on speculation that 50 would be sold. Most probably, not more than 35 actually saw distribution. Later, beginning on June 24, the Proof dies were used to make circulation strikes.

Breen (*Proof*, 1989) adds gratuitously without giving any basis for the comment: "Restrikes may exist but decisive evidence is lacking." Further, after noting S.H. Chapman's "notorious unreliability," Breen quotes Chapman's commentary in the Wetmore and Wilson sale catalogs, in which Chapman stated that the late John F. McCoy "stated to me that he knew only 30 [gold Proof sets] were struck, and some of these were remelted at the Mint."

Die Data and Notes. For characteristics of the obverse die, see information under Proof gold dollars of 1862, since the same die was used.

Auction Information (Proofs). The description of a nice example:

> *1939–11: William B. Hale Collection* (B. Max Mehl), lot 672: "1863 As perfect a Proof as I have ever seen. Sharp wire edge. Excessively rare. Limited coinage. Listed at $75, but in the remarkable condition is worth almost as much as any gold dollar." *Later offering: 1992–10: Floyd T. Starr Collection* (Stack's), lot 1098: "1863 Choice Brilliant Proof, nearly gem. Only 50 struck, the majority melted. Both surfaces fully brilliant, devices frosty. Fields nearly pristine. Rims and denticles fully struck. Extremely rare: Breen believed that fewer than a dozen Proofs survive and listed only six, the Starr coin being his number 6. David Akers could offer no estimate of survivors. Missing in Proof format from the Norweb sale. One specimen each permanently impounded in the National Numismatic and ANS Collections. The Starr coin is nicer than the Eliasberg: 51 plate, about equivalent to Trompeter: 9, ex Garrett (1976): 409. As a date, this is the rarest gold dollar of the 1860s. From B. Max Mehl's sale of the William B. Hale Collection, November 28, 1939 lot 672."

AMERICA AND NUMISMATICS IN 1864

Federal issues of paper money continued to proliferate, dominated by Fractional Currency for lower value transactions, Legal Tender notes in denominations from $1 upward, and National Bank notes from $5 upward. Silver and gold coins were nowhere to be seen, continuing a situation that would extend for many years. Gold dollars were redundant to commerce and were made only in nominal quantities.

W. Elliot Woodward offered at auction the John F. McCoy Collection in May and the Levick, Emery, Ilsley, and Abbey Collections in October. As he stated in his catalogs, his policy was to buy collections outright, then offer them in the saleroom. *Banker's Magazine* carried this review of the McCoy sale in its June issue:

> Another sale of coins has just terminated at the auction rooms of Bangs, Merwin & Co., New York, having continued five days. We give below a few quotations, from which our readers will see that the interest in rare coins and medals is on the increase . . . The sale of the American portion of the catalogue commenced with a dollar of 1794—the first of the series—and having the reputation of being the finest specimen known, its possession was contended for with a determination seldom witnessed. It was sold at the high price of $285. The first colonial coin in the catalogue was a New-England shilling, which brought $22.50. A small coin, known as the George Clinton copper, brought $110. A Washington half dollar of 1792 was sold for $85. A cent of the same date for $110, and a scarce medal, with the bust of Washington, and known as the Fame Medal, reached the high price of $125.

Bronze two-cent pieces were issued for the first time, and were the first federal coins to bear the motto "In God We Trust." Cents were switched in composition from copper-nickel to bronze. By this time the shortage of one-cent pieces in circulation had ended, and earlier Flying Eagle and Indian Head cents came out of hiding.

The American Numismatic Society, which had expired in 1859, was revivified under the name of American Numismatic and Archaeological Society, the expansion intended to draw a wider membership base. Archaeology never became important to the group, and years later, in 1907, the designation was dropped.

The Union registered many victories in the Civil War in forays throughout the South. On March 10, General U.S. Grant was given the command of all army divisions. General William Tecumseh Sherman ravaged much territory, including Atlanta and a wide swath extending through Georgia to the sea. Confederate paper money fell to such a low level that none was issued after this year.

In the North on August 11, an all-time record was set when it took $285 in currency to buy $100 in gold coins from a bank or exchange office. Amid outcries against profiteering, there were many manipulations in financial circles, several shenanigans and "corners" in the stock market, and other financial games. In November, deposed General George McClellan challenged Abraham Lincoln for the presidency, but the incumbent won handily. Many votes for McClellan were placed to express dissatisfaction with the ongoing war (which by this time had rendered both sides great tragedy and harm) rather than in support of the merits of the candidate.

1864

Circulation-Strike Mintage
5,900

Proof Mintage
50

Enlarged 2x
(actual size 15 mm)

Whitman Coin Guide (WCG™)

VF-20	EF-40	AU-50	AU-55	MS-60	MS-63	MS-65	PF-63	PF-65
$375	$500	$750	$950	$1,200	$3,000	$6,000	$8,500	$14,000

CERTIFIED POPULATIONS

G-4–EF-45	AU-50–58	MS-60–62	MS-63	MS-64	MS-65	MS-66	MS-67	MS-68–70
9	39	34	10	22	2	5	11	9
PF-50–58	PF-60–62	PF-63	PF-64	PF-65	PF-66	PF-67	PF-68–70	
0	2	4	4	5	4	1	0	

Key to Collecting. Mint State 1864 gold dollars are rarities. Among those that exist are some superb gems, although the typical piece is apt to be below that level. Although the mintage is slightly less than that of 1863, a few more 1864-dated dollars exist at all grade levels. Over the years the appearance of a choice or gem 1864 has been ample reason to expend a few extra words in catalogs.

Estimated Total Population (Mint State). 100 to 150. Many are MS-60 to MS-62, with "loose" grading often seen, in view of the rarity of this date. However, gems have been sprinkled among auction offerings—far more than for the 1863—to which this date is sometimes compared. The cluster of coins graded MS-67 and higher is remarkable and has no counterpart in the 1863 issue, a date with which 1864 is often compared. *Certified population, MS-63 and higher:* 60.

Estimated Total Population (Circulated Grades). 170 to 220, mostly in EF and AU grades. This coin is very rare, especially in the context of the great demand for coins of this denomination.

Characteristics of Striking and Die Notes. Often with date numerals weakly struck, but with some notable exceptions. Planchets are often defective and show streaks or small laminations. Dies were incompletely finished, and high-grade examples show parallel striae. Some higher grade specimens also show clashmarks in the fields, typically on both obverse and reverse.

Numismatic Notes

Die Data. 1864 four-digit date logotype: The digits 18 are close together, 86 are closer still, and 64 are virtually or completely touching on most impressions. The 1 has a lower left serif longer than its lower right serif; the base of the 1 is higher than the base of the 8. The 8 is slightly flattened at top and bottom and somewhat angular rather than rounded (but not as much as on the 1863). The 6 has heavy upright portions, its left upright slanting slightly to the right as it goes upward, and its ball close to the curve below it. The 4 has a thick upright, without a crosslet on the crossbar. The upper right side of the crossbar is small and extends slightly farther to the right than the serif below it. This logotype was used on all dies.

Mintage. Two deliveries of circulation strikes were made, 2,400 on February 23, 1864, and months later, 3,500 on December 6 [per Breen (*Encyclopedia*, 1988)].

Auction Information. As with the 1863, the elusive nature of the 1864 was recognized at an early date. A few early listings:

> *1893–05: Nicholas Petry Collection* (S.H. and Henry Chapman), lot 331: "1864 dollar. Uncirculated. Mint luster. Extremely rare."

1897–04: M.A. Brown Collection (S.H. and Henry Chapman), lot 211: "1864 Fine. Pierced over head. Excessively rare."

1898–12: James T. Callender Collection (Lyman H. Low), lot 371: "1864 Slight scratches near ST in STATES, otherwise Extremely Fine. Exceedingly rare."

1908–12: D.M. Kuntz Collection (Henry Chapman), lot 241: "1864 Very Fine. Hole drilled over head, cutting E out of STATES. Very rare."

1909–06: Henry L. Jewett Collection (S.H. Chapman), lot 952: "1864 Very Fine. Very rare."

PROOFS

Estimated Total Population and Key to Collecting. 12 to 15. The 1864 Proof gold dollar is an incredible rarity, a landmark issue among Proof gold dollars dated after the 1850s, and one of several nearly impossible-to-find dates of this decade. It is likely that no more than 25 or so pieces were distributed from the Mint figure of 50 coins struck.

Die Data and Notes. According to Breen (*Encyclopedia*, 1988): "Proofs are of the so-called 'heavy date' variety, with numerals 6 and 4 touching from the logotype being punched very deeply in the die. Minted on February 11, 1864. The obverse is the same used in 1863, with polish in the topmost feather and below ear. The 1864 Proofs are about as rare as the 1863 Proofs."

For characteristics of the obverse die, see information under Proof gold dollars of 1862, since the same die was used. This supersedes Breen's commentary (*Proof*, 1989, under the 1864 listing, p. 125) that the 1863 and 1864 Proof gold dollars share the same obverse, but which makes no mention that this die was used to strike other Proofs as well.

Auction Information (Proofs). A few listings with pertinent information:

1941–06: William Forrester Dunham Collection (B. Max Mehl), lot 1839: "1864 Struck in yellow gold; sharp impression. The most perfect and magnificent brilliant Proof of this rarity I have ever seen. Perfectly and evenly struck with slightly raised borders and wire edge. Not the slightest mark or spot to mar its beautiful appearance. While this date is rare in any condition, but in this remarkable state I consider it even more rare than the 1875. For my own satisfaction I looked through the catalogs covering a period of more than 25 years, and including of course all of the important sales held during this period. I found that there were a great many more 1875 Proof gold dollars offered than that of 1864, and not a single specimen matched this one. It is simply superb. I may be enthused about it, but it is really a thrilling coin to look at and more thrilling to own. If I had this coin in stock, I would not part with it for less than $100, which I think is a fair price for it." *Later offering: Floyd T. Starr Collection* (Stack's), lot 1099. "1864 Choice Brilliant Proof. Only 50 struck, the majority unsold and melted. Lovely, deep yellow to pale orange gold in color. Both fields fully brilliant, devices frosty. Full LIBERTY. Mint flash visible in feathers of headdress, hollow under ear, some letters on coronet, portions of reverse wreath. Lightly hairlines both sides. Struck from the perfect states of the dies. Very rare: fewer than 15 survivors are believed known. Breen listed nine, the Starr coin being his number 4; inaccurately listed one in the Norweb Collection, overlooked a second in the Smithsonian, leaving his total census unaffected. Missing in Proof format from the Eliasberg, Norweb, and Kaufman sales. Two specimens are permanently impounded in the National Numismatic Collection (ex Mint and Lilly Collections), one in the ANS Collection. The Starr coin is nearly the equal of the Trompeter example. From B. Max Mehl's sale of the William Forrester Dunham Collection, June 3, 1941 lot 1839."

1946–06: 93rd Catalog Sale (Barney Bluestone), lot 1071: "1864 Brilliant glittering Proof, In my opinion this is a much rarer coin in Proof than the 1875. In the past three decades I have handled at least twenty 1875 gold dollars whereas only two 1864 actual brilliant Proofs passed my hands." Bluestone, whose office was in the Hotel Syracuse in the New York state city of the same name, handled many important coins. His catalogs have been overlooked by nearly all researchers.

1950–05: Golden Jubilee Sale / Jerome Kern Collection (B. Max Mehl), lot 264: "1864. Perfect brilliant Proof. Here is a rarity the real value of which and the real rarity of which has not been recognized by most collectors. While the 1864 gold dollar is available in Uncirculated condition, in Proof condition I consider it extremely rare. The Dr. Green Collection, which had a complete set of the gold dollars almost all in Proof, did not have an 1864 in Proof. There is no mint record of the number of Proofs struck, but there were only 25 Proofs struck in 1865 and I doubt very much if that many Proofs were struck in 1864. Auction record $115 and certainly worth it."

1992–02: Ed Trompeter Collection (Superior), lot 10: "1864 Grade Gem Brilliant Proof. Same obverse as 1862, repolished (note die polish below ear); heavy date, 64 touching, minutely further right than on business strikes (which have 6 4 apart). Description: Identifiable by a tiny mark just right of right ribbon end, from foreign matter adhering to die at striking . . . A list of major gold dollar auctions lacking it would be pages long. Only a single example has been graded by the services, it grading Proof-63 (PCGS)."

AMERICA AND NUMISMATICS IN 1865

The Mint introduced the nickel three-cent piece, intended to be useful in the continuing scenario in which neither silver nor gold coins were seen in commerce. These proved to be popular, to the detriment of the recently inaugurated bronze two-cent coins, the production of which dropped sharply. To encourage more use of Fractional Currency bills of denominations from 5¢ to 50¢, the legal tender status of the bronze cent and two-cent piece was limited to a total of just 4¢ in a given transaction.

W. Elliott Woodward conducted just two sales this year, but each was highly important—the Bache, Bertsch, and Lightbody Collections in March, followed by the Bache, Bertsch, and Colburn Collections in December. The only other notable sale of the year was held by Bangs & Co., general auctioneer (books, antiques, coins, etc.) in New York City. Featured was one of several collections formed by Joseph N.T. Levick, a numismatist whose interests, ranging from memorable early copper cents to incredible tokens and medals, changed over time—but resulted in fascinating records of the activity of the period.

The fortunes of the Confederacy continued to decline. In January on the London market, where both American and Confederate money was actively traded, $100 in federal bills could buy gold worth $46, while the same amount in Confederate paper was worth just $1.70 in gold. Soon, CSA paper depreciated to nearly the vanishing point—but not quite—since there was a speculative interest that, somehow, at least a partial redemption might be made.

On April 9, General Robert E. Lee surrendered to General U.S. Grant at Appomattox Court House, Virginia. The Civil War was over. The toll stood at more than a million casualties plus untold damage to homes, civic buildings, businesses, and government property. It would take many years for America to return to normal. A few days later, on April 14, President Lincoln was assassinated at Ford's Theatre in Washington, by actor John Wilkes Booth. Vice-President Andrew Johnson became the chief executive. It was widely anticipated that the chaotic monetary situation would return to normal.

1865

Circulation-Strike Mintage
3,720

Proof Mintage
25+

Enlarged 2x
(actual size 15 mm)

Whitman Coin Guide (WCG™)

VF-20	EF-40	AU-50	AU-55	MS-60	MS-63	MS-65	PF-63	PF-65
$400	$650	$825	$1,050	$1,750	$3,750	$6,500	$8,500	$14,000

CERTIFIED POPULATIONS

G-4–EF-45	AU-50–58	MS-60–62	MS-63	MS-64	MS-65	MS-66	MS-67	MS-68–70
10	16	24	5	10	11	8	4	1
PF-50–58	**PF-60–62**	**PF-63**	**PF-64**	**PF-65**	**PF-66**	**PF-67**	**PF-68–70**	
0	3	0	5	11	6	1	0	

Key to Collecting. In Mint State, the 1865 gold dollar is second in rarity only to the 1863 (among Philadelphia Mint issues). The elusive nature of this date was recognized at an early time. Many late 19th- and early 20th-century catalogs make liberal use of adjectives in this regard, and for modern catalogs there is no limit on the excitement. Although the mintage of this date was very low, some choice and gem Mint State coins seem to have been saved as souvenirs or for other purposes. Most of these made their debut on the market toward the end of the 20th century. Do you wonder where they were earlier?

Estimated Total Population (Mint State). 70 to 90. Usually of high quality, although lower end pieces can be overgraded. Gems come on the market often enough that finding one will not be a problem. *Certified population, MS-63 and higher:* 41.

Estimated Total Population (Circulated Grades). 125 to 160. A key issue in the series. Usually seen EF or AU.

Characteristics of Striking and Die Notes. High-grade circulation strikes nearly always show heavy die striae. Some planchets show slight lamination marks or streaks. Dies were clashed after only 1,000 or so had been struck. A few pieces display relapping of the reverse die, with disconnected elements to the left and right sides of the wreath and at the lower right outside of the wreath. All circulation strikes were produced from the same pair of dies, with the date ever so slightly slanting up to the right, and about *twice as far* from DOLLAR as from the ribbon bow tip.

NUMISMATIC NOTES

Die Data. 1865 four-digit date logotype: The digits 18 are very close together; with 86 farther apart, and 65 the farthest. The 5 leans slightly right, but not enough to be called italic or slanting; the left side of its ball is about even with left side of the upright above it. This logotype was used on all dies this year.

Auction Information. Many Uncirculated coins have been offered over the years. Selected citations:

> *1890–01: Robert Coulton Davis Collection* (New York Coin & Stamp Co.), lot 949: "1865 Sharp Uncirculated; rare."
>
> *1905–12: A.H. Lockwood and Samuel W. Treat Collections* (S.H. and Henry Chapman), lot 353: "1865 Uncirculated. Mint luster. Brilliant, beautiful specimen and extremely rare thus."
>
> *1911–03: 48th Public Sale, William H. Woodin Collection* (Thomas L. Elder), lot 878: "1865. Brilliant Uncirculated. Coinage given as only 3,725 pieces, being several thousand less than coined in either 1863 or 1864. The price realized at this sale should be correspondingly large." Realized $47.
>
> *1940–09: 54th Catalog Sale* (Barney Bluestone), lot 723: "1865 Uncirculated. Brilliant. Exceedingly Rare. Was purchased as Proof."
>
> *1941–06: William Forrester Dunham Collection* (B. Max Mehl), lot 1840: "1865 Brilliant semi-Proof; just about equal to a perfect Proof. Sharp and perfect in every respect, with raised borders and wire edge. A magnificent specimen of this rarity. Listed up to $75 and certainly worth it in this remarkable condition." Realized $67.50.
>
> *1947–10: H.R. Lee Collection* (Stack's), lot 916: "1865 Brilliant Uncirculated. Proof like surface, a sharp impression that makes it look like a real Proof. A rare and valuable coin." Realized $105.
>
> *1981–07: Auction '81* (Paramount), lot 1360: "1865, Superb Gem Uncirculated 67 . . . It is fully struck with a high wire rim and razor sharp details. The coin has light gold color and all of its full original mint luster. It was struck from lightly clashed dies. The surfaces are absolutely pristine except for one tiny and insignificant mark in front of the nose that is mentioned more for future identification than anything else . . . We have never seen or heard of a comparable business strike and we feel that this could very well be the finest known 1865 gold dollar . . ."
>
> *1983–11: Virgil M. Brand Collection, Part I* (Bowers and Merena Galleries), lot 33: "1865 Choice Brilliant Uncirculated, MS-65 . . . Walter Breen notes that one pair of dies was used to strike original pieces (in addition, pieces which he designates as restrikes, struck only in Proof, were made from another die). 'For the record' we note that the present die, the original die, is hallmarked by having a tiny 'island' to the right of the numeral 6 in the date."

PROOFS

Estimated Total Population and Key to Collecting. 16 to 22. Proofs are very rare, but many dozens of auction appearances (in some instances representing the same single coins) have taken place over a long period of time. In today's era of buying and selling "trophy coins" without holding them for a long time, the chance of finding one without a long wait is very good.

Mintage. Delivered on March 8 (25 specimens). There are no official Proof production records for this and certain other years, but R.W. Julian has located some Proof deliveries, including for *full gold Proof sets* from the 1860s onward. The *total* Proof mintage for gold dollars was more likely closer to 50 than to 25.

Die Data and Notes, Including About Restrikes. Proofs were minted on March 8 and probably other times. John Dannreuther has identified three different dies used to make Proofs this year:

1. The first die used had in irregular or "wavy" surface in areas, perhaps due to improper hardening, or there may have been a problem with basining or some other preparation process. The reverse is more "dished" than normal, from the basining process. This die can be identified by having the peak of the ribbon below the left edge of the 6. The date slants slightly up to the right. It is much closer to the ribbon tip than to DOLLAR. Walter Breen called this a "restrike," but by examining the state or progression of the same *obverse* die mated with this and the two other 1865 reverses, Dannreuther determined this was the *first* used. After making only a few impressions, this die was replaced with another.
2. The second die is not known to have had any problems. However, it was used for just a short time. The Smithsonian Institution coin is from this die. Today, this is the only known example. The date slants slightly up to the right. In relation to dies 1 and 3 it is higher, but still slightly closer to the ribbon tip than to DOLLAR. Perhaps the die cracked soon after its use, or there was another problem. The common obverse die used on all three varieties was lightly polished before striking this variety. Likely, coins from dies 1 and 2 were in the delivery of March 8.
3. The third die is the one typically seen on Proofs of this year with another slight polishing before striking this variety. The date is level and is much closer to the ribbon tip than to DOLLAR. The logotype is punched very deeply into the die, slightly distorting the level of the field surrounding it.

Auction Information (Proofs). Several selected citations.

1950–05: Golden Jubilee Sale / Jerome Kern Collection (B. Max Mehl), lot 265: "1865. Brilliant Proof. Die break on upper obverse, making the upper portion of the obverse a trifle 'higher.' Very rare. Catalogs $150." Realized $135.

1972–06: Russell C. Heim Collection (Stack's), lot 777: "1865 Proof. From our Rawls Sale, June 1970. This was the first example we have seen of this date struck from buckling dies. Possibly the last one struck before the die shattered. Rare." *Later offering: 1973–12: Westchester Collection* (Stack's), lot 1309: "1865 Brilliant Proof . . . Ex Russell C. Heim Collection."

1982–10: Eliasberg Collection (U.S. Gold Coin Collection) (Bowers and Ruddy Galleries), lot 53: "1865 Choice Brilliant Proof-65. With small unpolished die area on the reverse near the top of the wreath, as made . . . *From the John H. Clapp Collection, 1942. Earlier from Charles T. Steigerwalt, November 1893.*"

1992–10: Floyd T. Starr Collection (Stack's), lot 1100: "1865 Choice Brilliant Proof . . . Both sides are deeply mirrorlike, while the devices are pleasingly frosty. Hidden lint mark at top of obverse under ES. Die chip between 65 in date, near the opening of 6, as seen on the Norweb, Eliasberg, and Trompeter Proof specimens. Reverse die perfect, like the Trompeter coin, not clashed with outlines of Liberty's head in the wreath as on Norweb: 1904. Very rare: of the 25 struck fewer than 15 are believed to survive. This specimen is the eighth listed by David Akers in his survey of auction appearances of Proofs. Among the finest known: finer than the Kaufman coin, missing from our 1976 Garrett sale. Quality overall equivalent to Trompeter: 11, Eliasberg: 53, Garrett (1979): 410, and the Norweb example. From Numismatic Gallery's sale of the 'Memorable Collection,' March 1, 1948 lot 21; earlier from the same firm's sale of the 'World's Greatest Collection' (F.C.C. Boyd), January 25, 1946 lot 20."

AMERICA AND NUMISMATICS IN 1866

"In God We Trust" appeared for the first time on silver denominations from the quarter to the dollar and on gold from the $5 to the $20. The nickel five-cent piece, authorized under the Act of May 16, 1866, appeared in circulation in the summer. The design featured a shield on the obverse and stars and rays on the reverse. Defying expectations, silver and gold coins continued to be hoarded. The lowest exchange rate for the year was reached on March 24, when $125 in paper was needed to buy $100 in gold coins. The high, on June 18, required $167.75 in paper to buy $100 face value in gold. Speculation in precious metals was intense, and large profits were made by traders.

In May the American Numismatic and Archaeological Society began publishing the *American Journal of Numismatics (AJN)*, the first general magazine in the field of United States coins, tokens, and paper money. This continued to be issued for the next four years, but was never profitable. The magazine was transferred to the Boston Numismatic Society, which changed its frequency from monthly to quarterly, after which it was issued well into the 20th century, serving as a record of many events.

The auction of the Francis Hoffman Collection conducted by W. Elliot Woodward prompted this review in the June issue of the *AJN*, reflecting the tenor of the current market and postwar uncertainty. No longer were Washington pieces the darling series of investors:

> The sale of coins April 24–27 was tolerably successful when judged by the standard of other recent sales, but compared with former ones was far from encouraging. In Mr. Hoffman's collection were many very desirable pieces, some of which brought scarcely more than nominal prices, while, in a few instances the bids exceeded those on any former occasion. A noticeable feature of the sale was the falling off in the prices of the rare gold coins . . . The Washingtons sold at ruinously low prices. The Naked Bust [today called the *Roman Head*] which sold in the McCoy sale for $480, brought, in this, no more than $220. A rare medal in silver, weighing nearly four and one half ounces, with fine bust of Washington and inscription commemorative of his birth and death, sold for $12, though the bidder was authorized to pay as high as $150. Pattern pieces, which have been constantly going down since the United States Mint passed into the hands of the present *family*, showed the actual falling off only in a more marked degree. For rare store cards and catalogues quite an eager competition existed.

The last sentence reflected a truism that is still in effect today: When one sector of the market fades, another is in the ascendancy. Collectors continue to collect and dealers to deal, but with different emphasis.

The Civil Rights Act, passed by Congress on April 9 over President Andrew Johnson's veto, decreed that all native-born Americans would automatically become citizens, *Indians excepted.* In the meantime the rebuilding of the South, termed Reconstruction, was well underway, replete with many injustices and scandals. Carpetbaggers, as they were called, came from the North, carrying few possessions in a cloth bag, or similar unit, and set themselves up in prominent positions in the disarrayed governments of cities, counties, and states. Western Union acquired two telegraph companies and became the first significant industrial monopoly in the United States. Pithole, an oil town in Pennsylvania, was connected by petroleum pipeline to a rail head five miles distant, the first such pipeline in the United States.

1866

Circulation-Strike Mintage
7,100

Proof Mintage
30

Enlarged 2x
(actual size 15 mm)

Whitman Coin Guide (WCG™)

VF-20	EF-40	AU-50	AU-55	MS-60	MS-63	MS-65	PF-63	PF-65
$375	$500	$725	$875	$1,150	$2,250	$3,500	$8,500	$14,000

CERTIFIED POPULATIONS

G-4–EF-45	AU-50–58	MS-60–62	MS-63	MS-64	MS-65	MS-66	MS-67	MS-68–70
6	28	41	21	23	14	12	9	5
PF-50–58	**PF-60–62**	**PF-63**	**PF-64**	**PF-65**	**PF-66**	**PF-67**	**PF-68–70**	
0	2	3	8	11	16	4	0	

Key to Collecting. The 1866 is another gold dollar from rarity-spangled mid-1860s. Whenever a nice one comes up for auction, the cataloger has the justifiable opportunity to be quite enthusiastic. A flurry of gem offerings occurred in the 1980s and 1990s, before which coins in such high grades were viewed as especially rare. Since then, "trophy rarities" of all kinds have played musical chairs, being frequently reoffered in the sale room. Auction opportunities to acquire a choice or gem coin are now frequent, but were once very occasional. This translates into *opportunity* if you are seeking one.

Estimated Total Population (Mint State). 140 to 180, of which perhaps half are choice and gem specimens. *Certified population, MS-63 and higher:* 85.

Estimated Total Population (Circulated Grades). 190 to 240. Most are in grades of EF and AU. The 1866 in any grade is a highly desirable coin and has been for many generations.

Characteristics of Striking and Die Notes. Striae are seen on nearly all high-grade coins, these being from the die-preparation process, and especially prominent on earlier strikings. Later, striae wore away on the dies or were removed by relapping (a process which in turn either created other striae, or resulted in a prooflike surface, depending on the procedure).

Nearly all circulation strikes show clashmarks. On many pieces these are very heavy, especially on the reverse, including the word LIBERTY in raised letters below the date, transferred by clashing from the obverse inscription in Miss Liberty's headband. Still other coins are from relapped dies, with most of the clashmarks gone on the obverse and all gone on the reverse, but with extensive die striae.

Some are highly prooflike and are difficult to distinguish from Proofs unless you check the identifying features.

NUMISMATIC NOTES

Die Data. 1866 four-digit date logotype: The digits 18 are slightly farther apart than the others. The 1 leans right. The 8 has nicely rounded curves, and its top interior space is very slightly smaller than its bottom interior space. Both 6s have thick sides, thin top curves, thin bottoms, and heavy balls very close to their top curves. Both lean slightly right. The last 6 can appear to be slightly larger, and to have a larger interior space at the bottom. This logotype was used on all gold dollar dies and also on *half dime* dies.

Mintage. 1,100 were delivered on January 27 and 6,000 on February 9.

Auction Information. Selected auction offerings, mainly emphasizing prooflike coins, were made from a very wide field.

> *1900–06: Parcel Sale* (Lyman H. Low), lot 663: "1866 Uncirculated, brilliant, equal to Proof. Very rare." Realized $6.50. An early mention in a long list of auction entries over the years that reveals prooflike Mint State coins are sometimes virtually indistinguishable from Proofs.
>
> *1901–07: Dr. Ellwood E. Hopkins and Harrison Collections* (S.H. and Henry Chapman), lot 525: "1866 Uncirculated. Brilliant mint luster resembling a Proof. Beautiful specimen and very rare."
>
> *1904–04: John G. Mills Collection* (S.H. and Henry Chapman), lot 646: "1866 Uncirculated, with Proof surface. Rare." Realized $6.
>
> *1926–02: Cary, McGill, Heaton, Havemeyer, Kinports, Craddock, Little, Morris, and Haller Collections* (Thomas L. Elder), lot 1793: "1866 In brilliant Mint State, almost equal to a Proof struck at the mint. I regard this date just as rare as 1864. In a lot of 4,000 gold dollars examined by me there was only one dated 1866. This proves beyond a doubt its great rarity."
>
> *1997–04: John J. Pittman Collection, Part I* (David W. Akers Numismatics, Inc.), lot 901: "1866, Gem Uncirculated. A magnificent specimen with full prooflike fields, a very sharp strike, and beautiful light to medium orange gold toning. There are a few faint hairlines in the field behind Liberty's head, but the overall quality of the coin is outstanding, and this certainly ranks as one of the finest specimens known of this rare date. Obviously this coin is a very early strike, minted before the dies clashed, and it is very similar in overall appearance to a Proof. Even JJP was unsure, since on his coin envelope he has written, 'Sent to Abe (Kosoff) for checking.' apparently to get Kosoff's opinion . . . Note: In Breen's *Encyclopedia*, he states, 'Proofs have tops of wreath joined, business strikes have tops of wreath separate." The latter part

of his statement is not correct, as this specimen clearly shows, so one should not use the Breen criterion for determining the Proof or Uncirculated status of an 1866 gold dollar. The easy and decisive test is to look at the leading feather of the headdress. All 1866 Proofs were struck using the Proof obverse die of 1862–1873, which shows a distinct polished area within the first feather. On all business strikes, the feather is 'solid.'"

Proofs

Estimated Total Population and Key to Collecting. 15 to 20. The number of extant pieces can only be a guess, due to many past offerings of prooflike coins as full Proofs. The Garrett and Eliasberg coins each had dark spots.

Mintage. 25 Proofs were delivered on January 15 and a further five on June 8. Whether this constitutes the entire production is not known.

Die Data and Notes. There are two obverse dies used with a common reverse die to create the two varieties of 1866. The Proof-only die was used for nearly all Proofs from 1862 to 1876 (only 1874, some 1876 issues, and this date used a different obverse than that of 1862). For the characteristics of the first obverse die, see information under Proof gold dollars of 1862. The Bass Collection Sale (Part III, lot 43) contained an example of the second obverse die used for a few 1866 Proofs. In that sale, the author noted: "John Dannreuther notes that this Proof is from an obverse die that is not usually associated with Proofs of this era. Interestingly, Harry Bass had noted on his insert that this coin matched the ANS specimen, which is in their complete run of Proof gold dollars from 1854–1889." Besides the ANS coin, another example of the second obverse die was the Proof with a perfect first plume feather; a little "pool" of Proof surface below the earlobe; and a die crack from the center of a dentil to the top of the E (UNITED). This appeared in the Bowers and Merena Galleries sale of November 2002.

Auction Information (Proofs). A sample of offerings from a wide field:

1911–03: 48th Public Sale, William H. Woodin Collection (Thomas L. Elder), lot 879: "1866. Brilliant, glittering Proof. Judging by the number of times this piece has been offered at public sale, it is as rare as either 1863, 1864 or 1865. Collectors should value it accordingly. Very rare." Realized $16.

1921–02: Dr. G.F.E. Wilharm Collection (B. Max Mehl), lot 21: "1866 Brilliant Proof, sharp. Extremely rare, nearly as rare as the '63 or '64, and in Proof condition should bring equally as much." Realized $18.

1992–02: Ed Trompeter Collection (Superior), lot 12: "1866 Grade Choice Brilliant Proof. Only the one variety; few faint die file marks slant down to the left from curl above and left of ear. Description Minor hairlines on the obverse, but these are more than made up for by the deep mirrors . . . In all, 7 examples have been graded by PCGS (none by NGC), with the finest being a Proof-66."

1999–10: Harry W. Bass Jr. Collection, Part II (Bowers and Merena Galleries), lot 163: "1866 Proof-63 (PCGS) . . . Just 30 Proofs were minted with perhaps half that number surviving today. Walter Breen noted in his *Encyclopedia* that Proofs have the top of the wreath joined while business strikes have the wreath separated. In the present sale, however, both the currently offered Proof and the business strike also offered in this sale have the wreath joined at top. Whether or not the tips of the wreath are joined or separated has nothing to do with a change in the design or even a slight variation. Rather, the master die had the wreath tips joined. If impressed to less than its deepest extent into the working die, certain low-relief features on the master die would not be transferred to the working die, and the wreath might appear open on such a working die. Alternatively, a working die that was deeply impressed by the master die and which had the tips joined, could have the tips later separated if it was relapped, that process causing the grinding away of lower relief features. It is seen in the latter instance that a given die could exist in two different states—with tips joined and with tips separate, if the die was relapped after some use. These same general comments can be extended to the $3 gold series as well, that denomination having a similar reverse design. Purchased from Stanley Kesselman, October 5, 1967."

AMERICA AND NUMISMATICS IN 1867

There had been several changes in the Mint directorship since 1861, when James Ross Snowden had been replaced by James Pollock. Now, in April 1867, Dr. Richard Henry Linderman was named to the post. Linderman, an avid numismatist, was in the enviable position to make his own rarities, and that he did with reckless abandon. He served two terms: April 1867 to April 1869 and April 1873 to December 1878. Linderman, a medical doctor, was a brilliant man, but, as was the case with every other Mint director since Snowden in the 1850s, he could not resist the temptation of secretly making restrikes and rarities. This practice continued under others until the summer of 1885. Philadelphia dealer John W. Haseltine, son-in-law of William K. Idler, was the main sales outlet from Mint officers to the rare coin market.

A new portrait lathe, the invention of J.C. Hill in England, was purchased by the Mint and used to reduce engravers' models to coin-hub diameter, leading to the making of dies. Apparently, this device did not work as well as the Contamin portrait lathe purchased in France and used at the Mint since the late 1830s. In Philadelphia, E.B. Mason Jr., began publishing *Mason's Coin and Stamp Collector's Magazine*, which endured until 1873 and was later followed by other titles from Mason. It was the first significant dealer-published journal of importance in the United States.

On February 9, the editor of the *Portsmouth* (New Hampshire) *Journal* reported his visit to a local bank, where as a trustee he spent two hours observing activities, including this: "It fell to our lot last week . . . to examine the assets of the bank and ascertain whether the institution really holds all the money, stocks, and securities which are reported on the book of the treasurer. The heavy iron door of the vault was thrown open, and the committee being seated at a large table, the contents of the vault shelves were removed and placed before them. It was no glittering display of the precious metals, for of silver there was a single dime, of gold a half eagle accompanied by a little dollar was the whole metallic display, except one nickel three-cent piece."

The boundaries of the United States were expanded greatly with the purchase of Alaska from Russia for $7,200,000, as negotiated by Secretary of State William Henry Seward. This amounted to less than two cents per acre. Nebraska was admitted to the Union, becoming the 37th state. The Midwest was on the cusp of an era of settlement and exploitation, which would continue until the late 1880s. Bison in vast numbers roamed the plains, furnishing great sport for hunters, including those who fired rifles from the windows of railroad passenger cars. The economy in that area was generally strong, as more settlers moved in and built settlements and towns.

1867

Circulation-Strike Mintage
5,200

Proof Mintage
50

Enlarged 2x
(actual size 15 mm)

Whitman Coin Guide (WCG™)

VF-20	EF-40	AU-50	AU-55	MS-60	MS-63	MS-65	PF-63	PF-65
$425	$550	$725	$875	$1,200	$2,100	$4,000	$7,000	$14,000

CERTIFIED POPULATIONS

G-4–EF-45	AU-50–58	MS-60–62	MS-63	MS-64	MS-65	MS-66	MS-67	MS-68–70
4	40	43	10	18	7	8	5	3
PF-50–58	PF-60–62	PF-63	PF-64	PF-65	PF-66	PF-67	PF-68–70	
1	8	2	6	5	0	0	0	

Key to Collecting. The 1867 is another in the lineup of rare gold dollars of this era. As is true of other rarities after 1863, memorable gems have been offered multiple times, although sometimes these offerings constitute recycling of the same coins. Worn coins are rare as well, an aspect not fully realized by market prices. The rarity of this date is often overlooked.

Estimated Total Population (Mint State). 75 to 110. For the most part, these are of choice quality. Still, in absolute terms these are very rare, and securing one for your collection may entail a wait. *Certified population, MS-63 and higher:* 47.

Estimated Total Population (Circulated Grades). 150 to 200. Most are EF or AU.

Characteristics of Striking and Die Notes. Nearly all 1867 gold dollars are sharply struck, often with wire rims. Most high-grade pieces show clashmarks and striae, the latter from the die preparation process. Some of these include, again, the word LIBERTY below the date on the reverse.

Numismatic Notes

Die Data. 1867 four-digit date logotype: The digits 18 are closely spaced, 86 are slightly wider apart, and 67 slightly wider yet. The 1 has a lower left serif larger than its lower right serif; the base of the 1 is slightly higher than the base of the 8. The top interior of the 8 is slightly larger than its bottom interior, and the 8 leans slightly right. The 6 has a somewhat flattened and heavy left side, and leans slightly right. A fancy 7 shows a particularly large upper left serif, the serif slanting down to the left; the lower right of base of the 7 is squared off rather than a gentle curve. This logotype was used on all dies.

Mintage. Delivery took place on January 24.

Auction Information. Selected offerings from generations past:

1871–10: Jno. A. Nexsen Collection (Edward Cogan), lot 845: "1867 Uncirculated. Very Fine." "Very fine" meant "very nice" in this context.

1905–09: XVIII Mail Auction Sale (Ben G. Green), lot 136: "1867 Uncirculated, has been a Proof. Very rare." Realized $9.25. Green gives us an interesting status transmutation—from Proof to Uncirculated—actually an impossibility.

1921–12: John Story Jenks Collection (Henry Chapman), lot 5834: "1867. Extremely Fine. Very rare; in fact, as far as the number of specimens passing through my hands would indicate, it is equal to 1863, '64, '65 as to rarity."

1923–10: Charles Wellinger Collection (B. Max Mehl), lot 24: "1867 Brilliant Uncirculated, with Proof surface. Nearly equal to a brilliant Proof. Extremely rare."

1963–05: Emerson Gaylord Collection (Mayflower Coin Auctions), lot 51: "1867 Brilliant Uncirculated with full proof-like lustre. A first strike and very choice. A most unusual and interesting pattern of die breaks appear both obverse and reverse. The reverse shows some evidence of the word 'Liberty' transferred through planchet from the obverse. The first example of this variety that your cataloger has ever seen." Maurice M. Gould was the primary cataloger for Mayflower sales.

Proofs

Estimated Total Population and Key to Collecting. 14 to 17. This is a great rarity, a challenger to the elusive 1864 Proof of the same decade.

Mintage. Proofs were minted in two batches, with 25 delivered from the coiner on March 5 and a further 25 on July 2. Despite this, relatively few are known today.

Die Data and Notes. For characteristics of the obverse die, see information under Proof gold dollars of 1862, since the same die was used. David W. Akers has pointed out that on the reverse rim between 6 o'clock and 7 o'clock there is a tiny triangular raised die lump—a feature not seen on any circulation strikes.

Auction Information (Proofs). Selected citations:

1869–09: Edward B. Taylor Collection (Edward Cogan), lot 476: "1867 Dollar beautiful Proof; scarce." Notable mention of scarcity soon after the coin was minted.

1911–03: 48th Public Sale, William H. Woodin Collection (Thomas L. Elder), lot 880: "1867. Proof. Less coined this year than in 1864, and I am unable to find where it has been offered before in this condition. Extremely rare." Tom Elder did not do much looking at other catalogs!

1935–04: E.H. Adams and F.Y. Parker Collection (Thomas L. Elder), lot 1895: "1867 Proof. Very rare in this condition, or any other condition."

1937–05: Dr. Clifton Wheeler, Sigmund Von Lieven and Dr. George Ross Collections (Thomas L. Elder), lot 919: "1867 Brilliant Proof. Very rare gem, first we have had in many years in Proof." "Many years"?

1939–11: William B. Hale Collection (B. Max Mehl), lot 676: "1867 Proof. Extremely rare. I consider it as rare as any of the 60's." Realized $34.

AMERICA AND NUMISMATICS IN 1868

At the Mint, those with possession of appropriate dies continued to make numismatic delicacies. Included were curious varieties of gold dollars, such as Proofs struck in copper and aluminum. Silver and gold coins remained absent from circulation in the East and Midwest, but were widely used on the West Coast. Such pieces were worth a premium in terms of paper money. Liberty Seated silver dollars were made in quantity for the export trade, mainly to merchants in Canton, China.

Reconstruction programs continued in the South, while in the North it was debated whether it would be best to simply seize properties as spoils of war and punish the former Confederate territory, this being called "retribution." In the November election the inflation of value of paper money was a key issue, with Democrats favoring the repaying of old government bonds in Legal Tender bills, while the Republicans, with Civil War hero U.S. Grant as their candidate, felt that the value in gold coins should be given. Grant won. Later historians generally agreed that Grant made a fine military leader but a poor chief executive.

1868

Circulation-Strike Mintage
10,500

Proof Mintage
25+

Enlarged 2x
(actual size 15 mm)

Whitman Coin Guide (WCG™)

VF-20	EF-40	AU-50	AU-55	MS-60	MS-63	MS-65	PF-63	PF-65
$275	$400	$525	$625	$1,100	$2,100	$3,750	$7,500	$13,000

CERTIFIED POPULATIONS

G-4–EF-45	AU-50–58	MS-60–62	MS-63	MS-64	MS-65	MS-66	MS-67	MS-68–70
12	65	67	28	17	8	5	4	5
PF-50–58	PF-60–62	PF-63	PF-64	PF-65	PF-66	PF-67	PF-68–70	
0	3	2	7	5	2	0	0	

Key to Collecting. The 1868 gold dollar is scarce in all grades. Mint State examples are usually in lower ranges, but in recent decades there have been quite a few offerings at the MS-65 level and higher, some doubtless being the same coins reoffered.

Estimated Total Population (Mint State). 100 to 140. Most are in the range of MS-60 to MS-63. Superb gems have been graded all the way to MS-69. *Certified population, MS-63 and higher:* 67.

Estimated Total Population (Circulated Grades). 250 to 450. Without a doubt, it is the most available gold dollar of its immediate era. However, in terms of American numismatics overall, a field of 250 to 450 coins hardly makes a piece common. Most circulated pieces are EF or AU.

Characteristics of Striking and Die Notes. Striking is often sharp, but some specimens show lightness at the higher parts. The luster on high-grade pieces tends to be somewhat satiny, sometimes "greasy," rather than deeply frosty. The "clashed dies problem," endemic among earlier dollars of the decade, seems to have abated in 1868. Most high-grade coins show die striations from the die finish process.

Numismatic Notes

Die Data. 1868 four-digit date logotype: Larger numerals were used than for dies of closely preceding years. The digits 18 are very close together, and 868 are farther apart, and evenly spaced. The 1 has a lower left serif heavier than its lower right serif; it leans slightly right; the bases of 1 and 8 are on same level. Both 8s have top interior spaces ever so slightly smaller than their bottom interior spaces. The first 8 leans slightly right. The 6 is slightly larger and leans slightly right. This logotype was used on all dies.

Mintage. Delivery took place on February 25.

Counterfeits. This gold dollar date has been widely counterfeited. Thousands of fake 1868 dollars were distributed in Europe as early as the 1950s and 1960s. Time was when European banks, curio shops, and even coin dealers (not the better-known ones, however), if they had an American gold dollar or two, were apt to have fakes dated 1868. Authentication or certification is mandatory if you are not knowledgeable. Most fakes trade outside of numismatic circles, including at antique shows, on the Internet, etc., where people with very little knowledge jump at the chance to buy "bargains." Your best protection is to buy examples certified by the leading services.

Auction Information. Selected citations:

> *1885–12: Auction* (H.G. Sampson), lot 579: "1868 Dollar Uncirculated. Mint lustre. Very rare." Realized $1.75.
>
> *1898–09: F.P. Bradish Collection* (Ed. Frossard), lot 528: "1868 Brilliant Mint State, equal to a Proof. Rare." Realized $9.
>
> *1905–09: XVIII Mail Auction Sale* (Ben G. Green), lot 137: "1868 Uncirculated, has been a Proof. Rare." Realized $6. Note the status switch from Proof to Mint State—an impossibility.
>
> *1945–03: William A. Knapp Collection* (B. Max Mehl), lot 888: "1868 Brilliant Uncirculated, almost equal to a Proof, and was originally purchased as a Proof . . ."
>
> *1956–04: Thomas G. Melish and Clinton W. Hester Collections* (A. Kosoff), lot 1784: "1868 Uncirculated gem, proof-like. In fact, it was originally acquired as a Proof."
>
> *1984–07: Auction '84* (Paramount), lot 821: "1868 MS-65+. 100% full strike and extraordinary lustre and color. Very nearly as choice as the Auction '81 specimen or the Brand coin sold last fall and certainly in the top 8 or 10 of all known 1868 gold dollars. Ex McNally Sale (NASCA, 1976), lot 542, where it was described as 'possibly the finest known specimen.'" This was in the era when MS-65 represented just about the ultimate designation used by catalogers; today, the same coin might well grade MS-67 or MS-68.
>
> *2000–11: Harry W. Bass Jr. Collection, Part IV* (Bowers and Merena Galleries), lot 74: "1868 MS-64 . . . According to notes recorded by Harry Bass, the thin vertical scratch on Liberty's neck is actually a die characteristic. Nearly perfect dies with traces of clash marks along Liberty's profile. From Stack's sale of the Shapero Collection, October 1971 lot 708."

Proofs

Estimated Total Population and Key to Collecting. 12 to 16. This is one of the most elusive issues in a decade laden with rarities. No accurate figure will ever be known, for many circulation strikes are highly prooflike, and some have been cataloged as Proofs in the past. Nearly all have the dies misaligned—obverse and reverse in the same direction—but very few auction listings have mentioned this. This coin is also known with the reverse misaligned about 30º (Floyd Starr Collection, Stack's, October 1992).

Mintage. Proofs numbering 25 pieces were delivered on February 20. Probably, others were delivered later.

Die Data and Notes. For characteristics of the obverse die, see information under Proof gold dollars of 1862, since the same die was used. The reverse has the date logotype low, with the 6 above the point of the ribbon and fairly close to it, and with the date slanting down to the right (easily discernible by comparing to the baseline of the letters above it).

Nearly all known Proofs have the dies oriented in the same direction, rather than the customary 180° apart; this is also true of *all* known $3 gold coins of this date. However, the Floyd Starr 1868 Proof gold dollar (Stack's, October 1992, lot 1102) had "reverse die alignment offset right by about 30°." Walter Breen mentioned that Proofs with the correct (180°) orientation exist.

Auction Information (Proofs).

1869–09: Edward B. Taylor Collection (Edward Cogan), lot 477: "1868 Beautiful Proof; scarce." Realized $2.

1884–01: Steigerwalt's Coin Journal (Charles Steigerwalt, Lancaster, Pennsylvania), fixed-price offering: "1868 Gold dollar, Proof impression. $2."

1884–12: 25th Sale, Washington Collection (Dr. George W. Massamore), lot 959: "1868 Proof, rare." Realized $2.10.

1906–05: Harlan P. Smith Collection (S.H. and Henry Chapman), lot 377: "1868 Brilliant Proof. Rare."

1909–11: 34th Public Sale (Thomas L. Elder), lot 510b: "1868 Proof. Very rare."

1911–03: 48th Public Sale, William H. Woodin Collection (Thomas L. Elder), lot 881: "1868. Brilliant Proof. I find but one record of its having been offered outside of a Proof set in this condition. Extremely rare." Realized $13.50. Elder forgot the stand-alone specimen he had offered slightly over a year earlier as lot 510b in his November 1909 sale—and he did not look very far in competitors' catalogs.

1992–10: Floyd T. Starr Collection (Stack's), lot 1102: "1868 Gem Brilliant Proof. Only 25 struck, all on February 20 of the issue . . . Struck from the late state of the obverse, thin die break on neck. Near normal reverse die alignment, offset right by about 30 degrees." This is an interesting and anomalous reverse die alignment.

AMERICA AND NUMISMATICS IN 1869

The branch mint at Carson City, Nevada, under construction for several years, neared completion. By year's end it was set and ready to go, but no dies were on hand. Coinage commenced in 1870, and never included gold dollars. E.B. Mason Jr. issued a sheet titled "Mason's Photographic Gallery of Coin Collectors of the United States, No. 1," with 48 tiny photographs of numismatists, all male, published as a tip-in to *Mason's Coin and Stamp Collectors' Magazine.* Edward Cogan issued three catalogs in 1869, one of them, for the Mortimer MacKenzie Collection in June, being the first in America to have photographic plates. In the same year the *American Journal of Numismatics* issued a photographic plate featuring large copper cents of 1793. Photography had entered the hobby in grand style.

On May 10, 1869, the "golden spike" was driven into a tie, and the Union Pacific and Central Pacific rail lines joined to complete a connection from East to West. The first through-trip passenger cars traveled the line from California to New York in July of the next year. The typical journey took eight days.

Speculation in gold had been a lively trade in New York City ever since the early days of the Civil War. The first of several notable "black days" in financial history occurred on Wall Street on "Black Friday," September 24, 1869, which saw many speculators ruined. Jay Gould, James Fisk, and others, one of whom was President U.S. Grant's brother-in-law, attempted to corner the market on gold. They drove the price up to $162 per ounce, at which point Secretary of the Treasury George Boutwell began to sell government gold holdings to drive down the price.

1869

Circulation-Strike Mintage
5,900

Proof Mintage
25

Enlarged 2x
(actual size 15 mm)

Whitman Coin Guide (WCG™)

VF-20	EF-40	AU-50	AU-55	MS-60	MS-63	MS-65	PF-63	PF-65
$350	$475	$700	$800	$1,200	$2,250	$3,500	$7,500	$13,500

CERTIFIED POPULATIONS

G-4–EF-45	AU-50–58	MS-60–62	MS-63	MS-64	MS-65	MS-66	MS-67	MS-68–70
13	45	65	29	16	9	4	11	5
PF-50–58	PF-60–62	PF-63	PF-64	PF-65	PF-66	PF-67	PF-68–70	
0	2	4	8	3	1	0	0	

Key to Collecting. The 1869 gold dollar is scarce in all grades. Among Mint State examples, some have prooflike fields and may have been struck from Proof dies, but on a regular press using circulation-strike planchets. Auction catalogs and fixed price lists reveal that a supply of Uncirculated 1869 dollars was on hand in early times—unlike certain earlier issues which were gathered here and there, often in worn grades.

Estimated Total Population (Mint State). 130 to 180. Among these are some choice and gem specimens. *Certified population, MS-63 and higher:* 74.

Estimated Total Population (Circulated Grades). 175 to 275, mostly in higher circulated grades challenging the Mint State level. AU pieces are more often seen than are EF examples, and anything graded lower is *very rare* (not that it makes any difference).

Characteristics of Striking and Die Notes. Striking is inconsistent among gold dollars of this date, and many are lightly impressed, especially on the reverse. Some have bulging in the right obverse field. Early impressions of circulation strikes have parallel raised die ridges on the reverse. Slight doubling of the obverse inscriptions and a raised "teardrop" below Miss Liberty's eye are hallmarks of the circulation strikes, but not Proofs.

Numismatic Notes

Die Data. 1869 four-digit date logotype: The date is in larger numerals than for 1868. Digits 18 are nearly touching, with 86 and 69 each slightly farther apart but not by much; on deep impressions they could appear to touch. The 1 has an overly long lower left serif. The upper interior space of the 8 is significantly smaller than its bottom interior space. The 6 has a heavy ball nearly touching the curve below it, and it does touch on deep impressions. The 9 is *not* from an inverted 6 punch used on this die, but from another punch, with a differently shaped interior opening—its ball has a point, and is distinctly separated from the curve. This logotype was used on all dies.

Mintage. Delivery took place on February 15.

Auction Information. Many 1869 dollars have crossed the auction block, quite a few of which have been described as prooflike.

Proofs

Estimated Total Population and Key to Collecting. 12 to 15. Another very rare Proof from a decade in which extreme rarity is the rule for several issues. Auction appearances are often spaced over a period of years (but with some exceptions of clusters of offerings). For years, examples were encountered only when large collections came to market. Today, most are traded apart from collections, often as "trophy coins."

Mintage. Proofs were delivered on February 19 (following the delivery of circulation strikes on February 15). It is not known if this represented the only delivery of Proofs. However, if additional pieces were struck, the number must have been small.

Die Data and Notes. For characteristics of the obverse die see information under Proof gold dollars of 1862, since the same die was used. On the reverse within the wreath there are multiple raised die finish lines.

Auction Information (Proofs). These selections are from dozens reviewed.

> *1888–11: Rev. W. Foster Ely Collection* (Scott Stamp & Coin Company, Ltd.), lot 93: "1869 Proof, scarce." Realized $3.70.
>
> *1911–03: 48th Public Sale, William H. Woodin Collection* (Thomas L. Elder), lot 882: "1869. Proof. Mint record gives for this piece a smaller coinage than 1864. Adams gives only one record of a sale, in Proof condition. Very rare." Realized $23.
>
> *1937–05: Dr. Clifton Wheeler, Sigmund Von Lieven and Dr. George Ross Collections* (Thomas L. Elder), lot 921: "1869 Brilliant Proof. Extremely rare. (We haven't had one in many years)."
>
> *1939–11: William B. Hale Collection* (B. Max Mehl), lot 675: "1866 Variety with light die breaks on obverse; apparently from a very early impression of the die. Proof; perfect and sharp with wire edge." One of the earliest descriptions encountered with die details. Perhaps a prooflike circulation strike.

AMERICA AND NUMISMATICS IN 1870

In the *Annual Report of the Director of the Mint*, 1870, James Pollock commented on the continuing absence of certain coins in circulation:

> The Mint work is necessarily hindered and restricted by the continued suspension of specie payments. We are doing less than was done many years ago, when there was a much smaller population and far less wealth . . . Emerging from a tremendous Civil War which shook every social interest to the very foundation, it is no wonder that our currency continues in an abnormal condition. Most of our people rarely get the sight of a gold or silver coin.
>
> They know, by the state of the money market, the relation between the precious metals and current paper notes, and they must be kept advised of this to understand what is the real value of those notes; but the gold by which the measure is made, is almost as much out of sight as the sacred pound troy, or kilogram, carefully guarded as the final resort. But the people at large will never give up the idea that the real money is made of gold and silver; made of definite weight and fineness, and certified by government stamp. They will use paper, and its use will increase; its imponderable property makes it a very great convenience. Still it is only paper; a little fire or water destroys it; and if it does not bear a market relation to gold, it may be kept safe, and yet will buy nothing.

In San Francisco the cornerstone was laid for a new and long-overdue Mint building. Gold dollars were struck there, the first branch mint issues since 1861, and the last for the remainder of the series.

The decennial census of this year placed the population of the United States at 38,558,371. America continued to recover from the effects of the Civil War, but there was much dissatisfaction and distress with the Reconstruction program in the South. The Democratic donkey was born on January 15, 1870, in a cartoon in *Harper's Weekly*. The arrival of the Republican elephant would not happen until 1874.

1870

Circulation-Strike Mintage
6,300

Proof Mintage
35

Enlarged 2x
(actual size 15 mm)

Whitman Coin Guide (WCG™)

VF-20	EF-40	AU-50	AU-55	MS-60	MS-63	MS-65	PF-63	PF-65
$300	$425	$625	$750	$1,100	$2,100	$3,500	$7,250	$13,500

CERTIFIED POPULATIONS

G-4–EF-45	AU-50–58	MS-60–62	MS-63	MS-64	MS-65	MS-66	MS-67	MS-68–70
11	81	77	30	36	12	5	11	4
PF-50–58	**PF-60–62**	**PF-63**	**PF-64**	**PF-65**	**PF-66**	**PF-67**	**PF-68–70**	
1	6	3	4	6	1	0	0	

Key to Collecting. The 1870 is yet another gold dollar in a lineup of scarce and rare issues. The wonder is how and why these seldom-seen coins have escaped the widespread attention of the collecting community. Except, perhaps, for some landmark high-grade certified coins, prices are eminently reasonable. Most examples have good eye appeal.

Estimated Total Population (Mint State). 150 to 220, mostly in the range of MS-60 to MS-63, although superb gems are known, as reflected by the certification data. *Certified population, MS-63 and higher:* 99.

Estimated Total Population (Circulated Grades). 130 to 180. Most are EF or AU. Worn specimens are rarer than Mint State examples.

Characteristics of Striking and Die Notes. The obverse die used to make circulation strikes was left over from 1869 and has minor repunching on the O (OF) (see Breen, *Encyclopedia*, 1988). Usually seen well struck on the obverse, but somewhat lightly defined on the reverse. On some examples, the reverse is highly prooflike—probably from relapping the die.

Numismatic Notes

Die Data. 1870 four-digit date logotype: The date is in thin figures. Numerals 18 and 70 are slightly closer together than are 87. The top serif of the 1 is slightly longer than the lower left serif; the base of the 1 is higher than the base of the 8. The 8 has a smaller top interior space than bottom space, and leans slightly right. A fancy 7 has a rounded base. The 0 leans slightly right (best determinable by noting the orientation of the interior space). This logotype was used on all dies of the Philadelphia and San Francisco mints.

Mintage. Delivery took place on January 20.

Auction Information. As is the case with most Philadelphia Mint gold dollars of this era, listings tend to be basic—with not much in the way of historical information or research notes, but there are occasional exceptions. Many have been described as prooflike, with the Woodin specimen (sold by Thomas L. Elder in March 1911) listed as: "1870. Uncirculated, reverse Proof. Very rare."

Proofs

Estimated Total Population and Key to Collecting. 12 to 15. This is one of the rarer dates of the era. Though it isn't the case for certain other gold dollar dates of the era, in 1870 a number of well-known early numismatists acquired Mint State coins instead of Proofs. Mint records (as examined by R.W. Julian) reveal that 25 Proofs were delivered on February 3, followed by 10 more on June 1; although the first group was probably not depleted. The number actually sold is not known.

Die Data and Notes. For characteristics of the obverse die, see information under Proof gold dollars of 1862, since the same die was used.

Auction Information (Proofs). Several selections:

> *1876–06: Collection of Gold, Silver and Copper Coins and Medals* (Edward Cogan), lot 920: "1870 Proof dollar. Scarce." This comment indicates that scarcely six years after its mintage, the Proof gold dollar of 1870 was considered scarce—although Cogan often applied such terms as *scarce* and *rare* indiscriminately, even to common coins.

1912–06: George H. Earle Jr. Collection (Henry Chapman), lot 2628: "1870 Proof. Very rare in this condition." For many different gold dollar dates, Earle acquired Proof examples as well as high-grade circulation strikes, considering each to be a challenge to collect.

1938–03: A.R. Gray and D.P. Dickie Collections (Thomas L. Elder), lot 2775: "1870 A brilliant Proof. Probably not over fifteen examples struck in Proof state this year . . ." *Later offering: 1992–10: Floyd T. Starr Collection* (Stack's), lot 1104: "1870 Brilliant Proof. Only 35 struck. Both surfaces fully brilliant, devices lightly frosty. Mint flash in first feather of headdress, ERTY on coronet band, hollows of leaves in wreath. Lightly hairlined. Reverse die lapped, venation in uppermost leaves nearly gone now. Very rare . . . From Thomas Elder's March 23, 1938 sale."

1947–06: Will W. Neil Collection (B. Max Mehl), lot 2319: "1870, Brilliant Proof, sharp, with broad borders on obverse. Rare date in rare condition." *Later offering: 1997–04: John J. Pittman Collection, Part I* (David W. Akers Numismatics, Inc.), lot 905: "1870 Proof. 35 Proofs minted. Deep mirror fields and attractive, but irregular coppery gold color. Light to moderate hairlines throughout the fields, and one scrape at the tops of AT in STATES . . . Very rare with only 14–17 Proofs still in existence. Purchased from B. Max Mehl's sale of the Will W. Neil Collection."

1870-S

Circulation-Strike Mintage
3,000 (possibly 2,000 without mintmark)

Enlarged 2x
(actual size 15 mm)

Whitman Coin Guide (WCG™)

VF-20	EF-40	AU-50	AU-55	MS-60	MS-63	MS-65
$475	$800	$1,250	$1,600	$2,700	$7,000	$17,500

CERTIFIED POPULATIONS

G-4–EF-45	AU-50–58	MS-60–62	MS-63	MS-64	MS-65	MS-66	MS-67	MS-68–70
12	45	45	6	8	9	1	0	0

Key to Collecting. The 1870-S dollars were a popular curiosity in circulation in San Francisco in the 1870s and 1880s, and jewelers and others kept an eye out for them, resulting in many being saved. Quite a few were employed in the making of pins, brooches, etc. (these are not included in certification data today).

Although 3,000 of these were coined, it is likely that 2,000 lacked the S mintmark (see notes below). Accordingly, in terms of apparent distribution, 2,000 should be deducted from the San Francisco mintage and added to the Philadelphia total.

Estimated Total Population (Mint State). 35 to 50. Most are MS-60 to MS-62. The number of *different* specimens of the 1870-S dollar known to exist is somewhat of a puzzlement. This issue has had much publicity over the years, due to its unique status as the only mintmarked gold dollar after 1861. *Certified population, MS-63 and higher:* 24.

Estimated Total Population (Circulated Grades). 90 to 120. Most are in EF or AU grades. Some of the most important American cabinets have lacked a full Mint State coin. In addition to these, perhaps just as many others exist in impaired grades from use as jewelry. Many listings for such jewelry pieces have appeared in catalogs over the years.

Characteristics of Striking and Die Notes. Typically well struck.

Numismatic Notes

Die Data. In December 1869, two pairs of 1870-dated dies were sent from Philadelphia (where all dies were made, including for branch mints) to San Francisco, but inadvertently lacked the "S" mintmark. On May 14, 1870, this telegram was sent by the superintendent of the San Francisco Mint and received the same day in Philadelphia:

> LETTER S OMITTED ON ONE AND THREE DOLLAR DIES SENT TO THIS BRANCH FOR THIS YEAR. 2000 PIECES COINED. CAN THEY BE ISSUED. O.H. LAGRANGE SUPT.

Soon thereafter, two more dies, these with the S, were shipped by transcontinental railroad and arrived on May 28.[54] Apparently, only one reverse die was used, with the S slightly repunched on the lower part. On May 27, the S-less gold dollar die and the $3 die in which an S had been cut by hand (in order to create an 1870-S $3 for placing in the San Francisco Mint cornerstone), were shipped back to Philadelphia.

Today, it is not known whether the 2,000 S-less gold dollars struck in San Francisco were melted, or if they were released. If the latter, then the mintage figure of 3,000 1870-S dollars would consist of 2,000 that appeared to be Philadelphia Mint coins (without mintmark) and only 1,000 appearing as 1870-S coins.

Last San Francisco Gold Dollar. The 1870-S was the only San Francisco Mint gold dollar made after 1860. Unlike the situation in the East and Midwest, where gold dollars were held by the Treasury Department and paid out only when a premium was offered, in the West, gold dollars readily circulated at par. It seems likely that the 1870-S gold dollars were turned into the channels of commerce, where most acquired light wear.

Heaton Writes About S-Mint Dollars (1893). In 1893, Augustus G. Heaton, in his monograph, *Mint Marks*, offered the first in-depth study of branch mint issues. For gold dollars he commented: "The San Francisco issues are seven: "1854, '56, '57, '58, '59, '60, and '70, all being obtainable but the latter, which is excessively rare and the only one of the gold dollar mintmarks which we do not possess."

Notes on Contemplated 1871-S Coinage. Two pairs of dies for 1871-S coinage were received at San Francisco on December 16, 1870, but remained unused.

Auction Information. Below is a selection from many appearances, in the early years to the 1950s. The adjective *excessively* has been used excessively in many descriptions.

> *1903–07: A.C. Muma, Thomas Adam, George Giffen, and E.M. Turner Collections* (Lyman H. Low), lot 349: "1870-S Very Fine. Excessively rare. Auction records in 7 years, 2 fine specimens, $110, $105." Realized $71.
>
> *1905–09: XVIII Mail Auction Sale* (Ben G. Green), lot 140: "1870-S Uncirculated. Excessively rare. Has brought $110 at auction." Realized $125.
>
> *1906–05: XXIII Public Auction Sale, A.L. Schuyler Collection* (Ben G. Green), lot 337: "1870-S Very Fine. Faint solder spot on edge. Excessively rare."

1907: Superb Collection of United States and Foreign Gold, Silver and Copper Coins, Fractional Currency, Etc., Fixed Price List (Elmer S. Sears), lot 562: "1870 San Francisco Mint. Beautiful, Uncirculated impression in full mint bloom. Absolutely the finest specimen of this great rarity known. Excessively rare. $150."

1907–03: David S. Wilson Collection (S.H. Chapman), lot 308: "1870-S Extremely Fine. Excessively rare." Realized $50.

1911–03: 48th Public Sale, William H. Woodin Collection (Thomas L. Elder), lot 883: "1870-S. Uncirculated, mint luster. Record for this date made in one of my recent sales, $137.50. The second rarest gold dollar." Realized $100.

1922–12: H.E. Rawson, Dr. A. de Yoanna, and David Strasser Collections (B. Max Mehl), lot 90: "1870-S Uncirculated, with bright mint luster, considerable Proof surface, the obverse could be passed as a Proof. Excessively rare and valuable, especially so in this wonderful condition. Old record well over $100." Realized $105.

1932–04: Sale 278, Collection of U.S. Gold, Silver and Copper Coins (J.C. Morgenthau & Co.), lot 242: "1870-S About Uncirculated, Proof surface. Exceedingly Rare."

1939–10: 45th Catalog Sale (Barney Bluestone), lot 975: "1870-S Unc. Brilliant gem. One of the very best known. Excessively Rare in this magnificent state of preservation."

1943–11: 79th Catalog Sale (Barney Bluestone), lot 99: "1870-S Uncirculated. Considered one of our very rarest gold dollars. Auction record of years ago $135. In my 35 years of experience in the numismatic business, I have handled more 1861-D gold dollars than the 1870-S."

1944–02: Belden E. Roach Collection (B. Max Mehl), lot 1117: "1870-S The most beautiful and perfect specimen of this, the rarest gold dollar of this mint, that I know of. It is a perfect brilliant Proof. Raised borders. Perfect in every respect. It is supposed that no Proofs were struck at the branch mints. This may and may not be true, but this specimen is certainly everything I claim for it as above described. It is the most remarkable specimen of this rarity I have ever seen, and as such, it is worthy of a new high record for it." This must have been a truly fantastic coin.

1956–11: 48th Sale, Thomas L. Gaskill Collection (New Netherlands Coin Co.), lot 900: "1870-S. Brilliant Uncirculated, proof-like lustre. The hypercritical perfectionist with a glass will see a few minute abrasions, doubtless inflicted in the bag, and an insignificant rim bruise or so. This coin is still the equal of any that we have seen, including two described as 'gems.' As dealer Kosoff said, in his catalog of the Melish collection: 'Has record, in lesser condition, to $300.' In addition to the EF-AU Melish piece at $245, we have located sixteen other records for the 1870-S gold dollar. Two had loops removed, one was a plugged piece that made the round for years, and only three were described as brilliant Uncirculated. One of these was really nice, that being the 'World's Greatest Collection' example sold in 1946." An inadvertent reflection of the depth, or lack thereof, of Walter Breen's reference library; 16 earlier citations found by him constitute but *a small fraction* of the public auction appearances before that time. In the 1950s, Breen stood almost alone in publishing auction catalog information that bespoke scholarship, and few questioned his statements.

AMERICA AND NUMISMATICS IN 1871

The Act of March 3, 1871, endeavored to end a glut of bronze cents and two-cent pieces by revising their legal tender status, limited at just 4¢ per transaction, and making them exchangeable for Legal Tender currency when presented in amounts of $20 or more. It provided for the melting of millions of unwanted two-cent pieces as well as worn Indian cents, to be recoined into new cents, which happened in a significant way beginning in 1873.

In 1871 the average annual wage in America was $415, rising to $418 in 1872 and falling back to $401 in 1873. During the next decade the average annual wage remained lower and did not reach $418 again until the year 1900. In approximate terms, $1 in 1871 was equivalent to about $100 today. So many double eagles were sailing off to foreign ports, where they were melted and converted into other coins, that Secretary of the Treasury George S. Boutwell decreed that these could no longer be exported, and that only small denominations could be shipped abroad. This caused a great outcry, and the policy was soon abandoned.

In the South, blacks continued to be second-class citizens, at the mercy of whites in most business, educational, and social situations. Congress declared that Indian tribes had no further status and were simply wards of the government, and that no more treaties would be made with them. By this point, white men had broken every important treaty ever made and had driven most Native Americans from their home territories. On October 8 and 9 in Chicago, a cow owned by Mrs. O'Leary kicked a lantern—so legend has it, or whatever the cause—a fire ravaged over three square miles of the downtown business district.

1871

Circulation-Strike Mintage
3,900

Proof Mintage
30

Enlarged 2x
(actual size 15 mm)

Whitman Coin Guide (WCG™)

VF-20	EF-40	AU-50	AU-55	MS-60	MS-63	MS-65	PF-63	PF-65
$300	$425	$575	$675	$1,000	$2,000	$3,500	$7,250	$15,000

CERTIFIED POPULATIONS

G-4–EF-45	AU-50–58	MS-60–62	MS-63	MS-64	MS-65	MS-66	MS-67	MS-68–70
10	40	63	34	38	16	10	6	9
PF-50–58	**PF-60–62**	**PF-63**	**PF-64**	**PF-65**	**PF-66**	**PF-67**	**PF-68–70**	
0	1	1	3	2	1	0	1	

Key to Collecting. As the mintage might suggest, the 1871 gold dollar is rare at all levels. Most are in Mint State, some of which have been run through the certification services multiple times. The eye appeal is usually quite good.

Estimated Total Population (Mint State). 160 to 210. This coin is elusive in Mint State, but not a great rarity. *Certified population, MS-63 and higher:* 111.

Estimated Total Population (Circulated Grades). 110 to 160. AU is the usual grade. Auction data suggest that worn pieces are rarer than Mint State ones.

Characteristics of Striking and Die Notes. Most high-grade coins are quite prooflike, giving rise to certain of them being called, in the days before certified grading, full "Proofs." On lustrous examples, a little "Proof" patch is seen below Miss Liberty's ear.

Typically, gold dollars of this date are somewhat lightly struck at the center of the reverse, including at the 87 of the date, and on the obverse, at the hair above Miss Liberty's forehead. This was probably due to incorrect die spacing.

NUMISMATIC NOTES

Die Data. 1871 four-digit date logotype: The digits 18 and 71 are very close together, but the 87 are much farther apart. The base of the first 1 is slightly high; its lower right serif is slightly longer than its lower left serif. The top interior of the 8 is slightly smaller than the bottom interior, and the 8 leans slightly right. The second 1 is similar to the first 1. This logotype was used on all dies.

Mintage. Circulation strikes were delivered on February 15, 1871.

Auction Information. Listings are as expected for a gold dollar of this era: adjectives denoting scarcity have been used with frequency, many have been described as prooflike or even purchased as Proofs, and in recent times ultra-grade coins have commanded lengthy descriptions showcasing this aspect.

PROOFS

Estimated Total Population and Key to Collecting. 9 to 11. The 1871 is a landmark rarity—a focal point of Proof gold dollars of the era—sharing the limelight with the Proof 1874. Proofs were delivered on February 20. Based upon the rarity today, it is likely that no more than 20 were sold. As is true of all Proofs of this decade, offerings are few and far between in the marketplace. In the past, many prooflike circulation strikes have been offered as "Proof."

Die Data and Notes. For characteristics of the obverse die, see information under Proof gold dollars of 1862, since the same die was used. This supersedes Breen's commentary (*Proof,* 1989) that 1871 and 1872 Proof gold dollars were from the same obverse die. He did not mention the same die's other uses.

Auction Information (Proofs). The dozens of auction citations located basically described the grade and rarity. In recent decades, die characteristics (as explained above) have been part of some listings, as have population reports.

AMERICA AND NUMISMATICS IN 1872

At the Mint, the production of many different varieties of pattern coins continued, some of the best specimens being kept by Mint officers and employees and secretly filtered into the market. Accordingly, numismatists had no way to obtain such prizes as the 1872

Amazonian silver and gold (including the gold dollar) by Chief Engraver William Barber, except to try to buy them from John W. Haseltine or another favored dealer. Mintages of many series, including Indian cents, two-cent pieces, silver trimes, and lower denomination gold, were low. Specie payments continued in suspension, and by now many children had grown to adulthood without ever seeing a Liberty Seated silver or Liberty Head gold coin.

An equine plague known as the Great Epizoötic swept through the East and killed an estimated four million horses. In some cities, men were employed to draw rail cars on the streets. In November a great fire ravaged Boston and destroyed an estimated 766 buildings, the greatest conflagration ever for a New England city. President U.S. Grant, who had turned in a dull performance, stood for re-election and triumphed over Horace Greeley, editor of *The New York Tribune*.

1872

Circulation-Strike Mintage
3,500

Proof Mintage
30

Enlarged 2x
(actual size 15 mm)

Whitman Coin Guide (WCG™)

VF-20	EF-40	AU-50	AU-55	MS-60	MS-63	MS-65	PF-63	PF-65
$300	$400	$575	$700	$1,000	$2,250	$4,000	$7,500	$15,000

CERTIFIED POPULATIONS

G-4–EF-45	AU-50–58	MS-60–62	MS-63	MS-64	MS-65	MS-66	MS-67	MS-68–70
24	52	38	21	29	6	3	10	3
PF-50–58	**PF-60–62**	**PF-63**	**PF-64**	**PF-65**	**PF-66**	**PF-67**	**PF-68–70**	
2	5	2	5	8	3	3	0	

Key to Collecting. All 1872 gold dollars are rare. Most are at high AU levels or low Mint State categories. Superb gems are in the minority. Nearly all have excellent eye appeal. Many are highly prooflike.

Estimated Total Population (Mint State). 110 to 150, with MS-62 to MS-64 being typical grades. Gem pieces are rare, although over the years some of the "name" collections sold at auction have included them. Today, certified coins reach the MS-69 mark. Likely, as time progresses, some ultra high-grade coins will move up to even higher designations. *Certified population, MS-63 and higher:* 73.

Estimated Total Population (Circulated Grades). 110 to 160, most of which are in higher grades such as AU.

Characteristics of Striking and Die Notes. This date usually is found very well struck, a contrast to gold dollars of the year before. This simply means that during the production of these pieces, the dies were spaced closely together, so that the metal from the planchet flowed in both directions to completely fill the recesses in the obverse and reverse dies.

Many if not most circulation strikes have DO (DOLLAR) slightly filled in. Some high-grade coins have prooflike surfaces, enough to be mistaken for full Proofs (unless the die characteristics are examined).

Numismatic Notes

Die Data. 1872 four-digit date logotype: The date is in small, heavy numerals. The digits 18 are close together, 87 widest apart, and 72 in-between. The 2 is significantly low. The 1 has a heavy upright, heavy flag, and short bottom serifs; its base is slightly higher than the base of the 8. The top interior of the 8 is about the same size as the bottom interior, and the 8 leans right; its base slightly lower than the base of 72. The 2 is fancy, with small ball at the upper left close to the curve below (and touching it on some die impressions); its curved base has a small spur at the lower left bottom of the curve. This logotype was used on all dies.

Mintage. Three deliveries were made, on March 18 (1,000), October 21 (500), and December 18 (2,000).

Auction Information. Many coins have been described as prooflike, some as Proofs. An example of the last is provided by lot 5839 sold by Henry Chapman in December 1921 as part of the John Story Jenks Collection: "1872. Brilliant Proof, slightly hairmarked, small dent in center of edge swells the beading on border on lower edge of reverse the size of a pin head. Very rare." This descended to Floyd T. Starr, whose collection was auctioned by Stack's in October 1992, with this description: "Lot 1108: "1872 Choice Brilliant Uncirculated, prooflike."

In the same vein, in March 1945 the William A. Knapp Collection coin was described by B. Max Mehl: "Lot 892: 1872 Uncirculated with Proof surface, originally purchased as a Proof."

Proofs

Estimated Total Population and Key to Collecting. 14 to 18. The 1872 Proof dollar is extremely rare. Some of those offered as "Proof" years ago are now attributed as prooflike circulation strikes.

Mintage. 30 Proofs were delivered on February 3.

Die Data and Notes. For characteristics of the obverse die, see information under Proof gold dollars of 1862, since the same die was used. This supersedes Breen's commentary (*Proof*, 1989) that 1871 and 1872 Proof gold dollars were from the same obverse die—which did not mentioning the same die's other uses.

Auction Information (Proofs). Selected citations. Certain of these "Proofs" may have been prooflike circulation strikes.

1911–03: 48th Public Sale, William H. Woodin Collection (Thomas L. Elder), lot 886: "1872. Brilliant Proof. In this condition, one of the rarest of gold dollars." Realized $14.75.

1913–05: Malcolm N. Jackson Collection (U.S. Coin Co.), lot 319: "1872 Brilliant Proof. very rare, especially so in this condition." Realized $14. This firm was a partnership operated by Wayte Raymond and financed by Elmer S. Sears.

1985–05: Dr. Jasper L. Robertson Collection (Mid-American), lot 1157: "1872 Choice Proof (64/64). This is a very rare issue, with a reported Proof mintage of just 30 pieces. Breen estimates that less than 17 examples still survive (we believe that number may even be on the high side) . . . Both the obverse and reverse exhibit the bright, 'orange-peel' surfaces that are so characteristic of Proofs from this era. The fields are deeply mirrored, and the devices are frosted and 'cameo' in appearance. Just a few faint hairlines separate this coin from the gem class (in fact, most catalogers would grade it as such)."

AMERICA AND NUMISMATICS IN 1873

The Coinage Act of February 12, 1873, most of which was drafted by Comptroller of the Currency (and numismatist) John Jay Knox—one of the most brilliant men to occupy an important post at the Treasury Department in the 19th century—eliminated the two-cent piece, silver three-cent piece, and the half dime, created the trade dollar, and adjusted the weights of the dime, quarter, and half dollar (these three coins thereafter bore arrowheads at their dates, through 1874). Henceforth, the Treasury department would mint dimes, quarters, and half dollars (no mention of silver dollars) for the account of the government, to better control the supply of coins—a departure from the prevailing practice of matching mintages to the requests of depositors. Gold dollars were not affected. The head of the Philadelphia Mint was afterward designated as the superintendent, with that office moved to the Treasury Building in Washington, D.C.

In Philadelphia, the *North American* reported on March 4:

> The United States Mint has commenced melting the first installment ($1,000,000) of twenty millions $1 gold pieces, which, during the ensuing month are to be re-coined into larger denominations. These pieces were of inconvenient size, and the government has experienced trouble in issuing them in large quantities. This induced the government to take them from the Sub-Treasury in New York, where they have been idle the past few years, and place the metal in a more desirable shape. From 1849, when the first one-dollar gold pieces were coined at the Mint in this city, to 1867, when the coinage was stopped, there has been $17,709,442 made in the Philadelphia Mint alone. It is presumed that the whole issue of $1 gold pieces will amount to over thirty millions. One million of gold dollars, when first issued by the Mint, will weigh 3,686 pounds avoirdupois, or a fraction over one ton (twenty cwt.) and four-fifths. In twenty millions of dollars we have nearly thirty-three tons. The loss by abrasion in one million dollars is $4,408.37. In other words, $20,000,000, used ten years, loses $88,167.40. If the twenty million pieces to be melted were piled in a perpendicular line, they would reach eleven and five-sixths miles. Were the pieces laid flat on a level plain, they would extend 158 miles.

The 1873 Proof set included more coins than any set before or since: Indian Head cent, two-cent piece (last year of the denomination), nickel three-cent piece, silver three-cent piece (last year of issue), Shield nickel, half dime (last year of issue), dime without arrows at date, dime with arrows at date, quarter without arrows at date, quarter with arrows at date, half dollar without arrows at date, half dollar with arrows at date, silver dollar, trade dollar, gold dollar, quarter eagle, $3 gold piece, half eagle, eagle, and double eagle. Because sets sold early in the year contained coins without arrows, and later sets had arrowheads on the dime, quarter, and half dollar, and since certain other sets lacked all denominations, collectors had to assemble such full sets on their own.

Ever since the end of the Civil War in 1865, the American economy had been growing. The process was hardly smooth, due to problems with Reconstruction in the South, political incompetence and scandals, and more. Railroads were the great growth industry of the period, and vast amounts of money were spent to project and build lines into many sectors, including to areas in which there was no realistic hope of earning a profit. By late summer, there was apprehension in many financial houses. On September 8 the Warehouse Security Company of New York City, important in lending money and handling securities in the grain and produce businesses as well financing the Missouri, Kansas & Texas Railroad, announced that it could not meet its obligations. Immediately, several brokerage houses and banks failed, soon taking down the Union Trust Co., National Trust Co., and Commonwealth National Bank in New York City and the First National Bank in Washington, D.C. Most startling was the collapse of Jay Cooke & Co., the most important dealer in government bonds and securities. For the first time ever, the New York Stock Exchange locked its doors, and remained closed for ten days. Fright and consternation swept the country, and the Panic of 1873 went into full swing—the first such event since the Panic of 1857. The economic malaise lasted through 1877.

The presidency of U.S. Grant was rocked by scandals and charges of incompetency, never mind that his second term was just beginning. Most prominent in the news was the Crédit Mobilier enterprise, the investigation of which began in 1872, and revealed that many congressmen received cheap or free stock to encourage them to vote for certain railroad appropriations. This had its genesis when the directors of the Union Pacific Railroad feared that its huge profits would cause unwanted attention, and formed a new entity to siphon off much of the money—with a nod of appreciation to Congress, which made it all possible.

1873, Close 3

Circulation-Strike Mintage
3,500 to 5,000 (estimate)

Proof Mintage
25

Enlarged 2x
(actual size 15 mm)

Whitman Coin Guide (WCG™)

VF-20	EF-40	AU-50	AU-55	MS-60	MS-63	MS-65	PF-63	PF-65
$425	$775	$1,100	$1,250	$1,700	$4,250	$13,500	$15,000	$29,000

CERTIFIED POPULATIONS

G-4–EF-45	AU-50–58	MS-60–62	MS-63	MS-64	MS-65	MS-66	MS-67	MS-68–70
12	71	58	15	23	3	4	0	0
PF-50–58	PF-60–62	PF-63	PF-64	PF-65	PF-66	PF-67	PF-68–70	
1	2	0	2	5	1	0	0	

Key to Collecting. This variety seems to have been discovered by Thomas L. Elder by 1927 (see citation below), although the late Harry X Boosel (his middle name/initial was X, without a period) claimed the credit. Boosel estimated 1,800 as the mintage, a figure that has been generally accepted by many catalogers. I suggest that while the mintage was but a fraction of that of the Open 3 variety, it was still considerably more than 1,800, perhaps in the range of 3,500 to 5,000. With regard to the status of prooflike circulation strikes vis-à-vis Proofs, and the accuracy of the mintage figures, there are some unresolved questions.

The 1873 Close 3, called *Closed* 3 by some catalogers, was not publicized until the late 20th century. Accordingly, earlier specialized collections of gold dollars did not include the variety. Today it is deemed essential for the specialist.

Estimated Total Population (Mint State). 80 to 120, most being in the MS-60 to MS-63 range. *Caveat:* In the early years, certain certification services did not attribute 1873 dollars by varieties of the numeral 3; accordingly, current population reports are partly corrupted. *Certified population, MS-63 and higher:* 35.

Estimated Total Population (Circulated Grades). 110 to 160. Very rare. The Close 3 gold dollar population estimates admit to a large amount of guesswork, because auction and catalog data are inconclusive.

Characteristics of Striking and Die Notes. Many, if not most, Mint State coins are prooflike. All have a die scratch (*raised* on the coin) on the Miss Liberty's throat. Some show evidence of clashed dies. In the headdress, the letters IBERTY are often weak or missing. The center two digits in the date, 87, are lightly defined on many, while others show just the 7 weak.

Walter Breen (*Encyclopedia*, 1988) stated that the weakness in the word LIBERTY on certain dies of 1873 (also 1874) was "a result of *wear* on the hub," which to the present writer seems unlikely, since the attrition of the letters was not gradual. Whatever the reason, according to Breen, "William Barber in 1874 raised another obverse hub from the master die of 1856, indistinguishable in detail from its predecessors. This served for the remaining low-mintage years through 1889, probably fewer than 50 working obverses in all."

John Dannreuther suggests a cause for the weakness in LIBERTY was the excessive polishing of the working dies, because LIBERTY was incuse on the working hub (and coins), while it was raised on the working dies. It would be nearly impossible to remove the incuse lettering on the working hub without creating a dished area, which would have caused a bulge in the working die and a subsequent dished area in the coins struck from such a die.

Numismatic Notes

Die Data and Explanation of Close 3. 1873 Close 3 four-digit date logotype: The date is in small numerals. The digits 18 are closest together, the 87 and 73 are each wider, and each is about the same distance apart as the other. The 1 has a heavy upright; the base of 1 is slightly higher than the base of the 8. The top interior of the 8 is smaller and narrower than the bottom interior. The base of the 7 is lower than the base of the 8. The 3 has a heavy right side, a thin top and bottom, and prominent ends or balls that virtually touch—with little or any space in between—the "Close 3."

On January 18, 1873, A. Loudon Snowden, chief coiner at the Philadelphia Mint, wrote to James Pollock, director of the Mint:

> I desire in a formal manner to direct your attention to the 'figures' used in dating the dies for the present year.
>
> They are so heavy, and the space between each so very small that upon the small gold and silver and upon the base coins, it is almost impossible to distinguish with the naked eye whether the last figure is an eight or a three. In our ordinary coinage many of the pieces are not brought fully up, and upon such it is impossible to distinguish what is the last figure of the year's date. I do not think it creditable to the institution that the coinage of the year should be issued bearing this defect in the date. I would recommend that an entire new set of figures, avoiding the defect of those now in use, be prepared at the earliest possible day.[55]

Auction Information. A few samples, including an early description of the Close 3, follow. As can be seen, attributions of Proof vis-à-vis prooflike can be a matter of question:

1927–12: Dr. Daniel W. Valentine Collection (Thomas L. Elder), lot 144: "1873 With figure 3 closed. Uncirculated, Proof surface. Rare." Very significant as an attribution of the Close 3 style (the same catalog had a Open 3 dollar; see later citation).

1992–02: Ed Trompeter Collection (Superior), lot 19: "1873 Grade Choice Brilliant Proof Variety Closed 3. Incomplete top feather, but apparently not the 1866–72 die as it does not show the die file marks from ringlet near ear; die polish in other feathers, dentils spaced apart. Description The plurality of the 12 to 15 survivors show lint marks, including this one (on cheek and throat, near chin and C(A), and near large 1); these are not to be counted as defects, as they come from extraneous matter adhering to dies at striking. Otherwise, everything is bold, and very close to gem class. Liberty, in particular, is nice and frosty against the reflective field . . ." *Later offering: 1992–08: Orlando Sale* (Superior), lot 541: "1873. Closed 3. PCGS MS-65. The Ed Trompeter coin . . . In our Ed Trompeter Sale we referred to this piece as a Choice Brilliant Proof having mintage of 25 (all struck February 18, 1873). The grading service has chosen to grade in MS-65 . . . To date, this is one of only 2 examples in its grade category, with 1 higher." *Later offering: 2004–11: Palm Beach Sale* (Heritage), lot 8059: 1873 Closed 3 MS-65 PCGS. Ex: Trompeter . . . Trompeter considered the present piece to be a Proof and it was part of his fabulous collection of Proof gold coinage. It does match Breen's proof diagnostics, which include an incomplete feather in headdress below the second T in STATES, an open top of the wreath, and a slightly rising date. The date location is seemingly identical to the Proof offered in our 2001 FUN Sale as lot 8057. Regardless of its Proof or business strike status, this is a very rare gold dollar, since only 25 Proofs were struck and PCGS has certified a mere four business strikes as MS-65 with two finer." *The rest of the story:* The coin was purchased by John Dannreuther in partnership with another dealer. His comment (via correspondence):

> It is a Proof! It is now in a PCGS PR65 holder. The Proof-only obverse die of 1862 is an infallible test for 1873, as there is another die (see your Bass citation below—I still own that coin and it is NOT a Proof, as it does not have the tiny raised line from the ringlet . . . it is a single line, not the 'die file marks from the ringlet near ear' noted in the Superior Trompeter description). I also bought an 'MS' coin that Frank Van Valen catalogued, which also is now in a PR holder. The obverse die is definitive for all Proofs 1862–73 and 1875, while there are second obverses for 1866 and 1876. 1874 stands alone, as you know. The Smithsonian Institution coin from an intact gold Proof set was the example I used to 'prove' to PCGS that the Trompeter coin was a Proof. Interestingly, in 1875, after a year's hiatus, the obverse of 1862 was REFROSTED, as the 1875 Proof obverse of two years later is fantastic! It is the only instance that I know about (although some believe the 1827 quarter obverse was re-frosted) where a die was re-frosted—undoubtedly with acid, as there is a slight spillover around Miss Liberty on some 1875 Proofs.

1995–10: 60th Anniversary Sale, Seymour Finkelstein Collection (Stack's), lot 1392: "1873 Closed 3. Choice Brilliant Uncirculated . . . The variety with the raised die line on the neck, often seen on the more common Open 3. This would suggest a marriage of a Closed 3 reverse die with an Open 3 obverse die, unlisted by Breen. This unusual coin may be a real 'find' for a specialist in this series." Lot 1393: "1873 Closed 3. Another. Brilliant Uncirculated. Deep yellow gold with numerous tiny contact marks. A distinctly different obverse die than the preceding specimen, this one with a tiny raised die lump on the neck. Scarce."

1999–01: FUN Sale (Heritage), lot 7921: "1873 Closed 3 MS-66 (PCGS). One of the scarcest coins in the series and certainly one of the most under-publicized. Of the 1,800 business strikes minted, perhaps 75–85 examples survive in all grades."

2000–11: Harry W. Bass Jr. Collection, Part IV (Bowers and Merena Galleries), lot 80: "1873 Close 3. MS-63 . . . LIBERTY is strong and complete, with digits 87 weak . . . There are a numerous clashmarks above the Indian's head-dress and into the legend. Rare but unappreciated as such. From Paramount's Davies-Niewoehner Sale, February 1975 lot 473." Lot 81: "1873 Close 3. MS-62 (PCGS) . . . Although certified as Mint State, this may be a Proof as recorded by Harry Bass in his notes. Believed to be a Proof by Mr. Boosel and by RARCOA, and cataloged by them as: 'Only 25 struck as were all the gold Proofs of this year. Lovely Brilliant Proof with some hairlines and die lint marks, which are characteristically found on these Proofs.' Perfect dies. The first feather is incomplete, characteristic of Proofs of this era. From RARCOA's sale of the Harry X Boosel Collection, April 1972 lot 670."

PROOFS

Estimated Total Population and Key to Collecting. 9 to 12. All known Proofs of this year are of the Close 3 style, struck to the extent of 25 coins. This is one of the great rarities in the Proof gold dollar series. See important note about Proofs at the end of the Ed Trompeter Collection citation above. Proofs were made from poorly finished dies this year, giving them a curious appearance, and causing some to be mistaken for prooflike circulation strikes. In a study of this issue, John Dannreuther commented:

> Upon examining actual coins it is immediately obvious that Proof 1873 gold dollars were poorly made, as the obverse die is not worn, proven by its use in 1875 for the well-made Proof gold dollars of that year. The hair and wreath both lack detail and have a granular look. This indicates that the dies were not properly spaced when this coin was struck. The patchy nature of the frost on the face is also indicative of a planchet that did not completely fill the die cavity. Since only 25 Proofs were believed struck, these delivered on February 18, one must think that the lack of demand because of financial strife must have tempered any complaints that collectors might have voiced at the time about the poor quality of these coins.

Die Data and Notes. For characteristics of the obverse die see information under Proof gold dollars of 1862, since the same die was used. For the 1875 Proof gold dollar, the marker, "no thorn or line protruding from jaw," is another way to differentiate these from circulation strikes. The obverse die was treated with acid to recreate the frosted surface, which was mostly gone in its last use in 1873 (1874 Proofs used a different obverse die). Therefore, Proof 1875 gold dollars have great cameo appearance, equal to those of 1862–1869.

Auction Information (Proofs). The dozens of auction citations located basically describe the grade and rarity. In recent decades, die characteristics (as explained above) have been part of some listings. Among them is this somewhat curious listing:

> *1979–11: Garrett Collection, Part I* (Bowers and Ruddy Galleries), lot 410: "1873 Closed 3. Choice Brilliant Proof. Struck from the Proof dies identified by Walter Breen by a conspicuous unfinished feather in the headdress located below A in STATES, as well as various other characteristics which he described in detail. This pieces also possesses some hints of mint frost, especially when viewed at a distance with a strong light source to accent this feature. Undoubtedly a Proof in its context as part of an original 1873 Proof set, this piece has caused a decided difference of opinion among several respected authorities when examined out of context today; at least one of whom has designated it as *prooflike Uncirculated.* To avoid future controversy, we are offering the coin as a Proof in our opinion. All who contemplate competing for this piece would be well advised to examine it personally and formulate their own determination. From W. Elliot Woodward, September 5, 1883; earlier from the Ely Collection." *Later offering: 2005–01:* FUN Convention Sale (Heritage), lot 8505: "1873 Closed 3 PR-65 Cameo NGC. Garrett Collection . . . In the Garrett catalog in November 1979, Bowers was careful to state his uncertainty about this coin's status as a proof or first-strike prooflike, even though he did state that this piece showed a 'conspicuous unfinished feather in the headdress located below the A in STATES.' Nine years later Walter Breen published this as the sole diagnostic of genuine Proofs in his *Complete Encyclopedia*, where he stated: 'have incomplete feather below T (ES).' We disagree with both and see the incomplete feather actually below the second T in STATES. Each side shows a number of lint marks from the dies having been wiped with a cloth and the lint adhering to the dies and then being transferred to the finished coin. The Proof 1873 is one of the rarest coins in the entire gold dollar series. Only 25 proofs were struck and it is doubtful that more than half that number are extant today as recognizable proof strikings. The fields are nicely mirrored but lack the depth that one might expect of a Proof striking from this period. Even orange-gold coloration covers each side. An extremely rare opportunity for the gold dollar collector or aficionado of the 19th century Proof gold." Today it is generally agreed, and has been affirmed by David W. Akers, that pieces struck from the obverse die with unfinished feather details are Proof pieces. However, the rest of the story may yet be told.

1873, Open 3

Circulation-Strike Mintage
123,300

Proof Mintage
None

Enlarged 2x
(actual size 15 mm)

Whitman Coin Guide (WCG™)

VF-20	EF-40	AU-50	AU-55	MS-60	MS-63	MS-65
$165	$210	$235	$265	$375	$1,350	$2,500

CERTIFIED POPULATIONS

G-4–EF-45	AU-50–58	MS-60–62	MS-63	MS-64	MS-65	MS-66	MS-67	MS-68–70
62	522	1,651	629	350	70	18	0	1

Key to Collecting. The 1873 Open 3 is frequently seen in the marketplace, usually in Mint State and highly lustrous. Many have weak areas with LIBERTY partially or completely missing. The luster and eye appeal are generally good.

Estimated Total Population (Mint State). 2,500 to 3,500, many of which are of choice or gem quality. Over the years the writer and consultants for this book have had several mini-hoards of one to two dozen specimens, and it has not been unusual for a single auction to include multiple specimens. Most Mint State 1873 Open 3 gold dollars are lustrous and frosty, but some have a partially prooflike surface. *Certified population, MS-63 and higher:* 1,125.

Estimated Total Population (Circulated Grades). 1,250 to 1,750, mostly in higher grades such as EF or AU.

Characteristics of Striking and Die Notes. Some show die clashing, but such coins are in the minority. Most examples have the word LIBERTY in the headdress weak or even completely missing. Some have a prominent *raised* die scratch on Miss Liberty's neck; these are plentiful; this line is known on both the Close 3 and Open 3 varieties.

Numismatic Notes

Die Data. 1873 Open 3 four-digit date logotype: *Made from the 1873 Close 3 punch, now with the last digit reworked.* The knobs of the 3 have been mostly cut away and made smaller, and now have a wide separation between them.

Auction Information. Selected offerings:

1927–12: Dr. Daniel W. Valentine Collection (Thomas L. Elder), lot 143: "1873 Open figure 3. Mint State, Uncirculated." Very significant as an attribution of the Open 3 style (the same catalog had a Close 3 dollar; see earlier citation).

1937–03: VII Auction Sale of U.S. Coins (Ira S. Reed), lot 688: "1873 Was Proof, Uncirculated." Today, numismatists would view such a description with humor, as a Proof cannot change to become a high grade circulation strike.

1963–05: Emerson Gaylord Collection (Mayflower Coin Auctions), lot 59: "1873 Open 3. A Beautiful Gem Uncirculated first strike. Full proof-like lustre and another good example of what is being sold by many as Proofs today."

1969–10: Auction Sale (Lester Merkin), lot 387: "1873. Open 3. Brilliant proof-like gem Unc., early strike from new die with full original polish; looks like a Proof except for the usual sharpness of Unc. Coin with regular border. A real showpiece, one of the most beautiful gold dollars of this date we have seen."

1999–05: Herman Halpern Collection (Stack's), lot 2870: "1873 Open 3. Choice Brilliant Uncirculated. Lustrous, frosty yellow gold surfaces are brilliant and appealing. A prominent long vertical die file line extends from Liberty's earlobe through the truncation of neck. This feature is seen on many specimens. The coin is generally well struck. Only the LI of LIBERTY in headband shows, a characteristic always seen on this die variety."

AMERICA AND NUMISMATICS IN 1874

In his *Annual Report* for the fiscal year ended June 30, 1874, Mint Director James Pollock commented:

> It seems a remarkable omission in our laws, that there is not limit at which our coins shall cease to be a legal tender on account of *wear* . . . In some sections where gold is much used, as on the Pacific Coast and in the extreme Southwest, the wear is very marked. Quarter eagles may be met with, not really worth more than $2.40, and gold dollars still more deficient in proportion. It would be well to declare by law that gold coins shall be a legal tender at their stamped value, so long as they weigh within 1% for the smaller denominations and 1/2 of 1% for the larger. But then the question arises, who shall lose the difference when the coin becomes uncurrent? . . .
>
> Whenever the specie basis shall have been reached, large coinage of the half and quarter eagles, will be necessary, but the mints can manufacture the same as rapidly as would be required or the bullion could be supplied for the purpose. We now have six different denominations of gold coin, which is a greater variety than is required. This being the case, and the three-dollar piece corresponding so nearly, as to weight, value, and size, with the quarter eagle, and rarely used, its coinage should be discontinued. The gold dollar is not a convenient coin, on account of its small size, and it suffers more proportionately from abrasion than larger coins. Its issue should, therefore, be confined to actual demands for it by the depositors of bullion, and the requirements for change and retail transactions should be met with silver coin.

The price of silver had been declining on world markets since the early 1870s, when several European countries demonetized the metal and moved exclusively to the gold standard. At the same time, in America the production of silver increased sharply, from new mines in the West. The national economy remained slow.

1874

Circulation-Strike Mintage
198,800

Proof Mintage
20

Enlarged 2x
(actual size 15 mm)

Whitman Coin Guide (WCG™)

VF-20	EF-40	AU-50	AU-55	MS-60	MS-63	MS-65	PF-63	PF-65
$165	$210	$235	$265	$375	$1,350	$2,500	$10,000	$30,000

CERTIFIED POPULATIONS

G-4–EF-45	AU-50–58	MS-60–62	MS-63	MS-64	MS-65	MS-66	MS-67	MS-68–70
74	723	2,709	1,245	800	225	79	63	8
PF-50–58	PF-60–62	PF-63	PF-64	PF-65	PF-66	PF-67	PF-68–70	
0	1	0	7	3	1	0	0	

Key to Collecting. The 1874 gold dollar is very common in nearly all grades. Striking and eye appeal can vary widely. Many have been certified as gems. Some effort has been made by catalogers to interest collectors in the many coins with partial LIBERTY or with this word missing altogether, but the response has been an unstifled yawn. When buying, cherrypick for sharply struck details.

Estimated Total Population (Mint State). 4,500 to 6,000, perhaps even more. A generous mintage late in the series, combined with a high conservation rate, yields a large supply in existence today. Many 1874 gold dollars are choice or gem quality and have frosty luster. *Certified population, MS-63 and higher:* 2,488.

Estimated Total Population (Circulated Grades). 3,000 to 5,000. Usually in higher grades such as EF and AU.

Characteristics of Striking and Die Notes. Sometimes there is slight granularity or planchet roughness on the high points of the date numerals and certain letters on the reverse. Some are lightly struck at the center two date digits (87) and/or at the letter O (DOLLAR). These are often weakly defined at LIBERTY in the headband with just the L showing, similar to the 1873 coins in this regard. It is not unusual to find the word missing entirely.

Numismatic Notes

Die Data. 1874 four-digit date logotype: The digits are large and rather "bulky." The are very closely spaced, the 18 close at the base, 87 close at the top, and the 7 and 4 fairly close to each other. The 1 has a thick upright, short bottom serifs with right side shorter, and a base slightly higher than the base of the 8. The upper interior of the 8 is slightly smaller than the bottom interior, the 8 leans right. The base of the 7 is about level with the base of the 4. The 4 has a very heavy upright; its diagonal is thicker near the top of the numeral, and there is no crosslet on the bar; the right tip of the bar is about equal with the right bottom serif. This logotype was used on all dies.

Mintage. The large mintage for this year resulted from the recoinage of worn gold coins brought to the Mint and melted. Further, it was anticipated that gold coins would be paid out by the Treasury in the near future, and a supply was coined to have specimens on hand (as it developed, gold coins did not circulate freely until late December 1878.

In 1873 and 1874, the Treasury Department contemplated paying out silver and gold coins once again (gold had not been distributed at par since late December 1861), and some silver coins were paid out beginning in the former year. It could have been that fairly large quantities of gold dollars were minted in 1873 and 1874 to provide for this procedure. However, while silver dollars were paid out in small numbers at the time (not in substantial quantities until April 20, 1876), gold coins remained sequestered until December 1878. The high gold dollar mintages of 1873–1874 were ready and all set, but had nowhere to go. With an adequate supply of gold dollars on hand, the Treasury Department called for only small mintages in the next several years.

Auction Information. Auction listings often mention the absence of the word LIBERTY on the obverse. M.H. Bolender's March 1951 sale of the Fox Collection included this: "Lot 952: 1874 AU. Only L in LIBERTY is struck up. This is almost characteristic of this date. In our last sale, a collector returned an 1874 gold dollar, a choice specimen, with a remark: 'How could it be Uncirculated when LIBERTY is all worn off?'" A small percentage of listings note a prooflike surface.

Proofs

Estimated Total Population and Key to Collecting. 9 to 11. The mintage figure of 20 represents the number of Proofs known to have been delivered as part of full Proof *sets*. It may be the case that some additional single Proofs were made, but if so, the number was small, for the 1874 is a great rarity today, a top-echelon prize *far rarer* than the 1875 (see following section).

Die Data and Notes. Proofs were struck with or without the word LIBERTY (or with just the beginning of the word) visible on the headband, the without-LIBERTY variety being the more available of the two. This would indicate two production runs of Proofs.

AMERICA AND NUMISMATICS IN 1875

The government was bound and determined to restore silver and gold coins to circulation, but some recent efforts in the silver direction achieved little. In December 1874 the Senate approved a bill, taken up by the House on January 7, 1875, and passed that day, mandating that gold coin payments would resume on January 1, 1879. To make this possible, a provision was made for the secretary of the Treasury to sell bonds, *without limit*, to raise the necessary amount of money to have an appropriate quantity of gold coins on hand. In the meantime, silver and gold coins traded at a premium in relation to paper money. The 20¢ piece was introduced, but circulated only in the West, and only for a short time before the denomination was discontinued.

Early American Coins, by Sylvester S. Crosby, was published, a landmark reference that today remains essential to any numismatic library. In New York City in October, Edward Cogan's sale of the Col. M.I. Cohen collection took place. The 2,400 lots included an 1804 silver dollar that realized $325. The coin market was neither hot nor cold, but was treading water, and prices in the sale were modest. A complete gold Proof set of 1875, containing the $1, $2.50, $3, $5, $10, $20, for a total face value of $41.50, brought $46.50, or not much more than face value (considering the exchange rate for paper money). This was to be expected, for similar coins could still be ordered from the Mint. However, to do so, other gold coins, obtainable from brokers and exchange houses, had to be submitted in payment, this being the practice ever since 1862.

President U.S. Grant continued in office, bumbling his way along (per the view of later historians). In New York City a new Court House building, estimated to cost $250,000, was completed for $13,000,000, thanks to graft by "Boss" Tweed and his Tammany Hall ring. In this era Thomas Nast was the foremost political cartoonist. Many of his sketches showed Tweed as a monster. One showed him as a vulture, leading his brood, saying, "Let us prey." The United States Hotel opened at Saratoga Springs, with nearly 1,000 rooms; the Palace Hotel started business in San Francisco with 755 rooms; and in Chicago the new Palmer House Hotel took the place of the hostelry by the same name that was reduced to ashes in the 1871 Chicago fire. Society events glittered in the cities in the cooler months, and in the summer those who could afford it would often take the train to a country or mountain resort and enjoy leisure pursuits.

1875

Circulation-Strike Mintage
400

Proof Mintage
50 to 60 (estimate)

Enlarged 2x
(actual size 15 mm)

Whitman Coin Guide (WCG™)

VF-20	EF-40	AU-50	AU-55	MS-60	MS-63	MS-65	PF-63	PF-65
$2,350	$3,900	$5,250	$5,750	$8,000	$11,500	$25,000	$16,500	$14,000

CERTIFIED POPULATIONS

G-4–EF-45	AU-50–58	MS-60–62	MS-63	MS-64	MS-65	MS-66	MS-67	MS-68–70
8	22	32	9	12	9	3	0	0
PF-50–58	PF-60–62	PF-63	PF-64	PF-65	PF-66	PF-67	PF-68–70	
1	1	2	4	7	7	0	0	

Key to Collecting. The 1875 is the most famous single date in the gold dollar series, due to its low production. For generations this has been a great object of desire, both by serious specialists as well as seekers of "trophy coins." Most examples are well struck and have excellent eye appeal. All are highly prooflike.

There is no reason to doubt the published figure of 400 circulation strikes. However, rather than being intended for circulation, it seems likely, at least to the writer, that some of these were struck for the numismatic market. Others were acquired by jewelers, who fashioned them into various articles.

Estimated Total Population (Mint State). 40 to 60, some of which have been called Proofs. All seen have had full prooflike surfaces.

The number of extant prooflike Mint State coins vis-à-vis Proofs is a matter of debate and probably will never be ascertained. No matter. Mint State or Proof, the 1875 is the darling of the gold dollar series. Most are in high grades and nearly all have nice eye appeal. *Certified population, MS-63 and higher:* 33.

Estimated Total Population (Circulated Grades). 30 to 40, mostly at the AU level, invariably with prooflike surfaces. The population of the 1875 circulation strike is difficult to measure, since the coins are rarities and have a high degree of visibility in print. *Estimated total population (impaired, used as jewelry):* 40+. At least 40, perhaps more, are known that have been mounted for use as jewelry or are otherwise impaired; many auction offerings of such coins could be cited. This dramatically reveals that jewelry makers were important "consumers" of gold dollars during this era.

Characteristics of Striking and Die Notes. Usually well struck and always with prooflike surfaces.

Numismatic Notes

Die Data. 1875 four-digit date logotype: The digits 18 are close together, but 87 and 75 are each wider at about the same distance. The 1 has a heavy upright; its lower left serif is slightly longer than its lower right serif; a tiny thorn protrudes from the lower right serif and nearly extends to the adjacent 8; the base of the 1 is higher than the base of the 8. The 8 leans right. On various dies (depending on the depth and angle of the punch, etc.) the top and bottom openings of the 8 can be the same size, or one larger or smaller than the other. The 5 leans slightly right; its heavy flag extends right to about the same distance as the curve below it; the ball at bottom is of minimal size and very close to the upright. This logotype was used on all dies.

David W. Akers discovered (and Breen used that information) that Mint State coins have a tiny raised spine extending from Miss Liberty's jaw into the field. Using this as a criterion, it seems that Mint State coins are fairly often available, although for many years before this was published there were more "Proof" listings in auction catalogs. The certification services use the Akers criterion, and thus pieces listed as Mint State are with thorn.

The writer would not be at all surprised to learn that many of these with-thorn pieces were made specifically for the collector market and sold as Proofs, perhaps after the first run of without-thorn Proofs had been completed.

Die Notes on the Bass Collection, Part I Coin, Lot 195. Obverse: The die is highly polished, as on the Proofs, but probably not intended as a Proof. There is a thorn extending from below Miss Liberty's chin near where it meets the neck, and several parallel minute raised die finish lines in the field below I (UNITED). There is no Proof surface in the headdress or in the recesses of LIBERTY, and C (AMERICA) is filled with material. This is a completely different die than the Proof in this sale, not a different state of the same die. Reverse: The die is quite similar to the Proof, highly polished. The date position is slightly more to the right. The amount of filling of DOLLAR and part of the 5 are the same. Above the left side of the rightmost ribbon, there is no Proof surface extending deeply into the crevice.

Auction Information. Most listings of this date have been classified as Proofs. Today, it is impossible to sort out which were actually circulation strikes. Modern listings of Mint State coins usually mention David W. Akers's finding that these are distinguished by a tiny thornlike projection extending from the lower jaw into the field.

Proofs

Estimated Total Population and Key to Collecting. 25 to 30. True Proofs are very rare in comparison to the never-ceasing demand for this landmark date, but are much more available than are Proofs of such years as the super-rarities of 1871 and 1874.

Conventional wisdom has it that 20 Proofs were made this year, this being the number delivered on February 13 as part of *sets*. It is a virtual certainty that others were made, but no record has been located to prove it. Per conventional wisdom, *1874* Proof gold dollars were also coined to the extent of 20 pieces in sets, but *far fewer* have ever come on the market. Similarly, 20 gold Proof sets were made in 1876, but Proof gold dollars dated 1876 are much rarer than are those dated 1875.

It is my view that somewhat more than 20 Proof 1875 gold dollars were made. Douglas Winter agrees (via correspondence), suggesting that an additional 20 or 30 were made to fill collector demand. It would stretch credulity to suggest that the Proof 1875 $20, also with a reported mintage of 20 Proofs (as part of the sets), was made in the same total quantity as the Proof dollar. The 1875 Proof $20 is an incredible rarity in Proof state, while the 1875 dollar, while rare, appears on the market with regularity. As long ago as February 1944 in his sale of the Belden Roach Collection, B. Max Mehl, in the offering of an earlier-dated Proof dollar, stated this relative to the 1875: "1859 Perfect brilliant Proof. Sharp wire edges. Extremely rare and certainly worth far more than its listed price of $25. I doubt if there are as many Proofs of this date as there are of the 1875. I know one thing, that in my own experience, I have handled at least ten 1875 Proofs to one of this date." However, Mehl probably confused certain prooflike circulation strikes with full Proofs.

Die Data and Notes. For characteristics of the obverse die, see information under Proof gold dollars of 1862, since the same die was used. For the 1875 Proof gold dollar, David W. Akers's marker, "no thorn or line protruding from jaw," is another way to differentiate these from circulation strikes.

Description of Proof 1875 from the Bass, Part III Sale. The obverse has tiny raised rust areas in the field below Miss Liberty's chin and at the lower left of the F (OF). The first feather is incomplete. The reverse is deeply polished to give "orange peel" effect to finished coins, but with some stray die polish lines remaining. There is a double outline to the wreath and denomination 1. The wreath apex is joined at the top. The centers of D, O, and A filled in—without polish. Four-digit date logotype: The digits 18 are close together, and 87 and 75 are each wider at about the same distance. On the 1, the lower left serif is longer than the lower right serif; a tiny thorn protrudes from the lower right serif and nearly extends to the adjacent 8. The 8 leans right, and its top interior is slightly smaller than the bottom interior. The 5 leans slightly right. Its ball is minimal sized and is very close to the upright. In the die, the base of the 7 is above and slightly to the right of center of the highest ribbon point.

Because circulation strikes are prooflike, the rarity of Proof 1875 gold dollars appears lower than it actually is—this despite a very *generous* quantity of Proof auction appearances. As an example, the Virgil M. Brand Collection, Part II specimen lot 988, described by the present writer in June 1984 as "MS-67, full prooflike surface," was bought by Brand as a Proof.

It is likely that dozens of prooflike *Mint State* pieces have been offered as *Proof* in past years, and that this has inflated the auction data.

Auction Information (Proofs). A tiny selection from *hundreds* of listings is given. In contrast, there are relatively few citations for Proof $5, $10, and $20 coins of 1877, *said to have been of the same mintage.*

1880–11: S.K. Harzfeld's 15th Sale, lot 648: "1875 *Proof, excessively rare.*" Realized $4. In contrast, the next three lots in the same sale, Proofs of 1876 to 1878, realized $1.10 each, or scarcely above face value.

1882–03: 40th Auction Sale, John W. Scott Collection (Scott & Co.), lot 140: "1875 Indian Head; Proof; excessively rare." Realized $6. This coin was the highlight of Scott's personal gold dollar set, arranged by dates (without mintmarks), but lacking many of the dates in the 1860s and 1870s.

1911–03: 48th Public Sale, William H. Woodin Collection (Thomas L. Elder), lot 889: "1875. Perfect Proof. Excessively rare, the record at public sale has exceeded $100, and the previous steady advance in price will doubtless continue." Realized $86.

1911–06: 50th Public Sale, Summers Collection (Thomas L. Elder), lot 319: "1875. Bright Proof. Extremely rare. Records up to $100 at public sale."

1911–09: 52nd Public Sale (Thomas L. Elder), lot 591: "1875 Brilliant Proof. Extremely rare. Records over $100. At public sale."

1917–10–0: F. Ramsdell, H.H. Butler, and James I. Brown Collections (Thomas L. Elder), lot 640: "1875 Brilliant Proof. Exceedingly rare. I have not offered one since the Woodin Sale in 1911. This coin should bring $200 to $250 judging by its actual rarity. Most gold dollar collectors do not have it and some have not even seen it. The prize coin of this sale." Elder forgot two he had offered since Woodin (see above).

1934–04: Clara B. DeHaven Collection (Thomas L. Elder), lot 2548: "1875 All Want It But Few Have It! [Headline] Proof. Very rare, the rarest Philadelphia Mint dollar. Records to $135 in these sales."

1955–04: 45th Sale (New Netherlands Coin Co.), lot 780: "1875 Mostly brilliant Proof. Only 420 examples (of all kinds) coined. More than twice as rare in numbers made than the vaunted 1895 Morgan dollar, and, to our minds, potentially worth twice as much."

AMERICA AND NUMISMATICS IN 1876

The Centennial Exhibition in Fairmount Park in Philadelphia opened on May 10, with President U.S. Grant officiating. He sent a signal, and a giant Corliss steam engine launched into power, throwing machines into motion. At the Mint, George T. Morgan, an English engraver, was hired as an assistant to William Barber.

At long last, silver coins began to reappear in general circulation in late April. Once again, Liberty Seated coins were seen in commerce. Fractional Currency notes were discontinued, creating a numismatic demand for them, while at the same time the bills of the Confederacy were popular with collectors.

By 1876, "Silverites," affected by the drop in price and demand for bullion wanted the government to give silver legal tender status in unlimited amounts, and mandate that 16 ounces of silver in coin form would be equal to one ounce of gold. Seemingly, this would have resulted in people using silver coins to pay debts, even to the government—including some obligations that had been backed at least with the implication that the dollar would be as good as gold. Foreign financiers were aghast at the prospect that Americans might seek to pay their obligations in silver, accelerating a great export of coined gold to Europe and elsewhere. (This would have fortuitous results for later generations of numismatists who repatriated many double eagles, far and away the most popular denomination used for this purposes.) No gold dollars are known to have been exported for use in settling international payments.

The presidential election was particularly nasty, a situation that did not improve after November, when Democrat Samuel J. Tilden captured the most popular votes, but the win went to Republican Rutherford B. Hayes, who it seemed gained the needed Electoral College votes, 185 in number. Frauds and irregularities including unfair rules and false counts were charged in Louisiana, Florida, South Carolina, and Oregon, with different officials giving different tallies. The matter was placed into the hands of 15 men, comprising five Supreme Court justices, five senators, and five representatives, whose political persuasions divided into eight Republicans and seven Democrats. As might be expected, Hayes was declared the victor.

In Montana, Sioux Chief Sitting Bull and his comrades wiped out Lt. Col. George Custer and his Army contingents, after which Custer was viewed as a martyr in the American press, in keeping with prevailing sentiment that Indians had little or no status.

1876

Circulation-Strike Mintage
3,200

Proof Mintage
45

Enlarged 2x
(actual size 15 mm)

Whitman Coin Guide (WCG™)

VF-20	EF-40	AU-50	AU-55	MS-60	MS-63	MS-65	PF-63	PF-65
$285	$350	$500	$600	$775	$1,200	$3,000	$6,000	$14,000

CERTIFIED POPULATIONS

G-4–EF-45	AU-50–58	MS-60–62	MS-63	MS-64	MS-65	MS-66	MS-67	MS-68–70
6	53	83	42	62	15	4	2	0
PF-50–58	PF-60–62	PF-63	PF-64	PF-65	PF-66	PF-67	PF-68–70	
1	0	3	15	10	5	1	0	

Key to Collecting. The 1876 gold dollar is rare, as its low mintage suggests. Relatively few seem to have been saved by collectors or dealers, with the result that Mint State coins are very elusive. Many circulation strikes have highly prooflike surfaces.

Only rarely is the quality of strike of this or any other Philadelphia Mint gold dollar date mentioned in print, and certification holders do not mention it either. Thus, it is proper to know that some lightness of strike is to be expected for an 1876 gold dollar, and a piece described as "lightly struck" may be every bit as nice as one with no mention of the striking characteristics.

Estimated Total Population (Mint State). 225 to 325. When encountered, the usual Mint State coin is apt to grade in the MS-60 to MS-63 range. The 1876 can be compared to the 1878 in this regard. However, in choice and gem grades, the 1876 is a bit more available than the 1878, and it is likely that several dozen exist. *Certified population, MS-63 and higher:* 125.

Estimated Total Population (Circulated Grades). 110 to 130. Examples are elusive in all circulated grades. When seen, the typical coin is apt to be lightly worn and in the AU category. Not counted here are many coins that were used in jewelry.

Characteristics of Striking and Die Notes. Often lightly struck on the high points of the obverse portrait, such as at the hair and headdress plumes. On some (*e.g.*, the Virgil M. Brand Collection sale, November 1983, lot 54) the central two date figures, 87, are lighter than the outside figures, due to metal flow requirements. On some pieces the ribbon knot is lightly defined.

Numismatic Notes

Die Data. 1876 four-digit date logotype: The digits are about evenly spaced, with 18 very slightly closer than the others. The 1 is thick; its lower left serif is slightly longer than its lower right serif. The 8 has a top interior space slightly smaller than the bottom interior space; it leans slightly right. The 6 is thick at left; its small irregular ball nearly touches the curve below it, and touches it on some deep impressions. This logotype was used on all dies.

Circulation strikes seem to have been produced from a single obverse die with a raised rust spot on Miss Liberty's neck.

Auction Information. Below are several selected offerings from hundreds studied.

1904–04: John G. Mills Collection (S.H. and Henry Chapman), lot 656: "1876 Uncirculated, with Proof surface. Rare." Realized $2.75.

1905–11: Philip D. Hoch Collection (Lyman H. Low), lot 548: "1876 Very Fine; fifth in rarity from the Philadelphia Mint." Realized $3.75. The 1876 was not usually characterized as rare in early listings; this is an exception.

1924–04: A.C. Nygren Collection (Henry Chapman), lot 3: "1876 These dollars have been in a necklace or other piece of jewelry, show it on the edge and sometimes on the reverse—very slight evidences of where the solder has been removed, a process probably responsible for a sweated or plated appearance that all have. Fine. Scarce. 50 pieces." An interesting group reflecting what was the fate of many gold dollars of various dates over the years.

1982–10: Eliasberg Collection (U.S. Gold Coin Collection) (Bowers and Ruddy Galleries), lot 65: 1876 Choice Brilliant Uncirculated, MS-65, prooflike surface. With the date level (on Proofs it slants slightly down to the right). The obverse displays hairline die breaks at the top of the F in OF and at the top of M in AMERICA and connecting ER of the same word. Among the reverse numerals of the date, 1 and 7 are the most heavily impressed into the die, with 6 being next and being the most lightly impressed. The reverse displays some mint-origin planchet adjustment marks in the field, a feature visible under magnification. *From the John H. Clapp Collection, 1942. Earlier from the Harlan P. Smith Collection (Chapman brothers, May 1906). Graded as Brilliant Proof in that sale.*"

1983–11: Virgil M. Brand Collection, Part I (Bowers and Merena Galleries), lot 54: "1876 Choice Brilliant Uncirculated, MS-65. Central two figures lighter than the outer two." Lot 55: "1876 Choice Brilliant Uncirculated, MS-65, prooflike. From the same dies as the preceding, but with the two central figures bolder—probably due to a microscopic adjustment in die spacing. As such, very unusual. An examination under magnification of the various business strike 1876 gold dollars shown here reveal that they are all from the same reverse die, but the obverses are with a number of variations from coin to coin. The reverse die is characterized by several features, including recutting to the right side of the letters OLL of DOLLAR, and a tiny connection between the knob of the 6 to the curve below."

Proofs

Estimated Total Population and Key to Collecting. 25 to 35. Rare in relation to the demand for them. The higher figure for 1876 may have been in anticipation of sales at the Centennial Exhibition held in Philadelphia this year. The Mint was invited to have a coin display at the fair, but declined (the original 1836 steam-powered press was on view, however, and was used to strike tiny brass souvenir tokens). Many visitors to the event made side trips to the Mint.

Mintage. Two deliveries were made, February 19 (20) and June 13 (25).

Die Data and Notes. A key identification feature for *some* Proofs of 1876: The vertical element of the leftmost feather in the headdress plume is mostly polished away in the obverse die, giving Proof field in this area. This die was used to strike Proof gold dollars from 1862 to 1873, in 1875, and in some of 1876; the area of polish was increased as the years went by; it was employed for some circulation strikes (not Proofs) of 1879, and, relapped (producing more polish areas in the headband) to make certain circulation strikes (not Proofs) of gold dollars in 1888 and 1889. Breen, in his Proof-coin reference (1989), describes what seems to be another obverse die: "No rust pit on neck; some extra outlines on UNI (UNITED) MERICA; die file mark through base of A toward M."

Proofs have the date numerals aligned slightly low at the right side (in contrast with circulation strikes, for which the date is level or oriented slightly upward). A short die line through the right base of the first A in AMERICA almost reaches M and is diagnostic of Proofs, according to Walter Breen.

A proof die for an 1876 gold dollar in the Bass, Part III sale was described as having an obverse with an unfinished feather and rusty spots in the exact same places as just described for the 1875. Its reverse had a low date logotype (as in the circulation-strikes die). On the Proof, the ribbon is centered below the space between 8 and 7, while on the circulation strike, the highest part of the ribbon is farther to the right, below the left side of the 7. As another measure, on the Proof the second L (DOLLAR) is above the 7 and slightly to the left, with the left side of the L, if extended downward, contacting the left edge of the 7; on the circulation strike the L is virtually perfectly centered above the 7.

Auction Information (Proofs). A few selected citations from hundreds found:

> *1880–11: S.K. Harzfeld's 15th Sale lot 649:* "1876 Proof, scarce." Realized $1.10. This was little more than face value and is one of many contemporary evidences that collectors owning Proof gold often found it more expedient to spend the coins than to consign them for auction.
>
> *1927–12: Dr. Daniel W. Valentine Collection* (Thomas L. Elder), lot 150: "1876 Brilliant Proof. With LIBERTY on coronet. Rare." No listings have been seen for a Proof *without* LIBERTY.
>
> *1943–01: 74th Catalog* (Barney Bluestone), lot 1054: "1876 Figure 8, struck weak, Proof." Realized $9.70. Multiple listings for Proof 1876 dollars can be found in Bluestone catalogs of the 1930s and 1940s.
>
> *1985–07: Auction '85* (Paramount), lot 1398: "1876 Gem Proof (65+/67). Deep golden toned Proof with exceptional brilliance, lustre and 'flash.' Apparent 'hairlines' in the fields are *not* really hairlines at all but rather are planchet lines not fully struck out in the minting process."
>
> *1997–04: John J. Pittman Collection, Part I* (David W. Akers Numismatics, Inc.), lot 912: "1876, Choice Proof . . . This Proof was struck using a new obverse die that shows none of the die lapping and polishing inside the leading feather on the headdress that characterizes the Proofs from 1862–1873, and 1875. The die is easily identified, however, by the die file mark that runs under the right foot of the first A in AMERICA toward the M. Some other Proofs of this year have the die lapping (cf. Trompeter: 22), so it is clear that the old 1862 obverse die was used for some, but not all, of the Proof run of 1876, and this new obverse die was also used for an unknown quantity. Although certainly rare, the 1876 issue is the most 'common' gold dollar in Proof prior to 1881; at least two dozen exist, perhaps even as many as 30."

AMERICA AND NUMISMATICS IN 1877

Silver coins became commonplace in circulation, soon developing into a glut. Since there was little need for new pocket change, Indian Head cents were made in small quantities and nickel three-cent and five-cent pieces were not made for circulation at all (but about 1,500 or so of each were struck as Proofs for collectors).

Despite travails in the national economy, the numismatic market had been strong in recent years, and in 1877 this continued. Part of this dynamism was caused by the availability of coins in frequent auctions, the continuing popularity and news content of the *American Journal of Numismatics*, and publications by dealers. The *Coin Collector's Journal*, launched by J.W. Scott in 1875, was riding strong, and in 1877 it was joined by *Numisma*, published by dealer Édouard Frossard, former editor of the Scott magazine. With so much to read and with intense activity, the hobby drew thousands of new participants.

The November 1876 election dispute was settled on March 2, 1877, with Rutherford B. Hayes declared the winner, barely in time for him to be inaugurated on March 4. In ensuing years many observers, including the editor of the *Washington Post*, would refer to Hayes as a fraud and impostor.

The economy, not strong since the days before the Panic of 1873, experienced more tremors in what some called the Panic of 1877, but its effects did not deserve that title. From this point the economy would strengthen, largely built on expansion of railroads and growth of towns and cities in the prairie states.

Alexander Graham Bell's telephone, demonstrated at the 1876 Centennial Exhibition, went on general sale in May 1877. On November 27, Thomas A. Edison demonstrated his phonograph, consisting of a cylinder covered with tinfoil into which a stylus impressed marks transferred from a tiny tympanum. The "Free Silver" movement gained momentum, backed by Western mining interests. Bankers, university professors, and circuit-riding speakers held themselves out as experts, attracting buyers for their pamphlets and audiences for their speeches. If silver could replace gold as the coinage metal of choice, prosperity would spread across the land, money would become cheap, old debts could be paid off easily, and other benefits would occur. Few speakers or writers had any real knowledge of American monetary or coinage history.

1877

Circulation-Strike Mintage
3,900

Proof Mintage
20

Enlarged 2x
(actual size 15 mm)

Whitman Coin Guide (WCG™)

VF-20	EF-40	AU-50	AU-55	MS-60	MS-63	MS-65	PF-63	PF-65
$275	$350	$525	$600	$775	$1,250	$3,000	$7,000	$14,000

CERTIFIED POPULATIONS

G-4–EF-45	AU-50–58	MS-60–62	MS-63	MS-64	MS-65	MS-66	MS-67	MS-68–70
12	66	110	47	36	12	14	27	11
PF-50–58	PF-60–62	PF-63	PF-64	PF-65	PF-66	PF-67	PF-68–70	
0	3	1	7	6	5	0	0	

Key to Collecting. As a low mintage date of which many examples are in numismatic hands, the 1877 has been popular for a long time. Still, the total number known is only a fraction of the 3,900 minted. Dollars of this date seem to have been saved by dealers and collectors, but only in modest quantities. Many of the higher grade coins are highly prooflike and closely resemble Proofs, sometimes leading to confusion in attribution. Cherrypick for quality, because there are many nice coins in the marketplace.

The "magic" of the 1877 date—due in large part from the well-known rarity of certain low-denomination coins of this date (Indian cent, three-cent pieces, Shield nickel, and 20-cent piece) has transferred to higher denomination issues, creating demand for gold dollars and other gold coins. Further, the published mintage figure of 3,900 acts like a beacon for intending buyers.

Estimated Total Population (Mint State). 250 to 350, this being a rather low figure in relation to the demand for them. Gems, while in the minority, appear on the market with regularity. Most Mint State coins are in ranges from MS-60 to MS-63. Choice and gem specimens can be located and have appeared in auctions on multiple occasions, but are quite scarce. *Certified population, MS-63 and higher:* 148.

Estimated Total Population (Circulated Grades). 150 to 210. Circulated coins are apt to be in higher grades such as EF or AU. Worn coins are rare, but who cares? It is likely that some coins called "Uncirculated" years ago would be called AU today. The 1877 is always in strong demand, including in circulated grades.

Characteristics of Striking and Die Notes. Usually seen sharply struck, however sometimes the letter C (AMERICA) is soft, and on some the central date numerals can be weak. As is the case with just about any gold dollar date from the 1870s onward, occasional pieces are seen with tiny lint marks (from threads adhering to the die) or minor planchet roughness. It has been suggested that circulation strikes are distinguished by having a tiny rust pit (raised on the coin) below Miss Liberty's ear on the obverse, and doubled letters in DOLLAR on the reverse.

Numismatic Notes

Die Data. 1877 four-digit date logotype: The digits are closely spaced, with 18 slightly closer than the others. The 1 is thick; a tiny spine from the upper right of its right serif touches the 8; the base of the 1 is slightly higher than the base of the 8. The 8 is upright (not leaning); its top space is slightly smaller than its bottom space. Both 7s have very heavy tops. This logotype was used on all dies.

Auction Information. Typical offerings describe prooflike surfaces. Recent auctions of ultra-grade coins devote much space to this aspect.

Proofs

Estimated Total Population and Key to Collecting. 11 to 14. Very rare. When seen, Proofs are apt to be of very high quality. The mintage of the Proof 1877 dollar is widely quoted as 20, as per the total of the two deliveries given below—this being the number of gold Proof *sets* sold this year. For this and any other Proof gold dollar it is possible that other stray pieces may have been struck to fill demand for single coins.

Die Data and Notes. The die used to strike Proofs of this year is described by David Akers under lot 913 in the John Jay Pittman Collection, Part I sale: "This Proof was struck from an entirely new obverse die which is different from the 1862–1875 die, as well as the second Proof obverse die of 1876. This new die is characterized by die file marks within the U of UNITED, and running from the right side of U into the field. I have seen no indication that this die was used for any Proofs after 1877, and it also does not seem to have been used for circulation strikes of any date."

A Proof in the Bass, Part III sale was described as having an obverse die with a complete feather. Harry Bass noted that his other Proof, and also the one in the American Numismatic Society Collection, showed evidence of die clashing; this one did not. Some raised marks on Miss Liberty's jaw included what appeared as a tiny raised L (imaginatively a privy mark for Longacre, but probably simply a die artifact) and a pimple on the neck junction(closer to the hair than to the front). The reverse had the highest ribbon point under the space between 8 and 7. The wreath tips joined at the top. (On a circulation strike in the Bass Collection, the highest point of the ribbon is below the first 7, slightly to the left of the center of the first 7.)

Mintage. Deliveries were made on February 24 (10) and May 31 (10).

Auction Information (Proofs). Certain "Proofs" may have been prooflike circulation strikes, a comment that holds true for other dates in this era. There have been many listings over the years.

AMERICA AND NUMISMATICS IN 1878

Western silver-mining interests called on their senators and representatives for help, and the result was the Bland-Allison Act passed on February 28, 1878, calling for the government to purchase millions of ounces of the metal and coin it into silver dollars ("Morgan" dollars). Hundreds of millions were made, creating what is the most popular 19th century numismatic specialty today. The design was copied from one of Morgan's pattern half dollars of 1877. It was hoped that this would help with the "Silver Question," (the position of Westerners that silver should be just as important as gold in coinage and in international transactions), but it did not. The market price of that metal continued to slide. In time, the Treasury issued a new class of currency, Silver Certificates, backed by stored silver dollars.

In the meantime, legislation had mandated that gold coins be exchangeable at par for paper beginning on January 1, 1879. The market anticipated the date, and on December 17, 1878, parity was achieved. Contrary to the expectations of bankers, the Treasury Department, and many observers, there was no rush to obtain gold. With the knowledge that bills could be redeemed in gold at any time, the public elected to keep using paper. An exception was the West Coast, where gold coins had been in circulation continuously in the 1860s and 1870s and continued to be popular.

The Panic of 1877 continued its scourge, and in 1878 more than 10,000 businesses shut their doors. Money was tight, many projects slowed or were halted, and there was little optimism.

1878

Circulation-Strike Mintage
3,000

Proof Mintage
20

Enlarged 2x
(actual size 15 mm)

Whitman Coin Guide (WCG™)

VF-20	EF-40	AU-50	AU-55	MS-60	MS-63	MS-65	PF-63	PF-65
$275	$325	$525	$600	$775	$1,250	$4,000	$6,500	$13,000

CERTIFIED POPULATIONS

G-4–EF-45	AU-50–58	MS-60–62	MS-63	MS-64	MS-65	MS-66	MS-67	MS-68–70
5	84	113	51	33	16	11	2	0
PF-50–58	**PF-60–62**	**PF-63**	**PF-64**	**PF-65**	**PF-66**	**PF-67**	**PF-68–70**	
0	2	1	8	10	3	0	0	

Key to Collecting. The 1878 is the last date of the old order, so to speak. After this year, large percentages of gold dollar mintages were saved by dealers and collectors. Today, the 1878 is a scarce date in any grade. Those that do exist are mainly in Mint State. Gems are extremely rare, and probably fewer than a dozen exist. When Mint State 1878 gold dollars are encountered they are likely in lower levels such as MS-60 or a few points above (although with "gradeflation" the numbers seem to be creeping upward). Even Virgil M. Brand, who often had the best of everything, including rarities, had to be content with a group of 1878 gold dollars grading from AU-55 to MS-60.

On December 17, 1878, gold coins achieved parity with paper money for the first time since the waning days of December 1861. Now, all was set for gold dollars to enter circulation again and see wide use. This did not happen. These coins continued to be made in small quantities. They were not generally available at face value through banks, and a premium had to be paid to get them. Jewelry companies gobbled up large quantities, making low mintages even rarer from a numismatic viewpoint. We know that thousands of gold dollars of various dates were used this way, as evidenced by Mint comments and correspondence complaining of the practice. Today, gold-dollar jewelry is not often seen. I can only surmise that when gold dollar bracelets, necklaces, and bangles fell out of fashion, most were sold as scrap and melted, particularly in the 1930s when the government called in gold.

Estimated Total Population (Mint State). 225 to 275. The rare nature of the 1878 gold dollar in Mint State vis-à-vis the rather plentiful 1879 gold dollar in Mint State, and a comparison of their mintages, makes an interesting study, considering that both dates had a production of 3,000 coins. The few coins that grade MS-65 or finer, and have good eye appeal, are special prizes. *Certified population, MS-63 and higher:* 148.

Estimated Total Population (Circulated Grades). 110 to 145, most of these being lustrous and at the AU level.

Characteristics of Striking and Die Notes. These are usually seen well struck. On many if not most pieces, the second 8 (1878) is partially filled or exhibits lines in the interior.

Numismatic Notes

Die Data. 1878 four-digit date logotype: The numerals are widely spaced, quite unlike the case for the several preceding years; the 18 closest, the 87 wider, and the 78 widest. The 1 is thick, slightly heavier at the top, and with the lower right serif incomplete at the base; the base of the 1 is higher than the base of the 8. The top and bottom spaces of both 8s are about equal size; both lean slightly right. The base of the 7 is lower than the bases of other numerals. This logotype was used on all dies.

Auction Information. Here are two selections:

> *1939–11: William B. Hale Collection* (B. Max Mehl), lot 687: "1878 Brilliant semi-proof; was originally purchased as a Proof and is just about equal to it. Listed at $25 for a Proof, and this coin is worth just about its highest listed price." Realized $7. An early comment concerning the Proof vis-à-vis circulation strike confusion.
>
> *1986–07: Auction '86* (Paramount), lot 1858: "1878, Gem Uncirculated (65/65). A wholly prooflike gem with amazing brilliance and lustre and all of its original yellow gold color. Distinctly underrated in gem condition. In fact, it has been our experience that this date is considerably harder to obtain in MS-65 than the 1877, for example, which for some reason unfathomable to us, almost always brings a higher price."

Proofs

Estimated Total Population and Key to Collecting. 11 to 14. The Proof mintage figure of 20, representing full sets of Proofs, may have been supplemented by striking a few extra pieces. Proofs have been rare since day one.

Mintage. Delivery took place on February 9.

Die Data and Notes. A description of a certified 1878 Proof gold dollar from the Bass, Part III sale stated that a short die line connects the right base of A in STATES with the first plume in the headdress; this was a different die from that used in 1877 and not the "incomplete feather" die used on certain other Proof issues of the era. On the reverse, diagonal die lines fill the interior spaces of the final 8. The date logotype is low, with the highest point of the ribbon appearing just to the left of the 7.

Auction Information (Proofs). Certain of these "Proofs" may have been prooflike circulation strikes.

> *1882–03: 40th Auction Sale, John W. Scott Collection* (Scott & Co.), lot 142: "1878 Indian Head; Proof." Realized $1.35.
>
> *1901–10: Haigh Collection Of Coins, Masonic Medals, Etc.*, (C.F. Libbie & Co.), lot 730: "1878, brilliant Proof."
>
> *1944–02: Belden E. Roach Collection* (B. Max Mehl), lot 1071: "1878 Brilliant Proof. Raised borders. A gem, and as such, rare and valuable. One of the most difficult dates to find in Proof condition. Catalogs at $25." Realized $27.50.
>
> *1945–11: Catalog of Rare United States Coins Mail Bid Sale* (J.S. Schreiber), lot 1227: 1878 Proof." Schreiber was related to Art and Paul Kagin of Hollinbeck Coin Co., but operated independently.
>
> *1982–10: Eliasberg Collection* (U.S. Gold Coin Collection) (Bowers and Ruddy Galleries), lot 67: 1878 Choice Brilliant Proof-65. Only 20 Proofs of this issue were coined, and probably no more than a dozen or so survive today. Struck from dies with the final 8 of the date filled, a characteristic observed on the Garrett Collection coin as well. *From the John H. Clapp Collection*, 1942. *Earlier from the David S. Wilson Collection (S. H. Chapman, March 1907). Part of a gold Proof set purchased at that sale.*"

1992–02: Ed Trompeter Collection (Superior), lot 24: "1878 Grade Choice Brilliant Proof. Extra outlines on UNITE MERICA and lower part of device; scattered rust pits at curl behind eye, below ear, and on neck. Reverse: Extra outlines on left wreath, bows, ribbons, and 1 DOLLAR; wreath tops not joined; right top leaf hollow; DO and final 8 filled. Pedigree Ex N.M. Kaufman: 647; the 'tack marks' affect only the reverse knife rim at top and bottom. The RARCOA cataloger thought enough of this piece to illustrate it both in text and on Color Plate III." The Kaufman coins were tacked to a backing and displayed on the wall of a bank in Marquette, Michigan. Interestingly, the "tack marks" mentioned by Superior seem to have been missed during the certification that took place after this coin was sold. *Later offering: 2001–05: Fairchild Family Trust Collection* (Ira & Larry Goldberg Coins & Collectibles), lot 1210: "1878. PCGS graded Proof 65 Ex Trompeter. Tied for the finest graded of this date, only 20 were coined in Proof, and PCGS has graded 6 this high, with none graded higher. A superb example for the advanced collector."

AMERICA AND NUMISMATICS IN 1879

Horatio C. Burchard became director of the Mint in February, succeeding Dr. Henry Richard Linderman. He remained in office through June 1885. Behind-the-scenes capers continued in Philadelphia, including striking silver and gold denominations in copper and aluminum. Pattern $4 Flowing Hair gold Stellas were made, but apart from those given out to congressmen and senators, the Mint held on to them tightly—causing a furor hotly discussed in catalogs and other publications of the era. Other varieties of 1879 and 1880 $4 coins were made secretly.

In June, *Banker's Magazine* ran an article noting that "the great bulk of the gold coinage at the United States mints consists now, and has consisted for the past twenty-five years, of double eagles, which, from their size, do not get into common circulation, but are used as public and banking reserves, or exported as so much stamped bullion." The only way to make small-denomination gold coins popular in circulation would be to eliminate paper money of under $25, as many foreign countries did.

The numismatic hobby remained active, continuing a growth that would last for more than a decade. In Philadelphia, brothers S.H. and Henry Chapman, who had left the employ of John W. Haseltine in 1878 to start their own business, conducted their first auction sale. Held on October 9, 1879, the catalog described 604 lots and had four photographic plates. In time, the Chapman brothers would rise to the top of their profession, handling the lion's share of important collections during the next several decades. Late in the year there was an investment scramble to buy Proof trade dollars and to secure regular circulation-strike gold dollars. The trade dollar boom ended in 1880, but gold dollars continued to be avidly sought for the next ten years.

The country emerged from its economic doldrums, helped in great part by massive exports of grain to Europe, to assuage the effects of crop failures there. Interest in prairie-land real estate intensified. During the next decade the Midwest would enjoy boom times financed by money from the East, attracted by interest rates often as high as 7% to 10%. In Colorado, there was a great increase in silver mining, adding to the market oversupply and further decreasing the price. The "Silver Question" remained the prime topic in politics.

On October 21, Thomas A. Edison announced that after hundreds of experiments, he had finally found a suitable filament for his incandescent light bulb. Although he was not the inventor of this boon to mankind, his product was the first to achieve commercial success, which it did in a short time. Electricity was coming into wide use as improvements were made in transmitting it to distant locations. Most interior lighting was by gas or kerosene lamps. Steam engines drove factories and mills, excepting those tapping water power.

1879

Circulation-Strike Mintage
3,000

Proof Mintage
30

Enlarged 2x
(actual size 15 mm)

Whitman Coin Guide (WCG™)

VF-20	EF-40	AU-50	AU-55	MS-60	MS-63	MS-65	PF-63	PF-65
$195	$275	$375	$475	$600	$1,400	$4,000	$5,750	$13,000

CERTIFIED POPULATIONS

G-4–EF-45	AU-50–58	MS-60–62	MS-63	MS-64	MS-65	MS-66	MS-67	MS-68–70
4	57	82	42	114	91	57	12	0
PF-50–58	**PF-60–62**	**PF-63**	**PF-64**	**PF-65**	**PF-66**	**PF-67**	**PF-68–70**	
0	1	3	10	4	5	0	0	

Key to Collecting. This year begins a continuous run of gold dollars, extending to 1889, for which collectors, dealers, and investors saved significant quantities at the time of issue. Gold dollars were not seen in circulation, and when bank tellers had them they usually charged a small premium. At the same time, the other denominations ($2.50, $3, $5, $10, and $20) were readily available at face value, although $3 coins were never popular with banks and were not widely stocked.

Philadelphia dealers in particular bought large quantities of gold dollars from the Mint at the time of issue (see notes below). Today, choice and gem examples are easily located. Many are highly prooflike. The low mintage figure is enticing for 1879—as it is for most later years—and as a result these coins have always found a ready market.

Estimated Total Population (Mint State). 700 to 900. Mint State specimens are usually highly prooflike. I have handled several hundred Mint State specimens of each of the 1879, 1880, and 1881 gold dollar dates, and other groups have appeared elsewhere on the market (see notes below). It seems that most of these have not yet reached the certification services. The offering of prooflike gems at auction has furnished many opportunities for catalogers to use enthusiastic descriptions and high grades not normally encountered in the gold dollar series until the years from 1879 onward. Trophy coins abound of the later dates—with MS-66 and higher certified examples appearing on the market with regularity. *Certified population, MS-63 and higher:* 323.

Estimated Total Population (Circulated Grades). 150 to 225. Rare, simply because the hoard coins were Mint State, as were those saved by investors and speculators. None reached general circulation. Thus, any circulated piece was mishandled by an investor or speculator. Probably only a few hundred pieces below MS-60 exist, and I have never seen a well-worn one.

Characteristics of Striking and Die Notes. The majority of pieces are highly prooflike, sometimes resembling full Proofs, except that the rims of circulation strikes are not as sharply struck, and in some instances the dentils are mushy or run together. On some pieces the obverse is fully prooflike, while the reverse is partially so, or even frosty.

The dies clashed at one time, and a few pieces (*e.g.*, Patterson Collection, Bowers and Merena, March 1985, lot 3004; also Auction '87, Superior, lot 1619) show traces of clashmarks, mostly on the reverse. It seems that the same die pair was used to make certain Proofs (see below) as well as circulation strikes.

Numismatic Notes

Die Data. 1879 four-digit date logotype: The numerals are widely spaced, with 18 closest, 87 wider, and 79 widest. The lower left serif of the 1 is heavier than the lower right serif. The base of the 8 is lower than that of other numerals; its top interior is slightly smaller than the bottom interior. The 9 has a small ball close to the curve above it, but separated from it on most dies. This logotype was used on all dies.

The obverse die used to strike many pieces has most or all of the letters in LIBERTY (in Miss Liberty's headband) missing, reminiscent of 1873 gold dollars. Breen (*Major Varieties of U.S. Gold Dollars*, 1964) states, "[On the headband] BER weak on all seen." John Dannreuther's explanation for the missing LIBERTY on several dates is that, since the word was *raised* on working dies, it could be easily removed (or partially removed) by indiscriminate polishing.

Woodward Misled by the Mint. In his sale of the William Clogston Collection, April 1881, W. Elliot Woodward included this on lot 1019: "1879 Splendid Proof. In the catalog of my 33rd sale, No. 1508 is '1879 gold dollar, far rarer than the 1858 silver dollar.' This statement is an error which I will explain. On the 22nd day of December, 1879, I called at the Mint in Philadelphia, and in conversation with one of the officers or clerks, he gave me the information that only 27 gold Proof sets had been struck up to that date, and that a large proportion of that small number remained unsold; he also informed me that 27 was the entire number struck of gold dollars and three dollar pieces, and that there would probably be no more made during the year. Influenced by this statement I purchased a gold set, and until recently was not aware that the actual issue of these two coins exceeded one thousand each. I beg to offer an apology to collectors for so far forgetting myself as to make any statement for fact, based on information obtained from the Mint of the United States."

Speculation in Gold Dollars, 1879–1881. Beginning in 1879 there was a popular speculation in certain United States coin series, especially the gold dollar, but to a lesser extent the silver trade dollar and the $3 gold denomination. Large quantities of gold dollars bearing the dates 1879, 1880, and 1881 were bought by a Baltimore investor, whose identity is not known today, although it has been suggested that T. Harrison Garrett, an heir to the Baltimore & Ohio Railroad fortune, is a likely candidate. If so, these gold dollars were not transferred to The Johns Hopkins University in 1942 when T. Harrison Garrett's coins were gifted to the institution by one of his sons, John Work Garrett.

A glance at the circulation-strike mintage figures reveals enticingly low production quantities for circulation-strike gold dollars of these three years:

1879: 3,000

1880: 1,600

1881: 7,620

Quantities were set aside, and began appearing in large numbers in the 1940s. Among the advertisers in *The Numismatist*, April 1947, Scott Stamp & Coin Company, Inc., devoted a full page to offering 1879 and 1880 gold dollars for sale in Uncirculated grade at $15 and $20 each, respectively.

In the 1950s and 1960s, glittering prooflike gem gold dollars of 1879, 1880, and 1881 were available in the market in quantity, especially through the offices of Abner Kreisberg in California and Thomas Warfield of Baltimore (these in addition to a hoard of 300 handled by John J. Ford in the 1950s). It was generally acceded at the time that the source for these coins was a Baltimore bank vault, but no other details were given. In a comment made to the in 1996, Abner Kreisberg recalled that he had purchased some of his coins from old-time dealer Joe Block (who also had large quantities of 1938-D Buffalo nickels).[56]

I was involved in the numismatic distribution of these pieces and acquired examples to the extent of many hundreds of each date. There were more of 1881 than of the other two. Today, high-grade gold dollars of all three dates are often encountered and are highly prized for their quality and their low mintage.

Walter Breen (*Encyclopedia*, 1988) gives as the source for this hoard Charles E. Green (Chicago dealer) and Horace L.P. Brand (of Chicago, a brother to super-collector Virgil M. Brand and co-heir of the fabulous Brand estate following Virgil's death in 1926). If Brand had been the source, further information could be found in the extensive Brand archives in the library of the American Numismatic Society, New York. However, examination of those records by John Dannreuther revealed that the only date Brand bought in a group was the 1889, of which he acquired 50 pieces. Brand was numismatically active from the 1880s until his death, but probably not as early as 1879 through 1881, for he was still a teenager then and it is unlikely that he would have bought gold dollars in large quantities.

Auction Information. Auction listings from this year onward generally impart very little useful numismatic information. Nearly all are devoted to grade, perceived rarity, and appearance.

PROOFS

Estimated Total Population and Key to Collecting. 14 to 17. Authentic Proofs are very rare. However, prooflike circulation strikes closely resemble Proofs, and since it seems that Proof dies were also used to make circulation strikes, the difference is often fuzzy. Consulting historical listings is of no use in computing rarity, due to this fuzziness as well as to the practice of offering prooflike Mint State coins as "Proofs." Proofs that meet current die criteria are very rare and constitute only a tiny fraction of those offered as "Proof" in past auction catalogs and price lists. Proofs are usually seen with "orange peel" fields and cameo contrast to the letters and devices.

Mintage. The following were delivered as part of full gold Proof sets. (These figures come directly from original Mint records as studied by R.W. Julian.[57]) Second quarter: seven. Third quarter: four. Fourth quarter: ten. Walter Breen states (*Encyclopedia*, 1988) that 20 Proofs were delivered on January 25, these with criss-crossed lines in the left bow opening; these dies were also used to make circulation strikes, sometimes very prooflike, and later showing clashmarks. On November 22, ten additional Proofs were delivered "from drastically repolished dies" (to remove clashmarks) which do not show these lines.

Die Data and Notes. Walter Breen in his Proof coin work (1989) states that on Proofs "BER (LIBERTY) is always weak." However, this may be true of some circulation strikes as well. Light repunching is seen at the lower outside right of the 8.

An 1879 Proof in the Bass, Part III catalog was described as having an obverse die with mirrorlike fields. This was a different die from that on the 1877 or 1878 Proof dollars in the Bass, Part III offering. Raised rust marks appear on the neck below the jaw, about opposite the left curve of the topmost of the two curls. On the reverse, the highest point of the ribbon is just left of the 7.

Auction Information (Proofs). Listings abound, but likely most have been for prooflike circulation strikes.

AMERICA AND NUMISMATICS IN 1880

Nearly 50 coin auctions were held this year in a field now crowded with dealers. The venerable W. Elliot Woodward, who had left numismatics to concentrate in developing real estate in Roxbury, Massachusetts, had resumed his activity in the late 1870s, and in 1880 cataloged a remarkable eight sales. John W. Haseltine turned out nine; the Chapman brothers held three; and Ed. Frossard, S.K. Harzfeld, E.B. Mason Jr., the combination of H.P. Smith and H.G. Sampson, Bangs & Co., J.W. Scott, and George W. Massamore created others.

The typical auction catalog of the period had few if any illustrations and gave very brief descriptions to federal coins, often simply a word or two, such as "Brilliant Proof, rare." On the other hand, colonials, tokens, and medals were often granted a sentence or two, and rarities a paragraph. There were no grading standards or agreed-upon interpretations, and one person's "Proof" might be another's polished Extremely Fine. Generally, collectors did not bid by mail, but placed commissions with favored dealers who attended the sales in person, viewed the lots, and bid. Auctions proceeded at a slow pace, punctuated by many interruptions, sometimes including last-minute inspection of coins (usually on view on tables in the same room).

Most numismatists interested in federal coins collected copper cents and early (pre-Liberty Seated) silver. Gold coins of 1795 to 1834 were pursued with passion, as were gold dollars from 1849 to date, but there was little interest in other denominations, and scarcely any at all for the $5, $10, and $20 issues. Coins were collected by *date*, not by mintmark. In 1880, no one paid attention to or cared about Carson City, San Francisco, or other issues that later became recognized as rare. Tokens and medals were very popular, as were Fractional Currency and Confederate paper notes. Patterns always attracted attention at auction sales. Like as not, the typical numismatist of 1880 had a few foreign coins in addition to American issues.

In the 1880 census, the American population was recorded at 50,155,783. Most people lived on the East Coast. It was a presidential election year; many Republicans wanted U.S. Grant to run for a third term. At the nominating convention delegates were stalemated on the matter, until the 36th ballot, when James Abram Garfield was chosen. The Democrats fielded Winfield Scott Hancock. In November, Garfield was the winner.

1880

Circulation-Strike Mintage
1,600

Proof Mintage
36

Enlarged 2x
(actual size 15 mm)

Whitman Coin Guide (WCG™)

VF-20	EF-40	AU-50	AU-55	MS-60	MS-63	MS-65	PF-63	PF-65
$185	$275	$325	$400	$575	$1,400	$4,000	$5,500	$13,000

CERTIFIED POPULATIONS

G-4–EF-45	AU-50–58	MS-60–62	MS-63	MS-64	MS-65	MS-66	MS-67	MS-68–70
1	15	66	38	83	112	156	191	47
PF-50–58	PF-60–62	PF-63	PF-64	PF-65	PF-66	PF-67	PF-68–70	
1	8	7	13	8	3	3	0	

Key to Collecting. Choice and gem Mint State coins are very plentiful, since many, if not most, were saved by collectors, dealers, and speculators. Some are highly prooflike and closely resemble Proofs. The 1880 has always been in great demand due to the low mintage figure.

Estimated Total Population (Mint State). 1,000 to 1,200, this representing *most of the mintage!* Nearly all were saved by investors and speculators at the time. However, unlike certain later gold dollars of the decade, those dated 1880 seem to have remained in groups until the present century. Relatively few have reached the grading services so far. However, the 1880 gold dollar is of enduring popularity, and whenever a nice specimen appears on the market it sells readily. Nearly all examples are choice or gem quality, often with prooflike surfaces. Moreover, each is usually a visual treat. Any auction offering of a gem coin invariably attracts enthusiastic bidders drawn by the enticingly low mintage figure and the spectacularly high grade—although for 1880 we are talking about super-gems in the MS-68 range or higher. *Certified population, MS-63 and higher:* 627.

Estimated Total Population (Circulated Grades). 90 to 120. A worn 1880 gold dollar would be a *rarity*, simply because most were carefully preserved in Mint State. So far as is known, only a few pieces at best reached circulation. David Akers (1975) located many dozens of citations for Mint State coins at auction, but only one coin in VF grade and only one in EF.

Characteristics of Striking and Die Notes. These are usually very well struck. Some show slight repunching at the central 88 (1880) figures.

Numismatic Notes

Die Data. 1880 four-digit date logotype: The digits 18 are closely spaced; 88 and 80 are also close, but not so close as 18. The bottoms of 1 and 8 are about on the same level. The first 8 is slightly higher than the second 8, and the top opening smaller on both. The bottom of the 0 is higher than that of the adjacent 8, and it leans slightly right. This logotype was used on all dies.

A description of circulation strikes from the Bass, Part III offering: 1: The obverse die is highly polished and prooflike, but different from any *Proof* die seen. The reverse has the highest point of the ribbon below the second 8, just about below the left side of the bottom interior of the 8. The date is very close to the ribbon point. 2: Another die shows the date 1880 slightly to the left of the preceding. On both dies, the date is close to the ribbon below, with the highest point of the ribbon being below the center of the 8 or slightly to the left of it.

Hoard Note. John J. Ford Jr. handled a hoard of about 300 pieces in the 1950s (and a similar number of 1879; see earlier listing).

Auction Information. Listings abound, with adjectives usually concentrating on prooflike character and high grade.

Proofs

Estimated Total Population and Key to Collecting. 22 to 27. True Proofs are very rare. Many old-time listings are apt to have been prooflike Mint State pieces rather than Proofs. The entire situation is quite confused, and historical citations are almost impossible to reconcile to Proof vs. Mint State unless the pieces are re-examined today.

Die Data. A description of Proof characteristics by David W. Akers, of lot 917 of the John Jay Pittman Collection, Part I, October 1997: "The wreath tops are solidly joined, in contrast to the business strikes where they are not. There is also a broad frosted area around the top end of each side of the wreath that is much more prominent on Proofs than it is on the business strikes. Finally, when viewed edge-on, Proofs are decidedly different from the business strikes, since the edge of a Proof is broad and square, as well as 'thicker' due to the double striking under extra pressure."

A description of a PCGS-certified 1880 Proof coin in the Bass, Part III Sale says the obverse die is highly polished, unlike any Proof dies seen in the Bass sale. The centers of letters are filled and have frosted surfaces. The reverse has the highest point of the ribbon below the left edge of the second 8. The wreath is not joined at top, but is separated by a small distance.

Mintage. The following were delivered as part of full gold Proof sets: (These figures come directly from original Mint records as studied by R.W. Julian.[58]) First quarter: 17. Third quarter: 5. Fourth quarter: 10. The several other Proofs were delivered singly.

Auction Information (Proofs). Listings abound, but likely most have been for prooflike circulation strikes.

AMERICA AND NUMISMATICS IN 1881

Silver coins from the dime to the half dollar were a glut in commercial channels. No more were needed, but the Mint continued the production in small quantities for circulation, to prevent them from being rare. In January 1881, S.K. Harzfeld included this in an auction catalog: "lot 1081a: 1880 half dollar, quarter, dime. Uncirc., bright. 3 pieces. The Superintendent of the U.S. Mint, Colonel A.L. Snowden, has authorized me to state, that he will furnish on application, to every bona fide collector, two sets of these Uncirculated coins, at face value. As was done in 1879, speculators (not the legitimate coin dealers) tried to secure these coins and to sell them at fancy prices, claiming that only 100 sets were struck. Colonel Snowden, however, stopped at once the sale to these speculators, and had a sufficient number struck ($1,000 worth of each denomination) to supply all bona fide collectors."

Archibald Loudon Snowden, a nephew of former Mint Director James Ross Snowden, was living a lie and was deeply involved in the secret coinage of patterns and other rarities for private profit. There was no demand for additional gold dollars for circulation either, since paper dollars were used instead. A small coinage was effected and was mostly taken up by numismatists and speculators, plus jewelry manufacturers.

Financial, commercial, and banking journals featured discussions as to why the public was not using gold coins now that they were available, and had been since the waning days of 1871. The *Annual Statement* of the New York Chamber of Commerce noted this:

> A gold coin is but seldom met with in the ordinary transactions of life. From this it can only be inferred that the paper currency of the country is amply sufficient to meet the daily wants of the people. The history of all currencies shows that the one "having the least value will circulate, the natural tendency of man being to hold on to that which he most esteems. The only manner, therefore, by which gold can be brought into circulation is by withdrawing a part of the already sufficient paper currency."
>
> If it is intended to affirm that the paper currency we now have, consisting of greenbacks and National-bank notes, is of less value than gold, and that this is the reason why the paper circulates rather than the gold, we most decidedly dissent on both points. The paper will exchange for as much as the gold in the market, and will pay debts equally well, in any part of the country. Nowhere in the United States, is the slightest premium obtainable upon gold, in exchange for the paper. If the paper is circulated in preference to gold, it is because the paper is the most convenient, and because the people do not choose to lumber themselves up with gold, when something, equally valuable and available and more portable, can be had as a substitute. Without doubt, gold can be forced into circulation by withdrawing paper, but before a measure so repugnant to the habits of our people, and so certain to subject them to annoyance, is adopted, it will be necessary to assign some substantial reason for it.

President James A. Garfield said: "Whoever controls the volume of money in any country is master of all its legislation and commerce." On July 2, 1881, Garfield was mortally wounded by a gunshot from a rejected office-seeker, Charles J. Guiteau, and on September 19 he died. Succeeding him in office was his vice president, Chester Alan Arthur. The Supreme Court ruled the Federal Income Tax Law of 1862 unconstitutional.

Growth continued in the Midwest, and many new towns and cities were laid out. In the East investors eagerly purchased stocks and bonds, and for banks the high-yielding bonds brought new strength to their investment portfolios (or so it was thought).

1881

Circulation-Strike Mintage
7,620

Proof Mintage
87

Enlarged 2x
(actual size 15 mm)

Whitman Coin Guide (WCG™)

VF-20	EF-40	AU-50	AU-55	MS-60	MS-63	MS-65	PF-63	PF-65
$185	$275	$325	$400	$575	$1,400	$4,000	$5,500	$13,000

CERTIFIED POPULATIONS

G-4–EF-45	AU-50–58	MS-60–62	MS-63	MS-64	MS-65	MS-66	MS-67	MS-68–70
3	24	105	126	120	95	159	186	86
PF-50–58	**PF-60–62**	**PF-63**	**PF-64**	**PF-65**	**PF-66**	**PF-67**	**PF-68–70**	
1	5	8	22	8	10	2	0	

Key to Collecting. The 1881 gold dollar was hoarded at or near the time of issue. Groups and clusters of this date remained intact until the 1950s and 1960s, similar to the situation for 1879 and 1880, although more exist of 1881. As a result, choice and gem specimens are readily available today, although most have not been submitted to the grading service. Because the mintage was fairly low this year, coins of this date have always been in very strong numismatic demand.

Estimated Total Population (Mint State). 1,500 to 2,000. Nearly all are choice or gem, often with full prooflike surfaces (often sold as Proofs until recent times, when die data became available). The typical Mint State 1881 gold dollar is apt to be a visual treat. *Certified population, MS-63 and higher:* 626.

Estimated Total Population (Circulated Grades). 40 to 60. A worn 1881 gold dollar is a *rarity*, simply because most were saved close to the time of issue and survived in Mint State.

Characteristics of Striking and Die Notes. A few pieces show light clashmarks. Some circulation strikes show indistinct areas among the dentils. On some pieces the two central date digits, 88, show doubling in their interiors (*e.g.*, the Walter H. Childs Collection coin, Bowers and Merena, August 1999, lot 557).

Numismatic Notes

Die Data. 1881 four-digit date logotype: The date is very widely spaced, with 18 wide but not as wide as the others, and 81 in-between. On both 1s the lower left serif is slightly more prominent than the lower right serif. The interior of both 8s is somewhat irregular. This logotype was used on all dies.

Auction Information. Selected citations reflect the prooflike character of many coins.

1890–09: 39th Sale, Maj. William J. Thomsen (Dr. George W. Massamore), lot 801: "1881 Uncirculated. Almost equal to a Proof."

1900–03: Leopold Gans Collection (Lyman H. Low), lot 27: "1881 Uncirculated, brilliant, about equal to Proof. Rare."

1913–05: Malcolm N. Jackson Collection (U.S. Coin Co.), lot 328: "1881 Uncirculated, Proof surface." Realized $2.75.

1963–05: Emerson Gaylord Collection (Mayflower Coin Auctions), lot 74: "1881 A superb Gem Uncirculated specimen with full proof-like toning and high edge. An example of the proof-like pieces being sold today as Proofs."

1964–08: ANA Convention Sale (Federal Brand Enterprises), lot 2404: "1881—Brilliant Uncirculated, prooflike surface. A Gem first strike. (Purchased as Proof)."

1981–07: Auction '81 (Paramount), lot 1385: "1881 Superb MS-67. Brilliant, wholly prooflike 'first strike' that is virtually indistinguishable from a true Proof. Sharply struck with a high wire rim, deep mirror surfaces and incredible brilliance. Just a hint of light copper toning."

Proofs

Estimated Total Population and Key to Collecting. 40 to 50. So many prooflike Mint State coins have been sold as "Proof" in the past, that it is impossible to build an accurate record of historical citations.

Die Data and Notes. David W. Akers related (1975) that in 1973, Paramount International Coin Corporation handled an interesting group, the Leon Lindheim hoard of 1881 "Proof" gold dollars. "Lindheim, a well-known Cleveland collector and numismatic writer (with a regular column in the Cleveland *Plain Dealer*), set out to acquire as many specimens as he could from the reported 87-piece Proof mintage for this date, and over a period of many years he purchased many. As it turned out, *only eight coins* were actually Proofs, the rest being circulation strikes. Some were fully prooflike circulation strikes, but many others were only partially prooflike or were frosty . . . The true Proofs of 1881 are distinguishable by a small unfinished area in the die between the lower left part of the D in DOLLAR and the wreath."

Notes on a certified Proof in the Bass, Part III sale describe it as having the left side of the interior of the first 8 (1881) slightly shaded. The DO (DOLLAR) and A are filled in, but the top and bottom of the R show Proof surface.

Mintage. The mintage figure of 87 Proofs was located by Walter Breen as part of the chief coiner's records at the Mint.[59] This is higher than the "official" record which indicates 60 Proofs.

Auction Information (Proofs). Listings abound, but likely most have been for prooflike circulation strikes.

AMERICA AND NUMISMATICS IN 1882

The Chapman brothers printed a catalog of unprecedented lavish quality, with 12 photographic plates, describing several thousand coins, tokens, and medals from the celebrated collection of Charles I. Bushnell. Much effort was expended in giving lengthy and often interesting descriptions to scarce and rare issues. The catalog delighted collectors but was received with consternation by other dealers, who considered the Chapmans, both in their twenties, to be brash young upstarts. During the year more than 50 other auctions were conducted, so many that it was almost impossible to keep track of them. These were heady times in the coin hobby, the market was strong, and collectors and dealers had smiles on their faces.

It was an era of big business, and in many industries there were mergers to create trusts, including the Standard Oil Trust, captained by John D. Rockefeller, which controlled 95% of the American petroleum industry. In the West, railroad monopolies raised rates so as to deprive farmers and others of their profits. "Captains of industry" tried to outdo each other by erecting palatial homes in San Francisco, New York City, and other commercial centers.

Jumbo the elephant, brought to America from England by P.T. Barnum, was exhibited in Madison Square Garden, New York City, and was a sensation whose name soon became a synonym for large size. Opera houses were built in most towns and cities during this period and served to showcase actors, musicians, and others, including repertory companies as well as traveling troupes. Railroads were the main method of inter-city transportation, and tracks extended to just about everywhere. In villages and towns most people walked to their local destinations, since few had horses or carriages. At local stores patent medicines were among the best sellers, the demand being stimulated by outrageous claims in advertising. There were no rules or restrictions to be obeyed.

1882

Circulation-Strike Mintage
5,000

Proof Mintage
125

Enlarged 2x
(actual size 15 mm)

Whitman Coin Guide (WCG™)

VF-20	EF-40	AU-50	AU-55	MS-60	MS-63	MS-65	PF-63	PF-65
$185	$275	$325	$400	$575	$1,400	$4,000	$5,500	$13,000

CERTIFIED POPULATIONS

G-4–EF-45	AU-50–58	MS-60–62	MS-63	MS-64	MS-65	MS-66	MS-67	MS-68–70
1	29	86	65	76	45	62	77	17
PF-50–58	PF-60–62	PF-63	PF-64	PF-65	PF-66	PF-67	PF-68–70	
0	9	4	30	25	22	2	0	

Key to Collecting. The enticing low mintage figure of 5,000 has made this gold dollar a perennial favorite. Very few if any 1882 gold dollars were placed into general circulation, a commentary that is relevant for all dates of gold dollars of 1879 to 1889. Thus, an exceptionally high proportion of circulation strikes survives today, mostly in Mint State, and often choice or gem. While the gold dollars of 1879, 1880, and 1881 seem to have been hoarded in just a few places, later to appear on the market, in contrast, gold dollars of 1882 and years through 1889 seem to have been put away singly or in small groups. Today, the 1882 gold dollar is common in choice and gem Mint State. Likely, percentage-wise more have been submitted to the certification services than is the case for 1879 to 1881 coins.

Estimated Total Population (Mint State). 1,200 to 1,600. Most specimens are choice to gem and are typically very attractive. *Certified population, MS-63 and higher:* 684.

Estimated Total Population (Circulated Grades). 60 to 100. Very rare, since most survivors are Mint State. This issue never circulated. Worn pieces, when seen, are apt to be EF or AU.

Characteristics of Striking and Die Notes. The 1882 gold dollar is usually seen well struck, although a few are weak at the top of the date numerals (due to the demand for metal flow into the portrait on the *obverse* die, opposite the date numerals when both dies were in the coining press). Examples can be highly lustrous or with nearly full prooflike surfaces, or something in between.

Reflective of the need for expertise to differentiate prooflikes from Proofs is this citation from David W. Akers' cataloging of an 1882 dollar in Auction '82, lot 1852: "1882. MS-65. Boldly struck with deep mirror fields and beautiful copper toning. 'First strike' Uncirculated that is almost indistinguishable from a true Proof."

Some pieces are from clashed dies, although such citations are sparse in the literature; an example being RARCOA's 1882 dollar in Auction '83 lot 1354, "Struck from boldly clashed dies." On some circulation strikes, the 2 (1882) is slightly filled.

NUMISMATIC NOTES

Die Data. 1882 four-digit date logotype: The numbers 18 are closer together than the other digits, with 88 widest, and 82 nearly as wide. The base of the 1 is higher than the base of the 8. Both 8s slant slightly right (best determined by examining the position of the interior spaces). The 2 has thick (can vary) upper right and heavy bottom elements, the ball at its upper left is very small and imperfectly formed, and close to curve below it; the tip of the tail of the thick base of the 2 approaches the curve of the 2 and touches it on some impressions. This logotype was used on all dies.

Auction Information. Listings are aplenty, usually concentrating on prooflike character and high grade—not particularly a "good read" except for numismatists for whom ultra-high grade is the main factor in acquiring a coin.

PROOFS

Estimated Total Population and Key to Collecting. 60 to 80. Proofs are readily available, this in stark contrast to rarities of the 1870s and earlier. Certification data are useless in determining the number of *different* specimens of this and other Proof gold issues, due to resubmissions of the same coins. The issue is complicated by the fact that years ago, prior to the rise of the certification services, some prooflike Mint State coins were offered as Proofs. Perhaps the state of the art is coming full circle, and the value of the professional numismatist comes to the fore, with his or her expert opinion being just as good, if not even better than accumulated citations. The Proof attributions of the *leading* certification services conform to currently published die criteria. As is evident from citations throughout this text, there is still more to be learned about Proof characteristics of certain years.

Die Data and Notes. Proofs of this date (and era) often have lint marks from careless manufacturing and/or handling marks, the latter also acquired at the Mint. Proofs were made on multiple occasions this year (thus furnishing the possibility for slightly differing die characteristics), deliveries being widely spaced and in groups of 25, 33, 24, 15, 16, and 12 coins, to yield the total of 125.

Notes concerning a Bass, Part III 1882 gold dollar certified by PCGS: The obverse die shows interiors of all letters frosty, as seen in most other gold dollar Proofs of the era. The reverse has the highest ribbon point below the left side (not left edge) of the second 8. The date logotype slants slightly up to the right, usually determinable by noting that the 1 (1882) is farther below the O (DOLLAR) than the 2 is below the A. The interior of the second 2 is nearly completely filled in, except at the bottom.

Auction Information (Proofs). Listings abound, but likely most have been for prooflike circulation strikes.

America and Numismatics in 1883

In January the Liberty Head nickel, the design of Chief Engraver William A. Barber, was placed into circulation. The denomination on the reverse was given simply by the Roman numeral V, logical enough since the nickel three-cent piece had borne the Roman numeral III for many years. However, sharpers gold plated the nickels, sometimes added reeding to the edge by filing or milling, and passed them off as $5 gold coins of similar diameter. This erupted into a major scandal, Treasury agents were dispatched to track down the malefactors, and the design was quickly modified to add the word CENTS below the V. Rumor spread that the Mint would recall all of the CENTS-less coins and they would become rare and valuable. This news electrified the nation and prompted citizens to check their change in hopes of finding a rarity. The community of numismatists expanded greatly.

Gold dollars continued to be popular with numismatists and investors, who ignored quarter eagles, $3 pieces, and larger denominations, except for a few who acquired Proofs each year. Auction action continued its frenetic pace in the hobby, with, on average, a sale every week. In June, sales were conducted by Ed. Frossard (two events), H.G. Sampson, John W. Haseltine (two), W. Elliot Woodward (three), Lyman H. Low, and Charles Steigerwalt.

America enjoyed prosperity, with special focus on continuing growth and expansion in the prairie states, as towns and villages were laid out, built, and occupied. In publishing during the decade there was emphasis on books delineating town and county histories, plus atlases, some of which were very large and impressive.

1883

Circulation-Strike Mintage
10,800

Proof Mintage
207

Enlarged 2x
(actual size 15 mm)

Whitman Coin Guide (WCG™)

VF-20	EF-40	AU-50	AU-55	MS-60	MS-63	MS-65	PF-63	PF-65
$185	$275	$325	$400	$575	$1,400	$4,000	$5,500	$13,000

CERTIFIED POPULATIONS

G-4–EF-45	AU-50–58	MS-60–62	MS-63	MS-64	MS-65	MS-66	MS-67	MS-68–70
6	60	197	144	182	110	127	197	14
PF-50–58	**PF-60–62**	**PF-63**	**PF-64**	**PF-65**	**PF-66**	**PF-67**	**PF-68–70**	
1	16	8	19	15	16	7	0	

Key to Collecting. Very few, if any, 1883 gold dollars were placed into general circulation, a commentary that is relevant for all dates of gold dollars from 1879 to 1889. Thus, an exceptionally high proportion of circulation strikes survives today, mostly in Mint State and often choice or gem. Finding one that is "just right" will be no problem.

Estimated Total Population (Mint State). 900 to 1,300. Many pieces are prooflike and closely resemble full Proofs, but typically lack the "pebbly" or "orange peel" surface in the fields. The typical Mint State 1883 is a very attractive coin. Ultra-grade coins beckon to those with well-fortified bank accounts. *Certified population, MS-63 and higher:* 350.

Estimated Total Population (Circulated Grades). 80 to 120. Very scarce, since this issue was never released into general circulation. Worn pieces, when seen, are apt to be EF or AU, with the "wear" due to handling as souvenirs; the same commentary is relevant for all gold dollars of the 1880s.

Characteristics of Striking and Die Notes. Many if not most have areas of weak striking at the dentils, with the projections appearing mushy. This is true of prooflike pieces as well as those with frosty luster. Many specimens show die lapping.

Numismatic Notes

Die Data. 1883 four-digit date logotype: The figures are widely spaced: 18 closest, 88 slightly wider, and 83 extremely wide. The base of the 1 is higher than the base of the 8. Both 8s lean slightly right (as evidenced by their center interiors). The 3 is somewhat irregular at left, with its top ball larger and better formed than its bottom ball, which is somewhat truncated at its top. This logotype was used on all dies.

For circulation strikes, the date logotype position is similar to that on Proofs. The wreath apex is open (not joined, as on some or all Proofs).

Auction Information. Listings abound, again mostly concentrating on prooflike surfaces and high grades.

Proofs

Estimated Total Population and Key to Collecting. 50 to 75. The Proof coinage figure for this likely represents the *numismatic* demand for Proofs of the era, this in contrast to the largely expanded Proof figures of later dates, mostly for coins bought by the jewelry trade, it seems. Today, Proof 1883 gold dollars are elusive. In the past many prooflike Mint State coins have been offered as Proofs, thus somewhat obscuring the numbers known. However, it is likely that all pieces certified by the major services are Proofs. Moreover, Proofs lack the indistinct border striking of many prooflike Mint State coins. Curiously, the *flat rims* on many Proof gold dollars of this decade are irregular or imperfect.

Die Data and Notes. Breen (*Encyclopedia*, 1988) stated: "Proofs and circulation strikes come with or without repunching in the two central date numerals."

Some Proofs have elements of the date repunched, especially at the upper loops of both 8s and around the 3 (*e.g.*, Walter H. Childs Collection coin, B&M, August 1999 lot 559). A Floyd Starr Collection example (Stack's, October 1992), Proof lot 1122, was described as a: "Perfect date variety, the numerals filled, but not repunched."

Notes concerning Bass III 1883 Proof gold dollar certified by PCGS: Obverse die with U (UNITED) part of second S (STATES), most of first A (AMERICA) all of C, and all of second A filled in. Other interior areas with Proof surfaces. Same reverse since the interior of the first date is filled in as is the top interior of the second 8 and partially the bottom interior.

Auction Information (Proofs). As is true for most gold dollars of the 1880s there are many auction listings, but likely most have been for prooflike circulation strikes.

Mint Correspondence. It seems that on November 20, 1883, Superintendent Snowden of the Philadelphia Mint was annoyed that depositors of gold bullion were requesting tiny gold dollars in exchange. At the time, gold dollars were a nationwide fad, and all were selling at a premium. He would have preferred to make $20 gold double eagles, involving less time and trouble. The answer came to him on November 21, from Horatio Burchard, Director of the Mint, whose office was in Washington, D.C. (and had been since 1873):

> I have received your letter of the 20th instant stating that you are in receipt of many orders for gold dollars, and that in view of the fact that the Mint is running after hours to meet the current demand for silver dollars and minor coin you request to be informed if you should coin gold dollars.
>
> Section 3519 of the Revised Statutes provides that 'any owner of gold bullion may deposit the same at any Mint, to be formed into coin for his benefit,' and Section 3544 provides that 'in the denominations of coin delivered, the Superintendent shall comply with the wishes of the depositor, except when impracticable or inconvenient to do so.'
>
> Under these sections of law you cannot refuse to receive a deposit of gold bullion to be returned in gold dollars if so requested, but if you have no coin of that denomination in your bullion fund and it is inconvenient to coin the same, the depositor must wait until such time as you can conveniently coin them or else receive other denominations in payment for his deposit.
>
> I am clearly of the opinion that you should not run after regular working hours for this purpose; you should not pay them for other moneys, but only in settlement for deposits of gold bullion for coinage into gold dollars.

Get Them Before They Are All Gone. In June 1884, *Mason's Monthly Illustrated Coin Collector's Magazine* reported that recently-coined 1883 gold dollars were "rapidly going out of circulation." Actually, they never were in general commerce.

AMERICA AND NUMISMATICS IN 1884

During the calendar year $23,991,756.50 face value of gold coins was minted, with extensive coinage occurring in San Francisco, near the source of gold bullion. At the Philadelphia Mint only Proof $20 coins were made in 1883, 1884, and 1887—and none for general circulation—this because facilities of larger presses in Philadelphia were mostly devoted to the making of Morgan silver dollars, which had been made in huge quantities since implementation of the Bland-Allison Act in 1878. Uncle Sam stored vast quantities of such dollars, which, except for limited use in the West and South, were still unpopular with the public. Gold dollars continued to be in demand by investors and jewelers, some of whom ordered them from the Mint through their banks. Three-dollar coins scarcely ever reached the news, and production continued quietly, with many simply going into storage at the Philadelphia Mint, joining quantities on hand from prior years. A Treasury report estimated that $463,537,000 in gold coins was held in the United States, including $171,553,000 by the government.

The numismatic hobby remained dynamic, building on general enthusiasm for all kinds of hobbies as well as the afterglow from the said-to-be rare and soon valuable 1883 CENTS-less nickels.

In early 1884, there was fear of a financial panic when in New York City several important commercial firms failed, causing a decline in the prices of stocks and bonds. Fortunately for all concerned, the distress did not become widespread, and it was soon forgotten.

In the meantime, towns and cities in the Midwest continued to enjoy great expansion funded by extensive sale of bonds at high interest rates to banks and investors in the East.

The value of silver bullion continued to decline, keeping the "Silver Question" in the forefront of American politics. Most everyone seeking election to public office had to take a stand of pro-silver (the Western sentiment) or anti-silver (the East). Europeans continued to be worried that Americans would seek to redeem bonds and other obligations in silver dollars rather than gold, and for this reason large quantities of double eagles left the country.

In November, Democratic candidate Grover Cleveland was elected president, defeating James G. Blaine. Popular sentiment had it that Blaine would be a shoo-in, until a minister, seeking to be helpful, stated that the Democratic Party was based on "rum, Romanism, and rebellion." (Romanism referred to the Catholic church.) This aroused the ire of many Democrats, who turned out in large numbers at polling places, determining the outcome.

1884

Circulation-Strike Mintage
5,230

Proof Mintage
1,006

Enlarged 2x
(actual size 15 mm)

Whitman Coin Guide (WCG™)

VF-20	EF-40	AU-50	AU-55	MS-60	MS-63	MS-65	PF-63	PF-65
$185	$275	$325	$400	$575	$1,400	$4,000	$5,500	$13,000

CERTIFIED POPULATIONS

G-4–EF-45	AU-50–58	MS-60–62	MS-63	MS-64	MS-65	MS-66	MS-67	MS-68–70
6	40	127	102	70	52	31	28	10
PF-50–58	PF-60–62	PF-63	PF-64	PF-65	PF-66	PF-67	PF-68–70	
1	8	9	29	26	32	16	2	

Key to Collecting. The 1884 gold dollar is yet another that is easily available in choice and gem Mint State. The ease of finding them, plus the satisfaction of contemplating the low mintage figures, has made all dollars of this decade numismatic favorites for a long time.

Estimated Total Population (Mint State). 1,300 to 1,700, mostly choice or gem quality. Some Mint State coins have nearly full prooflike surfaces and could easily be mistaken for Proofs. *Certified population, MS-63 and higher:* 787.

Estimated Total Population (Circulated Grades). 125 to 200. Very scarce, since it is likely that this issue was never released into general circulation. Worn pieces, when seen, are apt to be EF or AU, with the "wear" due to handling as souvenirs; the same commentary is relevant for all gold dollars of the 1880s. Of course, a worn specimen is always less expensive than a Mint State coin.

Characteristics of Striking and Die Notes. Usually seen well struck. Some have clashmarks on the obverse and reverse (*e.g.*, Bass Collection, Part II, lots 236, 239, and 241). Breen (*Major Varieties of U.S. Gold Dollars*, 1964) stated that "[One of three reverse die varieties seen has a] crack from rim down through left side of final S in STATES, cf. Lot 982, New Netherlands 54th Sale."

Numismatic Notes

Die Data. 1884 four-digit date logotype: This shows larger numerals than used in the several preceding years. Digits 18 and 88 are about the same distance apart, with 84 very close and touching on deep impressions. The 1 is higher than the others and leans slightly right. The top interiors of the 8s are smaller than the bottoms. The first 8 leans slightly right. The 4 has thick upright; a horizontal line without crossbar extends about the same distance as the lower right serif above it, both being short. This logotype was used on all dies.

Copper Toning. Some pieces have copper toning areas due to imperfect mixing of the alloy. This occurs regularly on United States gold of the general period from the 1880s to at least 1910, and extends to circulation strikes as well as Proofs.

Mason's Commentary (1884). In June 1884, Ebenezer Locke Mason Jr. wrote this for his journal, *Mason's Monthly Illustrated Coin Collector's Magazine:* "It is not generally known that the pretty little gold dollars have been gradually going out of circulation: at least this is the fact in regard to those coined in 1883 and 1884. A gentleman connected with the United States Mint in Philadelphia writes as follows: '[To] Mason & Co., *Boston.* [From] *U.S. Mint, Philadelphia, April 9:* The Proof sets for this year are ready for delivery. Five cent nickels can be had at any time, but the silver ten cent pieces can only be had in sums of five hundred dollars, and only upon application to the Secretary of the Treasury. Gold dollars can only be had in Proof condition, as there are none coined for circulation. M.H.'"

The information proved to be incorrect, for later in the year, the Mint did make circulation strikes.

Auction Information. Once again, auction listings usually emphasize high grade and prooflike quality. The particularly scarce nature of the 1884, in relation to other dates of the decade (excepting 1886), is not widely noticed.

Proofs

Estimated Total Population and Key to Collecting. 100 to 140. Most Proofs are very attractive. Insist on certification by a leading service, since many prooflike Mint State coins have been marketed as "Proofs." As with other high-mintage Proof gold dollars of the decade, the number of 1884 examples known in collections today is only a small fraction of the published production figure of 1,006 coins. For this and other high-mintage Proofs through 1889, it is likely that jewelers, who had an insatiable demand for gold dollars, but who could not get them through banking channels, simply paid a small premium and bought Proofs—which were then incorporated into bracelets, brooches, etc. Still, enough were sold to collectors and dealers that finding a Proof today will be no problem.

Die Data and Notes. On the reverse, the highest point of the ribbon is below the interior right side of the third digit (second 8). The digits 18 are sharply repunched in the die; apparently the logotype was entered first at a crazy angle, slanting from lower left to upper right, then effaced (but now with traces still visible under magnification). However, Walter Breen (*Encyclopedia*, 1988) commented that "the same dies were used to make Proofs *and circulation strikes;* several varieties known." Further from the same writer (*Proof Coin Encyclopedia*, 1977, 1989): "At least three of the five varieties [of gold dollars known for the year] come in Proof state."

The Breen narrative was effectively challenged by David W. Akers in his commentary under lot 922 in the Pittman Collection, Part I (1997): "The numerals 18 in the date are dramatically repunched with the initial numerals much lower than the corrected ones. There is also a trace of repunching visible on the diagonal of the 4. Purchased from French's 2/59 sale lot 69, for $56. Although Walter Breen states a contrary opinion, both in his Proof *Encyclopedia* and in his 1988 *Complete Encyclopedia*, I can say that I have never seen a Proof 1884 gold dollar that was not from these dies, and conversely, I have never seen a business strike that was minted from these dies."

AMERICA AND NUMISMATICS IN 1885

Col. Oliver C. Bosbyshell, who had been at the Mint since May 4, 1869, then as register of deposits, followed on December 1, 1872, as assistant coiner, and since September 1, 1877, as chief coiner, tendered his resignation, effective February 1, 1885. A few years later (1889 to 1894), he served as superintendent of the Mint. While serving as coiner, somehow he was able to acquire rarities for himself, such as pattern 1877 half dollars (which were not openly available to anyone). Likely, the existence today of low-mintage 1884 and 1885 Proof trade dollars can be laid at his doorstep. On July 1, 1885, Superintendent A. Loudon Snowden was succeeded by Hon. Daniel Fox. Soon thereafter, Bosbyshell sold many rare pattern 1877 half dollars and other rarities to George W. Cogan (son of dealer Edward Cogan), who sold many of them to T. Harrison Garrett, the Baltimore numismatist.

There was a change in the Mint directorship in Washington, and in July, James P. Kimball took the place of Horatio C. Burchard. After Bosbyshell, Snowden, and Burchard left the Mint, the creation of numismatic delicacies slowed to a stop. By that time, secret rarities for the year included an estimated five 1885-dated trade dollars and several Proof sets struck in aluminum instead of the proper metals.

Big businesses, trusts, the erection of huge mansions in cities as well as at the seaside, and the perceived excesses of "high society" of the 1880s would furnish fodder for later generations of writers who were eager to prove that average citizens were suffering and hardly ever enjoyed themselves. However, a close examination of the facts reveals that although working conditions were often unsatisfactory, the average home was a happy one, and American citizens thoroughly enjoyed their amusements.

1885

Circulation-Strike Mintage
11,156

Proof Mintage
1,105

Enlarged 2x
(actual size 15 mm)

Whitman Coin Guide (WCG™)

VF-20	EF-40	AU-50	AU-55	MS-60	MS-63	MS-65	PF-63	PF-65
$185	$275	$325	$400	$575	$1,400	$4,000	$5,500	$13,000

CERTIFIED POPULATIONS

G-4–EF-45	AU-50–58	MS-60–62	MS-63	MS-64	MS-65	MS-66	MS-67	MS-68–70
6	87	179	125	141	114	87	36	3
PF-50–58	PF-60–62	PF-63	PF-64	PF-65	PF-66	PF-67	PF-68–70	
3	21	30	56	39	47	19	2	

Key to Collecting. Although the mintage of the 1885 gold dollar was small, many were saved by collectors, dealers, and investors. Others, perhaps the majority, went to jewelers, who seemed to have an insatiable demand for these coins. Today, enough choice and gem coins survive that finding one will be no problem. If you would like to have a "showpiece" gold dollar, quality-wise, the 1885 date is one of a string of nice possibilities from the 1880s.

Estimated Total Population (Mint State). 600 to 900, including pieces at the choice and gem levels. Many Mint State coins are prooflike and closely resemble full Proofs. *Certified population, MS-63 and higher:* 294.

Estimated Total Population (Circulated Grades). 110 to 150. In keeping with other gold dollars of the decade, the 1885 is very scarce, since this issue was never released into general circulation. Worn pieces, when seen, are apt to be EF or AU, with the "wear" due to handling as souvenirs; the same commentary is relevant for all gold dollars of the 1880s.

Characteristics of Striking and Die Notes. Some have a die bulge below STA (STATES) on the reverse and a light die crack from D (UNITED) to Miss Liberty's forehead. Some are softly struck at the highest points of the portrait of Miss Liberty. Delicate clashmarks are not unusual.

Numismatic Notes

Die Data. 1885 four-digit date logotype: Digits are of medium size, similar to 1884; they are fairly evenly spaced, although upon close inspection the 18 is close, 88 wider, and 85 closest of all. The 1 leans slightly right; its bottom is about on the same level as the base of the 8. The top interiors of the 8s are slightly smaller than their bottom interiors; both 8s lean slightly left. The 5 is slightly slanting, not enough to be called italic; its ball is close to but not touching the upright; its flag is pointed. This logotype was used on all dies.

Seven dies were prepared for this coinage, a combination of obverses and reverses. Not all were used.

Auction Information. Listings abound, with adjectives usually concentrating on prooflike character and high grade.

Proofs

Estimated Total Population and Key to Collecting. 140 to 180. Included in the population are many choice and gem pieces. Although this Proof issue has a generous mintage of 1,105, it is doubtful if more than 200 Proofs were ever distributed to collectors. Examples are scarce today, but enough are offered that finding one will be no problem.

Die Data and Notes. Some true Proofs have an "orange peel" character to the fields and are sharply struck at the dentils and border. Other Proofs were poorly made and have crumbling at the dentils and can have irregular rims (source: John Dannreuther, correspondence). Breen's comment (*Encyclopedia*, 1988) does not simplify the situation: "Five varieties of circulation strikes, four of them also known in Proof." While this information is interesting, the present writer does not necessarily consider it to be definitive. Often, Breen too readily accepted the "Proof" attributions of others without questioning them. Also, as is evident from many of Breen's descriptions in the fore part of his Proof coin *book*, if a coin had a prooflike surface, he often considered it to be a Proof.

While today, buyers often look at a "Proof" label on a certified holder and ask no questions, as a matter of fact, even the experts are sometimes undecided about what is a Proof and what is not. The situation is reflected in this expanded narrative by David W. Akers regarding a coin cataloged by Walter Breen and sold by Lester Merkin, then sold in 1997 in the John Jay Pittman Collection, Part I as lot 923:

> 1885, Very Choice Uncirculated, fully prooflike, or possibly Proof. Slightly cloudy surfaces and attractive orange gold toning. There is a tiny copper/carbon spot at the top of the forehead in the field, and a few light hairlines under the film. This is an extremely deceptive coin with deep mirror fields that even have considerable 'orange peel' surface. Furthermore, there are lint marks at NI of UNITED and above the 1 in the denomination near the top of the wreath. In most instances, the combination of an 'orange peel' surface and lint marks will indicate that a coin is a Proof, but I do not feel that is the case with this coin. It has rounded rims and much less sharp individual reeding segments than Proof invariably have. There is also considerable crumbling in the denticles from die deterioration, something not usually seen on Proofs. It is barely possible that this coin is a poorly made Proof, but I feel that it is really just a highly prooflike first strike Mint State coin. Others may disagree, however, so prospective bidders are encouraged to examine this coin closely and draw their own conclusions. Purchased as a Proof for $45 in a private transaction with Lester Merkin at the 1960 FUN show.

Auction Information (Proofs). Listings abound, but likely most have been for prooflike circulation strikes, as implied above.

AMERICA AND NUMISMATICS IN 1886

Silver quarters and half dollars continued to be minted in very low numbers, just enough to keep them from being rarities. For quarters and half dollars, just 5,000 circulation strikes were made, plus 886 Proofs. The coin hobby and market continued to be dynamic. In this era many numismatists also collected other things such as Indian artifacts, fossils, stamps, and books, and many dealers traded in these, including the Chapman brothers and W. Elliot Woodward.

The price of silver bullion continued to slide, although Silverites kept up the drumbeat for free and equal coinage with gold on a 16-to-1 ratio, never mind that in London, the world center for metal trading, the ratio was 20.78 to 1.

In many areas laborers were becoming restless, strikes broke out (one of which resulted in the infamous Haymarket Massacre in May), and there were many problems. Generally, employers dealt with strikers by force, and laborers responded in a like manner. It was a time of secret societies, and just about every city and town had several, sometimes a dozen or more. Members met from one to several times a month, engaged in special rituals, and promised loyalty to each other. Most prominent were the Masons and, in the North, the GAR (veterans of the Grand Army of the Republic of the Civil War). While most societies limited their membership to men, several catered to women. Women's suffrage continued as a popular social movement. On October 28, *Liberty Enlightening the World*, familiarly known as the Statue of Liberty, was dedicated on Bedloe's Island in the harbor of New York City.

1886

Circulation-Strike Mintage
5,000

Proof Mintage
1,016

Enlarged 2x
(actual size 15 mm)

Whitman Coin Guide (WCG™)

VF-20	EF-40	AU-50	AU-55	MS-60	MS-63	MS-65	PF-63	PF-65
$185	$275	$325	$400	$575	$1,400	$4,000	$5,500	$13,000

CERTIFIED POPULATIONS

G-4–EF-45	AU-50-58	MS-60-62	MS-63	MS-64	MS-65	MS-66	MS-67	MS-68–70
9	55	207	130	131	57	32	17	0
PF-50-58	PF-60-62	PF-63	PF-64	PF-65	PF-66	PF-67	PF-68–70	
1	21	23	39	42	32	5	0	

Key to Collecting. The mintage of 5,000 coins was made to prevent this from being a Proof-only date. Likely, many were acquired by dealers and collectors, preserving choice examples for our enjoyment today.

Estimated Total Population (Mint State). 800 to 1,200. Among the survivors there are many choice and gem pieces, including examples with prooflike surfaces. No doubt, prooflike circulation strikes have been listed as "Proofs" in catalogs of past generations, especially before the modern era of certification. *Certified population, MS-63 and higher:* 471.

Estimated Total Population (Circulated Grades). 180 to 250. The 1886 is very scarce, for the same reasons that apply to other gold dollars of the era.

Characteristics of Striking and Die Notes. Some are seen with prominent clashmarks due to the dies coming together without an intervening planchet, resulting in much of the word LIBERTY appearing by transfer on the reverse.

Breen (*Encyclopedia*, 1988) notes that the so-called "Recut 6" variety is, in fact, from a clashmarked die; this variety, usually seen with a prooflike surface, was said by the same writer to constitute about one eighth of the known population of 1886 gold dollars.

Numismatic Notes

Die Data. 1886 four-digit date logotype: The date is widely spaced: digits 18 are closest together, 88 widest apart, and 86 in between. The 1 leans slightly right. The first 8 leans slightly right. The 6 has a small ball that touches or nearly touches the curve below it. This logotype was used on all dies.

Auction Information. Listings are numerous, but fewer than for most other dates of the decade.

Proofs

Estimated Total Population and Key to Collecting. 100 to 140. Proofs are much less available than the generous mintage figure suggests. Some have copper toning spots from incomplete mixing of the alloy, and many, if not most, have at least a few lint marks.

Die Data and Notes. A description of a Bass, Part III 1886 gold dollar certified by PCGS: The obverse Proof die had Proof surface within all letters except the bottom part of E (AMERICA). The reverse shows the date fairly high, with the highest point of the ribbon under the left side (not left edge) of the second 8. The interior of the 6 is filled in (no mirror surface).

Auction Information (Proofs). Today it is difficult to differentiate, among historic catalog listings, as to which were Proof and which were circulation strikes.

AMERICA AND NUMISMATICS IN 1887

Coinage of gold was low at the Philadelphia Mint, except for modest coinages to prevent rarities from being created. However, because double eagles were not widely sought, nor had they ever attracted investors, the mintage for this particular denomination consisted only of Proofs. Gold dollars were made in small quantities, of which many pieces were saved by dealers and collectors. The jewelry trade absorbed even more.

The coin hobby continued to be active, but a bit slower than in recent years. Perhaps the novelty of the 1883 Liberty Head nickels without CENTS had faded, for dealers had large stocks of them, and no longer was the hope held that they would become rare.

The Scott Stamp & Coin Co. issued a new edition of *Gold & Silver Coins.* Priced at 75 cents, it claimed to "give the market value of every American gold and silver coin in various degrees of preservation with the prices charged by the publishers." The poorly researched guide listed gold coins from dollars to double eagles, completely omitting mintmarks except for the gold dollar series. Prices were listed for just about every date, including rarities. Among selected citations, the 1861 Philadelphia as well as the 1861 Dahlonega issue were given at the same price, $1.50 Good, $2 Fine, $4 Proof—never mind that no Proofs were made at branch mints. The rare 1875 gold dollar was listed at $4 Good, $10 Fine and $15 Proof.

Railroads continued to dominate investment, commerce, and listings on the New York Stock Exchange. The owners of the lines were all-powerful, and they often determined where rails would be placed by means of extracting payments from villages and cities. Some bypassed locations became ghost towns. Traveling by train was very popular, and those paying for appropriate tickets could take advantage of elegant facilities in well-appointed sleeping, parlor, and dining cars. Similarly, ocean liners were often luxurious.

1887

Circulation-Strike Mintage
7,500

Proof Mintage
1,043

Enlarged 2x
(actual size 15 mm)

Whitman Coin Guide (WCG™)

VF-20	EF-40	AU-50	AU-55	MS-60	MS-63	MS-65	PF-63	PF-65
$185	$275	$325	$400	$575	$1,400	$4,000	$5,500	$13,000

CERTIFIED POPULATIONS

G-4–EF-45	AU-50–58	MS-60–62	MS-63	MS-64	MS-65	MS-66	MS-67	MS-68–70
3	59	239	180	228	150	111	47	3
PF-50–58	PF-60–62	PF-63	PF-64	PF-65	PF-66	PF-67	PF-68–70	
2	22	24	47	38	29	8	2	

Key to Collecting. Although the mintage of the 1887 is just 7,500 pieces, many of these were saved at or near the time of issue. In the intervening years many were damaged, or surrendered to the government in the 1930s, or met other fates. However, much of the mintage survives, and many coins are in choice or gem preservation. Finding a specimen that is well struck and having good eye appeal will be no problem.

During this era the Treasury Department had no need for gold $1, $2.50, or $3 pieces for depositors or circulation, but circulation strikes were made, in addition to Proofs, "enough to prevent overvaluation from immediate rarity."[60] In other words, the mintage quantity given above was to shortstop dealers and collectors from making a profit on current coinage.

Estimated Total Population (Mint State). 600 to 900, the result of many pieces being saved. Gems are easily found in the context of the series. *Certified population, MS-63 and higher:* 378.

Estimated Total Population (Circulated Grades). 120 to 180. Very scarce in worn grades, since this issue was never released into general circulation. Worn pieces, when seen, are apt to be EF or AU.

Characteristics of Striking and Die Notes. Most pieces are sharply struck. The surfaces are sometimes frosty, but many have a partial or full prooflike surface. The latter are sometimes mistaken for Proofs. Some pieces were struck on imperfect planchets. The alloy mix seems to have been well adjusted for this date, since the literature is nearly devoid of mention of copper spotting.

Numismatic Notes

Die Data. 1887 four-digit date logotype: Digits 18 and 87 are closely spaced, 88 slightly farther apart. The base of the 1 is slightly higher than the base of the 8. The base of the second 8 is slightly lower than the base of the first 8. The 7 leans slightly right; its upper left serif is not emphasized. This logotype was used on all dies.

Auction Information. Listings are plentiful, usually with little information other than grade and enticements to bid.

Proofs

Estimated Total Population and Key to Collecting. 110 to 140. Only a small fraction of the mintage went to numismatists. There are enough Proofs on the market, however, that finding one will be no problem. Often, these are acquired as "trophy coins," and are resold not long afterward. Typically, a given year offers multiple opportunities to bid on these at auction. Sometimes prooflike circulation strikes are offered as full Proofs; however, the circulation strikes are apt to have indistinct striking at the rims, and lack the "orange peel" surface characteristic of Proofs.

Die Data and Notes. According to Breen (*Encyclopedia*, 1988), Proofs have the top of the wreath closed and the digit 7 entirely below the A (DOLLAR). A certified Proof in the Bass, Part III sale has the interior of DO and A (DOLLAR) filled. Its wreath joins at the top.

Similar to circulation strikes, some Proofs seem to have been struck on imperfect planchets (*e.g.*, Auction '86, Superior lot 1332: "Flashy glittering Proof with deep golden orange mint bloom color throughout. Some trivial marks appear on the surfaces; most of which appear to be planchet imperfections that were present during striking.").

Notes concerning another Bass, Part III 1887 Proof gold dollar certified by PCGS: The reverse die is oriented about 330° in relation to the reverse. The obverse die shows Proof surface within most letters, except O (OF), both As (AMERICA), M, the bottom of E, and C. A patch of Proof surface occurs below the eyelid, before the eyeball. The reverse has the highest point of the ribbon above the lower left interior of the third digit.

Auction Information (Proofs). This description from 1960 reflects why historical auction listings of "Proofs" often were of prooflike circulation strikes.

> *1960–04: 54th Sale, Jonathan Glogower Consignment, Etc.* (New Netherlands Coin Co.), lot 988: "1887. Extremely deceptive 'semi-proof' first strike. Obtained as a Proof, inevitably; and we lingered over this one (like the 1884 in our 51st Sale) trying to decide whether or not it was actually intended to be a Proof. A 'gem,' despite a few lint marks. This one will go high." *Another:* lot 989: "1887. Later state of the same dies, but not as deceptive though the dies still show high polish. Obverse weak at N and C. Desirable, though not quite in class with the last."

AMERICA AND NUMISMATICS IN 1888

The rare coin hobby continued to be somewhat slow, causing many dealers to emphasize other areas of collecting, including Indian relics and books. However, this did not deter Dr. George M. Heath from launching a new magazine, at first called *The American Numismatist*, later simply *The Numismatist*, perhaps after he realized that the "American" title had been used in 1886 and 1887 (but no longer) by C.E. Leal in Paterson, New Jersey. Heath was a man of many interests, skills, and accomplishments. Over a period of time, in addition to his medical practice, he wrote articles and poems, traveled widely on train excursions, and served as mayor of his hometown, Monroe, Michigan.

The "Silver Question" continued to dominate politics. Advocates felt that the free and unlimited coinage of silver, beyond the Morgan dollars already being struck, plus liberal issues of paper money, would bring prosperity to the average working person who felt left out in the recent wave of business expansion and profits. Moreover, old debts could be paid with new lower value dollars. The Greenback Party attracted believers, and for a time was an influence in elections. Although prosperity remained in many sections of the country, there were signs of chill in the prairie states. In Richmond, Virginia, the first electric trolley car, drawing power from overhead wires, became a reality. At the time, municipal cars, often called omnibuses, were mostly horse-drawn, some on tracks and others roving freely. In New York City traffic jams were common on Broadway.

President Grover Cleveland, who sympathized with working people but who also wanted to prevent inflation from becoming rampant through the depreciation of currency, ran for re-election in November. His opponent was Benjamin Harrison, who advocated what was known as populism. (Populists wanted cheap money, like paper, not backed by gold or silver, creating an inflationary economy that would enable them to pay off old debts with new money earned by doing less work or delivering fewer goods than the same money earned when the debt was incurred.) Harrison won handily, with 233 Electoral College votes, compared to 168 for his rival.

1888

Circulation-Strike Mintage
15,501

Proof Mintage
1,079

Enlarged 2x
(actual size 15 mm)

Whitman Coin Guide (WCG™)

VF-20	EF-40	AU-50	AU-55	MS-60	MS-63	MS-65	PF-63	PF-65
$175	$275	$325	$400	$550	$1,350	$3,500	$5,000	$12,500

CERTIFIED POPULATIONS

G-4–EF-45	AU-50–58	MS-60–62	MS-63	MS-64	MS-65	MS-66	MS-67	MS-68–70
12	47	285	276	392	192	198	79	8
PF-50–58	**PF-60–62**	**PF-63**	**PF-64**	**PF-65**	**PF-66**	**PF-67**	**PF-68–70**	
1	34	31	62	57	27	8	3	

Key to Collecting. The 1888 gold dollar is usually found in Mint State, deeply lustrous (only occasionally prooflike) and in grades from MS-63 upward. At the time of issue they were a popular speculation with collectors and dealers alike, and many were saved. Others were acquired by jewelers, who furnished a steady demand for coins of this denomination. High quality and good eye appeal are usual for this issue, although prooflike pieces can have weakness in certain areas of the dentils.

Estimated Total Population (Mint State). 1,800 to 2,200. Large numbers of 1888 gold dollars were saved by investors among the general public (not serious numismatists). Today, the supply is widely scattered. Still, they are plentiful in the marketplace. Regarding gems, the old-time record seems to show that it is easier to buy a gem Proof than a gem circulation strike, but this is misleading, because it is likely that most of these "Proofs" were prooflike circulation strikes. *Certified population, MS-63 and higher:* 1,144.

Estimated Total Population (Circulated Grades). 110 to 150. The 1888 gold dollar is very scarce in worn grades, since this issue was never released into general circulation. Worn pieces, when seen, are apt to be EF or AU.

Characteristics of Striking and Die Notes. Most pieces are well struck with frosty surfaces, although some prooflike coins were made. Occasionally a high-grade coin with copper staining is seen, indicative of incompletely mixed alloy (10% copper and 90% gold) in the planchet. A few are struck from a rotated reverse die. As noted by Breen (*Major Varieties of U.S. Gold Dollars*, 1964), "ERT often weak."

Numismatic Notes

Die Data. 1888 four-digit date logotype: Spacing of digits 18 is closest, the first 88 is wider, and the second 88 is ever-so-slightly wider yet. The third 8 leans left. This logotype was used on all dies.

Auction Information. Listings abound, with adjectives usually concentrating on prooflike character and high grade. The John J. Pittman Collection, Part I offering, April 1997, by David W. Akers, gives useful information in this regard:

> Lot 925: "1888 Choice Uncirculated, fully prooflike, in fact, that it is virtually indistinguishable from a Proof . . . Purchased by JJP as a Proof from a Mike Kolman sale,

> 11/17/56 lot 1118, for $27. This is a variety that has generally been offered as Proof in the past, and it is possible that these were actually struck as Proofs; however, I consider them to be business strikes . . . This coin was struck using the obverse die that was previously used for Proofs from 1862 to 1873, then again for all Proofs in 1875, and next for some Proofs in 1876. (It was also used for some of the business of 1879, but not the Proofs.) The die has been heavily lapped since its last usage for Proofs in 1876, now showing mirrorlike brilliance in the band below the headdress; LIBERTY has a weak E and Y, and the R and the T are nearly eradicated . . . Although this coin certainly looks like a Proof in many ways, the edge is rounded, not sharp and square as it is on a Proof. There is also die crumbling in the denticles above ST in STATES and on the corresponding position on the reverse at K-8, uncharacteristic of a true Proof. In the entire gold dollar series, there is no more deceptive coin than this one, and I am sure comparable pieces will continue to be offered as Proofs in the future.

PROOFS

Estimated Total Population and Key to Collecting. 150 to 200. Among Proof gold dollars this is one of the more plentiful issues, as can be said for certain other dates of this decade. Estimates of known specimens have varied widely over the years, with figures ranging from as high as 500 to as low as 20 to 24. The author's estimate is given here. Today, it is likely that fewer than 200 Proofs exist, or less than 20% of the posted mintage. Fully prooflike circulation strikes, themselves rare, have been sold as "Proof" on many occasions in the past. True Proofs appear with frequency on the auction market—often representing "trophy coins" that have bounced around from one sale to another in the past 20 to 30 years—yielding appearance numbers far higher than the actual number of *different* specimens changing hands.

Die Data and Notes. Not making attribution of Proofs vs. circulation strikes any easier is Breen's comment (*Encyclopedia*, 1988) that at least two die pairs used to make circulation strikes were also employed to make Proofs. The difficulty of distinguishing Proofs from circulation strikes is illustrated by lot 925 in the John Jay Pittman Collection, Part I (David W. Akers), cited above. A certain obverse die was used to strike Proofs from 1862 to 1873, in 1875, and some in 1876.

Generally, true Proofs have an "orange peel" surface and very sharp dentils; prooflike pieces often have irregular striking at the rims. A few Proofs have copper stains and/or lint marks, the latter from foreign material adhering to the dies.

Notes concerning a Bass, Part III Proof 1888 gold dollar certified by PCGS: On the obverse, the interior of letters are mirrorlike except for the base of E (AMERICA), interior of R, interior of C, and interior of the second A. On the reverse, the highest point of the ribbon is above the lower left interior edge of the second 8. The date is high, and closer to the letters above than to the ribbon below. The wreath is not joined at top, but nearly so. The DO and A (DOLLAR) are filled in.

Auction Information (Proofs). Again there are many listings, but likely some have been for prooflike circulation strikes.

AMERICA AND NUMISMATICS IN 1889

The coin market continued to be low, the pace of auction sales dropped, fewer Proofs were ordered from the Mint, and many collectors left the hobby. In his *Annual Report*

Mint Director Edward O. Leech commented: "I have the honor to recommend that legislation looking towards the discontinuance of the coinage of the 3-dollar and 1-dollar gold pieces and the 3-cent nickel piece be requested of Congress. Further:

> With regard to the 3-dollar gold piece, it may be said that that denomination of coin serves no useful purpose, and that its present coinage is limited to Proof coins [an incorrect statement!] sold at a profit by the Mint, to meet the demands of numismatic societies and coin collectors. There is no demand for it by the business public. The same objections apply to the 1-dollar gold piece, with the additional ones that it is too small for circulation, and that the few pieces issued annually from the Mint are used almost exclusively for the purposes of ornament. So long as statutory authority exists to coin this latter denomination, the suspension of its coinage by the Secretary of the Treasury is of doubtful legality. The most he has ever felt warranted in doing was to limit its coinage to pressing demands about the holiday season, and to maintain, unbroken, the series of coin sets sold by the Mint. The very limitation of its coinage leads to favorites in the distribution of the few pieces struck annually and to speculation in them.

Banker's Magazine, November 1889, included this:

> *Gold Dollars for Ornament.* 'Almost all of our gold dollars,' says the *Philadelphia Record*, 'are being used for purposes of adornment, and their fate as a medium of exchange has long been doomed,' said an official of the Philadelphia Mint yesterday.
>
> 'We are only coining about 5,000 per year for monetary circulation, and this small amount is meant by the Treasury Department to be merely for the purpose of keeping enough on hand to make change in paying depositors of gold bullion. If it were not for this, probably the coinage of gold dollars would be suspended. If we coined 1,000,000 gold dollars yearly the demand would not be satisfied. A few days ago we received a letter from a man living in Cincinnati who wanted 100 gold dollars. We answered that we could not grant his request. He then wrote to the Secretary of the Treasury at Washington, and the letter was referred to the director of the mint, James P. Kimball, who wrote to the gentleman at Cincinnati that he could not be accommodated. Director Kimball has officially notified us by letter that the small coinage of gold dollars should be distributed from the Mint here with care, not to allow them to pass into the hands of manufacturers for mutilation incidental to conversion into articles of adornment.'

These denominations were made for the last time in 1889.

Advocates of the Free Silver Movement became increasingly worried as prices of that precious metal continued to drop. Now, over-production of silver, plus surplus quantities in Europe, plus declining economic conditions in the United States all acted to create a dismal prospect. The *Wall Street Journal* began publication on July 8, an expansion of a daily financial newsletter issued by Dow Jones & Company, owned by Charles Henry Dow and Edward D. Jones.

On April 22, per the proclamation of President Benjamin Harrison, 1,900,000 acres of open land in the Midwest, stolen (or otherwise obtained) by the government from the Indians, was thrown open to homesteaders. However, "sooners," went early and claimed for themselves some of the choicest spots. By the night of April 22, towns, including Oklahoma City and Guthrie, were formed in several places in the Oklahoma Territory, complete with banks set up in canvas tents. Otherwise, there was trouble in the Midwest, and many businesses closed their doors, and municipalities defaulted on their bonds.

1889

Circulation-Strike Mintage
28,950

Proof Mintage
1,779

Enlarged 2x
(actual size 15 mm)

Whitman Coin Guide (WCG™)

VF-20	EF-40	AU-50	AU-55	MS-60	MS-63	MS-65	PF-63	PF-65
$165	$265	$350	$400	$550	$1,350	$3,500	$5,000	$12,500

CERTIFIED POPULATIONS

G-4–EF-45	AU-50–58	MS-60–62	MS-63	MS-64	MS-65	MS-66	MS-67	MS-68–70
15	128	612	590	891	688	618	365	17
PF-50–58	PF-60–62	PF-63	PF-64	PF-65	PF-66	PF-67	PF-68–70	
0	16	13	30	19	16	4	1	

Key to Collecting. The 1889 gold dollar is very plentiful in Mint State. Regarding *choice* and *gem* Mint State pieces, there is no contest as to this year being the winner in terms of the number in numismatic hands. In contrast, certain earlier gold dollars circa 1849 through the early 1850s are plentiful in Mint State, but mostly at lower levels, not choice or gem. The 1889 is thus an ideal candidate for a type set.

Estimated Total Population (Mint State). 7,000 to 10,000, most of which are very lustrous and frosty, rather than the prooflike surfaces seen for dollars earlier in the decade. Occasionally a small group of these will come on the market from some long-ago accumulation. The John Beck Collection, auctioned by Quality Sales in 1976 and 1977, included a dozen Mint State coins, four of which were described as "frosty gem." Information on Virgil M. Brand estate coins revealed that a cache of 66 specimens was inherited by Virgil's brother Armin after the former's death in 1926; presumably, this represented a group of 50 purchased soon after the coins were struck, plus scattered later additions. A small hoard of a couple hundred or so 1889 gold dollars, each coin Mint State, frosty and lustrous (not prooflike), was sold by Maurice Storck to the writer in the 1950s. These had turned up in a safe deposit box in a bank in Maine and were stored together in a medium-size kraft paper envelope. *Certified population, MS-63 and higher:* 3,239.

Estimated Total Population (Circulated Grades). 250 to 400. The 1889 gold dollar is very scarce in worn grades, since it is likely that this issue was never released into general circulation. Worn pieces, when seen, are apt to be EF or AU. Because the 1889 had a particularly high mintage for the decade, more mishandled pieces exist than do for certain other dates.

Characteristics of Striking and Die Notes. This date is usually seen well struck, with sharp central details, sharp dentils, etc. Surfaces are usually lustrous and frosty, but some prooflike pieces come to market every so often and are mistaken for full Proofs. Some pieces have copper toning spots from imperfect mixing of the 10% copper alloy in the planchet.

As explained by David W. Akers in the Pittman Sale, Part I (1997), a certain obverse die used to strike Proofs of 1862 to 1873, 1875, and some Proofs of 1876 (distinguished by having the vertical element of the leftmost feather in headdress plume polished away, giving Proof field in this area) was also employed for some circulation strikes (not Proofs) of 1879. Then, relapped and now with polish areas also in the headband, it was used to make certain circulation strikes (not Proofs) of gold dollars in 1888 and 1889.

At least two or three reverses were used, differing in the position of the date. The relationship of the second 8 to the ribbon loop peak is a good reference point.

Breen stated (*Major Varieties of U.S. Gold Dollars*, 1964): "[One variety has] ERT weak as on 1888 coins and probably from the same die." These are seen with some frequency today. Clashmarks are occasionally seen on dollars of this date. Some have been listed as having double striking, such as lot 159 in B. Max Mehl's March 1938 offering of the Samuel H. McVitty Collection: "1889 Unusual variety, with the figure 1 and the word DOLLAR double struck or re-struck. Uncirculated. Rare." This would have been machine doubling caused by die chatter.

The Childs Collection coin (Bowers and Merena, August 1999), lot 565, had the reverse misaligned and was oriented 150° in relation to the obverse, instead of the normal 180°.

Numismatic Notes

Die Data. 1889 four-digit date logotype: Digits 18 and 88 are close together, 89 farther apart. The 1 has heavy bottom serifs; its base is slightly higher than the base of the 8. The base of the 9 is slightly low. The 9 has heavy left and right sides, a delicate bottom, and a small, imperfectly formed ball close to or touching its upper curve. This logotype was used on all dies.

Auction Information. In the 20th century several auctions included small groups of Mint State coins, usually described as Uncirculated, but with some exceptions. Thomas L. Elder, who specialized in gold dollars, sold many in his sales over the years, as per this example:

> *1912–11: 69th Public Sale* (Thomas L. Elder), lot 810: "1889. Last year. Bright Mint State." Lot 811: "1889. Bright Mint State." Lot 812: "1889. Bright Mint State." Lot 813: "1889. Bright Mint State." Lot 814: "1889. Bright Mint State." Lot 815: "1889. Bright Mint State." Lot 816: "1889. Bright Mint State." Lot 817: "1889. Bright Mint State."

The New Netherlands Coin Co. was well known for describing varieties, as here:

> *1960–04: 54th Sale, Jonathan Glogower Consignment, Etc.* (New Netherlands Coin Co.), lot 992: "1889. Last year. Tiny chip above final A in AMERICA. Rev. Date slants down to right; r. ribbon end triple cut; no border around r. terminal tassel at top of wreath. Brilliant 'gem' Uncirculated. Record of $29. In our 53rd Sale." Realized $33. Lot 993: "Another 1889, from the same dies. Uncirculated. Record $29. In our 53rd Sale." Realized $27. Lot 994: "A third. Different dies; obverse without chip at A, reverse exactly like the last two but with marked border around r. terminal tassel. Choice first strike; microscopic evidence of handling, but less than the preceding lot." Realized $29. Lot 995: "A fourth. Different dies; obverse similar to 1888, ERT very weakly cut. Rev. Lower date, the O in DOLLAR almost its own height above 1 in date. Brilliant Uncirculated, almost in a class with the last." Realized $27.

Proofs

Estimated Total Population and Key to Collecting. 65 to 75. The published figure of 1,779 for 1889 represents the high-water mark for Proof coinage of *any* gold coin minted before 1934. Most probably, jewelers were the main buyers, for the Mint resisted selling them circulation strikes for face value (although Philadelphia coin dealers could obtain them easily enough). Because the coin market was in a slump at this time, and interest in

Proof coins of all denominations had diminished, it is likely that relatively few pieces ever reached numismatic channels. I estimate that no more than 150 to 300 Proofs were sold to collectors, and many of those have disappeared in the years since then.

Die Data and Notes. Poignantly, in *Major Varieties of U.S. Gold Dollars* (1964), Walter Breen described the die characteristics of the different Proof gold dollars of the 1860s through the 1880s, but for the 1889 gold dollar alone, he stated that "I have not had the chance to examine any Proof 1889 dollars." However, he must have been skimming his notes quickly when he later wrote his 1977 (revised in 1989, but no revision of this particular coin) Proof coin *Encyclopedia*, when he stated: "The 1889 is the gold dollar most often encountered in Proof." Sometimes, the more one reads of Breen's writing, the more confused one becomes!

Some Proofs have the peak of the ribbon bow to the left of center under the second 8 (1889); the Starr Collection coin (Stack's, 1992) is an example. Others have the peak to the right of center; the James A. Stack, Sr. Collection coin (Stack's, 1994) is an example.

A Bass, Part III 1889 Proof gold dollar certified by PCGS was described as having the interiors of the letters prooflike, except for the top of the second A (AMERICA); headband had ERT (LIBERTY) missing. The reverse had the highest ribbon point over the bottom left interior of the third digit in the date. The interior of the D and the top half of the interior of the O (DOLLAR) were filled in. The wreath tips nearly, but not quite, touched.

The John J. Pittman Collection, Part I coin (David W. Akers Numismatics, Inc., April 1997), lot 926 was described as: "1889, Proof. 1,779 Proofs minted. Brilliant mirror fields, deep yellow gold color, full Proof luster. Very sharply struck with a square edge, sharply detailed milling, and a partial wire rim . . . Struck using the same obverse die as the preceding 1888 business strike, some business strikes of 1879, and all the Proofs from 1862 to 1873, as well as the Proofs of 1875 and a small portion of the Proofs dated 1876. Note: Not all Proofs of 1889 were struck with this obverse die. In fact, most examples I have seen were struck with a different obverse die, one with all the feathers 'solid.'"

Auction Information (Proofs). Listings for true Proofs are infrequent. While modern certified Proofs are not questioned, many early listings may have been prooflike circulation strikes.

A theory has been advanced by John Dannreuther in combination with Ron Howard (per correspondence): "Many of the prooflike Mint State 1889 gold dollars may be poorly made Proofs. Of course, no legitimate certification service will call them Proofs, as they don't look like Proofs. However, if one examines these 'semi-Proofs,' you can see that they are different than the circulation strikes. It's a subtle difference, but the 'look and feel' of them is different. Of course, jewelry accounts for some of the 'missing' 1889 Proof gold dollars, but there has to be another explanation, in our opinion. The carelessness with making Proof gold dollars in general during the 1880s makes us believe that many 'Proof' 1889 gold dollars are misidentified as MS coins. It is likely that many smaller-diameter Proof coins of this era were struck only a single time, instead of doubly as was the normal practice."

APPENDIX

GOLD DOLLAR AUCTION RECORDS SINCE JANUARY 2003

The following are record U.S. auction prices for gold dollars since January 2003, arranged from highest price to lowest. In the Date/Variety column, W-numbers are Winter numbers. Abbreviations for grades and grading firms are as described in the main text.

Price	Date/Variety	Grade	Firm	Date
$690,000	1849-C Open Wreath	NGC MS63PL	David Lawrence RC	Jul-04
$373,750	1855 Proof	PCGS PF66DC	Heritage	Jan-08
$316,250	1855 Proof	PCGS PF66DC	Heritage	Jan-07
$287,500	1855 Proof	PCGS PF65	Heritage	Jan-05
$149,500	1854 Type 2	NGC MS68	Heritage	Feb-08
$149,500	1855-D	NGC MS64	Ira & Larry Goldberg	Feb-07
$149,500	1861-D, W-12Q	NGC MS65	Heritage	Jan-08
$138,000	1861-D, W-12Q	NGC MS65	Heritage	Apr-06
$132,250	1855-D, W-7I	NGC MS64	Heritage	Apr-06
$115,000	1855	PCGS MS67	Stack's	Nov-07
$109,250	1855-D, W-7I	NGC MS64	Heritage	Jan-06
$97,750	1849-C Open Wreath, W-1A	NGC F15	Heritage	Jan-03
$92,000	1852	PCGS MS69	Heritage	Feb-06
$92,000	1854 Type 2	PCGS MS67	Stack's (ANR)	Jul-03
$90,275	1855	NGC MS67	Bowers & Merena	Jan-08
$86,250	1855	PCGS MS67	Heritage	Jan-05
$86,250	1861-D, W-12Q	NGC MS64	Heritage	Jan-07
$86,250	1861-D, W-12Q	PCGS MS63	Heritage	Jan-04
$80,500	1861-D	NGC MS64	David Lawrence RC	Jul-04
$77,625	1864	PCGS MS69	Superior	Feb-05
$74,750	1858-D, W-10L	NGC MS66	Heritage	Apr-06
$69,000	1849 No L	NGC MS68 Star	Stack's	Jun-07
$66,125	1854 Type 2	PCGS MS66	Superior	Feb-08
$64,400	1855	PCGS MS66	Stack's (ANR)	Jan-04
$63,825	1855	NGC MS66 Star	Bowers & Merena	Aug-04
$63,250	1856 Slanted 5 Proof	PCGS PF65	Heritage	Jan-07
$60,375	1854 Type 2	NGC MS65 PQ	Ira & Larry Goldberg	Jan-04

Price	Date/Variety	Grade	Firm	Date
$57,500	1855	Superb GEM BU	Stack's	Oct-05
$57,500	1860-D, W-12P	NGC MS64	Heritage	Apr-06
$56,350	1855-D, W-7I	PCGS MS62	Heritage	Jan-04
$54,672	1849 No L	NGC MS68 Star	Superior	Aug-06
$54,625	1855	PCGS MS66	Bowers & Merena	Mar-04
$54,625	1854 Type 2	PCGS MS66	Superior	Feb-05
$54,625	1856 Slanted 5 Proof	NGC PF65UCAM	Superior	May-04
$52,900	1861-D, W-12O	PCGS MS63	Heritage	Nov-03
$51,750	1855	PCGS MS66	Heritage	Jan-07
$51,750	1849 No L	NGC MS68	Heritage	Aug-07
$50,600	1852	PCGS MS69	Bowers & Merena	Oct-05
$50,600	1849-D	PCGS MS64	Stack's (ANR)	Mar-06
$48,875	1860-D, W-12P	NGC MS64	Heritage	Aug-07
$48,875	1881 Proof	NGC PF67UCAM	Heritage	Mar-08
$48,300	1858	PCGS MS68	Stack's	Aug-07
$48,300	1858	PCGS MS68	Stack's (ANR)	Mar-06
$48,300	1854 Type 2	PCGS MS66	Bowers & Merena	Jul-03
$48,300	1876 Proof	NGC PF67UCAM Star	Superior	Nov-03
$47,150	1855	PCGS MS66	Bowers & Merena	Oct-04
$47,150	1856-D, W-8K	PCGS MS62	Heritage	Jan-04
$46,000	1855-D, W-7I	PCGS MS61	Heritage	Jan-04
$44,850	1849 No L	PCGS MS67	Ira & Larry Goldberg	Feb-07
$43,700	1858 Proof	PCGS PF65DC	Ira & Larry Goldberg	Feb-08
$43,125	1855	PCGS MS66	Heritage	May-07
$43,125	1854 Type 2	PCGS MS65	Heritage	Jan-08
$42,550	1854 Type 2	PCGS MS66	Superior	Aug-07
$42,550	1871 Proof	NGC PF67UCAM	Stack's (ANR)	Aug-04
$42,263	1854 Type 2	NGC MS66	Heritage	Jun-04
$41,400	1856-D	PCGS MS62	Stack's (ANR)	Sep-03
$41,400	1856-S	PCGS MS63	Stack's (ANR)	Jul-05
$41,400	1875 Proof	NGC PF66UCAM	Ira & Larry Goldberg	May-08
$40,250	1856-D, W-8K	NGC MS62	Heritage	Apr-06
$40,250	1885 Proof	NGC PF68CAM	Heritage	Jul-07
$39,100	1852	PCGS MS68	Heritage	Jan-05
$39,100	1856-S	NGC MS64	Bowers & Merena	May-06
$39,100	1875 Proof	PCGS PF66	Bowers & Merena	Mar-04
$37,950	1856-S	NGC MS64	Bowers & Merena	Aug-05
$37,375	1851-D, W-3E	NGC MS65	Heritage	Apr-06
$37,375	1855-D, W-7I	PCGS AU58	Heritage	Jan-08

Price	Date/Variety	Grade	Firm	Date
$37,375	1858 Proof	NGC PF66CAM	Stack's (ANR)	Jan-05
$36,800	1854 Type 2	NGC MS66	Bowers & Merena	Oct-04
$36,800	1855-O	NGC MS64	Stack's	Jan-07
$36,685	1854 Type 2	PCGS MS65	Bowers & Merena	Dec-03
$36,225	1872 Proof	NGC PF67UCAM	Heritage	Feb-06
$35,650	1855	PCGS MS65	Heritage	Jan-03
$35,650	1854 Type 2	PCGS MS65	Heritage	Jan-03
$35,650	1861-D	PCGS MS61	Bowers & Merena	Jul-03
$34,500	1855	PCGS MS65	Stack's (ANR)	Jul-03
$34,500	1855	PCGS MS65	Stack's (ANR)	Jul-03
$34,500	1865	PCGS MS68	Heritage	Mar-08
$34,500	1850-D, W-2C	NGC MS64	Heritage	Apr-06
$34,500	1856-S	NGC MS64	Stack's (ANR)	Jul-05
$34,500	1856-S	PCGS MS63	Superior	Nov-04
$34,500	1857 Proof	NGC PF65CAM	Stack's (ANR)	Nov-04
$34,500	1858 Proof	NGC PF66CAM	Heritage	Mar-06
$34,500	1861-D	PCGS MS61	Stack's (ANR)	Jul-03
$34,500	1861-D, W-12-O	PCGS MS61	Heritage	Nov-03
$34,500	1863 Proof	NGC PF67CAM	Heritage	Jan-07
$34,500	1866 Proof	NGC PF67UCAM Star	Heritage	Nov-06
$34,500	1875 Proof	NGC PF66DCAM	Heritage	Dec-04
$33,925	1854 Type 2	NGC MS65	Heritage	Jan-08
$33,350	1875	NGC MS66	Heritage	Aug-07
$33,350	1861-D	PCGS AU58	Superior	May-05
$32,200	1855	PCGS MS65	Heritage	Jan-07
$32,200	1858 Proof	NGC PF66CAM	Heritage	Mar-06
$32,200	1866 Proof	NGC PF67UCAM	Heritage	Jan-07
$32,200	1884 Proof, B-6107	NGC PF68CAM	Heritage	Jan-06
$31,625	1856-D	PCGS MS61	Bowers & Merena	Aug-07
$31,625	1882 Proof	NGC PF67UCAM Star	Stack's	Feb-08
$31,050	1855	PCGS MS65	Superior	May-06
$31,050	1852-D, W-4F	NGC MS63	Bowers & Merena	Aug-04
$31,050	1854-S	PCGS MS65	Bowers & Merena	Oct-04
$31,050	1856-D	NGC MS61	Ira & Larry Goldberg	May-08
$31,050	1856-D	NGC MS61	Ira & Larry Goldberg	May-06
$31,050	1873 Close 3 Proof	PCGS PF65	Bowers & Merena	Jul-06
$30,475	1854 Type 2	PCGS MS65	Superior	Jan-04
$30,475	1876 Proof	NGC PF66UCAM Star	Heritage	Jan-06

Price	Date/Variety	Grade	Firm	Date
$30,188	1887 Proof	NGC PF68CA	Heritage	Jan-07
$29,900	1855	PCGS MS65	Bowers & Merena	Feb-06
$29,900	1860	PCGS MS67	Heritage	Mar-04
$29,900	1854 Type 2	NGC MS65	Stack's (ANR)	Jan-04
$29,900	1855-O	PCGS MS64	Superior	Feb-03
$29,900	1858 Proof	PCGS PF65CA	Heritage	Feb-05
$29,900	1859-D, W-11N	PCGS MS64	Heritage	Jan-05
$29,900	1872 Proof	NGC PF67UCAM	Heritage	May-07
$29,900	1877 Proof	NGC PF66UCAM	Heritage	Dec-05
$29,900	1883 Proof	NGC PF67UCAM	Heritage	May-07
$29,900	1884 Proof	NGC PF68CAM	Stack's	Oct-05
$28,750	1855	NGC MS65	Heritage	Jan-06
$28,750	1881	NGC MS69	Superior	May-08
$28,750	1851-C, W-4D	NGC MS66	Heritage	Oct-06
$28,750	1854 Type 2	PCGS MS65	Superior	May-06
$28,750	1855-D	AU+	Stack's	Mar-06
$28,750	1859-D, W-11N	PCGS MS64	Heritage	Sep-05
$28,750	1872 Proof	NGC PF67UCAM	Superior	Aug-07
$28,750	1873 Close 3 Proof	PCGS PF65	Heritage	Feb-08
$28,175	1855	PCGS MS65	Heritage	Sep-05
$28,175	1854 Type 2	NGC MS65	Bowers & Merena	Mar-05
$27,600	1855	NGC MS65	Stack's (ANR)	Jan-04
$27,600	1852-D, W-4F	NGC MS63	Heritage	Apr-06
$27,600	1860-D, W-12P	PCGS MS62	Heritage	Jan-04
$27,600	1862 Proof	PCGS PF65DC	Stack's	Feb-08
$27,600	1873 Close 3	NGC PF65CAM	Heritage	Jan-07
$27,600	1881 Proof	NGC PF67UCAM	Heritage	Dec-05
$26,450	1852	PCGS MS67	Superior	Feb-05
$26,450	1855	NGC MS65	Stack's	Sep-04
$26,450	1854 Type 2	PCGS MS65	Heritage	Nov-06
$26,450	1858 Proof	PCGS PF64	Heritage	Apr-06
$26,450	1861-D	NGC AU58	Superior	May-05
$26,450	1861-D, W-12Q	PCGS MS61	Heritage	Jan-04
$26,450	1878 Proof	NGC PF66UCAM	Heritage	Jan-06
$26,163	1861-D	NGC AU58	Bowers & Merena	May-04
$25,875	1851-O	PCGS MS66	Heritage	Dec-05
$25,875	1855-D	NGC AU58	Superior	May-05
$25,875	1887 Proof	NGC PF68CAM	Bowers & Merena	Apr-08
$25,300	1867	PCGS MS67	Bowers & Merena	Mar-04
$25,300	1869	PCGS MS68	Bowers & Merena	Oct-04

Price	Date/Variety	Grade	Firm	Date
$25,300	1853-D, W-5G	NGC MS64	Heritage	Mar-04
$25,300	1854 Type 2	NGC MS64	Superior	Feb-06
$25,300	1854 Type 2	PCGS MS64	Stack's	Oct-04
$25,300	1855-D, W-7I	NGC AU55	Heritage	Jan-07
$25,300	1855-D, W-7I	NGC AU58	Bowers & Merena	Oct-04
$25,300	1855-O	NGC MS63	Bowers & Merena	Oct-04
$25,300	1856 Slanted 5	PCGS MS68	Heritage	Mar-07
$25,300	1856-S, B-6045	PCGS MS63	Heritage	Aug-04
$25,300	1858 Proof	NGC PF65UCAM	Superior	Jan-04
$25,300	1862 Proof	PCGS PF65	Superior	May-06
$25,300	1879 Proof	PCGS PF66DC	Heritage	Jan-07
$25,013	1858 Proof	PCGS PF65CA	Heritage	Jul-04
$24,725	1872	NGC MS69	Superior	May-06
$24,150	1852	PCGS MS67	Stack's	Jan-07
$24,150	1853	PCGS MS68	Bowers & Merena	Jul-03
$24,150	1854 Type 2	NGC MS65	Superior	Jan-07
$24,150	1855-D	NGC AU58	Superior	Nov-05
$24,150	1855-D, W-7I	NGC MS60	Heritage	Jan-03
$24,150	1856-D, W-8K	PCGS MS60	Heritage	Jan-05
$24,150	1859-C, W-11M	PCGS MS63	Heritage	Jun-04
$24,150	1861-D, W-12O	PCGS MS60	Heritage	Jan-03
$24,150	1861-D, W-12Q	PCGS AU55	Heritage	Jan-05
$24,150	1877 Proof	NGC PF66UCAM	Stack's (ANR)	Nov-04
$24,150	1877 Proof	PCGS PF65DC	Stack's (ANR)	Jun-04
$23,575	1855	PCGS MS64	Heritage	Nov-04
$23,575	1863 Proof	NGC PF66CAM	Heritage	Nov-03
$23,265	1874 Proof	NGC PF66CAM	Superior	Aug-06
$23,000	1852	PCGS MS67	Stack's	Oct-07
$23,000	1853	PCGS MS68	Heritage	May-04
$23,000	1864	PCGS MS68	Heritage	Jan-05
$23,000	1866	NGC MS68PL	Bowers & Merena	Aug-07
$23,000	1866	NGC MS68PL	Heritage	Jan-07
$23,000	1851-O	PCGS MS66	Stack's (ANR)	Jul-05
$23,000	1852-C, W-7H	NGC MS65	Heritage	Feb-08
$23,000	1852-C, W-7H	NGC MS65	Heritage	Oct-06
$23,000	1852-O	NGC MS66	Heritage	Jul-05
$23,000	1854 Type 2	PCGS MS64	Stack's (ANR)	Jun-04
$23,000	1855-C, W-9K	NGC MS60	Heritage	Feb-05
$23,000	1855-O	NGC MS63	Stack's	Jan-07
$23,000	1856-D	PCGS MS61	Bowers & Merena	Jan-03

Price	Date/Variety	Grade	Firm	Date
$23,000	1858-D	PCGS MS63	Stack's (ANR)	Oct-04
$23,000	1858-D, W-10M	PCGS MS63	Heritage	Jan-04
$23,000	1859-D, W-11N	NGC MS64	Heritage	Apr-06
$23,000	1878 Proof	PCGS PF65CA	Ira & Larry Goldberg	Sep-07
$23,000	1881 Proof	NGC PF67UCAM	Stack's (ANR)	Jan-05
$23,000	1886 Proof	PCGS PF67	Superior	Aug-07
$23,000	1886 Proof	PCGS PF67	Heritage	Apr-06
$22,425	1852	PCGS MS67	Heritage	Mar-06
$22,425	1886 Proof	PCGS PF67	Superior	Feb-08
$22,138	1885 Proof	NGC PF67UCAM	Bowers & Merena	Nov-07
$22,101	1855-O	NGC MS63	Superior	Aug-06
$21,850	1855	ANACS MS60 rev rim dmg	Heritage	Jan-05
$21,850	1855	PCGS MS64	Ira & Larry Goldberg	May-04
$21,850	1855	PCGS MS64	Heritage	Jan-04
$21,850	1853-D, W-5G	NGC MS63	Heritage	Apr-06
$21,850	1854 Type 2	PCGS MS64	Stack's (ANR)	Jan-04
$21,850	1855-C	NGC AU58	Heritage	Jan-08
$21,850	1855-D	NGC AU58	Ira & Larry Goldberg	May-07
$21,850	1859-D, W-11M	NGC MS64	Heritage	Jan-03
$21,850	1860-S	PCGS MS65	Stack's (ANR)	Jan-06
$21,850	1861-D	PCGS AU55	Stack's (ANR)	Nov-04
$21,850	1861-D, W-12Q	ANACS AU55 scratched	Heritage	Jun-06
$21,850	1885 Proof	NGC PF67UCAM	Heritage	Mar-03
$21,275	1851	PCGS MS67	Bowers & Merena	Jan-08
$21,275	1855-D	AU	Stack's	Mar-06
$21,275	1858-D	PCGS MS63	Ira & Larry Goldberg	May-06
$21,275	1884 Proof	PCGS PF67CA	Superior	Nov-03
$20,988	1853-D	NGC MS63	Superior	Jan-04
$20,700	1851	PCGS MS67	Stack's (ANR)	Jul-03
$20,700	1855	PCGS MS64	Stack's (ANR)	Jul-05
$20,700	1855	PCGS MS64	Heritage	Sep-03
$20,700	1866	PCGS MS68	Stack's (ANR)	Mar-06
$20,700	1849-D	NGC MS63	Stack's	Oct-07
$20,700	1853-D	PCGS MS63	Superior	May-04
$20,700	1853-D, W-5G	NGC MS64	Bowers & Merena	Jul-04
$20,700	1853-D, W-5G	PCGS MS63	Heritage	Jan-04
$20,700	1854 Type 2	PCGS MS64	Bowers & Merena	Jun-03
$20,700	1854-S	PCGS MS65	Stack's (ANR)	Jul-04
$20,700	1855-D	CH EF	Stack's	Jan-06

Price	Date/Variety	Grade	Firm	Date
$20,700	1855-D	NGC AU55	Bowers & Merena	Jan-03
$20,700	1855-D, W-7I	NGC AU53	Heritage	Mar-05
$20,700	1858-D	PCGS MS63	Superior	Feb-07
$20,700	1858-D	PCGS MS63	Stack's (ANR)	Aug-06
$20,700	1861-D, B-6070	AU50	Stack's	Mar-08
$20,700	1863 Proof	PCGS PF65DC	Heritage	Mar-08
$20,700	1864 Proof	PCGS PF65DC	Stack's (ANR)	Nov-04
$20,700	1865 Proof	NGC PF66UCAM	Bowers & Merena	Apr-05
$20,700	1885 Proof	PCGS PF67CA	Stack's (ANR)	Jan-04
$20,700	1887 Proof	PCGS PF67CA	Heritage	Apr-07
$20,125	1854 Type 2	PCGS MS64	Heritage	May-04
$20,125	1877 Proof	NGC PF66CAM	Superior	Jul-05
$19,550	1851	NGC MS68	Heritage	Jun-04
$19,550	1855	NGC MS64	Heritage	Jan-08
$19,550	1855	NGC MS64	Heritage	Jan-06
$19,550	1851-O	ANACS MS65	Heritage	Sep-04
$19,550	1855-C	AU	Stack's	Jan-06
$19,550	1855-D	PCGS AU55	Superior	May-03
$19,550	1856-D, W-8J	NGC MS61	Heritage	Jan-03
$19,550	1860 Proof	NGC PF66CAM	Heritage	Jan-07
$19,550	1861-D	ANACS AU55 scratched	Ira & Larry Goldberg	May-08
$19,550	1866 Proof	PCGS PF66CA	Heritage	Jan-07
$19,550	1866 Proof	NGC PF66UCAM	Stack's (ANR)	Aug-04
$19,550	1888 Proof	PCGS PF67	Stack's (ANR)	Jun-04
$19,200	1881 Proof	PCGS PF66DC	Heritage	Mar-07
$18,975	1851	PCGS MS67	Ira & Larry Goldberg	Sep-06
$18,975	1857	PCGS MS67	Stack's (ANR)	Mar-06
$18,975	1858	NGC MS68 Star	Stack's (ANR)	Mar-04
$18,975	1872	NGC MS68PL	Heritage	May-07
$18,975	1855-D	NGC AU53	Bowers & Merena	Sep-03
$18,975	1884 Proof	NGC PF67CAM	Superior	May-06
$18,688	1855	NGC MS64 PQ	Superior	Jul-03
$18,612	1885 Proof	NGC PF67CAM	Superior	Aug-06
$18,400	1855	PCGS MS64	Heritage	Apr-06
$18,400	1855	PCGS MS64	Heritage	Aug-04
$18,400	1855	NGC MS64	Bowers & Merena	Aug-04
$18,400	1855	PCGS MS64	Heritage	Jul-04
$18,400	1855	PCGS MS64	Bowers & Merena	Jul-03
$18,400	1870	PCGS MS68	Heritage	Mar-06
$18,400	1872	PCGS MS67	Stack's (ANR)	Mar-06

Price	Date/Variety	Grade	Firm	Date
$18,400	1883	NGC MS69	Heritage	Jul-05
$18,400	1849 No L	PCGS MS67	Superior	May-06
$18,400	1851-C	PCGS MS65	Heritage	Jun-04
$18,400	1852-C	NGC MS64	Superior	May-06
$18,400	1854 Type 2	PCGS MS64	Heritage	Nov-05
$18,400	1855-C, W-9K	NGC MS61	Heritage	Jan-03
$18,400	1858-D	PCGS MS63	Ira & Larry Goldberg	May-08
$18,400	1860-D	NGC MS61	Bowers & Merena	Jun-03
$18,400	1861-D	NGC AU58	Superior	Jan-03
$18,400	1862 Proof	NGC PF66CAM	Stack's	Sep-05
$18,400	1862 Proof	PCGS PF65DC	Heritage	Jan-07
$18,400	1879 Proof	PCGS PF66DC	Heritage	Jul-03
$18,400	1881 Proof	NGC PF67UCAM	Stack's (ANR)	Oct-05
$18,112	1859-C	NGC MS62	Superior	May-05
$17,854	1855	PCGS MS64	Heritage	May-04
$17,825	1866	PCGS MS68	Heritage	Feb-05
$17,825	1849-C Close Wreath	PCGS MS63	Stack's	Jan-08
$17,825	1854 Type 2	PCGS MS64	Heritage	Aug-06
$17,825	1855-C, W-9K	NGC AU58	Bowers & Merena	Jan-05
$17,825	1858-D, W-10L	PCGS MS63	Superior	Jan-04
$17,825	1858-D, W-10M	NGC MS63	Heritage	Jan-05
$17,825	1860-D	NGC MS61 PQ	Ira & Larry Goldberg	May-06
$17,825	1865 Proof	NGC PF66UCAM	Superior	Apr-03
$17,825	1869 Proof	NGC PF66CAM	Heritage	Feb-03
$17,250	1855	PCGS MS64	Superior	May-07
$17,250	1855	PCGS MS64	Heritage	Jun-05
$17,250	1855	NGC MS64	Heritage	May-05
$17,250	1855	NGC MS64	Superior	Mar-05
$17,250	1864	PCGS MS66	Heritage	Sep-03
$17,250	1868	PCGS MS68	Stack's (ANR)	Mar-06
$17,250	1875	PCGS MS65	Bowers & Merena	Mar-03
$17,250	1849-D, W-1B	NGC MS64	Heritage	Apr-06
$17,250	1850-D	NGC MS63	Ira & Larry Goldberg	May-07
$17,250	1854 Type 2	PCGS MS63	Heritage	Aug-07
$17,250	1854 Type 2	NGC MS64	Heritage	Jan-07
$17,250	1854 Type 2	PCGS MS64	Heritage	Sep-05
$17,250	1854 Type 2	NGC MS64	Heritage	May-04

Selected Bibliography

Adams, Edgar H. and William H. Woodin. *U.S. Pattern, Trial and Experimental Pieces.* New York: American Numismatic Society, 1913.

Adams, John Weston. *United States Numismatic Literature. Volume I. Nineteenth Century Auction Catalogs.* Mission Viejo, Cal.: George Frederick Kolbe Publications, 1982.

—*United States Numismatic Literature. Volume II. Twentieth Century Auction Catalogs.* Crestline, Cal.: George Frederick Kolbe Publications, 1990.

Akers, David W. *United States Gold Patterns.* Englewood, Ohio: Paramount International Coin Corporation, 1975.

—*United States Gold Coins: An Analysis of Auction Records, Gold Dollars.* Englewood, Ohio: Paramount International Coin Corporation, 1975.

American Journal of Numismatics. American Numismatic and Archaeological Society, later the American Numismatic Society. New York and Boston; various issues 1866 to 1912.

Attinelli, Emmanuel J. *Numisgraphics, or a List of Catalogues in Which Occur Coins or Medals, Which Have Been Sold by Auction in the United States.* New York: 1876.

Bolles, Albert S. *The Financial History of the United States from 1774 to 1885.* Three volumes. New York, 1879–1894.

Bowers, Q. David. *United States Gold Coins: An Illustrated History.* Los Angeles: Bowers and Ruddy Galleries, 1982; later printings Wolfeboro, N.H.: Bowers and Merena Galleries, Inc.

—*The History of United States Coinage.* Los Angeles: Bowers and Ruddy Galleries, Inc., 1979; later printings Wolfeboro, N.H., Bowers and Merena Galleries, Inc.

—*Abe Kosoff: Dean of Numismatics.* Wolfeboro, N.H.: Bowers and Merena Galleries, Inc., 1985.

—*American Coin Hoards and Treasures.* Wolfeboro, N.H.: Bowers and Merena Galleries, Inc., 1997.

—"Collecting United States Gold Coins: A Numismatic History." Chapter in *America's Gold Coinage*, the proceedings of the Coinage of the Americas Conference, American Numismatic Society, November 4–5, 1989. New York: American Numismatic Society, 1990.

—*Harry W. Bass Jr. Museum Sylloge.* Wolfeboro, N.H.: Bowers and Merena Galleries, 2002.

Breen, Walter. *Major Varieties of U.S. Gold Dollars.* Chicago: Hewitt Brothers, 1964.

—*Walter Breen's Encyclopedia of U.S. and Colonial Proof Coins, 1792–1977.* Albertson, New York: FCI Press, 1977. Reprinted as *Walter Breen's Encyclopedia of U.S. and Colonial Proof Coins, 1792–1987.* Wolfeboro, New Hampshire: Bowers and Merena Galleries, Inc., 1989.

—*Walter Breen's Complete Encyclopedia of U.S. and Colonial Coins.* Garden City, N.Y.: Doubleday, 1988.

Bradfield, Elston G. "Double Eagle and Gold $1 in the 1849 Congress." *The Numismatist,* April 1949. Discussion of the legislation leading up to the Coinage Act of March 3, 1849.

Bressett, Kenneth E. and A. Kosoff; introduction by Q. David Bowers. *The Official American Numismatic Association Grading Standards for United States Coins.* 6th edition. Atlanta: Whitman Publishing, LLC, 2005.

Carothers, Neil. *Fractional Money.* New York: John Wiley & Sons, 1930.

Coin World. Sidney, Ohio: Amos Press, *et al.*, 1960 to date.

Coin World Almanac. 6th edition. Sidney, Ohio: Amos Press, 1990.

Dannreuther, John. "James Barton Longacre: A Maligned Artist." Adapted from a Groves Lecture presentation at the American Numismatic Society, New York, April 15, 2000.

Dannreuther, John, and Jeff Garrett. *The Official Red Book of Auction Records: U.S. Gold Coinage, 2003–2007.* Atlanta: Whitman Publishing, LLC, 2008.

DeLorey, Thomas K. "Longacre: Unsung Engraver of the U.S. Mint," *The Numismatist*, October 1985.

Dickeson, Montroville Wilson. *The American Numismatical Manual.* Philadelphia: J.B. Lippincott & Co., 1859. (1860 and 1865 editions were slightly retitled as *The American Numismatic Manual.*)

Eckfeldt, Jacob Reese, and William Ewing DuBois. *New Varieties of Gold and Silver Coins, Counterfeit Coins, and Bullion; With Mint Values.* New York: George P. Putnam, 1851.

Heaton, Augustus G. *A Treatise on the Coinage of the United States Branch Mints.* Washington, D.C.: published by the author, 1893.

Judd, Dr. J. Hewitt. *United States Pattern, Experimental and Trial Pieces.* Racine, Wis.: Whitman Division of Western Publishing Company, 1959 and later editions (through the 7th edition); 9th edition, edited by Q. David Bowers, Atlanta: Whitman Publishing LLC, 2005.

Julian, R.W. "United States Proof Coinage." Manuscript created in 1980 for *Coins* magazine, published sequentially between September 1980 and December 1982.

Mason's Monthly Illustrated Coin Collector's Magazine. Philadelphia and Boston: Ebenezer Locke Mason. Various issues of the 1860s, 1870s, and 1880s.

NGC Census Report. Sarasota, Fla.: Numismatic Guaranty Corporation of America, various issues 1980s to date.

Numismatic News. Iola, Wis.: Krause Publications, Various issues 1950s to date.

Numismatic Scrapbook Magazine. Chicago: Lee F. Hewitt; Amos Press, Sidney, Ohio. Various issues 1935 to 1976.

Numismatist, The. George F. Heath, Farran Zerbe, American Numismatic Association, 1888 to date. Currently published in Colorado Springs, Colo.

PCGS Population Report, The. Newport Beach, Cal.: Professional Coin Grading Service, Inc. Various issues, 1980s to date.

Pollock, Andrew W. *United States Pattern Coins and Related Pieces.* Wolfeboro, N.H.: Bowers and Merena Galleries, 1994.

Sumner, William G. *A History of American Currency.* New York: Henry Holt and Company, 1874.

United States Mint, Bureau of the Mint, *et al. Annual Report of the Director of the Mint.* Philadelphia, Washington, D.C.: 1849 to 1890.

Vermeule, Cornelius. *Numismatic Art in America.* 2nd edition. Atlanta: Whitman Publishing LLC, 2007.

Winter, Douglas. *Charlotte Mint Gold Coins, 1838–1861, a Numismatic History and Analysis.* Wolfeboro, N.H.: Bowers and Merena Galleries, Inc., 1987.

—*New Orleans Mint Gold Coins, 1839–1909, a Numismatic History and Analysis.* Wolfeboro, N.H.: Bowers and Merena Galleries, Inc., 1992.

—*Gold Coins of the Dahlonega Mint 1838–1861.* Dallas: DWN Publishing, 1997.

—Gold Coins of the Charlotte Mint, 1838–1861, (3rd ed.). Irvine, California: Zyrus, 2008.

Yeoman, R.S. *A Guide Book of United States Coins.* Kenneth, E. Bressett, editor. Racine, Wis. and Atlanta: Whitman Publishing Company (and Western Publishing Company, Inc.), now known as Whitman Publishing LLC, various editions 1946 to date.

Notes

1. Letter from Roosevelt to H.C. Hoskier, December 19, 1905, quoted by David Enders Tripp in "'Fear and Trembling' & Other Discoveries,'" *American Numismatic Society Magazine*, Winter 2007.
2. The idea of a dollar struck in gold was hardly new in the 1830s. Thomas Jefferson had suggested the coin in his 1791 recommendations for American coinage. Later, in a March 29, 1807, letter to Mint Director Robert Patterson (father of the holder of the office in 1849), Jefferson stated, "Indeed I wish the law authorized the making two cent and three cent pieces of silver, and golden dollars, which would all be large enough to handle, and would be a great convenience to our own citizens."
3. Presumably, these 1836-dated coins (restruck in 1844) depicted a liberty cap on the obverse and a palm branch and inscription on the reverse—from the 1836 dies. Possibly, these are the gold dollars with dies oriented in the same direction (instead of 180° apart).
4. Contributed by Gerald Tebben to *Coin World*, July 27, 1998. Perhaps such pieces were distributed to legislators and others. The die alignments of the 1844 and 1849 restrikes are not known, but one or both probably had the dies oriented in the same direction (instead of 180° apart).
5. The diary is preserved in the National Archives. Citations are from an article by Rick Snow in *Longacre's Ledger*, June 2001.
6. Original manuscript notebook kept by George J. Eckfeldt, acquired by Q. David Bowers; the notebook had not been examined by Walter Breen, since its existence was not known during his lifetime. This corrects the information related by Breen that on the next day, May 8, "a few Proofs" and 1,000 circulation strikes of the new gold dollar were coined. (Breen, *Encyclopedia*, 1988; and elsewhere).
7. The weight of silver dollars was not reduced, and therefore they did not circulate after 1853. This silver denomination was primarily used in the export trade, especially to China, but also to Central and South America. It was not until 1873 that the price of silver bullion on international markets dropped to the point at which it was no longer profitable to melt down silver dollars.
8. The silver dollar is the exception. On February 28, 1878, the Bland-Allison Act provided for the coining in large quantities of silver dollars, a denomination that had not been made since 1873. There was no particular need for silver dollars in circulation. The legislation was intended to subsidize the market for silver—the price of which had dropped sharply in the 1870s. (This had followed the dumping of large quantities of silver coins on the market in Europe and increased production of silver metal in the American West, particularly in Nevada.)
9. Ironically, a century and a half later, in 1999, the Mint's catalog of coins, etc., for sale included mutilated coins—such as current commemoratives made into watches.
10. The totals in the 1934 report do not necessarily agree with other figures and totals in the same report. Moreover, there may be instances in which coins reserved for the Assay Commission were not counted (although for most years they were), and that special presentation strikings may not be included for years prior to 1860 and some later years as well, etc. Thus, these figures, while they appear to be precise, must be regarded as approximate.
11. Certain information about the mints is adapted from *United States $3 Gold Pieces*, Q. David Bowers with Douglas Winter, 2005.
12. With a nod to R.W. Julian, correspondence, February 8, 2004.

13. In the catalog of Stack's January 2007 auction held in Orlando.
14. These were deflationary times in America. According to the secretary of the Treasury there was $1,588,871,729 total money in circulation on January 1, 1892, including about $100,000,000 in gold coins. That amounted to about $25 per capita for a population of about 64,000,000. This was a sharp reduction from about $48 per capita at the end of the Civil War (at which time most money was in paper in the East and Midwest). See James B. Weaver, *A Call to Action*, 1892, pp. 304-313.
15. *The Elder Monthly*, Vol. 2, No. 2, April 1907; reprinted from the *Providence Journal*, date not stated.
16. By 1889, Low had been in the coin trade for about a decade. In that year he was chief auction cataloger for the Scott Stamp & Coin Company sales. In late summer and autumn 1889, Low was in Europe scouting for rare coins.
17. *The United States Branch Mint at Dahlonega, Georgia*, pp. 64–65.
18. First noticed by John Dannreuther in 1999.
19. Randall was a well-known Philadelphia dealer and one of the few in the early 1880s to study federal gold coins by minute die varieties (his interest is better known with regard to silver coin die varieties; he is widely thought to have been the uncredited author of John W. Haseltine's 1881 *Type Table* of silver issues.
20. First noticed by John Dannreuther; communicated to the author, November 9, 1999.
21. *A Reference to United States Federal Gold Coinage: Volume I*, p. 74.
22. Adapted from *The Expert's Guide to Collecting and Investing in Rare Coins*, Q. David Bowers, 2005.
23. For detailed notes on this and other Charlotte gold dollars, see Douglas Winter, *Gold Coins of the Charlotte Mint, 1838–1861.*
24. Clair M. Birdsall, *The United States Branch Mint at Dahlonega, Georgia*, p. 60, mentions that coins in the North Georgia College and Elliott collections have this distinction.
25. This and certain other die data adapted from Clair M. Birdsall, *The United States Branch Mint at Dahlonega, Georgia*, Table VI, from R.W. Julian's research in the National Archives. Breen's data (*Encyclopedia*, 1988) differs on this particular variety: he says the dies were shipped from the Die Department of the Philadelphia Mint, June 2–4, 1849 (received in Dahlonega on June 16).
26. *A Reference to United States Federal Gold Coinage: Volume I*, p. 80.
27. In *Gold Coins of the Charlotte Mint 1838–1861*, Douglas Winter assigns a running sequence to obverse and reverse dies for gold dollars of this facility, beginning with 1-A in 1849.
28. *Fractional Money*, 1930, pp. 110 ff. The situation is expanded upon in *Hunt's Merchants Magazine*, Vols. 19–28; William G. Sumner, *History of American Currency*, 1874; and the annual Treasury reports on finances, 1851–1853.
29. Emmanuel Attinelli, *Numisgraphics*, 1876, p. 8. The sale of Professor Daniel E. Groux's coins and medals in Boston, 1848, may have realized as much or more, but no records of prices have been located.
30. The diary is preserved in the National Archives. Citations are from an article by Rick Snow in the magazine *Longacre's Ledger*, June 2001.
31. Clair M. Birdsall, *The United States Branch Mint at Dahlonega, Georgia*, p. 61.
32. Paul F. Taglione, *A Reference to United States Federal Gold Coinage:* Vol. I, p. 89.
33. *Ibid.*, p. 96.
34. *Ibid.*, p. 97.

35. Original manuscript notebook kept by George J. Eckfeldt.
36. Author's note: Any such Indian motif pieces would have been struck at a later time and pre-dated.
37. The Indian Princess design, in the form of the full figure of Miss Liberty with a plumed headdress, was used on certain pattern silver coins, dime to dollar, designed by J.B. Longacre in the late 1860s and continued in use after he died.
38. The double-punched date ("the effect is grotesquely lopsided") and the doubled obverse die are listed as Breen 6035 and 6037 (*Encyclopedia*, 1988).
39. George Parish Jr., *American Journal of Numismatics*, August 1866. Attinelli, *Numisgraphics*, 1876.
40. *A Reference to United States Federal Gold Coinage: Volume I*, p. 102.
41. Clair M. Birdsall, *The United States Branch Mint at Dahlonega, Georgia*, p. 62.
42. Author's interview with John J. Ford Jr., March 11, 2000.
43. Breen (*Encyclopedia*, 1988) gives different information, stating that the Philadelphia Mint shipped three pairs of 1856-D dies to Dahlonega on March 11, these being received on April 15—a transit time of three weeks.
44. Clair M. Birdsall, *The United States Branch Mint at Dahlonega, Georgia*, p. 63.
45. *Ibid.*, p. 35.
46. Breen (*Encyclopedia*, 1988) states the dies were shipped from Philadelphia in December.
47. As confirmed by examination under high magnification of a Proof 1859 dollar (with Reverse Die 2) and a Proof 1862 dollar in the Bass III sale; study conducted February 17, 2000.
48. Walter Breen, the cataloger of this coin, only rarely attended the auction sales or viewed the auction lots of other firms. *Ex cathedra*, he often made pronouncements that competitors rightfully viewed as unfair. This swipe at the Baldenhofer coin virtually indicates that he had little information about it on hand, otherwise he would either know it was the Baldenhofer piece or it was not.
49. Breen (*Encyclopedia*, 1988) says eight reverses and does not give shipping date.
50. *John Sherman's Recollections of Forty Years in the House, Senate and Cabinet*, 1895, p. 23.
51. *A Reference to United States Federal Gold Coinage: Volume I*, p. 125.
52. Blanked dies: cataloger's description for clashed dies, this also being terminology used in many Mint records.
53. *The United States Branch Mint at Dahlonega, Georgia*,1984, p. 64.
54. The final connection in the transcontinental railroad line was made in 1869. In earlier times dies, were sent via steamer from Philadelphia to Panama, connecting across land to another steamer on the Pacific side, to San Francisco.
55. Breen, *Major Varieties of U.S. Gold Dollars*, p. 21; *Encyclopedia* (1988).
56. From Edward L. Fletcher Jr., *The Shield Five Cent Series*.
57. Letter, June 25, 1996.
58. R.W. Julian, letter, March 29, 2000. Also, Julian, "Notes on U.S. Proof Coinage II: Gold," *Numismatic Scrapbook Magazine*, February 1967.
59. R.W. Julian, letter, March 29, 2000. Also, Julian, "Notes on U.S. Proof Coinage II: Gold," *Numismatic Scrapbook Magazine*, February 1967.
60. Quoted by R.W. Julian, "Notes on U.S. Proof Coinage II: Gold," *Numismatic Scrapbook Magazine*, February 1967. This differs from the *official* delivery records, which "record 40 complete gold Proof sets (delivered on February 9) plus 20 gold dollars and 10 three dollar gold pieces."
61. This was stated in the 1887 R*eport of the Director of the Mint*.